FINLAND AND EUROPE

THE NORDIC SERIES
Volume 7

FINLAND AND EUROPE

International Crises in the
Period of Autonomy 1808 – 1914

by
JUHANI PAASIVIRTA

translated from the Finnish by
Anthony F. Upton and Sirkka R. Upton

edited and abridged by D.G. Kirby

University of Minnesota Press
Minneapolis

Published by the University of Minnesota Press,
2037 University Avenue Southeast, Minneapolis MN 55414
Printed in Great Britain

ISBN 0-8166-1046-0

Published in Finnish by Kirjayhtymä, Helsinki,
in 1978, with the title *Suomi ja Eurooppa:
Autonomiakausi ja Kansainväliset Kriisit
(1908–1914)*

The University of Minnesota is an
equal-opportunity educator and employer

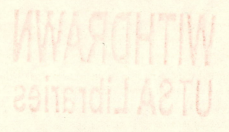

Contents

Preface

The history of Europe has generally been portrayed from two angles. The first and more traditional view looks at the role and development of nations and states, often within the framework of general political history or of international relations. The second line of approach, which has gained favour in recent decades, is to examine historical processes from a structural perspective, paying particular attention to such things as administration, social classes and groups, different occupations and cultures, all within a given territorial framework.

I have attempted in this work to bring together these two broad perspectives with Finland as the focal point. In spite of its peripheral position in Europe, Finland enjoyed an unusual and in many respects unique status. Separated from Sweden in 1808 and joined to the Russian empire, its geopolitical position nevertheless remained quite distinct within the northern Baltic area. Furthermore, different historical influences over the centuries left the country with a distinctive blend of eastern as well as western European characteristics.

During the nineteenth century, the national movement was born and grew to maturity in many European countries, including Finland. The fulfilment of national independence in the final stages of the First World War falls outside the scope of this book, although many of the problems with regard to Finland's relations with the rest of the world which are dealt with in the following chapters are of great relevance to the period of independence up to the present day.

If Finland's peripheral situation is examined from within, i.e. in terms of the structure of Finnish society, the delay in adapting to change is particularly striking. Although Finland enjoyed the privilege of autonomous government within the Russian empire, the political awakening of Finnish society occurred very slowly. The social role of the church was for a long time all-powerful, while the social structure was firmly moulded by the agrarian nature of the economy. Industrialisation only began to any marked degree at the end of the nineteenth century. Nevertheless, as changes occurred, an ever broader section of Finnish society began to react to international crises and events. Similar problems to those experienced in Finland occurred in other nations which were part of empires, such as Ireland and Bohemia.

In the years 1808–1914, Finland was to a greater or lesser extent affected by a number of international crises and major events in European history, and the way in which the country was affected has been examined in two ways. The first focusses attention on how the position of Finland was viewed abroad (in Sweden, Britain, France and Germany) in connection with international crises and events, and on what sort of interest Finland generally inspired there. The security policy of the Russian empire in the context of major events, and the general relationship between Finland and Russia, are also considered.

This first method of approach may be depicted schematically as follows:

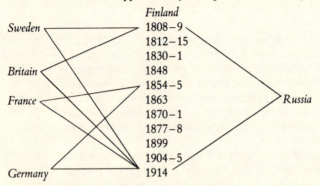

The second line of approach, schematically represented below, has been to see how Finland reacted to major events and crises, in terms of different social and occupational groups.

My research in Finland has been carried out partly in Helsinki — mainly in the National Archives, the library of the University, the library of the University's Theological Faculty, and the Labour Archives — and partly in Turku, in the libraries of the University of Turku and of Åbo Akademi. I have also made use of the major archives and libraries in Stockholm, Bonn, Hamburg, Paris, London and Vienna. In addition I have had the use of Russian materials from various sources.

I would like to acknowledge my gratitude to Professors Martti Ruutu, Lolo Krusius-Ahrenberg, Erkki Pihkala and Eino Murtorinne, and to the director of the Labour Archives, Matti Nieminen, all of whom went out of their way to read through my manuscript either in whole or in part. My thanks are also due to Professors Aulis Alanen, Helge Pohjolan-Pirhonen and Aimo Halila, and to

Drs Johannes Salminen, Pentti Airas and Tapani Vuorela. Of the many foreign colleagues who have discussed my work and helped me in various ways, I would especially like to mention Professors Pierre Renouvin, René Girault and François-Xavier Coquin and Dr Georges Déthan (France); Professors Hugh Seton-Watson and R.F.Leslie and Drs George Bolsover and David Kirby (Britain); Professors Georg von Rauch, G.Stökl, Eugen Lemberg and Walther Hubatsch and Dr Barbara Vogel (Germany); Professors Folke Lindberg and Åke Holmberg and Drs Carl-Fredrik Palmstierna, Sven Eriksson and Leokadia Postén (Sweden); and Professor Emil Niederhäuser (Hungary). In addition I have had the opportunity to exchange opinions about different aspects of my research with a number of historians in the Soviet Union.

In all the phases of my study, I have had valuable assistance from the young historians at the University of Turku, and I would like to thank in particular Drs Martti Julkunen and Juhani Mylly for their valuable criticisms and fresh ideas. My former colleague Keijo Korhonen and Professor Väinö Luoma also read through my manuscript and made a number of valuable comments.

I also acknowledge the assistance of the Finnish Academy, which granted me a senior scholar's award in 1977, and a number of different sources abroad which provided me with financial assistance.

Finally, I acknowledge my indebtedness to Anthony Upton of the University of St. Andrews and Sirkka Upton for their translation of the original text, and to Dr David Kirby of the School of Slavonic Studies, London, for his work in helping to edit the final text.

University of Turku, June 1981   JUHANI PAASIVIRTA

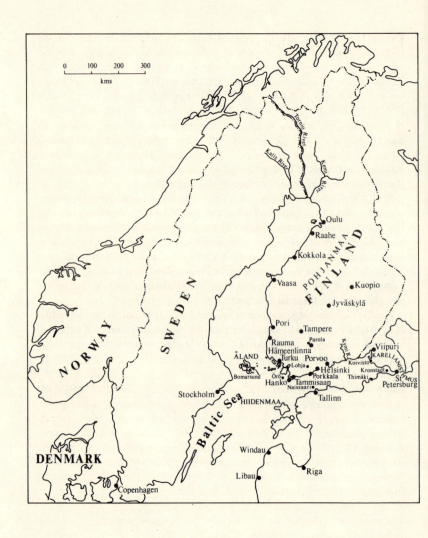

I. The final phase of Swedish rule

The Finnish question in international relations and the development of
political attitudes in Finland

In February 1808, Russian troops crossed the eastern frontier of the Swedish-Finnish kingdom. The conquest of Finland followed swiftly, and a great historical change began in that country. Finland's centuries-old connection with Sweden ended, and she became part of the Russian empire — although on the basis of her own special political status. The new era following this attachment to Russia was to link Finland with a new range of historical connections. As part of a great power and in terms of international politics and general international developments, she was drawn into a complex of political and other problems.

Even before the country was attached to Russia, the Finnish question had begun to some extent to be identified as a distinct question in international politics, especially in the eighteenth century.[1] Sweden's collapse as a great power in the Great Northern War (1700–21) had caused a certain disturbance among the ruling circles in Western European countries. From then on, when these circles turned their attention to Sweden, its eastern part — Finland — attracted more attention than before.

Of the European great powers it was France which, during the eighteenth century, supported Sweden's international position, in accordance with the policy begun by Richelieu. At the same time she used Sweden, along with Poland and Turkey, in the furtherance of her own political aims, which remained strongly anti-Russian throughout the eighteenth century. French foreign policy was later to influence Sweden in opening hostilities against Russia in 1741. In the ensuing conflict, Finland became a focus of international attention as an area occupied by Russian troops. At the end of the war in 1743, further eastern areas were detached from Finland and joined to Russia, as had happened in 1721. These two developments made the defence of what was left of Finland an important security problem for Sweden, and after the end of the war the French proposed to Sweden that fortifications be established before Helsinki. This speeded up the building of Sveaborg.

Thus Finland had earned some attention as a clearly distinguishable part of the Swedish kingdom in various international political contexts. However it did not follow from this that understanding of Finnish conditions was much increased abroad or that knowledge of some of the country's peculiar features was increased, for example about the Finnish language. Finland, seen from the power centres of Europe, was still unknown and peripheral.

Sweden again went to war with Russia in 1788 when the latter in turn was at war with France's old ally Turkey. But this time France, because of internal weakness, now sought to restrain the Swedish king, Gustav III, rather than

1

incite him to war. At the same time Britain too had begun to be suspicious of Russian foreign policy. Her general aim after the ending of the northern war was the preservation of a stable 'northern system' and because of this she was interested in a general balance in the Baltic area. However Britain saw this objective as under threat from the continuous enlargement of Russia's sphere of influence. In 1783, Russia annexed the Crimea, and Britain saw this as an attempt to extend her influence towards the eastern Mediterranean as well.

The war of 1788–90 between Sweden and Russia — with Finland again at the focus of events — attracted noticeable publicity both in western and northern Europe. Since there was fighting on two fronts simultaneously, in both northern and south-eastern Europe, diplomatic activity between the great powers was considerable. Britain, supported by Prussia, tried to protect the position of Sweden, Poland and Turkey as a counterweight to the strengthening of Russian influence; and to promote these diplomatic aims, she appeared as mediator at the peace negotiations between Russia and Sweden at Värälä (1790). However, there was dissatisfaction in both London and Berlin when the negotiations led to a peace on the basis of the *status quo ante* and there was no strengthening of Sweden's position.

Thus in the eighteenth century events in the area of Finland had attracted the attention of Europe's ruling circles through these wars. In all of them Sweden and Russia had been the antagonists, and Finland had been occupied by Russian troops; only the last, in Gustav III's time, had been an exception to this.

The Finnish question may also have been known of in Prussia and Austria, where the observation of Russian foreign activity was regarded as important, and in Denmark leading politicians had for many years been interested in collaboration with Russia: if they were to realise this aspiration, Sweden might find itself 'between the hammer and the anvil'.

In the course of the eighteenth century Finland had also begun to be distinguished from the rest of the Swedish kingdom by conditions in the country and the developing attitudes of the populace.[2] Especially after the war of 1741–3 and the 'little wrath' period of Russian occupation, criticism had begun to appear in Finland of the fact that the country's affairs were managed from Stockholm. The Finnish representatives in the Diet often made allegations that the eastern part of the kingdom was disregarded economically and its defence neglected. Representatives of the Finnish farmers complained that the status of the Finnish language too was disregarded. It was argued that there was indifference in Stockholm concerning Finnish problems.

Because Finland had become relegated to the role of a victim, this tended to unite the country's inhabitants, and it is possible to see a Finland-centred way of looking at affairs — a view that Finland had its own special interests — emerging alongside the habit of thinking of the kingdom as a whole. This became even clearer as the century advanced.

At the Diet the representatives of the eastern part of the kingdom might declare in different connections — transcending the lines between the Estates — that they represented the 'Finnish nation' or had the task of defending 'the rights and liberties of Finland'. In a sense, the Diet of 1765–6 saw the appearance of 'Finnish radicalism' when on the initiative of Anders Chydenius and others the question of granting certain coastal towns in Pohjanmaa rights to engage in overseas trade (the so-called staple rights) was raised.

In the last decades of the century divergent signs of change in Finnish conditions were apparent. Gustav III's reforms had benefited the eastern part of the kingdom in many respects. The Finnish burghers and farmers especially felt the economic expansion had improved their lot. But many specific matters like the execution of the great land re-distribution and the policy on home distilling caused dissatisfaction among the farmers. In Finland the burgher Estate was small in numbers and of limited importance, reflecting the slowness of urban development. The clergy carried out separately their task as advocates of various regional and local economic reforms. In the conditions of the time, certain regional differences also clearly emerged. Western and south-western Finland and some districts of Pohjanmaa were relatively prosperous whereas parts of the interior — like Savo — were relatively little developed. There had been no economic detachment of Finland from Sweden during the eighteenth century, and the Finns manifested the same dissatisfaction at the centralisation of the economic life of the kingdom as, for example, did the north of Sweden. However, in spite of these various expressions of dissatisfaction, there was a desire in Finland to emphasise loyalty and gratitude to the king of Sweden — but in a manner which showed that the Finns wanted their relationship to the king to be a special one, as a unit of their own. It was a special feature of the Finnish attitude that the ruler of Sweden was seen as a significant guarantor of security.

The academic circle in Turku generated its own influence in the development of attitudes in Finland at the end of the century. The intellectuals grouped round H.G. Porthan, besides being significant practitioners in different fields of learning, also typified to some extent a way of thinking coloured by a nationalist tendency, in which Finland itself was the focus. The cultural tendency directed by Porthan, while it stressed the national peculiarities, expressed at the same time firm loyalty to the state and a firm royalism.

After the outbreak of the war of 1788, criticism of Gustav III appeared within the officer corps, which came to a climax in accusations that it was the king who had really begun the war. The position of some Finnish officers at this stage was shown in the 'Liikala note', which was sent to Catherine II and expressed the wish for a restoration of peace between the two countries. A large number of Finnish and Swedish officers subsequently supported the peace effort and for that purpose created the so-called Anjala league. On the other hand, very little true political separatism, aimed at detaching the country from Sweden had appeared in Finland. It was mainly found among an aristocratic circle, whose central figure was Colonel G.M.Sprengtporten. However when war broke out in 1788, he had already moved to Russia and separatist phenomena were weakening.

Among the aristocracy in the Swedish kingdom — including Finland — certain attitudes clearly deviated from those of the rest of society. The characteristic feature — a certain cosmopolitanism — was also to be seen in aristocratic circles elsewhere in Europe at that time. In Sweden this novel attitude could include a degree of reserve when it was a question of relations to the king as the representative of authority and obligations to the state. International political developments were followed among the aristocracy more than in other spheres of society.

Among the different Estates in Finland the enhancement of Russia's role in foreign affairs claimed attention. At the same time, among the Finnish officer corps the image of Russia was changing: the eastern neighbour no longer appeared so much an enemy and a danger as before. But in Finland this new outlook came up against old traditions, which embodied a severely negative attitude to Russia, born of western cultural and Nordic social attitudes. In addition, the country's Lutheran faith was significant in emphasising the contrasts with Orthodox Russia. The attitude of the farmers to the eastern neighbour was absolutely negative — Russia was the country where serfdom was known to prevail.

In the eighteenth century questions of defence policy had received some attention among all levels of society in Finland, including the farming population.[3] There had for example been no opposition to furnishing reservists for the militia when a decision on this was made in the late 1770s. The Finnish clergy for its part displayed loyalty to the king during the war years 1788–90. By the 1790s there was no group in Finland actively following international affairs, as the officers had done in the preceding period, once the Anjala league had been judicially investigated. Since the Diet too did not meet in Sweden in this decade substantial groups of Finns had no opportunity to meet in an environment in which world events were discussed.

The French Revolution in 1789 was not experienced as any kind of great ideological turning-point by the narrow academic intellectual circles in Turku, on whom modern political ideas had not yet made an impact. In Stockholm, by contrast, events in Paris were already followed with interest, and the newspapers there divided into supporters and opponents of the Revolution. In the same way, even as far east as Königsberg, the Revolution could be felt as a significant sign of transition. However those circles in Finland which did follow events became more sensitive to the problems of defence policy because of the country's geographical position; this was influenced by the fact that during the 1790s the French Revolution and the partition of Poland caused considerable changes in the state frontiers of continental Europe, with whole countries disappearing from the map. This was illustrated by the attitude of Porthan, in whose stern criticism of the French Revolution there existed side by side conservatism and a desire for security, which included a fear of change. At this time fears were expressed that the waves of change on the continent might in some way reach as far as Finland. The close co-operation of the Finnish representatives at the Norrköping Diet of 1800 — including the nobility — expressed a certain general insecurity. Before that the fact that Gustav III had been succeeded by Gustav IV Adolf had served to remove the sharp edges which divided the Finnish Estates. Among the aristocracy there had been a fear of the 'Jacobin infection' spreading to Finland. The other Finnish Estates, influenced by their attitudes on defence policy, fear of Russia and traditional royalism, clung — in the uncertain international situation — more closely to the Swedish mother-country.

When Napoleon had risen to assume the direction of French policy, the great political changes in continental Europe only continued and the geographical framework broadened. However press censorship in the Swedish realm set obstacles and limits to the publication of news about these events, particularly concerning such a topic as the continuous growth of Napoleon's power.

The affairs of the Swedish kingdom were directed from Stockholm, and in ruling circles there it was well known what was really happening in the rest of Europe. Finland, however, was firmly isolated; in the eastern parts of the country it was primarily certain government officials, university professors and priests who had contact with Stockholm, and they brought back from their trips to Stockholm news about events in central Europe. Yet Finland lacked the kind of forum in which public affairs could be continually discussed.

In any case, some echoes of the clamour of events in continental Europe — the great political changes and continuing wars — were carried as far as Finland in various ways. Undoubtedly many rumours also circulated, and with uncertainty there was speculation that the continuing changes might soon reach northern Europe.

II. The union of Finland with the Russian empire as a consequence of the war of 1808

1. *The war between Russia and Sweden, the reaction of foreign powers to developments, and political attitudes in Russian-occupied Finland*

The genesis of the Russian attack upon Finland in February 1808 was linked to the phase of the Napoleonic wars in which the French sphere of influence was extended to the southern coast of the Baltic. In this phase three great powers — Russia and Britain as well as France — sought to develop a strategy in the Baltic area.[1]

In the immediate background to the attack, the turning-point was the broad agreement on co-operation between Napoleon and Alexander concluded at Tilsit in the summer of 1807. On the one hand it included a broad division of spheres of influence in the Balkans, and on the other an agreement on common measures in conformity with Napoleon's main objective, the so-called Continental System, whereby Britain should be totally excluded from commercial relations with the rest of Europe. With this aim in view, it was the intention to get Sweden and Denmark to join the continental blockade. When the British government came to know the content of the Tilsit agreement, the British fleet was ordered to bombard Copenhagen and subsequently the entire Danish fleet was destroyed: it was important for British interests to ensure that communications with the Baltic be kept open and to demonstrate to Napoleon and his allies in an unmistakable manner Britain's armed strength. However the blow suffered by Denmark had the opposite effect from what had been hoped in London: in the powerful reaction that followed, Denmark moved to Napoleon's side.

According to the Tilsit agreement, Alexander had the task of forcing Sweden to submit to the continental blockade; he was to choose the means and the definition of the overall objective. In this way the Finnish question began to emerge — on the basis of the great general division of Europe carried out by Napoleon and Alexander — although in the Tilsit negotiations nothing had been specifically decided about the fate of the country. Despite various kinds of pressure initiated by Alexander, Sweden and its king, Gustav IV Adolf, remained detached from the sphere of influence of the Alexander-Napoleon axis — encouraged to do so by the appearance of the British fleet in the Baltic after the bombardment of Copenhagen. However, Sweden was also being pushed into a kind of buffer position; at the same time as she tried to preserve her independent position, her territorial integrity was coming within the danger zone.

The situation following the Tilsit agreement was in many respects favourable

6

to Russia in the Baltic area, and it brought the Finnish question — as seen from St Petersburg — into focus. For a whole century Finland had been a kind of marginal question on Russia's north-west frontier from the point of view of her security requirements, although the experience of the Swedish army having twice — in 1741 and 1788 — used Finnish territory as a base for an attack towards St Petersburg had proved cautionary; in addition, on the latter occasion Russia had been tied down in a simultaneous war on another front. From 1700 onwards the territorial aims of Russian policy had been emphatically in the direction of the Balkans; in 1807–8 they were concentrated on Moldavia and Wallachia, but in that region there were no concessions to be had from Napoleon. This in itself had the effect of diverting the activity of Russian foreign policy away from the Balkans and almost directing it towards north-western Europe.

At the end of 1807, Alexander moved from diplomatic pressure in his relations with Sweden to a solution by military force; this involved many problems.[2] A complete change of direction in foreign policy towards a former ally had to be undertaken. The decision to begin military operations in Finland also demanded undertaking in advance extensive measures for equipment and supply, and in winter conditions too. This new front would be far from those areas where the Russian army had been concentrated hitherto — and this demanded time for preparation. The solution of these problems among the Russians themselves favoured meanwhile the most far-reaching diplomatic caution towards Sweden.

Russia began military operations on its Swedish frontier on 21 February 1808 without a declaration of war; in addition, she acted with concealed objectives in the opening phase of the campaign.[3] The fighting ability of the Swedish army and the attitudes of the Finnish population may have been problematical matters in St Petersburg, but the results in the first weeks were highly favourable to the Russian advance. Sweden was not at first prepared for concessions; but her position deteriorated when Denmark declared war against her on 14 March and Sweden-Finland was thus surrounded.

Military operations in Finland moved so swiftly that on 22 March Russian troops had occupied the country's capital, Turku, and continued their advance to the north. The Russians issued a proclamation dated 16/28 March, addressed to the foreign powers, declaring the part of Finland belonging to Sweden to be annexed to the Russian empire. This was repeated in another proclamation four days later.[4] 'Natural frontiers' were in themselves an important objective for Alexander, although this was not openly declared.

In the early months of the war, the Swedish army was forced to retreat to the north almost to the level of Oulu; Sveaborg surrendered and Åland was occupied by a Russian detachment. In the early summer, however, the Swedish army began a counter-attack both on the coast of Pohjanmaa and in Savo, and was supported by risings of the country people, especially in southern Pohjanmaa. A rising also broke out in Åland, forcing the Russian occupation force to withdraw from the archipelago. In addition Swedish troops made a diversionary landing near Turku, and a naval detachment was off the coast of Pohjanmaa. The Swedish advance in the summer months as far as southern Pohjanmaa compelled the Russian command to call up reinforcements, and the original invading force of some 24,000 men was more than doubled. This led to a new turn in the war in southern Pohjanmaa towards the end of August, and the approach of a British naval squadron towards the Gulf of Finland made the Russian army go for a quick decision. It also caused a wave of optimism in Sweden; Gustav IV Adolf hoped, in the early summer when the Swedish counter-attack was in progress in Pohjanmaa, that the British and Swedish fleets would make a joint assault on Kronstadt and other Russian bases.

Britain's policy, however, was to avoid definitive hostilities with Russia.[5] She was certainly prepared if necessary to protect the territory of Sweden proper, but was not prepared to commit herself to the reconquest of Finland. She sought to secure a certain state of equilibrium in the Baltic, which in the prevailing circumstances dictated a close liaison with Sweden. However Britain also had hopes the whole time that Russia would change her policy towards Napoleon, and therefore continuously avoided breaking relations off with St Petersburg.

The campaign in Finland, despite its peripheral position, aroused general European interest, as did the simultaneous campaign in Spain. In the spring and summer of 1808 *The Times* regularly published news of the campaign in Finland, relying largely on Swedish sources — which, however, were coloured by the wishful thinking prevalent there. For example, Sweden's counter-attack at the beginning of June in Pohjanmaa was given such prominence that her final defeat in the autumn caused great surprise.[6]

In Paris news about the war in Finland was to be obtained mainly through the official Russian newspaper *Journal du Nord*. From spring to autumn in 1808, it carried extensive reports of these campaigns. According to the account in the official French newspaper, *Le Moniteur*, at the end of September the Russian conquest of Finland was a demonstration of the kind of fate that awaited a country which ventured to oppose Napoleon.[7]

When Napoleon and Alexander met again at Erfurt in the autumn of 1808, the Russian Emperor received confirmation that Napoleon, who at this point was tied down fighting in Spain, had made an important concession: Finland — together with the Danubian principalities — was clearly acknowledged as belonging to the Russian territories, and furthermore without any territorial compensation to France.[8]

In the autumn of 1808, the Russians also secured their final military victory in Finland when the Swedish-Finnish main force suffered a major defeat at the battle of Oravainen on 14 September. In the armistice agreements of Lohtaja and Olkijoki — the latter concluded on 14 November — Finland was acknowledged to have come under Russian occupation. For Finland itself, the final solution of the conflict was dependent on the diplomatic settlement between

Russia and Sweden. In addition, the development of relations between the Russian occupiers and the Finnish population and the attitude of each side to this question would form its own complex of problems.

In conquering new territories, Russian policy had sought in various instances to create links with the local ruling groups. The aim had often been a measure of co-operation in which special privileges were conceded to certain groups in the population, and some areas had even been recognised in their entirety as having their own 'political existence'. For example, special privileges had been conceded to the nobility and burghers of the large towns in the Baltic provinces in the last phase of the Great Northern War. On the other hand, in some cases Russian policy was to annexe new territories directly to the empire as 'conquered lands'. This had happened in the partition of Poland, where the conditions in the conquered territories were made uniform with the Russian system.[9]

In the Finnish case, Russian policy came to follow the former line. Alexander's first proclamations, which were issued after the beginning of the war, contained promises to preserve the existing privileges of the Estates and freedom of worship. The emperor may have been thinking of giving the conquered areas of Finland roughly the same status as those which had been annexed to Russia in 1721 and 1743 and which had constituted the guberniya of Viipuri.[10] Swedish law had been in force and the Lutheran church active there, but otherwise these territories, known as Old Finland, had no special political status.

The granting of a special political status to Finland emerged only in the later phases of the war of 1808. It is a fact that in the summer months the Russians had met military resistance which, together with the popular risings, had surprised them. But from the autumn the international situation and the growing tension in Alexander's relations with Napoleon seemed to have reached a state which, from the conqueror's side, favoured speedy decisions on the 'pacification' of Finland; this would give the most secure possible outcome.[11] In addition, Russia had been forced to tie down considerable forces in Finland, which was still a secondary problem given her overall interests.

Traditionally the nobility was the important group in Finland when the Russian occupier began to establish relations with the Finnish leaders. Its position was based on its administrative role under Swedish rule and on the higher commands in the armed forces. Its growing cosmopolitanism during the eighteenth century, too, could not have remained unnoticed in St Petersburg. In addition, right from the beginning of the war the Russian occupier had sought contact with the leaders of the Finnish church,[12] a course of action in accordance with the policy pursued during the period 1714–21. The Russian occupier had then sought, with a view to preserving order, to maintain the church administration in the country since the secular officials had mostly fled to Sweden.[13] In Russian eyes, the Finnish Lutheran church had an important and respected position among the people. Russia now sought to use its leaders and the rest of its clergy as a channel of communication to maintain order in the occupied areas and as a means of 'winning the minds' of the population. This was a special kind of Russian pacification policy peculiar to Finland.

It was a striking feature of Alexander I's policy in Finland that already from the early summer of 1808 great attention was paid to the country's only university, Turku Academy.[14] Its significance was obvious — it trained civil servants and clergy — but the Emperor clearly also wished to recognise it as a centre of the highest intellectual culture in Finland. By promising to develop Turku Academy, he could display to the west an image of himself as a liberal ruler, which — as a security policy linked to the pacification policy — was not without significance. On the other hand, the actions of the Russian conquerors in Finland do not indicate that the country's burgher Estate was regarded as an important group, with which they should attempt — as in the Baltic provinces a century earlier — to establish special relations. The burgher Estate in Finland was neither prosperous economically nor socially significant. Nonetheless, the Russians showed a willingness to preserve the existing privileges of the Estate.

One special feature of Russian pacification policy in the transitional phase of 1808, which specifically concerned Finland, was that Russia also paid particular attention to the whole population, including the farmers.[15] In many respects Finland was treated in Alexander's policy as a traditionally 'Swedish land'; for example, promises were made to preserve the laws and general judicial system in force in the country. Also, the position of the Finnish farmers was recognised and acknowledged as different from what it would be in Russia. This acknowledgement implied that the Finnish farmers were a land-owning group enjoying legal security based on law.

Since Alexander's policy sought to preserve the general characteristics of Finland unchanged, the aim was specifically to influence the development of the political mood in the country, as a counter-balance to the fact of occupation. However there was a difficulty in that the government in St Petersburg hardly knew Finnish conditions. In addition, the exceptional circumstances created by the war had caused much loss and damage to the population, which had inflamed feelings — ultimately it was due to the indiscipline of the foreign troops.

As the conqueror of Finland, Alexander had also — from a general European viewpoint — certain general challenges before him. Finland was the most developed part of the Russian empire, and it was expedient to acknowledge this fact. At the same time, Europe was in a state of ideological ferment: the general European outlook pointed on the one hand to the world of ideas of the Enlightenment, on the other to the period of reform which had begun with the French Revolution, when various kinds of reform ideas were in the air. Great changes had taken place in those territories which France had conquered or which had felt the influence of Napoleon, such as the Rhineland. In Prussia too, for example, a great period of reform was in progress.

Change was the spirit of the times, and the nations were rising — more clearly than before — above the horizon of history. Alexander as a European ruler wanted to develop his empire, and in this he and Napoleon were clearly in competition. To grant autonomy to Finland after the country had been conquered could be presented, through Alexander's actions, as raising the nation up to a higher status.

The Finnish attitude to Russia was compounded of traditions that had developed over a long period. The general dissimilarity of conditions in the two countries — especially in culture, religion and society generally — had hardened the contrasts, which were further sharpened by various emotional factors from suspicion and contempt to outright hatred. Among Finland's lower social orders — notably the farmers and burghers — suspicion and a negative view of Russia were often more pronounced than in the upper class. In addition, the attitude of the clergy was generally critical and suspicious towards an empire which represented 'an alien religion'. Only the nobility saw conditions in Russia as not very different. Wars and periods of occupation had fuelled these sharply antagonistic attitudes: every generation of the eighteenth century had its own stock of experience and its traditions, superimposed on older elements, especially from the sixteenth century.[16] There had been little peaceful contact, connected with trade, between the Swedish and Russian states.

We should now look more closely at Finnish attitudes to the Russians in 1808 when they occupied the country. No flight of the members of the upper Estates and of civil servants to Sweden took place at the beginning of the war of 1808, as at the time of both the great wrath (1714–21) and the little wrath (1742–3). The surprise character of the campaign was undoubtedly one reason, but it was also influenced by the development of attitudes in the final stages of Swedish rule.

When the Russian occupation in southern Finland became an accomplished fact, fear and constraint were paramount, with the need to secure the inviolability of person and properly against the alien occupier. The new situation in southern Finland in the spring and summer of 1808 was one of forced coexistence of Finns and Russians.[17] When a great part of the country had been rapidly overrun, however, there appeared among the upper Estates in Finland an attempt to establish contact with the occupier. Great uncertainty prevailed over what Finland's fate was to be. The noblemen who came forward had an important virtue; they had grown up under the influence of the 'universal' European aristocratic culture of the Gustavian period, and as French-speakers had no language difficulties or inhibitions of manners in their new relations with St. Petersburg.

The new situation demanded of these Finnish leaders a quite different kind of responsibility than in the eighteenth century, when they had appeared as men of the opposition in the Swedish Diet, or been civil administrators in local government offices in Finland under the central administration of the kingdom. They now needed to call upon a new kind of judgement and initiative: they had to try to speak 'on behalf of Finland' — but without any sources of strength of their own. They were at the same time making a personal choice, which caused them to make a mental adjustment — in the midst of great uncertainty — from fear to gratitude. When definite results were within reach, C.E. Mannerheim and many other leading noblemen of the country also developed a pronounced monarchist attitude towards the Emperor. They began to praise his magnanimity, not only publicly but in private correspondence among friends.[18] This attitude differed completely from the relationship of the upper Estates to the sovereign in the final period of Swedish rule.

The leadership of the Finnish church saw dangers in the country falling into the power of Russia. The Lutheran church was being forced — in a situation dominated by armed force — into an empire in which the Orthodox faith had the ascendancy. The area of the Porvoo diocese was the first to recognise the military administration of Buxhoevden, the commander-in-chief, and make contact with it:[19] the geographical position of the diocese and the movement of the compaign had an influence on this development. Also, the Bishop of Turku, Jakob Tengström, was among those leaders of the country who sought actively to build up contacts with the occupiers, but the situation in his diocese did pose a number of problems; the Turku Chapter was hesitant in its attitude because, as the war continued in the spring of 1808, south-western Finland remained an uncertain border area; the Russians had been driven out of Åland and a Swedish landing had taken place near Turku. Bishop Tengström even left Turku for a time, clearly seeking his own personal safety since he had been an active representative of the policy of collaboration. The administration of the diocese came to a halt for a time.[20] When the war in Finland had been finally settled, representatives of the clergy took part in a special delegation of the Estates which travelled to St Petersburg in the autumn of 1808. There they claimed that the Lutheran church should have broad power in determining its own affairs; they wished to be free from dependence on Buxhoevden, who had indeed offered privileges to the church in the spring and summer of 1808, but had also used the clergy as instruments for his own purposes and had not been averse to coercive methods.

The change in national circumstances made a big impression. In the new conditions the church leadership began to stress the Lutheran tradition of submission to authority, and appealed to the Emperor along those very lines. It was a question of choosing a carefully thought-out 'middle way', in doing which they sought on the one hand to free themselves from interference by the Russian military administration and, on the other, tried to avoid for all time the solution adopted in Old Finland, which had led to a position where the civil administration had broad powers over church affairs.[21] From the church's point of view, the situation in the autumn of 1808 was considerably better than had been feared, which aroused Bishop Tengström's gratitude towards Alexander, whom he saw as a humane ruling figure. At this stage he was emphasising to the clergy even more consistently than before the importance of adapting to the new circumstances. [22]

The great upheaval of the French Revolution had been followed by the intellectual circle in Turku Academy without any desire for ideological participation and with reservations, as we have seen. However they had tried to follow the changes in Europe, which now — somewhat belatedly — were spreading their influence into Finland via the eastern route. The Academy continued to function and relations between it and the occupiers appeared to develop correctly. As early as June 1808, Alexander had signified to the vice-chancellor — again Bishop Tengström, — his favour towards the university and his desire to develop it. Among the academics there had been hardly any flight to Sweden before the arrival of the Russians. Even after the occupation a certain freedom of choice remained for those working at the Academy, and to move to the other side of the Gulf of Bothnia after 1808 might, for career and other reasons mean uncertainty. The Emperor's promise, moreover, seemed to secure the future development of the Academy.

Study and preparation for official careers — as judges, clergy, teachers and doctors — continued in the accustomed way. Later there was talk of expanding public offices, when the question arose of Finland getting its own central administration. But one fact was clearly visible: whether one worked in administration or education, it was always under the supervision of the higher administration. In Finnish society there were no free professions on offer to the intellectuals.

Among the burghers the desire to keep conditions unchanged was the predominant thought when they found themselves suddenly overtaken by the Russian occupation. Issues were examined, above all, from the point of view of the business community's overall position and of one's own livelihood; everything was linked to that. In the new situation they feared that they would become generally committed and oriented towards Russia in economic relations. When in the spring of 1808 the customs frontier between Russia and Finland was abolished, the decision was seen as pointing that way. In such a situation it was hoped, most of all in the burgher Estate, that trade with Sweden could continue unchanged, despite all the dissatisfaction and criticism it had occasioned previously. [23]

The farmers were the part of society which the campaign of 1808 and the occupation affected most severely. Town-dwellers, on the other hand, often got through with no more than a shock. The farmers' attitude to the Russian occupiers was that they represented a foreign language, an alien religion and an unfree society, and the popular risings of the farmers in southern Pohjanmaa in the summer of 1808 expressed their strong fear of the Russian system. [24]

There were also regional differences of adaptation to the new conditions. For example when in the summer of 1808 the war continued in Pohjanmaa, conditions in southern Finland had largely returned to normal in spite of the occupation. Swedish money was still in use, the previously existing laws were declared to be still in force, and official business could be transacted in Swedish. In southern Finland as a whole, the war of 1808 had left little trace. Life and property seemed secure, especially for town-dwellers. As early as the summer of 1808 festivities involving the local population and the Russian occupation troops were organised in Turku.[25] By contrast, in the country districts of southern Finland, where Russian military units were in transit and demanding billets and replenishment of their supplies, the mood was more restrained. The situation in southern Pohjanmaa, a region with a historic memory of strained relations between Russian troops and the local people from the times of the great wrath, was in many ways different and popular attitudes were also different. After the Russian troops had consolidated their position there, looting occurred in Vaasa, and in the countryside there were outbreaks of murders and arson.[26] As a consequence there was a rising of farmers in the region.

Although attitudes towards the Russian occupiers varied, there was essentially an adaptation to the new conditions in southern Finland. In this area lived almost the whole of the nobility and most members of the existing civil service. The occupier tried to influence the mood in the country favourably in a number of ways. For example, there was an order to reduce taxation in both town and country;[27] compensation was paid for damage and losses caused by the war; and the Russian military command punished soldiers for indiscipline, and by so doing made a favourable impression generally.

Among the measures taken by the occupiers, the administration of an oath of allegiance from the population of the occupied part of the country, begun in the spring of 1808, clearly proved double-edged. Since the war still continued in Pohjanmaa and the fate of the country had not yet been decided, such a measure was ill-received in many places, and even met resistance. The actual swearing of the oath was not always voluntary.[28]

In general, it is possible to discern two attitudes in Finnish society towards the Russian occupation as the autumn of 1808 approached.[29] Outwardly there appeared a desire for co-operation and submission to the political change that had occurred; here certain members of the nobility were leaders in making contact with the occupiers and with government representatives in St Petersburg. At the same time, however, passivity and reserve were apparent in the country. In the occupied areas, problems of adaptation often began at the individual level, from concern for personal safety and the inviolability of one's property; this concern was then manifested at a higher, political level. The central question was always whether the prevailing situation was final or merely provisional, and what kind of about-turns might still be in store — with perhaps a return to the past.

From the autumn of 1808, Finland was on the way to being isolated in relation to other countries. In accordance with the Tilsit agreement, Russia began to bring Finland under the regulations of the continental system; the import of

British goods into the Russian empire was forbidden, and in the summer of 1808 this ban was extended to Finland.[30] In the Atlantic and North Sea, British men-of-war posed a threat to merchant ships; and in addition, the southern Baltic had been drawn within the scope of the general war. To evade the continental system, Britain tried to maintain secret trade relations with the continent, using the Baltic area as a round-about supply route. Especially from 1807, her convoys sailed in the direction of the Sound, where Danish and French privateers gave chase. In the southern Baltic a naval war of 'limited operations' went on;[31] as an insecure and loss-making area it compelled Finnish merchant ships to curtail their movements. The consequences of this were a reduction of both exports and imports and signs of depression at home.

As a result of the Russian occupation, Finland had come to 'change sides' in European high politics as well. In regard to foreign trade, this meant that she neither had the advantage of Swedish neutrality, nor the official flag and military convoys which Sweden had used at sea to protect her merchant ships against interference by outsiders. The sudden change interrupted the possibilities of profiting from the exceptional demand created by the wars of the French Revolution and Napoleonic period in the international market — which, needless to say, aroused dissatisfaction in Finnish seafaring circles.[32]

Connections to Sweden from Finland had generally become disrupted by the autumn of 1808, when military operations on Finnish territory were coming to an end. The only newspaper in the country, *Åbo Tidning*, which had been published since the 1770s, did not contain — either then or throughout 1809 — any reports of general European political developments. Contact with the outside world had virtually been cut off.

2. *The Finnish question in the light of the Diet of Porvoo and the Hamina peace treaty*

In the autumn of 1808, as far as the Finnish question was concerned, the keys to political development were in the hands of the occupier. The development of the international situation came to be the external factor which influenced Alexander, in that way indirectly benefiting Finland. The growing tension and uncertainty in Russo-French relations caused Alexander to look for and also to make decisions with the purpose of guaranteeing rapidly, and as securely as possible, the pacification of Finland. The real value for Russia of its conquest of Finland appeared indirectly in those measures of Alexander's which affected the country.

The prevailing situation and the external constraints connected with it caused Alexander to go considerably further in the concessions to be made to Finland than had been contained in the promises he had given in the spring and early summer of 1808 'to preserve the law and religion unaltered'. The Emperor's decisions came perhaps to include such concessions as he might not have initiated in different circumstances.

In the autumn of 1808 a plan to give Finland a specially broader 'political existence' began to take shape. From a political-psychological point of view it was a question of the Finns being liberated by the emperor's measures from the fear and the attitudes born of the war and occupation. Thus there was an attempt to change the outcome of armed conquest into a positive approval of a new political situation. At this point the general situation in Finland was such that almost all civil servants had stayed at their posts. In addition, the administration of justice, the civil administration and the ecclesiastical administration — with certain limitations — also continued to function on the same basis as before. Thus a separate 'Finnish administration' functioned in the midst of an occupation. However, Finland lacked a central government — that had remained in Stockholm.

The granting of a separate 'political existence' to Finland raised the question of defining the administrative dividing-line between Finland and Russia in the new situation. This also meant that the role of the military authorities either had to be clearly limited or completely terminated. Alexander's decision on 1 December 1808 that business concerning Finland was henceforth to be presented directly to him, by-passing the officials of the Russian government machine, was a clear step in that direction. The decision also clearly implied that Alexander intended to maintain the existing legal system in Finland. In the same connection the office of Governor General of Finland was established, also directly subordinate to the emperor. A Finnish administration began to appear, which was clearly a distinct unit of its own, although it was still on a very provisional level. Also the fact that Alexander took as a new addition to his list of titles the name 'Grand Duke of Finland' emphasised this line of development.

The new arrangement for presenting Finnish business to the Emperor turned out to be unclear and vague in many respects, since the military administration in Finland continued to operate in a number of areas. Often high-ranking Russian civil servants managed to involve themselves in the preparation of Finnish business. Some of them found it difficult to accept that Finland constituted a special area within which their authority in the far-flung empire did not extend. In any case, on the basis of Alexander's decision of December 1808, a direct administrative link was initiated between Finland, forming a territorial unit, and the emperor acting in St. Petersburg.

The special political position of Finland was emphasised also by the separate 'Finnish Delegation', composed of representatives of the different Estates, which was summoned to St Petersburg. In negotiating on Finland's wishes in November 1808 this delegation refused to act with the authority of the Diet.[33] Alexander decided on 1 February 1809 that the Finnish Diet should meet at Porvoo at the end of March, this 'western' solution being quite novel within the borders of the Russian empire.

The summoning of the Diet in Finland, resulting from the emperor's action at a time when the diplomatic settlement of the war of 1808 had not yet been accomplished, showed beyond doubt that the annexation of the country to Russia was intended. An important and at the same time very visible move in Alexander's Finnish pacification policy was taking place. The 'Finnish Diet' which had received the summons was a national representative body such as had not existed till then. In addition, it was significant from a political point of view that the emperor himself announced that he would be coming to Porvoo to open the Diet. Alexander and the representatives of the Finnish people would thus appear side by side on this political occasion. The importance of the opening could also be emphasised by outward pomp and ceremony. It was clear in advance that through the representatives of the different Estates, knowledge of all that happened at Porvoo could later be spread over the whole country.

What was striking about the summoning of the Diet to Porvoo was the pronounced political staging connected with it. With the help of this new political institution, nominally representing the entire Finnish people, there was an attempt to encourage decisively the pacification of conditions and the obliteration of the negative side of the occupation among the country's population. At the same time it was the intention to bind the Finns and, under the emperor's direction, get them to participate in building the future of Finland on a new basis.

But the appearance side by side of Alexander and the Finnish Estates at the Diet of Porvoo was also a premeditated piece of political stagecraft, the essence of which it was desired to make widely known abroad as well. In this respect it was meant to be a 'show-case' for Alexander's policies. In the first place, it endeavoured to show the former mother-country, Sweden, that the Finnish people had broken away from their old political connection and had 'voluntarily' approved the foundations of the new political status. Secondly, Alexander wanted to notify Napoleon, that a new nation had joined his own sphere of influence, and was furthermore itself assisting the process.

The affirmation of the sovereign, given by Alexander at the opening of the Diet at Porvoo on 29 March 1809, renewed the Emperor's promise — already uttered on many previous occasions — that present conditions in Finland would be preserved unaltered. The affirmation did not contain anything completely new compared with earlier promises by the Emperor. However, in his affirmation the earlier promises were enlarged a little and made more precise. Instead of 'the preservation of the old laws and privileges of the Estates', Alexander's affirmation at the Porvoo Diet concerned 'the country's religion and constitution' and 'the rights and freedoms hitherto enjoyed by the different Estates — upper and lower — separately and together'.[34] The distinction between constitutional laws and ordinary laws made here was a 'western' distinction, unknown in Russia. However, the sovereign's affirmation contained no specific reference to the Gustavian constitutions of 1772 and 1789.

What was new in the Porvoo Diet was its presentation and outward pomp. The representatives of the Finnish people were hearing an Orthodox Emperor's

affirmation in the Lutheran cathedral of Porvoo. The Estates for their part —
in the same setting — swore an oath of allegiance to him. The historical and
ecclesiastical associations of the event were meant to give these assurances a
special value and significance, and at the same time emphasise that the political
change that had happened was irreversible for the Finnish people. As for
Alexander's general attitude towards Finland, the Porvoo Diet did not involve
anything new in principle, save that it had been summoned in accordance with
the traditions of Swedish rule. The tasks it was given continued from where the
Finnish delegation which had gone to St Petersburg had left off.

There was also a consistent endeavour to bind the Finns to build a new position for the country; the Estates were asked for opinions on many questions and
in addition they got the right to state their desires regarding the organisation of
conditions in the country in petitions. However, the emperor himself decided
on the matters which came forward; there was thus no question of any truly
common decisions or agreement between the parties. An exception to this
procedure was that the Estates themselves were allowed to choose candidates to
the country's new leading organ of central administration, the so-called government council. From the point of view of Mannerheim and the Finnish leaders
working with him, this procedure ensured that the Finnish emigrants who had
been in Russia since the 1780s did not obtain places in Finland's new ruling
body, by which they would have been able to achieve their hoped-for political
return. Sprengtporten, named Governor-General in December 1808, remained
the only emigrant who 'got in'. He had been in many ways Alexander's
counsellor in the preparation of Finnish business. But the emperor soon came to
realise that this was not a successful choice, and in 1809 Sprengtporten was
compelled to give up his office.

Although the simultaneous development of European political events
involved much of interest, the representatives at Porvoo made no reference to
foreign countries. This may be seen as expressing — indirectly — a certain
tension of the Estates among themselves. There was still uncertainty about what
would really happen in respect of Finland and how the emperor would react to
the various questions brought forward at the Diet, on which the Estates had
been asked for opinions. This was the central problem for the representatives of
the different Estates taking part in the Diet.

The only reference to foreign countries during the Porvoo Diet was to
relations with Sweden, in connection with the hope expressed by the burgher
Estate, in which the other Estates also joined, that they might carry on trade
from Finland to the former mother-country duty-free.[35] Even in this case it was
primarily a question of preserving Finnish conditions unchanged without reference to any international political events which perhaps the government in
St Petersburg would have considered sensitive.

Alexander's overriding objective was to make sure that the Finns would not
want to get back into union with Sweden. On the other hand, there was no
question at any time of Finland being subordinated to the political and social

system which Russia represented. The annexation of Finland to the Russian empire was not followed by a corresponding integration of the country's economy. On the contrary Finland's trade with Sweden was allowed to continue more or less on its former basis soon after the war ended. Moreover, after 1812 the customs frontier between Finland and Russia, removed in the spring of 1808, was reintroduced and thus Finland came to form a separate tariff area from Russia.

When negotiations for concluding a peace treaty between Sweden and Russia were conducted at Hamina in the summer and autumn of 1809, the fate of Finland was clear in every respect. Sweden had lost the war and its armies had withdrawn from Finnish territory; in addition, a *coup d'état* had occurred in Sweden in March 1809 in which Gustav IV Adolf had been thrust from the throne.

Because Russia was the victor in the war, she clearly held the initiative in the Hamina peace negotiations. However, the dangers of a crisis connected with Franco-Russian relations were a factor which made it important for the government in St Petersburg to achieve a peace treaty with Sweden without delay. The starting-point for the peace negotiations was to seal the annexation of Finland to the territories of the Russian empire. The real negotiations concerned certain more limited territorial questions and the more precise delineation of the new frontier between Sweden and Russia. On these questions clear differences emerged. The most important point of dispute was Åland, of which Sweden tried to keep possession because of its strategic importance. Åland was also important to Russia; its possession was seen as safeguarding Finland's union with the Russian empire. Because of the firm stand taken by Russia in the peace negotiations the Swedes were prepared to be satisfied with the demilitarisation of the Åland archipelago. But even so, that arrangement was seen as diminishing any future military danger from the east.[36] The Russians, however, saw that through the possession and complete control of Åland they could — besides securing possession of Finland — also establish broad military supervision of the northern Baltic sea. Therefore they did not consent to any limitation of their sovereignty where Åland was concerned.

Russia was ready for concessions to Sweden in another direction, which was less significant strategically. This covered the definition of the land frontier between the states from the head of the Gulf of Bothnia northwards. According to the original demand presented by the Russians, the frontier there should have run along the Kalix river, but in the final outcome of the Hamina peace talks, it ran along the Tornio and Muonio rivers. Although Russia made this concession to Sweden, she could in the new situation secure communications to the Arctic Ocean and to Norway through Finnish territory. The determination of the frontier between Sweden and Russia in this way was not based on national points of view; on the one hand, the Finnish-speaking population living in the part of Västerbotten west of the river Tornio remained on the Swedish side, on the other the Swedish-speaking population of Åland was attached to Russia. Geographically speaking it was however a natural frontier.

Characteristically, the Russian delegates at the Hamina peace talks insisted firmly that Russia's sovereign rights over Finland were in no way to be limited by the treaty; thus, for example, at the specific demand of the Russian delegation, all reference to Finland's autonomy was left out of the peace treaty. In this way Russia also avoided the possibility that Finland's special political status could in future come within the sphere of 'international supervision', so that, for example, Sweden could have made representations concerning it.

It was indirectly affirmed in the Hamina peace treaty that Sweden remained wholly an outsider in respect to Finland, when the King of Sweden stated that after the ruler of Russia had given assurances to the population of the country about their rights, he had no cause 'to propose conditions' on behalf of his former subjects (Article VI).

It is remarkable that in the whole Hamina peace treaty Finland is nowhere mentioned by name. In this way Russia wished to avoid giving rise to any ambiguities in the territorial sense. But obviously it was also one means by which they avoided the name Finland emerging at the international level as a distinct concept with political implications; the confirmation of Finland's special status at the Porvoo Diet thus remained an arrangement strictly within the frontiers of the empire. The areas ceded by Sweden to Russia were listed in the peace treaty by provinces; in addition, Åland was mentioned separately in connection with the province of Turku and Pori, and at the end of the list the area of Västerbotten east of the Tornio and Muonio rivers (Articles IV and V).

According to Article XVII of the treaty, the commercial relations between Finland and Sweden would continue almost unchanged — in spite of the new frontier between the states.[37] Since previous economic ties were not broken, but Finland was recognised as still belonging to the same trading area as Sweden, it was a great advantage at that stage both to Finland, for whom a contrary decision would have caused great disturbance of the country's economic life, and to Sweden.

The general significance of the Hamina peace treaty was that in confirming the annexation of Finland including Åland to the Russian empire, it thereby strengthened the empire's dominant position in the Baltic area and sharply altered and weakened the significance of Sweden. This major change in Russia's favour could not be prevented even by Britain, who for the previous century had been interested in keeping a balance in the Baltic and whose naval squadrons had continually moved about these waters during the sailing season.

However for Britain the important thing was the struggle then proceeding against Napoleon. As this was still undecided in 1809, it was most important for her on which side of the European divide Russia would be in the decisive phase. Therefore the British thought that relations with St Petersburg must be handled by means of cautious diplomacy and without letting some secondary Baltic question cause a breach of relations.[38]

3. *The Russian pacification policy; Finnish supporters of the new political direction; the dissidents in post-war Finland*

The transitional phase of the years 1808–9, embracing the Porvoo Diet and the Hamina peace treaty, had given an external frame to Finland's new position — its links with the Russian empire and its special political status within it. However, political attitudes had not yet crystallised. Finland was indeed a conquered country, but events on the continent of Europe reflected a continuing military and political mobility in which the two main participants, Napoleon and Alexander, represented ever more clearly forces opposed to one another. In Finland's new situation, the personality of Alexander had acquired a central position. On the one hand the emperor had been giving promises about the country's special political status, but on the other — and this could not be overlooked — his war of aggression had made Finland a conquered country.

From the end of 1809, people in Finland began to break out of that isolation from foreign countries which had followed the war, and to a certain extent obtained information about political developments outside its borders. It was possible to renew both trading contacts and personal relationships with Sweden, and through these channels, information of various kinds and political rumours about events on the continent of Europe entered the country. Also, *Åbo Tidning*, which in 1810 changed into the country's official newspaper under the name of *Åbo Allmänna Tidning*, obtained the right to publish foreign news, under the strict control of the country's government council; it had to avoid all writing that could give rise to unrest in Finland.[39] In any case the reader of *Åbo Allmänna Tidning* became well aware of the most important events happening on the continent and could draw conclusions about the general direction of international political developments there.[40]

Alexander's pacification policy sought continually from 1809 onwards to draw the leaders of Finland's upper Estates on to the side of the new system. The measures in this direction were manifestly realistic: economic privileges were distributed generously to those concerned, in the form of land grants, titles of nobility, medals and other rewards.[41] The starting up of Finland's own administration, particularly after the government council was established in the autumn of 1809, offered promising career prospects for civil servants. Before 1811, about seventy new offices were established, and the salaries of the civil servants were considerably enhanced. Never in Swedish times had such a large group of Finns had such careers, nor had they carried such responsibility. However, commitment to the new system was also a choice of a political line, which it would not be easy to abandon later.

One of the significant moves in the emperor's pacification policy was the rescript issued in 1810, on the basis of which Finnish officers could retain the official residences and estates they had enjoyed under the Swedes, or 'full salary', even after the army had been disbanded in 1809. This so-called officers' manifesto secured the future and the economic position of the whole of a broad section of the privileged classes. It naturally impressed those circles deeply and inspired gratitude towards Alexander. The scheme was also aimed at getting Finns to return home from Sweden.[42]

Leading the line of co-operation was a limited but socially influential group of Finns, comprising noblemen, civil servants, officers, church leaders and professors of Turku Academy. In the first two years after the occupation the most central members of this group were to be C.E. Mannerheim, who had led the delegation which visited St Petersburg in the autumn of 1808, and R.H. Rehbinder and C.J. Walleen, representing a younger generation. Mannerheim occupied a central post in th government council as vice-chairman of its economic department, and Rehbinder and Walleen entered the Finnish affairs committee set up later in St Petersburg. Bishop Tengström emerged alongside them as a prominent participant in politics.

An important phenomenon of the times was the move from Sweden to Finland in 1811 of two notable 'Gustavian' noblemen, G.M. Armfelt and J.A. Ehrenström, both of whom soon acquired central positions at the head of their country's affairs. The *coup d'état* of 1809 in Sweden had eased the break away from their earlier Gustavian milieu, and their choice influenced other Finns living on the Swedish side of the Gulf of Bothnia.[43] But during the transitional events there was an endeavour in Sweden to characterise those who went into the service of the new régime in Finland as 'traitors'. This immediately reinforced the view among those who had chosen to enter that service that if a turn in high politics were to bring about a drastic change in Finland's position, it would not be possible for them to return to the service of the old kingdom.[44]

The emperor's policy tried to take into account the wishes expressed by the burgher and farmer Estates as well as those of the upper classes. The preservation of previously existing trade relations with Sweden was realised, as has been mentioned above; this was facilitated by Swedish currency still remaining the medium of exchange in the country. The desires expressed by the farmers' Estate also concentrated on preserving conditions as they had been. An extreme case — expressing a general fear of change — was the petition from this Estate that the position of the Swedish language in Finland should remain as before. Here there were suspicions to that in one way or another there might be an attempt to bring Russian into use in the official life of the country.[45]

The core of the emperor's pacification policy was the recognition of a distinct 'Finnish way of life'. Confidence in this began to change Finnish attitudes after 1808–9, but this took time. It is difficult to discern precisely the progress of this change of attitude or to date it accurately. In districts such as Turku, which were labelled 'Swedophile' in the Russian government, shifts of opinion are difficult to make out. What can be said however is that the fear aroused by the occupation began to diminish and in its place a new feeling of security began to develop, which at the same time eliminated or at least reduced the attitude of hostility to the east created by war and tradition. The involuntary co-existence born of war and conquest began to change into a positive recognition of the new political situation of the country.

Both the leading groups of Finns who supported the new régime and the government in St Petersburg were, however, well aware of the existence of dissidents. In Armfelt's opinion a full break away from the influence of Sweden and the assumption of a position of clear loyalty in Finland might influence the emperor favourably. This, to his mind, was realistic politics, which would benefit Finland.[46] But the suppressed opinions of the dissenters in Finland were strengthened — in addition to the factors mentioned earlier — by the thoughts of revenge appearing in Sweden around 1810. They were fuelled by the bitterness of the defeat suffered in the war, but also by the insecurity felt in Sweden in the changed military situation, in which Åland too was occupied by Russian troops; a Russian attack on Sweden was even considered a possibility. The advocates of revenge in Sweden began with the automatic assumption that conditions in Finland were wretched and that the Finns generally wanted a return to union with Sweden. The election of the French Marshal Bernadotte as Swedish crown prince in 1810 strengthened the idea of revenge — news of which spread to Finland.[47]

A significant step, reflecting the pacification policy in the autumn of 1811 — when the relations of France and Russia were deteriorating even further — was the decision to unite Old Finland with the rest of Finland. This meant a return to the territorial unity of Finland, and it also eliminated the fear which had arisen, that conditions in Finland might deteriorate to the level of development of Old Finland. This important sign had a favourable effect on all levels of society, and it was felt in a very concrete way by the people living in the neighbourhood of the old frontier.

The special status of Finland in relation to Russia and the pursuit of the country's interests in St Petersburg were strengthened by another decision made in 1811, concerning the establishment of a special 'Finnish affairs committee' in the Russian capital. This new institution, which came to be led by Armfelt with Rehbinder and Walleen as members, confirmed in practice the earlier decision in principle that the presentation of Finnish business was to be made directly to the emperor. It is relevant to recall in this connection, as an instance of the strengthening of Finland's special status, that the customs frontier between Finland and Russia were established after 1812.

The question of re-establishing the Finnish armed forces after the disbandment order of 1809 also arose, but Finns were sharply divided as to the appropriateness of this measure. Those who hoped for a positive resolution of the issue believed that by this means they could get rid completely of the Russian occupation forces in the country. Those who opposed establishing their own army feared that the Finns might find themselves in battle against their former fellow-countrymen, the Swedes, if an international crisis broke out, especially if the attack came from the west.[48] The emperor for his part reacted negatively to all proposals aimed at the re-establishment of the Finnish army. In the Russian government the wounds of the war of 1808 were felt as being still unhealed. It was assumed that unrest could break out in Finland over the establishment of her own army; further the existence of Finland's own army was seen as easily feeding thoughts of revenge and a return to Sweden.

III. The overthrow of Napoleon and Finland's position and circumstances in a new transitional period

1. *Napoleon's Russian campaign, the Finnish question in the Russian-Swedish negotiations of 1812 and Finnish attitudes*

When relations between France and Russia were moving towards open crisis in June 1812 and Napoleon launched an attack on Russia, the Finnish question had re-emerged in the atmosphere of growing international tension as a small side-issue attached to the northern periphery of the respective spheres of influence of the two emperors.

Since the 1807 negotiations at Tilsit, Napoleon had used Finland as an instrument with which to entice Alexander into co-operation with him. As relations between France and Russia came to a head at the turn of 1811 and 1812, he began once more to exploit the Finnish question. Finland was the territorial promise which Napoleon offered to Sweden at this point, to induce her to join his side in a war against Russia.

Napoleon hoped to form a grand alliance against Alexander, and Sweden as well as Turkey was intended to take part in it. In the event of war breaking out, Napoleon had planned that two flank attacks would be made with the help of these countries, one from the Balkans into southern Russia, the other over the Gulf of Bothnia into Finland. In this way he believed he could develop a gigantic plan for the encirclement of Russia.[1] Turkey had had hostile relations with Russia in the past, but was still not ready to make a military alliance with Napoleon. On the contrary, just at the critical moment in June 1812, she made peace with Russia, ceding Moldavia and Wallachia.

When an offer of negotiation was made to Stockholm from Paris in February 1812, Sweden was already switching to a policy of rapprochement with Russia. Marshal Bernadotte, having become Swedish crown prince two years earlier, did not wish — to the surprise of many — to begin a war of revenge over Finland. He was of the opinion that Finland belonged geographically to Russia. Instead he showed an obvious interest in getting Norway for Sweden, believing that these two countries formed a united territorial whole. However, having come to the country from outside Bernadotte, found that the loss of Finland was still an 'open wound' to many Swedes.[2]

When negotiations between Russia and Sweden took place in St Petersburg in the spring of 1812, it was Alexander's aim to confirm the position of Finland as part of Russia. In this way the dangers threatening the security of St Petersburg from north-western Europe would be eliminated if (or when) war broke out between France and Russia. On the basis of a secret agreement concluded in April 1812, Russia and Sweden began a measure of co-operation which, however, was loosely defined. Each party recognised the territorial integrity of the other; consequently Sweden confirmed that Finland belonged to the Russian empire for the future. Russia for her part declared her readiness for certain diplomatic and military supporting actions the purpose of which was to influence matters so that Sweden might induce Denmark to cede Norway to her.[3] It was believed in the government in St Petersburg that in this way the idea of revenge for the loss of Finland, which existed in Sweden, would be moderated. The consultations carried on between Russia and Sweden meant in the last resort the development of the relations of both countries towards the position that if Napoleon began to attack Russia, Alexander and Sweden might undertake joint military action against him.

Government circles in Russia assiduously followed the emperor's Swedish policy even when, in late June 1812, Russia was attacked by Napoleon. At the end of August, when Napoleon's armies were already as far as the outskirts of Smolensk, Alexander and Karl Johan — Bernadotte adopted this name on becoming Swedish crown prince — met in Turku, and Alexander strove continuously in the discussions to confirm the co-operation of Sweden with Russia. However, Alexander also wanted to be assured of the strength of the new political attachment of Finland but he could not, when all Russia's forces were tied down in the empire's defence, offer Sweden any direct military support in obtaining possession of Norway. This part of the settlement had to be left for the future. Although the situation was very critical for Russia, Alexander acted firmly and consistently to the extent that he was not prepared — in contemplating Russian-Swedish military co-operation against Napoleon in the direction of the Baltic provinces — to concede Karl Johan's request for Finland in return for such help, even 'as a temporary pledge' until they should succeed in getting Norway for Sweden.[4]

The Turku negotiations were significant for Russia too in that Karl Johan had publicly acknowledged that he was an ally of Alexander. This strengthened Alexander's determination to continue the struggle against Napoleon. When at the same time news began to spread to Finland of the new direction in foreign policy adopted by Sweden, this influenced the moods and attitudes in the country and undermined belief in the realisation of revenge in Sweden.

Karl Johan, as the new leader of Sweden's foreign policy, had thus prepared for the possibility that Russia would ultimately emerge as the victor in the war against Napoleon. But he may not have left the alternative outcome completely out of consideration. If Karl Johan had succeeded at Turku in getting Finland into his possession as a temporary pledge, it would undoubtedly have given him a real basis for keeping a strong negotiating position and voice at the end of the war in Europe. Sweden's commitment to military co-operation with Russia was also planned to take place in accordance with so slow a timetable, that when the agreed moment arrived the military outcome of the Russian campaign must already be obvious or at least discernible on the horizon.

Napoleon's attack on Russia could not fail to influence those Finns who kept abreast of the times. How each one reacted in this situation depended partly on whether he had openly supported the new régime in Finland or not, partly on general adaptation to the new circumstances. The territory of Finland itself was in no danger of becoming an objective in Napoleon's campaign, if only because he had no fleet at his disposal.

When Russia's defensive action against Napoleon moved towards Moscow, the significance of Finland and Finnish attitudes became important for Russia. It would be doubly dangerous in such a situation if the Finns were to begin in some way opposing the Russians. The significance of Finland as a peaceful area only increased the further Napoleon's advance continued.

The Finnish affairs committee in St Petersburg was of the opinion that Finland should demonstrate clearly a desire 'to take part' in the fight against Napoleon.[5] Armfelt, an extreme opponent of Napoleon, also associated the fate of Finland with Alexander's success in repelling the attack because only when Napoleon was overthrown would the position of Finland, in his opinion, be secured. The members of the Finnish affairs committee in St Petersburg tried to act to produce some kind of activity in Finland and to influence the general attitude in the country in the middle of the crisis in the empire. At the same time, Alexander was also preparing the ground in Finland for objectives of his own through the agency of the Governor-General Steinheil.

The Emperor had given up his earlier negative attitude to establishing Finland's own military forces in the situation of the summer of 1812. In this he thought such a solution — limited in its framework — as reflecting clearly the favourable general attitude in Finland to Russia's defensive war. However, Alexander also wanted the Finns to appear to be taking the initiative themselves. Rehbinder acted to accelerate matters, and made a proposal on 5 August to the Emperor, who approved in principle the establishment of a small Finnish army. On 13 August, he also consented to the implementation of a general fund-raising in Finland so that volunteer forces could be established and equipped more easily.[6] The Finnish affairs committee from St Petersburg also directed that propaganda against Napoleon should be stepped up in Finland. For this task it chose J.A. Ehrenström, who tried to depict in colourful language the dangers which, according to him and his patrons, threatened the whole of Europe if it fell into the power of the tyrant — the most dangerous in history. Finland too would become a vassal of France and some general of Napoleon's would be appointed its ruler. The result could be suffering for all levels of the country's population.[7]

Ehrenström's purpose was also to detach the Finns from the view that Russia and Sweden continued to be enemies in the phase which had followed the war of 1808. Ehrenström also tried to make enlightened Finns aware of the rapprochement of Alexander and Karl Johan and the negotiations they had carried on; he emphasised that in the situation of 1812 the states led by these two men had to defend their independence and freedom against a common danger.[8] However, the efforts of leading personalities to influence the general attitude of the people in Finland proved difficult. Although the political atmosphere and mood had undoubtedly calmed down somewhat since 1808, passivity was evident generally when the question was raised of assembling an army in Finland to support the defensive battle Russia was fighting. Such passivity undoubtedly contained, consciously or unconsciously, an instinct of self-preservation and a desire to stand aside from great world events. The European situation had not been finally settled, and the possibility remained that Napoleon would win.

The course of Napoleon's Russian campaign was very well known to Finns who kept abreast of the times. *Åbo Allmänna Tidning* had been commissioned to publish the official Russian communiqués from the early stages of the war. On this basis it was possible to follow the important events in the advance of Napoleon's *Grande Armée* and the Russian retreat.[9] Apart from publishing Russian news material, the newspaper did not itself put forward any opinions about the historic battle that was in progress. Its very neutral attitude may reflect a certain political calculation and discretion. This line — for whatever reasons it may have been adopted — occasioned criticism among the Finnish leaders who represented the line of open collaboration. Mannerheim for example thought at the height of the crisis, in the late autumn of 1812, that the country's official newspaper was 'worthless'.[10]

By the emperor's order, the Finnish church had been drawn in to support Russia's defensive struggle. Governor-General Steinheil gave precise orders to the Chapters at the beginning of August on the prayers which were to be read out in church at every service for the embattled Russian army. There was little room for maneouvre. Bishop Tengström appealed to the loyalty of the clergy, pointing out that they knew how to value 'that security and peace which the Finnish people can enjoy under a gentle and well-meaning administration'.[11]

The attempts made in the country's leading circles to get the Finns to take part in Russia's struggle were not very successful in evoking a popular response. The organisation of conscription, characterised as voluntary, involved for example the magistracy in the towns and the crown bailiffs in the countryside, in addition to which there was an appeal to the church for support.[12] Ehrenström, in his second article, also called for the assembling of volunteer forces. The result of the conscription, however, remained very small and in some places, such as southern Pohjanmaa, it failed completely. The levying of volunteer troops also did not get very far. Because of this a decision was taken in the middle of September to resort to paid enlistment. The objective was to recruit three regiments.[13]

The significance of the Finnish regiments which were recruited came to be mainly symbolic. They were ordered to do guard duty in St Petersburg, whence the Russian troops had been taken to the front. In the higher levels of Finland's administration it was possible to present the measure as a demonstration of loyalty to the empire in the pevailing crisis; the task given to the Finnish troops was indeed a demonstration of confidence by Alexander. In the summer of the same year, alcoholic liquor was sent from Finland as a gift to Russian detachments fighting in Kurland.

2. *How were Napoleon's defeat in Russia and the later campaigns in central Europe reflected politically in Finland?*

After the French armies had completed their advance and occupied Moscow, Napoleon's Russian expedition began to turn into a general retreat from October-November 1812 and finally into an open defeat. This change soon began to be visible even in Finland: the danger of war had now disappeared beyond the periphery of the country.

The great transition that had taken place in Russia was soon evident, for example in that there was a change towards peacetime conditions at sea, while the war continued on the continent of Europe. Russia and Britain had made peace in July 1812, which had put an end to the break in relations which had gradually arisen between them since the time of Tilsit. As a consequence, Finnish trade, which had been able to follow the normal channels to Sweden since 1809, was also freed from political obstacles in Britain. At the same time Finland's foreign trade in its entirety began to break out from the pressure of the emergency which had lasted since the beginning of the revolutionary wars in the mid-1790s.

In spite of the removal of these obstacles Finland's trade with countries outside the Baltic got going only slowly. The coming of peace to the whole of continental Europe in 1815 did not yet mean a 'normal situation' for Finland's exports to western European countries. This was because the wars were followed by a slump in which export prices remained low. Nonetheless, Finland's trading relations with the Netherlands and France, and even with Portugal and Spain, gradually picked up.

On the other hand the revival of Finnish exports to Britain at the end of the war was held back by tariffs and restrictions which had come into force a few years earlier. Britain's experiences of the continental system had given her an object-lesson in what it meant when the country was completely dependent on imports of timber from Europe. Because of this Britain had negotiated the procurement of timber from Canada since 1809, and to support the new import trade she had raised duties on timber coming in from different parts of Europe.[15] All these wartime tariff increases remained in force on the return of peace, and they were further strengthened by resolutions in parliament in 1819. Only after the mid-1820s did these restrictions begin to be dismantled, and since market conditions were at the same time becoming more favourable, Finland's exports to Britain also began to increase again in that period.[16]

The political outcome of Napoleon's Russian campaign was quickly reflected in Finland. After the great turning-point when Napoleon continued to withdraw towards central Europe, the government is St Petersburg took care that the

Finns were kept systematically informed about the succession of victories by the Russian armies and generally about the key position of Russia in the battle against Napoleon. The principal contents of *Åbo Allmänna Tidning* in 1813 and 1814 were the proclamations and communiqués of the Emperor Alexander and General Kutuzov and other commanders, which told of the continuing advance of the Russian armies on the continent and the liberation of the peoples from the Napoleonic yoke.[17] On their own side the Russians had begun to refer to the victory they had won over Napoleon in his Russian campaign as 'the patriotic war'.

The Russian armies had repelled the invader by great exertions, including the resort to guerrilla warfare, and in consequence there was a powerful intellectual reaction in the empire. The ideals of Russian nationalism emerged into the foreground. Prominence was also given to the emperor, the achievements of the unconquered Russian army, the Orthodox church and the people, whose will to defend themselves and great sacrifices were lauded.[18] When the campaigns on the continent ended in the spring of 1814 and the Russian and allied armies marched as victors into the French capital, the defeat of Napoleon was depicted by the government in St Petersburg as the overthrow of the 'world tyrant'. At the same time Alexander was praised as a great emperor. At the intellectual level the result of the war was described as 'the victory of Moscow over Paris'.[19]

The St Petersburg government not only endeavoured to inform the Finns of the great achievements of the Russian army, but also to draw the Finns themselves into the celebrations of its victories. Governor-General Steinheil organised publicity activities over the whole country along these lines, which took on a strong flavour of political propaganda. At the same time numerous different festivities were organised, in which Steinheil involved both the Finnish civil administration and representatives of the church. In this way they could be certain in advance that the desired propaganda effect would be extended to the various parts of the country, even to the peripheries and to the different levels of the population including the farming community. In the festivities organised in Turku and in other towns in the country, for example, high dignitaries and representatives of different social groups were present. Their programmes included official communiqués about the latest victories of the Russian armies, on account of which the participants in the festivities raised their glasses in honour of the emperor, his family, General Kutuzov and the imperial army. Gun salutes were fired, and the burghers organised dances to round off the victory celebrations.[20]

The Church acquired a central role in celebrating the Russian victories because the government in St Petersburg sought to use it, especially in this connection, as a 'channel of communication', since the influence of the church extended throughout the country. Parish church services were the occasions when towns people and the farmers in the parishes could be given news of the campaigns on the European continent and of the fate of Napoleon. Soon after the great turning-point in Napoleon's Russian campaign, Alexander ordered (on 5 November 1812) announcements to be made in Finnish churches about the Russian army's victory and a special prayer of thanksgiving that Moscow had been saved from falling to the enemy.[21]

Special thanksgiving services and other festivities were organised in October 1813 in honour of the great victory won by Alexander and his allies near Leipzig. A detailed 'explanation' of how the campaigns in continental Europe had developed was read out in churches. This set forth that 'the down-trodden nations of Europe' had received the assistance of the emperor Alexander, who had assumed the task of 'defending the common cause and set himself and his whole military might against the common oppressor'. At the same time it was emphasised — according to the Finnish-language version of the explanation — 'what bravery and irresistible force the earnest love of the fatherland gives the soldiers, who are fighting for freedom against evil and violence'. These official statements to the Finns did not omit to mention also that Sweden had taken part in the battle of Leipzig against Napoleon.[22]

When it became known in Finland that Alexander and the allied armies had entered Paris at the end of March 1814, the Governor-General gave the order that this event be celebrated as a day of jubilee in Finland as in St Petersburg. Thanksgiving services were organised in all the churches in the country — for the second time — for the victories won in the war.[23] In the great festivity held in Turku, which was organised under the leadership of Steinheil, it was asserted of the allied entry into Paris that it was 'a common cause of rejoicing for the fatherland and mankind'.[24] The organisation of official celebrations became still more frequent as Napoleon was being overthrown, and the series was rounded off in the summer of 1814 by festivals of thanksgiving organised over the whole Russian empire.[25] The return of peace was in itself a significant fact, fully recognised in Finland. The country's leading circles added their own intellectual analysis of the overthrow of Napoleon. Bishop Tengström announced to the clergy of Turku diocese that 'the salvation of Europe had been brought to a conclusion and the independence and peace of the fatherland assured'.[26]

It was an unusual phenomenon in Finnish circumstances that at the same time examples of political pamphlets were published. In these the victories of the Russian army and the events connected with Napoleon's overthrow were depicted. Some of these publications had been translated from Russian into Swedish.[27] In all of them the official political slogans of the period were affirmed.

In the propaganda praising Alexander conservative and pacifist elements were put side by side. He was a noble 'prince of peace' who had undertaken as his mission to 'save the independence of Europe' and 'overthrow the tyrant of the world'. Napoleon was pictured as the heir of the Revolution who had caused wars and plundered most of Europe.[28] How, then, was the newest phase of this great political transformation actually perceived and experienced in Finland in the midst of all the official propaganda?

It was an indisputable fact, of which no Finn who even minimally followed events could be ignorant, that a major change of relative political strengths had occurred in Europe in favour of Alexander and Russia. It was repeatedly emphasised too that Sweden had been on the same side as Russia in the war and that Karl Johan and his army had participated in overthrowing Napoleon in central Europe. Thus there was a desire to make it as clear to the Finns as possible that the foreign policy of their new state and of their former mother-country had no differences — certainly of a nature which could justify political speculation.

Russian pacification policy in Finland was clearly changing in character after the transitional period of 1812. It was now marked by straightforward measures and an unconditional tone; it no longer appealed to the Finn's own interests in the same way as earlier, nor did it make proposals or show a desire for compromise. Russia's position of strength in world politics was clearly emphasised, and this also pointed the Finns towards simple submission. This was the hard logic of great world events in peripheral Finland. Now, at the very latest, all wishful thinking about a return to union with Sweden must have disappeared from the minds even of those who had still nurtured it until then, and who for some months in the latter part of 1812 had perhaps received some additional hope. Of course there were those who could not forget that the Russians had conquered Finland in a war of aggression. But it was dangerous to say anything of this kind, although it was not yet a decade since the war of 1808. The dissident really had room to maneouvre only in his own imagination, if he still wanted to return to the former times under Sweden.

A new period of history had irrevocably begun in Finland. For those, mainly of the upper classes, who had been in the service of the new régime from the beginning, it meant continuing as before. At the same time the Finns who worked in the central administration — whether in the Finnish affairs committee in St Petersburg or the government council in Helsinki — recognised the changed political atmosphere, which since the end of the general war had become an accomplished fact in Europe at large and in Russia in particular. An undeniable consequence of this was that the freedom of maneouvre of the central administration, which had appeared in the expression of their own views and the making of initiatives, was reduced from what it had been. This stemmed from the strengthening of patriarchal conservatism in St Petersburg.

In the post-1815 conditions, Finns in the various leading groups in society found themselves more frequently obliged to express their general political attitude than the burgher working at his own trade, to say nothing of the farmer, living isolated in the countryside. By sharply criticising Napoleon in public, a person could show loyalty to the empire and testify that he separated himself from all thought of change in the position of Finland. It was characteristic of these years that abuse of Napoleon could go to great extremes.[29] A special kind of dialectical feature was the repeated praise of Alexander in conjunction

with condemnation of Napoleon. This comparison of opposites was also connected with the conservative-pacifist spirit of the time. It became customary to
compare Napoleon as heir to the wars of the Revolution with Alexander's
image as a ruler who was restoring peace.

People obviously adapted themselves quickly in Finland both to criticism of
Napoleon and also to the officially inspired ruler-worship of Alexander;[30] nothing corresponding to it, either in content or level, had appeared in Finland in the
previous century. Certainly confidence had been expressed in the rulers in the
latter period of Swedish rule, but there had been no worship of the ruler. This
had been little in evidence among the upper class but more so in the rest of
society, especially among the farmers.

In the new conditions the central administration of Finland and the church
leadership seemed to adapt most rapidly to ruler-worship. These circles had supported the new régime from the start and were in many ways committed to it
too because of their own interests. But Finnish society as a whole seemed to
adapt to the worship of the ruler. It was certainly influenced to an important
extent by the emperor's pacification policy, particularly since this had been in
effect since 1809. In the shaping of Finland's new political position there had
been accommodation on both sides. On the other hand, it was clearly more
difficult for the Finns to accept and adopt the praise directed towards the
Russian army and the Russians in official proclamations and announcements.
Their reserve clearly concealed both irritation and even a certain anxiety. The
reasons for the reserve can be explained by the army in question having been,
from a Finnish viewpoint, an enemy in the very recent past.

Official propaganda had also sought to extend its influence to the farming
population, primarily through the church. However, this was conducted in a
language more suited to the so-called educated class. It was also difficult for
the farmers to follow these announcements, because of their lack of adequate
basic knowledge of European history and geography. Although the defeat of
Napoleon had been spoken of from pulpits for so long, it is uncertain whether
the farmers really had any idea even of who Napoleon was. The farmers had,
however, been made aware of economic change when the earlier lively demand
for timber and tar had been followed by a slump. Their views on these changes
might be altogether idiosyncratic and primarily derived from their own
environment. The name of Napoleon might conjure in their minds the image of
a gigantic buyer of timber in some distant land; now this person was perhaps
dead.[31] In the course of time information on the long period of war and such
events as Napoleon's Russian campaign were conveyed to the Finnish farmers as
well. Stories found their way to the Finnish countryside, according to which
generals 'Holodin' and 'Morosa' had inflicted a thorough defeat on the French
army, the soldiers of which experienced the severe winter on the Russian plains
dressed in silk.[32]

3. *The Congress of Vienna and the Finnish and Polish questions*

When the Congress of Vienna in 1814–15 discussed the organisation of European affairs after Napoleon, Finland's annexation to Russia had been an accomplished fact for some years. In addition, Sweden had recognised the change at the Hamina peace of 1809, which had been concluded outside the political system of Napoleon and independently of it.

The Finnish question was left out of the discussions of major territorial questions among the great powers at Vienna. Finland as a territory was clearly removed from the main channels of European politics, and besides it belonged primarily within the direct strategic and other interests of Russia — alone among the great powers that had overthrown Napoleon. Russia for her part let it be understood in advance that she did not accept the inclusion of the Finnish question on the agenda of the general negotiations of the great powers, announcing that she regarded everything that concerned Finland as being an internal affair of the Russian empire.[33] Thus she emphasised that the Finnish question was no longer in any way an open question — territorially or otherwise — which could have been dealt with at the international level.

In spite of the Russian position, the Finnish question was touched on at the Congress in the general exchange of views between the representatives of the great powers on the settlement of territorial questions in Europe. In these discussions the preservation of a certain balance in the relative strengths of the great powers was an important and also a controversial question. In dealing with this general question the British representative, Lord Castlereagh, touched on the case of Finland. Castlereagh wished to establish the point that Finland and Bessarabia were territories which Russia had been able to annex before the Congress,[34] and that they should not be forgotten in the overall assessment of the shares and advantages accruing to the victorious powers in territorial questions. It is worthy of note that Castlereagh's remark concerned territories in the Baltic and Black Sea areas — in which Britain had been concerned to maintain a balance in the previous century and specifically to prevent the strengthening of the Russian position.

On the other hand, Poland was on the agenda of the Congress as a problem involving the interests of several of the great powers. For this very reason, the solution which was reached over the Polish territories was a compromise. Thus the main part, known as Congress Poland, which was to be annexed to Russia, was not a national unit like Finland after the areas of Old Finland had been joined to it. The Polish question had been prominent in international politics and it involved centuries of political tradition, so it was difficult to believe that the organisation of the political status of the new Poland joined to Russia should remain Russia's internal affair. Alexander had to accept — with obvious reluctance — that Poland should receive an autonomous status on the basis of an international agreement concluded by the great powers at the Congress of Vienna.

Alexander would clearly have wanted the organisation of Poland's position to be settled through 'bilateral negotiations', such as his secret discussion with certain Polish leaders in 1811–12. Conceding 'international supervision' in the Polish question must have been displeasing to Russia if we recall how consistently she had acted on the Hamina peace negotiations to eliminate for the future all outside intervention in the Finnish question. In fact, the autonomy given to Poland strengthened to some extent the special status of Finland which, after 1815, was no longer unique in the Russian empire. Polish autonomy was somewhat more extensive than Finland's; Poland had its own army, the Diet met regularly, and at the head of its autonomous government there was a viceroy. Poland had in every way been better known than Finland, and the autonomy settlement was a kind of restoration of her political existence after the partitions which had taken place at the end of the eighteenth century. At the Congress of Vienna, the diplomats of the great powers recognised Finland as a territorial question, but the name was not connected with any politically conscious and active nation.

It is possible to take the view that among the territorial settlements of the Congress of Vienna, the decision whereby Norway was annexed to Sweden concerned Finland and its new position indirectly. The new definition of Norway's position, which took place through a special state decree (*riksakt*), was arrived at outside the settlement of the great powers. Norway was given as compensation to Sweden for the loss of Finland; so Sweden achieved a prestige victory after suffering military defeat and a political setback. The territorial solution balanced the 'historical burden' in the relations of Sweden and Russia and was thus an additional factor strengthening the new status and link of Finland to the empire.

After the Congress of Vienna, Russia was the dominant power in the Baltic. At the end of a transitional period, Finland with the Åland islands and Poland had been added to her territories. Of the states around the Baltic, Sweden and Denmark had both experienced military defeat. From 1815, in terms of international relations, the Baltic was a *mare russicum*.

IV. The position and state of Finland in the crisis period of the July Revolution and the Polish revolt, 1830 – 1831

1. *Finland's special political status, the buttresses of the new system and the bases of the national identity*

The succession of wars lasting three years which began with Napoleon's Russian campaign, in which the Russian armies carried the fight into central Europe, brought the central administration of Finland to a halt because Alexander was with his armies. This also hindered the further development of the central administration along the lines already established.[1] Officials of the central administration in Russia had issued orders and reports to the governing council in Finland and to other officials, and in other respects interfered in the country's internal affairs. When the continental war ended, these circumstances came to an end too, even if the return to normal was slow. Only by the spring of 1817 were the long unresolved items removed from the agenda, after which administration could function regularly, with Alexander once again residing mainly in St Petersburg.[2]

An important decision for clarifying Finland's special status was secured in 1816 when the governing council of the country was given the new title 'Imperial Finnish Senate'. This change, unlike the exceptional happenings of the war years, emphasised the direct contact of the supreme governmental institution of Finland with the emperor in preparing matters for decision. The word 'imperial' in the new title was meant to demonstrate equality with the governing Senate of Russia in its relationship with the ruler. With the change of title Alexander again gave assurances, in a general way, of the preservation of Finland's rights.

A small circle of leading Finnish officials held a key position in the practical implementation of Finland's special political status and the country's own administration. They started from the assumption that the outcome depended very much on the Finns themselves; and because the members of this circle had at an early stage chosen their political line, it would not have been easy for them to abandon it when difficulties arose. They formed the most important buttress of the new system in Finland.

As a general basis for their activities the leading circles in the civil service tried to develop their own special idea of Finland. Its starting-point was a clear break from Sweden — both from common historical memories and also spiritually. On this foundation they conceived of Finland as 'fatherland' and Russia as 'the great empire'.[3] In the new conditions one must learn to see the demands of the common good in new ways. The situation was not without danger, because Finland was linked to a state which was both large and in many ways very different from itself. They could see danger in the dissension and selfishness of the Finns. These civil servants in Finland's central administration were cautious in political decision-making and they observed patriarchal-bureaucratic methods of execution. The line of action of the leaders of the country may be termed a conservative security policy. The social aim of this policy was to keep the broad circles of the people away from politics and in general from involvement in public affairs. In the whole system a powerful direction from above was prominent; it was apparent both in the relations of the emperor and the civil service and between the latter and the people.

The behaviour of Finland's leading men reflected indirectly their consciousness that the foundations of the special political status of Finland were weak and that in general the country's own sources of real strength were minimal compared with Russia. They sought to build carefully on the promises which had been given by the emperor. At the same time, a fear of change in existing conditions was characteristic; for changes could mean a step into the uncertain and the unknown. There was also a fear that reforms might force them to abandon traditions.

Thus keeping things as they were, in the view of the civil servants in the central administration of Finland, was a general way of preserving the characteristics of the different fields of activity of Finnish society. They tried to handle affairs between Finland and St Petersburg diplomatically, but at the same time self-defence was their basic line. This meant working in an atmosphere of mutual suspicion. The aim was on the one hand to avoid conflicts with the government in St Petersburg, but on the other it was thought important that they should be able if necessary to draw conclusions from those attitudes of the emperor which concerned the general political development of Europe, so that they would be able to take appropriate decisions before there was interference from St Petersburg; Rehbinder in particular was considered skilled in such perception.[4] This policy of political caution could involve, for example, the prevention of foreign ideas, which were considered dangerous, from entering the country. This way of handling Finland's affairs might also imply that the people themselves should remain as inconspicuous as possible — and unheard. In the central administration this involved, after 1815, much calculated expediency since there was at that time a powerful paternalistic current in Russia, and the spirit of the reactionary and ruler-dominated Holy Alliance prevailed widely in continental Europe.

In the new circumstances under which the leading men in the central administration of Finland were forced to formulate policy, there were many unknown factors. They must try to tread some kind of middle way, as Rehbinder expressed it. On the one hand they had to protect the country's own legal system and its social and cultural traditions, but on the other Russian interests had to be recognised. This policy called for a fundamental change in the attitudes which had prevailed under Swedish rule. At the same time, to what extent they could now draw close to Russia? As a policy line Finland's relations with the emperor were a kind of dual defensive activity, and they were handled by both the leading civil servants in Helsinki and the Finnish affairs committee in St Petersburg. While they started from the assumption that Finland's political loyalty served the political security of the Russian empire on its north-west frontier, this loyalty was maintained by directing Finnish society by patriarchal methods.[5]

Even after the Senate had moved, in 1819, from Turku to Helsinki, the distance between the country's supreme administrative organ and the emperor remained considerable. This had the consequence that Alexander saw fit to leave final powers of decision to the Senate in many matters regarded as less important, which the King of Sweden had previously decided on the spot. The Governor-General of Finland, who was always a Russian after Sprengtporten's time, also acted as president of the Senate, thus keeping a watchful eye over Finnish civil administration. At the same time, as a high-ranking military man and commander-in-chief of the Russian forces in Finland, he was the special guardian of the security interests of Russia's north-west frontier.

In St Petersburg, alongside the Finnish affairs committee, there was a special Finnish secretary of state (later a minister-secretary of state), who was an important person, close to the emperor, and represented the views and interests of the country as a counter-weight to Russian influence. His loosely-defined duties were broadly those of a diplomat.[6]

In the patriarchal measures of the central administration in Finland, the direction of the official information service played an important part. *Åbo Allmänna Tidning*, still the country's only newspaper, came to have special significance from the middle 1810s onwards. Through it the readers, mostly civil servants, clergymen and academics, received information about both the government's official announcements and events abroad. The events of the Congress of Vienna were extensively reported,[7] but after the Congress, indeed, from the beginning of 1816, the content of *Åbo Allmänna Tidning* changed considerably, coverage of general politics and major political events disappearing almost entirely. In the latter half of the decade only two political news items in the paper concerned the countries of the Holy Alliance, both linked with the name of Alexander: the meeting of the Polish Diet in Warsaw and the Congress of Aachen, both in 1818; at the latter, the rulers of the great powers considered the affairs of post-war Europe.[8] Such news as *Åbo Allmänna Tidning* carried about Austria and Prussia was carefully positive in content, containing nothing that could be construed as critical of political conditions. These allies of Alexander's Russia represented the same autocratic structure and upheld the same system.

News about Britain, on the other hand, was not protected in the same way as that from Russia's allies. Britain was not a regular ally of Russia, although after 1815 it took part in the discussions between the countries of the Holy Alliance; in addition its political system was very different from Russia's. News about

Britain might reveal deficiencies in the country and scandals in the British royal family.[9] News about Sweden was strikingly sparse. This must have been because leading circles in the country wanted to encourage the isolation of the Finns from the former mother-country.[10]

It is difficult to be precise about the extent of the circle in Finland which, in the period after 1815, was interested in foreign affairs and in their own general conditions; primarily it included the nobility, representatives of the academic world, the clergy, civil servants and wealthy burghers. The scanty and colourless foreign news in the country's official and only newspaper clearly did not satisfy this circle. At the beginning of Russian rule, Swedish newspapers had their own value as a substitute for a non-existent Finnish political press. In 1819, the collective circulation in Finland of four Swedish newspapers (*Stockholms Posten, Post-Tidningar, Inrikes-Tidningar* and *Allmänna Journalen*) was about 400 subscriptions, an average of 100 subscriptions each. This approached the circulation of *Åbo Allmänna Tidning*, which in the same year had about 500 subscribers.[11]

It was suspected in the central administration of Finland that much of the political information which remained outside the supervision of the authorities infiltrated from Sweden; the Swedish newspapers which were read in Finland were either conservative or liberal. In 1820, subscription to the newspaper *Allmänna Journalen* was completely forbidden in Finland: it had contained views opposed to the general line of the Holy Alliance, and among other things described the Congress of Vienna as 'the great auction of the nations'.[12]

The content of Finland's special political status and the management of the country's internal affairs had been defined, in broad outline, in imperial proclamations, resolutions and practical measures during the transitional period. Yet the relationship of Finland to the empire remained unresolved in detail. There existed no legislation with the character of constitutional law; practice and political circumstances alone formed the basis of action.

Those in the central administration were very conscious of a prevailing state of uncertainty, involving dangers for Finland. It became the aim to fill this constitutional void and strengthen the general foundations of Finland's special status for the future. To realise this aim, from 1817 the circle of the Finnish affairs committee in St Petersburg and the leading civil servants in Helsinki speeded up plans for a separate constitution for Finland. Rehbinder, Walleen, Tengström, J.F. Aminoff and others who were involved in this design, seem also to have felt a special concern for the success of this policy. In a memorandum drafted by Walleen, the aim was defined as 'a firm and precise system, both in internal affairs and those which arise from the country's union with Russia'. The Polish constitution of 1815 was regarded as one possible model for Finland. The constitution of 1815 establishing the terms of union of Sweden and Norway may well not have been unknown to Rehbinder and Walleen, but it does not seem to have been referred to, perhaps out of caution, this being a foreign example.

To these general aims of strengthening Finland's position can be added schemes for a Finnish army. It was hoped that Finland could thereby get rid of at least the greater part of the Russian troops in the country. The separate army included in the Polish autonomy system may have encouraged plans for the same thing in Finland.[13]

Finland's leading civil servants believed in 1818 that if they succeeded in getting the Diet called into session they would also take a considerable step forward in preparing for these fundamental political questions. The fact that the Polish Diet was meeting in Warsaw at this time also encouraged such aspirations. The calling of the Diet was a kind of threshold for the planned reforms, which they hoped to persuade the emperor to accept. However, Alexander made no decision about calling the Finnish Diet. He had become emphatically cautious in everything which implied liberalism and could occasion unpleasant political surprises. He had had problems in Poland where the Diet had been 'restless'. On the other hand Finland had in one respect already received more than Poland, namely reunion of all Finnish lands. In 1818, after the overthrow of Napoleon, Alexander plainly wanted to cover up that 'show-case' towards Europe which he had been making of Finland a decade earlier, in the general interests of the empire. He also wanted to avoid foreign countries again taking an interest in the Finnish question. The fact was that the Polish Diet, to whose regular assembly the emperor was committed, had been written up surprisingly fully in foreign newspapers. Alexander's negative attitude to the summoning of the Finnish Diet also buried the idea of a separate constitution for Finland and with it the possibility of giving Finland's special status in relation to the empire greater precision.

In 1819, Alexander made an extensive tour of Finland. He visited the new frontier of the empire with Sweden and the area between the Tornio and Kemi rivers, ceded by Sweden on the basis of the Hamina peace treaty, which had not belonged administratively to Finland at all before 1808. Southern Pohjanmaa was also included in the emperor's journey. In the advance preparations for the visit, Rehbinder had depicted this well-known battleground of the 1808 war as still 'Swedophile' — according to him the spirit of the farming population in particular was 'bad'; Alexander thought that it should be included in his itinerary so that he could influence the mood of the people there.[14]

Alexander undoubtedly concluded on the basis of his inspection that Finland was fully pacified and that the Finns therefore did not constitute any special problem for the empire. The many stories that circulated after his visit describe the glittering impression his figure had left on the people. There was nevertheless still a feeling among leading Finnish civil servants of disappointment and even pessimism about the future of Finland. The emperor's visit had not brought a change of feeling among these circles. The political blow they had suffered can be seen in the memoirs written by Mannerheim at the end of the

1820s, in which he stated that the summoning of the Diet had not succeeded for an unknown reason, 'and obviously the question will never arise again.'[15]

The general political line that Alexander had followed in Finland since 1808–9 had endeavoured to get such institutions as the Lutheran Church, which had great influence on the people, and the country's only university at Turku as buttresses of the new system. In the case of the Church, it seems that the Lutheran doctrine on the respect due to authority could in practice be shifted fairly smoothly from the King of Sweden to the emperor. In the new circumstances Alexander gradually became, in the consciousness of the people, the ruler 'by the grace of God' supported by the declarations and general attitudes of the Church. The fact that the emperor had clearly recognised the inviolability of the country's Lutheran Church was also well received.

The proclamations for a day of prayer, drawn up by the emperor personally in 1818 and 1819, emphasised in many ways the significance of religion. At the same time they spoke, in contemporary fashion, of the subjects' duty of obedience and the importance of social tranquillity.[16] In the new conditions of the country the 'union of throne and altar' worked in support of both parties reciprocally. While the inviolability of the Finnish Lutheran Church was recognised by St Petersburg, obvious care had been taken from the beginning to ensure that the subordination of the Finnish Church to Sweden did not continue. For example, those parishes in the Tornio valley on the Finnish side of the frontier were required, after the peace of Hamina, to break off all administrative connections with the diocese of Härnösand, under which they had been administered hitherto.[17]

Initially the Turku Chapter and some other organs of the Church supported the preservation of ecclesiastical administration in the country's northern frontier area unchanged, while the government council and later the Finnish affairs committee had intervened and demanded that the church too, in its own administrative system, should observe the new state frontier. Thus interference from the government in St Petersburg was having an influence in the background. As a consequence, it was ordered that where the new frontier divided the area of an old parish, the part left on the Finnish side was to form a new and separate parish. In this reorganisation of Finnish church administration directed from St Petersburg, it became clear that the duties of a clergyman were also to include the role of a state official. This circumstance meant that the clergy was not outside political influence and could experience pressures of a political nature as well: it was now part of the clergy's duty to educate people in respect for the new authority and allegiance towards it.

The general position of the Finnish Church in the early nineteenth century is illustrated by the way in which the bishops, beginning with Tengström, were taken into the confidence of the ruler. The emperor might, when in contact with them, agree on important business and also direct the taking up and handling of matters which he himself desired. Furthermore the bishops had communications with the Senate and Rehbinder in St Petersburg. In the Church at this period, a small circle of leading men decided important matters. Since the duties of the bishops included the handling of many questions involving political considerations, the emperor gave special attention to the nomination of bishops. Without exception at the beginning of the nineteenth century, he 'elected' a different candidate from the one placed first in the episcopal election and generally one who had some connections with St Petersburg. Among the leading circles in the Finnish Church there was uncertainty in the early phases of Russian rule how active the Church could be, as an institution representing the Lutheran faith in a state in which the emperor and most of the population were Orthodox. However, it soon became clear that no political limitations were being set by St Petersburg in church affairs; on the contrary, it was desired to demonstrate the freedom of the Finnish Church as an example of Alexander's tolerance.[18] Hence the tercentenary of the Reformation in Finland was celebrated in 1817 as a great festival of the Finnish church and emphatically in the spirit of its creed. In connection with the celebrations, the emperor raised Tengström to the rank of archbishop.

It was obvious that under the leadership of its own archbishop the Finnish Lutheran Church would constitute an independent unit of its own. At the same time its relations with the nearest Lutheran archbishopric, Uppsala in Sweden, could be loosened.

The sovereign's recognition of the Finnish Church and its confessional inviolability was made apparent later when Nicholas I became emperor. The positive relationship of the new emperor to the Lutheran Church appeared for example in his ostentatiously favourable attitude towards the organisation of a special celebration in Helsinki, in June 1830, for the tercentenary of the Confession of Augsburg, on which occasion the foundation stone was laid for the new Lutheran church in Helsinki, the Nicholas church.[19] The speech by Bishop Molander, of Porvoo, on this great occasion compared Lutheranism and Catholicism in politically expedient language: Catholicism was the characteristic religion of countries prone to revolutions (there had been such in southern Europe in the early 1820s); by contrast, respect for authority and loyalty to the sovereign were particularly characteristic of Lutheranism.[20]

The great change in Finland's position from 1808 onwards did not in itself cause serious problems for those who worked at Turku Academy; its professors had figured little in politics in the latter period of Swedish rule, and they had taken no stand in support of the French Revolution. Nobody needed to undergo a political conversion or retract his previous views. Problems only arose in the Academy years later in indirect consequence of the change in the country's position. It was a question of the Academy's international relations, which in the latter half of the eighteenth century had been many-sided. They had extended outside Sweden to Germany — Porthan had made contacts with Göttingen — and to the Anglo-Saxon countries, including the United States.

In the new position of Finland the central administration, and especially the government in St Petersburg, did not look kindly on the continuation of academic connections with the west, which were suspected of spreading 'dangerous' ideas in Finland. Rehbinder tried to influence decisions, and he did not act on his own initiative.[21] The breaking of ties, above all with the former motherland, was one of the general aims of the establishment in Finland. Both Armfelt and Tengström used the influence which they wielded respectively as chancellor and vice-chancellor of Turku Academy. The leaders of the country saw the Academy's task as primarily to strengthen attachments to the existing order — to the sovereign, religion, the country's own legal system and everything that was native to Finland. Everything associated with the spirit of the French Revolution was to be condemned. Attempts to move in this direction were modest, but typical of the prevailing situation: there were plans to establish a periodical supported by the teaching staff of Turku Academy, with the title *Läsning för finnar* (Readings for Finns).[22] It was to have a cultural-social function, and emphasise certain types of political attitude. The impression remains, however, that the professors of Turku Academy had little desire to take part in public affairs, influenced by the fact that the attempts at activism clearly originated with leading political circles. The planned periodical, which was discussed many times at Turku Academy, remained unrealised. In any case, the Academy was to fulfil an important task training civil servants, clergy and teachers.

Finland, as it had developed since 1809, was a political structure which embraced only a very small portion of society. The civil servants and functionaries in the administration, church and university numbered only about 500-600. In this political structure the burgher Estate and the farmers formed a passive element. The burghers were engaged in economic activity, not politics. In the decades after the annexation to Russia, the possibilities for development which opened up for the burgher Estate in different areas of the economy, and the general economic prospects for the future, came to depend very much on its attitude to the new conditions in the country. The farmers tended to be traditionalist in their attitudes to public affairs and changed their opinions slowly. Although the farmers represented that part of Finnish society which had directly experienced war, Alexander's pacification policy did not include any elements which would have affected them in particular. To this stratum of society also belonged the numerous former militiamen who, after the Finnish army was disbanded in 1809 were deprived of the military allotments which many of them had been able to cultivate for a long time.[23]

The special political position of Finland and the many other new features in the development of the country constituted a kind of framework within which many new realities and a new viewpoint could be experienced. There began to emerge Finland's 'own circumstances', in which living, observing and acquiring a sense of awareness were all helping to shape a national identity.

Finland's frontiers enclosed an obvious territorial and geographical entity, albeit that communications between the different parts within it were poor. One feature which expressed the individuality of this territorial entity was its own administration, run by Finnish officials, which represented continuity at the levels of the Senate, and of provincial and local government. Although its decisions and orders did not much affect the daily life of the people, its existence could not be ignored. The civil servants could be criticised as reactionary bureaucrats but still they did form the country's 'own' administration, the mere existence of which gave substance to the consciousness of a national identity.

After the separation from Sweden, the Finnish Lutheran Church was a peculiar institution in a Greek Orthodox empire. When the pastor spoke from the pulpit of Luther's teaching as 'our own faith' he was at the same time emphasising the dividing line from the east. This affected the whole of Finnish society, and had its own significance in the development of national thinking.

When after 1808 Finland's economy began to break free from its traditional subordination to Sweden it was forced, more than before, to generate activity from its own resources. Although the customs duties between Sweden and Finland only came into effect over a longish period of time — they were raised gradually in 1817 and 1828 and from 1844 they became normal — the clear economic separation began to be a reality from the mid-1820s. Finland's own merchant navy grew quickly, especially from the 1830s, and it was distinguished by its size from all others within the Russian empire. It also became known abroad, even though it did not have its own flag or other distinguishing marks. Individuality was also to be found in the Finnish farming community, who as a land-owning group were in contrast to their Russian counterparts.

The awakening of a national identity, however, demanded a small self-conscious group which would take the initiative in making these realities into a national programme. In Turku Academy a new kind of spiritual ferment began to appear with the approach of the 1820s, influenced by two factors: on the one hand the young intellectuals were conscious of the great historical turn of fate which had occurred in Finland, and on the other, the new patriarchal-bureaucratic atmosphere was a powerful irritant. The young intellectuals had not yet had time to become bound to the power structure of society, and the small group at Turku Academy, which formed the only cultural-political organisation in the country at the time, was ready for action. They were painfully aware of the new frontier separating Finland from Sweden, while there was a stark difference in Finnish conditions compared with the rest of the Russian empire. They must try to create from the territory that was left between Sweden and Russia proper, a clearly distinct entity recognised as such in the country. In this there were many psychological factors — predominantly the instinct for self-preservation.[24]

To realise their objectives the young intellectuals began putting forward their own idea of Finland, notably the new concept of the 'the Finnish people'. In the beginning this was more an assumption or hypothesis than a reality; in any case, a need was felt to build round it some kind of activity. This awakening was stimulated also by similar intellectual-cultural influences from abroad, from Sweden and (through Sweden) Germany.[25] Awareness of broad ideological support encouraged belief in the achievement of a 'national awakening' in Finland too. Thus a small activist group desired to make the population of the country into a distinct Finnish nation.

The acceleration of the national awakening in Finland occurred in a different manner from the classical examples of this phenomenon on the continent of Europe, where the process had begun with a more developed nationality and culture. The starting-point in Finland was the feeling of the young intellectuals that they had been forced to break away from their previous links with a high-level culture and were therefore in a vacuum because Finland lacked a culture of her own. In their search, the representatives of the new style of thought, the so-called Turku romantics, seized on the Finnish language in which they saw concealed, for example in its folk-poetry, a peculiarly Finnish spiritual force. They wanted to develop the Finnish language into one in which literature could be published and which would also come to be used in the public life of the country.

The planned cultural and research activity did not divide the young academics of Turku along language lines. In the first place there was the problem of awakening national consciousness in the country. The intention was to mark out a boundary line to the west, but also a self-defensive position against the east, against the great empire and Slavism. The content of their own national identity had to be defined and society at large persuaded to recognise its existence. The Finland-idea that thus developed among the Turku romantics did not involve the adoption of any actual political position, much less political activity. They were far removed from the leading civil servants who were the country's decision-makers. The two groups had difficulty understanding one another, to say nothing of recognising one another, so different were their view-points. The young intellectuals were liable to label the activity of the top civil servants as reactionary or secretive, because they worked in a sheltered circle and directed patriarchally a people whom they mostly saw as an uneducated rabble. However, even the activity of the civil servants helped to promote the Finland-idea, and was an influence favouring the recognition of a national identity.[26] The basic question was, in a way, the same for both: the general direction of historical development in Finland and the conditions making for its individuality.

In the midst of this national cultural awakening there also arose a more uncompromising train of thought, represented by the young A.I. Arwidsson. In Arwidsson and his articles in *Åbo Morgonblad* was expressed the mood of protest created by the times and the wish of a representative of the young generation to oppose the old generation. In Arwidsson's opinion the leading circles cared primarily about their own careers.[27] Starting from a pessimistic conception of Finland at that time, Arwidsson wanted to produce a spiritual awakening or, as he put it, stir up the 'national spirit'. His outlook was basically liberal, for he stressed the importance of press freedom and the open exchange of views. He also sought to expose grievances, activate the relations between the ruler and the people, and generally introduce englightenment into the transaction of government business. He took a special interest in the problems of small nations alongside large ones, having been stimulated by writings from abroad — primarily Danish and German. By contrast he may not have especially followed political events on the continent; he had not been moved by the *Burschenschaft* phenomena of the German students or the revolts which broke out in southern Europe around 1820.

In striving to influence the awakening of the national identity, Arwidsson both stressed the boundaries which distinguished Finland both from east and west, and tried to activate the citizens politically, which was something to which the Turku romantics did not aspire. He disturbed the calm which the top civil servants wanted to preserve in Finland. Although his activity was prompted by Finland's internal conditions, which he saw as dismal, the country's leaders compared his activity with foreign phenomena, *inter alia* the *Burschenschaft* movement and even the revolutionary French Jacobins of the 1790s.

The international situation grew strained after the congresses of Laibach in 1821 and Verona in 1822, with Britain dissociating herself from collaboration with the three great conservative monarchies of continental Europe, Austria, Prussia and Russia. A consequence of this was that in those countries there arose ever greater distrust of any sign of political opposition and dangerous western ideas. The Helsinki bureaucracy and the Finnish affairs committee in St Petersburg could not fail to perceive these changes. Since the policy of caution they represented involved attempting on their own initiative to scorch in advance any dangerous developments in Finland, so as to avoid interference from St Petersburg, Rehbinder felt compelled to interfere, and chose a very severe course of action.[29] *Åbo Morgonblad* was suppressed in 1822 and a little later Arwidsson was dismissed from Turku Academy. The ideas of the bureaucracy and a young dissenter on what was right and possible in Finland were irreconcilable; Rehbinder, in the Finnish affairs committee in St Petersburg, feared all unrest in Finland, and Aminoff, the vice-chancellor of Turku Academy, sought to preserve a patriarchal idyll. Arwidsson for his part suspected that the Finnish bureaucrats could not get away from the wake, mentality and above all the opinions of the Russian ruling circles in St Petersburg.

The fate of Arwidsson undoubtedly had a great influence later on Finnish academic intellectual circles. His case showed clearly what kind of national activism, 'participation', was politically forbidden in intellectual circles in Finnish society. It could not of course in itself prevent the development of the national-romantic tendency, but as a dramatic experience it undoubtedly showed the limit which could not be overstepped. In any case, the area of activity concerned with language and culture remained; here was the possibility of studying the Finnish language and searching for the special characteristics of the Finnish people through the different sciences and arts.

2. *The Finnish press and international affairs in the 1820s*

As circumstances changed, gradually the possibilities for Finns to follow foreign political events improved as the 1820s advanced. By that time they were no longer dependent on one official newspaper for news. When the central administration finally moved to Helsinki in 1819, a new one, *Finlands Allmänna Tidning*, began publication in the new capital from the beginning of 1820. The existing official newspaper changed its name to *Åbo Tidningar* and continued to appear in the former capital under that name.

Other papers began to appear as well, so that from this time on one can speak, albeit modestly, of the country's press as a new phenomenon. *Mnemosyne*, which had appeared from the end of 1819 in Turku, represented the national-romantic circles there. *Turun Wiikko-Sanomat*, founded in 1820, was the only Finnish-language newspaper of the time aimed primarily at the advanced elements of the farming population. A further addition was *Åbo Morgonblad*, which from 1821 onwards published the above-mentioned articles by Arwidsson. The growth of the press was also a sign of the endeavour to break out of that 'quiet life' which had been characteristic of the half-decade after the fall of Napoleon.

In the early 1820s, revolts broke out against the reactionary governments in Spain and southern Italy, and the Greeks rose in revolt against the long domination of Turkey. The Finnish newspapers, including the official ones, covered these events very openly, without in any way concealing the real nature of the revolutionary happenings in the countries concerned. This was possible because it was not seen by the government in St Petersburg as against the interests of the empire. The revolts in Spain and Italy were a long way from the protective belt of Russian security policy in central Europe, and were not seen, at least at first, as being capable of causing the spread of insurrection. From the point of view of these events, Finland was very much on the periphery.

Finlands Allmänna Tidning published from time to time very extensive reports of events in Spain which brought out clearly the liberal objectives of the revolts. A constitution had been demanded, and the movement of the masses, supported by the army, pressed the king to make concessions.[30] That newspaper described the rebellion in Naples as of a similar character to that in Spain; there too the rebels demanded that the king should submit to governing the country according to the constitution. The official paper wrote of the demands for a 'free constitution' and of 'revolutions' which were happening in both these southern countries.[31] *Turun Wiikko-Sanomat* also published some general news items about these events.[32]

The revolt against Turkey, which broke out in Greece in 1821, became a central news item in several Finnish papers. Their attitudes turned out to be clearly anti-Turkish, which might have seemed harmless, in so far as Russian foreign policy had long been clearly directed againt Turkey. *Finlands Allmänna Tidning* depicted the Turks as barbarous and savage.[33] *Turun Wiikko-Sanomat* told of Turkish cruelties and murderous acts. The paper also highlighted the religious clash involved in the war: it was a battle of Christians against pagans.[34]

Thus the Finnish press took a clear stand on the Greek war of independence. Since at this stage there was not yet any kind of politicisation of Finnish society, the reasons for these attitudes must be sought elsewhere. Among the young intellectual academics in Turku, philhellenic attitudes appeared, as in many European countries at the time,[35] linked to appreciation of the ancient classical culture, not to political ideas. In Finland, the growth of this kind of interest was undoubtedly influenced as well by the simultaneous awakening of national romanticism, which the Turku romanticism represented. At this time religious factors also considerably influenced attitudes to public affairs: the Turks symbolised paganism, and hatred of them may be regarded as a traditional attitude of Lutherans, going back to Germany in the 1520s.[36]

Eighteen twenty-one marks the beginning of military intervention by the Holy Alliance to suppress the continuing revolts in southern Europe; at the Congress of Laibach, Russia, Prussia and Austria decided to send an army of intervention to Naples. Britain and France announced their intention to stand aloof from such a policy. Under Alexander I's influence, the Congress of Verona in 1822 decided that the Holy Alliance would also intervene in Spain, the task of military intervention being assigned to France.[37] Because of this, Britain withdrew entirely from joint action with the continental powers.

The changes in the general politics of Europe were reflected in the Finnish papers. *Turun Wiikko-Sanomat* described the decision of the Laibach Congress on military intervention in Naples, and explained that 'unruliness, savagery and mutual revolt' had gained control in southern Italy; the princes of Europe feared the outbreak of another French revolution if they did not, by joint action, take care of 'the common tranquillity'.[38]

Greece presented a difficult problem for the Holy Alliance. Unanimity could not be generated because Turkey was the legitimate party and Greece the insurgent. Russian and British military and commercial interests guided their policies, and the objectives was to weaken Turkey. Religion introduced a further element to this conflict, differing from the basic line of the Holy Alliance.[39] Any reference in the Finnish press to general politics in connection with the Greek war of independence, always emphasised the 'peace-loving' intentions of Alexander's policy.[40]

However, in the government in St Petersburg the intellectual enthusiasm with which the Finnish newspapers wrote about the Greek war of independence aroused suspicion, although it did not in itself conflict with the line of Russian foreign policy in the Balkans. Even more serious, the country's only Finnish-language paper, which circulated among the lower class, was most conspicuous in writing enthusiastically — and stridently — on behalf of a people who had risen in rebellion. Alexander intervened, and at the beginning of 1823 *Turun Wiikko-Sanomat* was forbidden to publish political news about foreign countries.[41] The paper had a little earlier begun to use the Swedish papers as a source.[42] After this only *Finlands Allmänna Tidning* continued to cover Greek events on its own. Thus the government in St Petersburg had been afraid of political unrest spreading specifically among the lower class in Finland.

Once a clear breach had occurred between the three great continental powers and Britain, because of the decision of the Congress of Verona, east-west ideological cross-currents were also stimulated.[43] Finland came to be placed in close contact with these conflicting influences, because in Sweden at the same time there was a clearly strengthening liberal orientation. This brought new problems for Finland's political position as well.

Because of this, political control in Finland was being intensified. An indication of this was the cautious way that *Finlands Allmänna Tidning* — unlike at the beginning of the 1820s — reported political events abroad.[44] The central administration in Finland constantly considered by what measures they could most effectively prevent dangerous foreign influences from entering the country. Foreign literature and newspapers became objects of suspicion, and from late 1823 the customs administration was instructed to carry out special surveillance duties by inspecting literature brought into the country.[45]

The Finnish affairs committee in St Petersburg was clearly concerned about the situation; it was afraid of the central administration in the country losing its grip and the Russians themselves intervening directly in Finland's internal affairs to intensify control of political opinions. At the same time, Rehbinder saw patriarchal holds being weakened when he noted, with obvious regret, how remarkably information published in newspapers guided public opinion, and that newspaper-reading had spread to 'the less educated sections of the population'.[46]

In the autumn of 1823 an imperial decree came into force in Finland empowering the authorities to start legal action over writings in newspapers and to order their suppression; such a decision, however, was to be submitted to the emperor for confirmation.[47] The general deterioration of newspaper activity is illustrated, for example, by the way a new paper, the *Åbo Underrättelser*, which had begun to appear in Turku in 1824, steered completely clear of covering politics and political events abroad.[48]

The inviolability of Finland's position, which the cautious line of Rehbinder and Walleen had tried to protect, was coming under pressure from ever-stronger forces in St Petersburg. After Steinheil, Zakrevski became Governor-General in 1823. He was a straightforward old Russian bureaucrat, and in his time (till 1831) the line of action pursued in Finland by the Governor-General clearly changed. Zakrevski, who distrusted alien nationalities, set himself the task of bringing 'the inhabitants of Finland closer to Russians'. The change from earlier practice was also demonstrated when he sought and succeeded in obtaining, in the discussion of Finnish affairs, a direct channel of access to the emperor, by-passing the Finnish secretary of state in St Petersburg. Zakrevski's position and prestige were further strengthened when, in 1828, he also became the imperial minister of the interior.[49]

The Decembrist revolt among the officer corps which broke out in Russia in 1825 shook Nicholas I, who had just come to the throne. This kind of revolt, in which western influences played their part, had not happened before in Russia, and its outbreak and suppression were most significant events. The purges and precautionary measures which followed were both effective and severe, and a truly reactionary phase set in. Nicholas I sought that the existing system be strongly protected against new revolutionary attempts.

The reactions to the Decembrist revolt were seen in Finland in a greater severity than before in Zakrevski's activity, in accordance with the 'law and order' line. As a result, fear and uncertainty intensified among leading Finns both in St Petersburg and Helsinki. They were afraid that the position of Finland and the internal conditions of the country could change. There was also cause for uncertainty in certain practical measures and business under consideration; in some of the emperor's measures concerning Finland the country's laws might be by-passed.[50]

A censorship decree based on that introduced in Russia in 1826 was issued in Finland in 1829. This required the advance censorship of all printed material, and its purpose was effectively to protect from criticism the prevailing system and its foremost supports in Finland. The decree forbade the printing of all matter that offended the emperor, the Christian religion, the government of the country and the fundamental laws.[51] The censorship decree muffled the public exchange of views considerably. Further, it decreased internal discussion in the church to the advantage of the church leadership. The decree also had an international dimension, in that it sought to protect from offence the governments of foreign nations in friendly relations with Russia, namely Austria and Prussia and the Holy Alliance countries in general.

The political isolation of the empire was paralleled in the second half of the 1820s by an attempt at economic isolation. Attempts were made to reduce Finland's trade with Sweden and correspondingly to enlarge it with Russia. This was apparent when Nicholas ratified the new trade agreement between Finland and Sweden in 1828. He also instructed the Senate to prepare such measures on trade and in other areas of the economy as would better correspond with Finland's new political position and at the same time deliver it from its state of dependence on Sweden.[52]

3. *The impact of the July Revolution in Finland*

The revolution which broke out in France in July 1830 meant the first serious blow at the Holy Alliance system. It arose when clear dissatisfaction with Charles X was expressed in the elections for the Chamber of Deputies, which he tried to evade by augmenting his own power. The consequence of this was political unrest among the masses, which led to the abdication of Charles X and the election of Louis Philippe as the new king.

The three great powers of the continent now saw themselves faced with a political threat aimed at the system which had prevailed for a decade and a half; liberalism and nationalism were rising as the new ideological driving forces, their supporters having clearly been activated against the politics of legitimism and the *status quo*. The immediate reaction of Nicholas I was that Russia should seek an agreement with Prussia and Austria to carry out a military intervention against the new authorities in Paris led by Louis Philippe. However, the emperor was forced to give up this intention because he could not get the support of his allies. The only result of the negotiations was an agreement made by the Russian foreign minister, Nesselrode, and Metternich at Karlsbad in August 1830, whereby they would not intervene but would not accept either possible interference by the new French government in the internal affairs of other countries. Nicholas was, however, on the alert and considerable Russian forces were concentrated in Poland for a possible march into western Europe.[53]

The revolt of the Belgians against Holland in August 1830 caused the government in St Petersburg to fear that the whole social system was imperilled as the revolt spread beyond the frontiers of France. Nicholas saw a general European revolution approaching, and in this new situation was again prepared to mount a military intervention to restore the old system in Holland and Belgium. Prussia announced her readiness to support such a plan, but Austria, tied down by her own problems, *inter alia* in northern Italy, declined to take part. The solidarity of the three great powers of the Holy Alliance was thereby virtually at an end.[54]

When discussions were held in St Petersburg at the end of August on the revolution in Paris, Governor-General Zakrevski was also summoned to receive instructions.[55] The emperor had given orders for various precautionary measures to maintain order, including strict political supervision over the whole empire. In these orders the Poles and the Finns were singled out as objects of vigilance. According to the special orders, all Russian subjects in France were to return at once to their own country. Here too the Poles and Finns were mentioned separately.[56]

As seen from St Petersburg, Sweden in particular posed a 'security risk' in Finland, since through Sweden dangerous channels of communications and news from continental Europe might develop. These apprehensions followed from the suspicions that had developed in St Petersburg in the later 1820s, because Sweden had been moving away from the policy line of 1812 in relation to Russia and liberalism had an increasing foothold there.

Since the severe censorship decree had come into force in Finland just the previous year, the authorities had, from the beginning of 1830, been taking measures to realise its aims. Lending libraries in different parts of the country were purged of 'unlawful' literature, and single numbers of Swedish newspapers were also from time to time ordered to be confiscated.[57] When news of the July Revolution in Paris began to reach Helsinki in August 1830, these control measures were put into practice in a number of ways. Before the outbreak of the July Revolution, the country's official newspaper, *Finlands Allmänna Tidning* had time to describe the political situation in Paris as very critical; when the king had declared a state of emergency the masses had run riot and a thousand people had died. After this the actual outbreak of revolution was no surprise to an observant reader, but because of the emperor Nicholas' visit to Helsinki in the middle of August 1830, no news about France was published for a couple of issues. When on 24 August, after the end of the imperial visit, *Finlands Allmänna Tidning* published news of the outbreak of revolution in Paris, it did so very cautiously and relying on official information from St Petersburg.[58] The character of the information in official paper changed somewhat as it began to base its news on information obtained directly from Paris, reporting in all its editions for about three weeks the political changes which were happening in France. The attitude of the paper at this point was generally informative and it did not adopt any sort of position.[59]

When *Finlands Allmänna Tidning* published the first news of the revolt in Belgium, on 21 September, it described the political disturbances as caused by the 'common rabble'. However the paper soon gave up this kind of reporting, which served the ends of conservative-pacifist propaganda, and already in the next issue explained that in Belgium it was a question of a real national uprising, with causes 'much deeper' than had at first been believed.[60]

The situation in Finland itself did not seem to the central administration of the country to be showing signs of danger. Nothing in St Petersburg pointed to military intervention in continental Europe, such as circles close to the emperor had been given to understand at the beginning of the unrest. Further, in Stockholm there appeared no special signs of political unrest. The authorities in Finland could find no effects of the revolution in Paris, which after all was far away. It took an average of twenty-four days for news from there to reach Helsinki.[61] So in its stand on the prevailing situation from August 1830, the Finnish central administration did not tighten its hold; rather the indications were in the opposite direction. Swedish newspapers, with a circulation in Finland of 400–500 copies, were scarcely confiscated at all in the latter half of 1830.[62] The revolutionary events in Paris and Brussels were examined more freely in the Swedish press, in some cases with considerable sympathy. Certain Finnish newspapers also tentatively published small items in which it was made clear that there had been a revolution in France, for example *Helsingfors Tidningar, Åbo Underrättelser* and *Turun Wiikko-Sanomat*.[63] It may not have been specifically forbidden to publish news of the revolutionary events in Paris in papers other than *Finlands Allmänna Tidning*, but the censorship decree of 1829 was in the background, emphasising the general supervision directed at the press.

The exchange of opinions on international political events was not wholly strange in elite circles in Finland. The way in which the July Revolution was viewed is well illustrated by the correspondence of J.A. Ehrenström and J.F. Aminoff,[64] both well-known representatives of the leading group among the upper classes, then already withdrawn from public life. The outbreak of revolution frightened Ehrenström, who had been a strong supporter of the existing system and in his time an open opponent of Napoleon. He saw Paris as the classic seat of revolution and it awoke in him the question whether the course of revolutionary events of 1789 had now begun again. He feared the coming of a long period of revolution and war. The Belgian revolt gave confirmation to the idea that the revolutionary movement was spreading. In September 1830 Ehrenström thought that events in western Europe would lead to a general European war; the news from St Petersburg of the extreme position of the emperor Nicholas may have reinforced this line of thought.

The Finnish church leaders automatically assumed that the upper levels of society were well aware of the July Revolution and political disturbances that had occurred elsewhere. They stressed, in the proclamation of a day of prayer issued at the beginning of December 1830, that it had been the good fortune of the Finnish people, in the year about to end, that the nation had been able to live 'in undisturbed peace'. No more substantial account of the 'political unrest' in continental Europe, which was very far away, was given in this connection, yet a clear reference was made to 'misleading doctrines'.[65]

The experience of the French revolution and the Napoleonic times, prompted seafaring circles in Finland's coastal towns to ask from the late summer of 1830 if the new political disturbances would lead to war. *Oulun Wiikko-Sanomat*, representing seafaring and merchant communities, from its foundation in 1829 had attentively followed foreign events.[66] Thus it too began to report the July Revolution, following the same line as *Finlands Allmänna Tidning*, but clearly differing from all other papers in southern Finland. *Oulun Wiikko-Sanomat* gave informal, brief reports of the events in Paris without mentioning its sources.[67] These may have been the country's official paper but — considering the distance — also some Stockholm papers. In addition, *Oulun Wiikko-Sanomat* contained, in the autumn of 1830, brief items on the Belgian revolt and political disturbances in Germany.[68] The paper covered the international situation from the point of view of those engaged in foreign trade and emphasised the resulting problems.[69] But because news of July Revolution reached the Finnish coastal towns in late August or early September, and news of the extension of revolution events in continental Europe about a month later, they scarcely affected Finnish seafaring circles, since the sailing season was already ending and the ships which usually sailed south in the winter season were probably already mostly on their way.

4. *The Polish revolt and the Finnish question in the development of events*

When revolt broke out in Poland at the end of November 1830, the government in St Petersburg faced a truly major problem. The danger which, after the July Revolution, Nicholas saw threatening the whole international system which had held sway in Europe since 1815 had moved inside the frontiers of the empire. The rebels, who included the Polish army, rapidly took possession of almost the whole area of Russian Poland. This rapid development neutralised Russia's capacity to intervene in Western Europe.

The Polish revolt not only threatened the integrity of the Russian empire, but at the same time it jeopardised Nicholas' international authority. Marshal Paskevich was given the task of suppressing the Polish rebels with the aid of the Russian army and returning Congress Poland to union with the empire. The differences that existed among the rebels made united action on their side difficult; they were made up of such different elements as conservative great landowners, poor peasants and radical intellectuals.[70] In spite of this the Poles defended themselves stubbornly. The mobilisation of the Russian troops took time, in addition to which they experienced great supply difficulties, and some military setbacks, while advancing into Poland. The revolt ended in September 1831 with the conquest of Warsaw and the surrender of the Polish troops. In western Europe and in Sweden, there was a powerful sympathy for the Polish liberation struggle. A newspaper and leaflet campaign was organised 'for Poland' in Stockholm. Liberals expressed extreme anti-Russian sentiments and criticised the emperor.[71]

In diplomatic circles in Vienna at one point, news circulated that Finland too would perhaps rise in revolt, and in Berlin the rumours went a stage further, contending that the Finns had already rebelled. In Stockholm a newly-arrived Polish émigré pursued his own free-lance diplomacy and launched rumours in which hope was changed into fact and Finland was on the point of 'participating'. Reports also circulated that arms were to be sent from Sweden into Finland. The Russian foreign minister, Nesselrode, ordered that the origin of all the rumours concerning Finland be traced, which brought a flock of reports to the Russian foreign ministry.[72]

The activity of the central administration of Finland in the crisis of the empire created by the Polish revolt was marked by emphatic loyalty and an endeavour to obey carefully all the security directives from St Petersburg. Nicholas' passionate reaction against the Polish rebels caused fear and uncertainty among the Finnish bureaucrats. Rehbinder had expressed a fear, right at the start of the Polish revolt, that the repercussions of its suppression might in some way endanger Finland's political position as well. In December 1830 he had written from St Petersburg to Walleen in Helsinki: 'The Poles have begun an insane action. Unless something wholly unexpected happens, they have lost their own case and also our own case, although we are innocent.'[73] There is little mention of the Polish revolt in the correspondence between the civil servants of the central administration in the Senate in Helsinki and in the Finnish affairs committee in St Petersburg.[74] There are only some references to the Russian military measures against the Poles, and further it was taken for granted that the rebels would lose. No question was raised about the appropriateness of the harsh measures adopted by the Russians. The sparse discussion of these matters may indicate the heightened sensitiveness of the subject. Suspicions could easily grown and secret informers were feared.

Nicholas ordered that Russia's military actions to suppress the Polish revolt were to receive 'full publicity',[75] a procedure which was part of the patriarchal practice of government and especially of the methods of autocracy. It was thus possible to make known to the population of the whole empire how the sovereign would punish 'misguided and criminal subjects'. This was also a general directive to the central administration in Finland. So that the official Russian announcements concerning the suppression of the Polish revolt should be really widely circulated in Finnish society, other newspapers in addition to *Finlands Allmänna Tidning*, both Swedish- and Finnish-language, were allowed to publish them. Thus for nine months from the beginning of 1831 the suppression was a central and very prominent topic in the Finnish press from *Helsingfors Tidningar* to *Oulun Wiikko-Sanomat*. According to the official version it was a question of a wicked crime against the emperor, a revolt brought about by the mindless rabble, and an iniquitous attempt to disturb the peace and order of the empire.[76] The official Russian military communiqués told from week to week how their army had advanced into Poland to carry out the emperor's orders. The Finnish press recognised the consistent harshness of Nicholas I's policy and allocated space generously for this official news material.[77] They clearly did not dare to embark on any other kind of reporting.

As soon as the Polish revolt broke out, Finland was isolated from communication with foreign countries on the orders of the central administration. The post between Sweden and Finland was completely severed for a long period in the early months of 1831. Those interested in the crisis had to accept that only official Russian accounts were in circulation.[78] The behaviour of the authorities was quite different from the period of the July Revolution; but the situation was also different in that there was enthusiasm for the Polish cause in Stockholm, and the emperor was not spared criticism in the Swedish press. Postal communications were subsequently restored from Sweden to Finland but the censor carefully inspected the Swedish newspapers that came into the country. The ones most often confiscated were the new liberal *Aftonbladet* and *Stockholms Posten*, *Dagligt Allehanda*, *Journalen* and *Conversationsbladet*.[79] The number of issues of foreign papers confiscated in 1831 rose to over 1,000, Swedish papers being the majority.[80] However news was 'smuggled' over the Swedish frontier, because trade links offered numerous possibilities and in the coastal towns Swedish papers could be read. The censorship authorities also kept an eye on German papers, of which a small number were subscribed to in Finland. The *Hamburger Correspondent* and *Hamburger Börsen-Halle*, especially, were, objects of official examination because in them could be found, for example, eyewitness accounts of battles in Poland, and dramatic interviews with Polish refugees and their stories of the activities of the Russian army.[81]

In one respect, the repression of the Polish revolt directly concerned Finland: the Finnish Guard Battalion was sent to the campaign in Poland along with the other troops of the Guard in the middle of January 1831. The official Russian communiqués publicised the battalion's 'participation' in military actions and praised the skill and bravery of the Finnish soldiers.[82] This also made clear the kind of obligations that Finland's membership in the Russian empire could place on her in a crisis.

Although the official Russian information service on the Polish revolt carefully filled the front pages, we must examine separately whether the Finns had their own ideas about this revolt, whether they pondered it closely and whether people in Finland generally reacted to events in Poland. On the whole, there was no positive image of Poland in Finland. Old traditions, dating from as far back as the sixteenth century, when Poland had stood actively for Catholicism, had influence as a negative factor. The confused internal situation of Poland before the partitions had steered conceptions in the same direction. In Finland, even those circles which followed events a little more extensively were clearly not familiar with the political dissatisfaction which emerged in Poland because that country did not have her national unity in the new situation after 1815. All political thinking that looked beyond autonomy was very remote to the Finns.

There were always those in high-ranking circles in Finland who followed general European developments extensively. Leading civil servants did so, but they were very reserved in expressing their opinions. During the Polish revolt Ehrenström again set out his ideas in his letters to J.F. Aminoff;[83] perhaps it was the fact that he had retired that made him less cautious. Ehrenström thought the Polish revolt senseless, when there were three militarily powerful great powers surrounding the country. Because of this the outcome of the insurrection was in his opinion self-evident. He examined both sides in the Polish question very independently: he observed in March 1831 that Russia had only managed to mount her military counter-measures very slowly and thought that the Poles were fighting with unexpected enthusiasm and bravery, although their resources were clearly small. Ehrenström was clearly concerned at the Finnish Guard Battalion being involved, which had the character of a civil war within the empire. He was aware that the battalion had suffered considerable losses in the difficult conditions, even before it went into action. Ehrenström saw the general European situation as very problematical. He noted cynically that cholera was spreading from east to west and revolutionary fever from west to east. 'No mortal knows where the latter will stop, and how to act against it.'

Another Finnish nobleman, C.G. Mannerheim, who in addition had contacts in St Petersburg, expressed the view in March 1831 that Russia would once and for all abolish the former autonomy of Poland,[84] which made him dubious about what might happen to Finland. Ehrenström believed that a consequence of the Polish insurrection would be growing distrust of Finnish loyalty in St Petersburg and the initiation of very unpleasant measures of control.

As for the circle of young Finnish academic intellectuals, at the beginning of the 1830s the atmosphere in Helsinki was not such as would have stimulated them to take a stand. Since the University had moved to the country's new capital in the year after the fire of Turku in 1827, it had not had time to group into communities in the new surroundings. University circles were somewhat confused after the move and had difficulty in finding a new basis for activity in the new environment. Attitudes were in many ways enfeebled, at least at first. Of the Polish revolt, the young intellectuals were only spectators;[85] cultural Finnish nationalism, or 'fennomania', had no political dimensions. In addition to the national romantic way of thought, they were fixed in the intellectual inheritance of the general European Enlightenment, above all in a positive belief in the victory of progress. Thoughts and aspirations moved on the level of spiritual and cultural development; political participation had not yet become a reality.

Among the burghers too there were no signs of politicisation. As a social group, because of Finland's peculiar circumstances, they had not formed a distinct entity, and were in many ways in a kind of transitional and intermediate phase.[86]

Turku, the ancient centre of the country, had received a blow in the fire of 1827, which also left its mark on the city's burghers. In Helsinki, the development of which as a commercial centre was only just starting, the burghers functioned in some isolation from the rest of society; those of Viipuri, which had belonged to Old Finland for a century, integrated slowly with the rest of Finland; and those of the coastal towns of Pohjanmaa were, for geographical reasons and because of communications, fairly separated, but were economically active. These circumstances and the state of the academic intellectuals may do much to explain why nothing happened in Finland in 1830–1.

The Polish revolt came up afterwards in Finland in various connections. When in the latter half of 1831 Polish refugees travelled through Finland to Sweden, some young intellectuals may have been in personal contact with them;[87] in any case, when knowledge of the experiences of the participants and their bitterness spread among certain groups of Finns, they began to see the events in Poland from Polish viewpoint of the Poles themselves. It was impossible for the young to avoid seeing the fate of Poland as something deeply tragic and the Poles as models of honour and heroism. J.J. Nervander expressed such thoughts in a letter to J.V. Snellman at the end of 1831.[88] Such influences, which came from the other side of the Gulf of Bothnia, provided the material for a poem which Fredrik Cygnaeus wrote in 1832 about the hero of Polish liberty, Kosciuszko.[89]

The leadership of the Finnish church came to terms with the revolutionary phenomena in Europe in 1830–1. The church was very conscious of its own special position as one of the buttresses of the prevailing system and its alliance with the sovereign. The proclamation for the day of prayer in December 1831 condemned, on the basis of a religiously inspired conservatism, the lack of trust which had arisen 'in many places in our continent' between ruler and people.[90] The reason was that people had rejected the guidance of God and allowed human selfishness and inflammatory doctrines to guide their activity.

The return home of the Guard Battalion from Poland in the spring of 1832 had a variety of after-effects. News of the considerable losses it had suffered had preceded it. When, following the battalion's homecoming, a review was held on the Kaartintori in Helsinki in April 1832, the human side of the affair was clearly revealed. Casualties had been heavy when reckoned according to the number both of the fallen and those who had died from other causes on this campaign. The review was described in subsequent memoirs as an occasion when the relatives were gloomy and despondent.[91] The official account of the campaign was different. The battalion received from the emperor the banner of the Knights of St George, in recognition of its courage and daring in battle against the Polish rebels.[92] On this occasion its commander, Lieut.-Colonel A.E. Ramsay, strongly emphasised the significance of loyalty to the empire and said: 'Let our banners be there in the future to call Finland's sons to display the highest virtues of citizenship, duty and loyalty towards the ruler.'[93] By conspicuous loyalty they might support Finland's position and the inviolability of her rights. This was a Finnish security policy, bound up with the spirit of the Holy Alliance.

At the same time, a quite different phenomenon made itself felt among the people of Finland: the spread of cholera from Russia towards the west and to Finland. It was continuously discussed by the Senate, the church and the official newspaper from the end of 1830,[94] and in it one can assume that the European crisis of 1830–1 — including the Polish revolt and its supression — were put in the shade by the threat of cholera in Finnish society at large and especially among the farming community. The question also arises whether the government in St Petersburg used the cholera danger for political advantage.

5. *The Finns and Finland's position in Russian security policy in the 1830s and 1840s*

The transitional phase which began with the July Revolution also led to changes in the system of international relations on the continent. The Holy Alliance, after losing its hold on western Europe, was forced to retreat. France and Belgium, where the political system had changed, had Britain at their side and formed a western European group of states, emphasising liberal principles and clearly distinguished from the countries of the Holy Alliance.

Thus a confrontation of east and west had formed in Europe, of which there had been signs, since the Congress of Verona in 1822. The political interests of the two sides were clearly divergent, in addition to the ideological division under the banners of conservatism and liberalism. In the new era Russia, Prussia and Austria continued to defend the tradition of the Holy Alliance and saw western ideas as a growing threat to the political and social system they represented.[95]

The split in the general European power structure which had appeared raised new problems for Russia in the Baltic area as well. From a military point of view, the phase in which the Baltic was a *mare russicum* had ended.

Britain, whose interests in the period after 1815 had been strongly directed outside Europe, began to play a greater role within it. Moreover, she found herself opposed to Russia both in the Black Sea and the Baltic. The issue at stake on both sides was one of influence and commercial interests. Rumours which circulated in the late 1820s alleged that Britain was trying to acquire a naval base somewhere in the Baltic area. In that area, the general European division along ideological lines was plainly visible: in Sweden the struggle of liberalism against conservatism was intensified, which also meant that Karl Johan's pro-Russian foreign policy was losing its support. The growing strength of the liberals meant that Sweden no longer had its previous significance for Russia as an 'ideological barrier' against the west.

The change in Europe's general development and the situation in the Baltic, after the interlude formed by the years 1815–30, put Finland in a new position in Russian security policy. The appointment of Menshikov in 1831 as the new Governor-General after Zakrevski eloquently testified to the newly enhanced significance of the country's position; Menshikov held at the same time the post of chief of the Russian naval staff in St Petersburg.

In the new international situation a broad overall plan for the defence of St Petersburg itself was formulated.[97] On Åland fortification work began, works were begun centering on the fortification of Bomarsund in the east of the archipelago. From the siting of this future base it can be deduced that its purpose was not to put pressure on Sweden, but generally to strengthen Russia's military position in the northern Baltic.

The defences on Finland's south coast were strengthened in 1832 with the refurbishing of the fortifications at Sveaborg. In addition a Finnish marine detachment, suited to the country's coastal conditions, had been established in May 1830, to replace the disbanded rifle battalions; like them, it was a force of paid, enlisted men.[98] Kronstadt, whose fortifications were strengthened, and the new defences built on the south of the Gulf of Finland at Tallinn and Dünamünde formed a continuation of the military systems on the north coast of the Gulf. This so-called Peter and Paul triangle of fortifications was meant to strengthen the considerable fleet which Russia began to build in the Baltic under the direction of admiral Menshikov. It was divided into three squadrons, of which two were usually based at Kronstadt and one at Sveaborg.[99]

In contrast to the considerable strategic significance of the south coast of Finland, the rest of Finland was secondary to the defence of St Petersburg. Finland as a territory, extensive and with poor communications, did not entice a potential enemy, and if such an enemy landed somewhere on the Gulf of Bothnia, this presented no direct threat to St Petersburg. In Finland there were some Russian land forces: one division of regular infantry divided into twelve battalions, and one regiment of Cossacks. These forces totalled over 10,000 men.[100] These forces were intended to strengthen the local defence of the fortifications on the south coast and as a covering force against small enemy landings; the transfer of the Finnish line battalions from Åland to Viipuri also points to this.[101] Later the peacetime grouping of these troops was partly altered, when some battalions were also stationed on the west coast.

In the empire's military planning the potential enemy was generally thought of as Britain, but in this case Sweden also posed a question. The repelling of any military surprises coming across the Gulf of Bothnia was important too, because even a small enemy success might lead to dangerous consequences in Finland, for example risings in certain areas of the west coast.

Of the officers of the Russian units stationed in Finland about half were generally Finnish, graduates of the cadet school founded at Hamina in 1812. In this way it was possible to use the knowledge of local conditions and the knowledge of the country's languages. By contrast the Russians were not prepared to initiate any 'Finnish solution' in organising the country's defence. From the plans to establish Finnish enlisted battalions a decision was made at the end of the 1840s to organise only one.[102] The Russians had learned from their experience of Poland, where the Poles' 'own' army had joined the insurrection. The staff of the Russian units stationed in Finland were small, which indicates that their operational planning was carried out in St Petersburg. In peace time these so-called Finnish units had no specific joint commander either; the Governor-General was *ex-officio* the commander of all military forces in Finland.

Nicholas I saw revolution as an international threat, an enemy always ready for action,[103] and in central Europe, Austria and Prussia formed an ideological bulwark against it. Their task was to stop a possible revolutionary wave set in motion again from Paris, which France was suspected of exploiting to destroy the international system of 1815. In the north, Finland was a continuation of the central European buffer zone, and thus had an important task. It was especially a matter of protection against dangerous intellectual influences coming from Sweden: attention was now also directed at the 'pro-Swedish spirit' in Finland, which had earlier aroused distrust at high levels.[104] The intensification of political control against Sweden was regarded as important for two reasons. Liberalism there had a strongly anti-Russian tendency and its supporters were prone to criticise the activity of the central administration in Finland. And of course all political information crossing the Gulf of Bothnia was for language reasons easily received in Finland.

One way to break connections with Sweden was to reduce the permits given for foreign travel. In practice merchants had no difficulty in obtaining passes, in contrast to university teachers, students and members of the upper classes.[105] In the first half of the 1830s, one group of Swedish newspapers after another was forbidden entry to Finland,[106] because of their postscripts on the Polish revolt and their liberal politics. The control of foreign literature generally continued, and as more public libraries were established, the literature in them became subject to pre-censorship by the authorities. All works dealing with Napoleon or the July Revolution were forbidden. The authorities also reacted suspiciously to foreign religious literature. An extreme example of the controlling bureaucracy's attitude was that even the scientific publications which Helsinki University received in exchange from foreign institutes of higher learning were liable to be inspected.[107]

When the government in St Petersburg considered measures against the 'pro-Swedish spirit' in Finland, it drew a practical dividing line which was in some respects significant. They began to tolerate the national-romantic movement because it seemed to constitute a break in Finland's traditional connections with Sweden. Its new phase of 'Helsinki romanticism' rested firmly on a native foundation, and was not supported, like the previous phase of Turku romanticism, by Swedish influences. Of course the government in St Petersburg did not actually approve of the national-romantic tendency in Finland, but they wanted to use it as a tool for their own ends. Hence in 1831, the Finnish Literary Society (*Suomalaisen Kirjallisuuden Seura*) was permitted by the emperor to begin its activity. At the same time it was decided to establish a Finnish-language lectureship in Helsinki University.

The political isolation of Finland from the west also involved measures with the main purpose of distancing Finland from Sweden economically. The new direction of trading relations which had begun at the end of the 1820s was continued. When, in 1830, all the inhabitants of town and country were given the right to export within the Baltic, the consequence was that Finland's trade with Russia — a part of which was conducted by farmers using their own boats — increased both with St Petersburg and the Baltic provinces. Soon after the new trade agreement between Finland and Sweden was concluded in 1834, clearly reducing their trade, an important reform was made in organising Finland's trade with Russia. According to a decree issued in 1835, there would be Finnish commercial agents in St Petersburg, Tallinn and Riga, to assist the setting up of commercial contacts for the Finns.[108]

The new tendency was also influenced by the fact that St Petersburg, as a major city, was in itself commercially attractive. Old Finland, now joined to the rest of Finland, was already integrated economically with Russia — on St Petersburg's terms. The districts of the coastal area of southern Finland and the eastern lake region benefited particularly from the increasing trade with Russia. The areas north of Saimaa, which had suffered particularly from their isolation caused by the frontier of the peace of Turku (1743), were organically incorporated into this area of new trade with the east. Finland's exports to Russia rose during the 1840s to 35–40 per cent of the country's total exports, while exports to Sweden, which had still been about 50 per cent in the 1820s, fell in the mid-1840s, when all special provisions ended, to under 10 percent. The share of imports in both cases was roughly the same. It was the coastal towns of Pohjanmaa which suffered most from the changes in the trade between Sweden and Russia.[109] Currency reform was also carried out in Finland in 1840 by eliminating the use of Swedish money and decreeing the Russian silver rouble as the only medium of exchange. This drew Finland into greater economic contact with the east than before.

The government in St Petersburg also sought to promote Finland's adaptation as a political buffer-zone against the west by quite different means. It was thought important that economic reforms could be carried out in Finland and that economic development was clearly going forward. The contentment of the Finns with conditions within their country would strengthen political loyalty to the empire and, indirectly, immunity against western ideas.[110]

Powerfully though the French revolution was hated in the entourage of Nicholas I and alien as the British political system was, the government in St Petersburg could not remain wholly indifferent to western reforms. Of course in Russia itself submission and obedience were taken by the autocracy for granted, but the Finnish question could not be handled in the same way if it aimed to achieve results. Because St Petersburg regarded reform policies in Finland as necessary, it also acknowledged that the country was a special case of its own within the empire. The aims pursued by Zakrevski as Governor-General, above all his favouring of the Russian language and attempts to bring Finnish society closer to Russia, did not suit the general line of Russia's new policy. There had also been criticism of Zakrevski in St Petersburg, by Menshikov among others. The change of Governor-General was therefore directly linked to Russian security policy. Menshikov recognised the integrity of the Finnish way of life and the need for internal reform.

In Finnish government circles the fact that, after the revolt, Poland lost her autonomous status and on the basis of the organic statute of 1832 came under a military governor and was ruled by offices functioning in St Petersburg, made a powerful impression. Consciousness of this followed the leading Finnish administrators like a long shadow through the whole succeeding period.

A strong paternalism continued to characterise Finland's central administration. Submission and obedience were declared the most important social virtues; criticism of political conditions was not permitted, and everything pointing to political participation was regarded with suspicion. It was seen as disloyalty to the system itself, because the paternalistic point of view almost equated such criticism with rebellion. Activity indicating rebellion was most feared in connection with international crises.

The central administration of Finland was also subjected to political pressure in the 1830s and 1840s from the government in St Petersburg, which sought to involve the country in certain imperialist and assimilationist endeavours. The most notable of these was the attempt by the Russian ministry of the interior to direct the work of codifying Finnish law into compatibility with the Russian system, which would thereby have endanger the inviolability of the Finnish legal system. Menshikov opposed this argument.[111] His basic argument was the importance of Finland remaining tranquil and loyal, for which reason it was necessary to preserve inviolate all aspects of the native Finnish way of life. Among the Finns two leading men of the new era, Alexander Armfelt (1842–76), who succeeded Rehbinder as minister-secretary of state in St Petersburg, and L.G.von Haartman, who became vice-chairman of the economic department of the Senate in 1841, actively defended the inviolability of the country's legal system. Nicholas I approved Menshikov's view, as far as Finland was concerned, and let the codification project drop, considering the political loyalty of the Finns to be paramount, on which basis they clearly differed from the Poles.

The central administration of Finland from the 1830s onwards acted vigorously along the general lines adopted by the government in St Petersburg to promote economic reforms in the country.[112] In agriculture they tried to develop self-sufficiency in bread-grains, develop dairy farming and initiate training in agriculture. They began to support industry by easing the supply of capital. They also sought to increase the state tax revenue by reorganising tariffs.

In the conditions of the 1830s the position of the church leaders as a buttress of the prevailing system was clear. The position of the bishops as trusted servants of the ruler was emphasised when the emperor repeatedly let political considerations influence preferments to vacant sees. After Tengström, E.G. Melartin, who came second in the Chapter's list of candidates, became Archbishop of Turku in 1833. When C.G. Ottelin was appointed Bishop of Porvoo in 1837, it was a demonstration of the emperor's favour more than any indication of the confidence of the clergy. Ottelin had long enjoyed confidential relations with the central administration, and had studied in St Petersburg. It was a peculiarity of his appointment that he had got on to the short list only after the candidate who came third in the election had — yielding to obvious pressure — resigned. Once appointed, Bishop Ottelin was in every respect a firm supporter of 'the alliance of the throne and the altar'.[113]

The emperor began to place more emphatic demands on the church, which from the early 1830s he regarded as an ally. To fulfil the role he envisaged for it, the church must also be internally united and an institution directed in an authoritarian way from above. In this sense, in its role as guardian of social morality, it was to be an effective spiritual buffer against all rebelliousness and a support of the country's administration in any possible crisis.

Among ruling circles in St Petersburg there had been suspicion of the revivalist movements which had been active in Finland from the last years of the reign of Alexander I; they were regarded as weakening governing authority in the church and fomenting unrest. Because of this, from the 1820s trials had been held in different parts of the country of certain revivalist groups. The question acquired a broad political significance when Nicholas I took it up in conversation with Archbishop Melartin in 1837, after which extensive counter-measures against the revivalists were started.[114] Revivalism was a popular religious movement which disregarded or flouted the regulations and prohibitions about church assemblies. Revivalism occurred under a self-appointed leadership, and could be directed against the clergy and the leaders of the church, whom the revivalists regarded as subordinating the work of the church to the service of a worldly system. The movement Revivalism affected in particular the farming community, who in central administrative circles were classed as 'the ignorant folk'. It was strong in Pohjanmaa, which had been labelled a politically unreliable area after 1808, but in other parts too. The revivalist movement led to allegations that 'republican' ideas were spreading from Sweden to Finland.[115]

The trials — about ten in all — which began in 1838 of numerous revivalist leaders were not in themselves a new phenomenon in Finland, but they were emphatically a government-inspired fight against the revivalists.

The task of the leaders of the church was to determine the grounds of the prosecution. The accused clergy were dealt with severely, but the farmers gently.

The performance of the leaders of the Lutheran church in Finland clearly satisfied the emperor and his advisers, and it is worth noticing that St Petersburg began at the same time to support conversion work on behalf of the Orthodox church in the Baltic provinces.

In the 1830s, of the institutions intended to support the prevailing system, Helsinki University came under pressure from two directions. The fact that, in Poland, Warsaw and Vilno universities had been closed was not in itself alarming, because there the reason was the revolt. But Nicholas saw the universities as forums which transmitted western ideas to the empire, and in Russia they were indeed the only institution for free political discussion. Hence the ruling circles of the empire were planning various measures to intensify control, among others by drafting new statutes for the universities.[116] The administration of Helsinki University sought to preserve the University undisturbed and for that reason to carry out measures thought appropriate to preserve order. In this way they believed they could ensure that Helsinki University would not be involved in the intensified control of the universities in the empire.

The student corporations, as new forums of activity, caused friction between the University administration and the students; student activity was clearly increasing in Finland. The direct or indirect influence of the government in St Petersburg was clearly reflected in the measures of the University administration. In the spring of 1832 the compulsory wearing of uniform by students was decreed. The decision made in 1833 to split up some of the student fraternities, was a measure designed to weaken them as forums for discussion and as bases for mass activity.[117] In fact this decision was only carried out slowly.

The application of paternalistic control in the University created a continuous state of tension between the rector and the consistory on the one side and the students on the other. The maintenance of order was interpreted by students as petty interference in their affairs and their readiness to express dissatisfaction was interpreted on the other side as irresponsibility.

When Nicholas I visited Helsinki in 1833, his purpose was to obtain a general picture of the situation and mood in Finland after the transitional years 1830–1. Afterwards, the Emperor felt assured that loyalty prevailed in the country along with 'order and good manners', the fruit of the 'patriarchal' system. Nicholas' satisfaction was expressed a little later in his letter to Marshal Paskevich: 'How wonderful it would be for us if thinking was everywhere as sound.'[118] It was typical of his style of government that as soon as he had left on his return journey to St Petersburg, *Finlands Allmänna Tidning* published a statement describing the activities of courts-martial in Poland and the severe sentences they had inflicted.[119] Here was a clear reminder to the Finns of how differently the emperor treated his loyal subjects from the rebellious Poles.

The same purpose underlay the visit which Nicholas made at the same time to the Baltic provinces: he was satisfied with this tour of inspection too. Finland and the Baltic provinces together constituted that sector of Russia's western frontier for the security of which the emperor alone took responsibility, without the support of allies. When in addition Russia succeeded in July 1833 in concluding a favourable treaty on the Bosporus, which prohibited the passage of all foreign warships, Nicholas could concentrate, together with Austria and Prussia, on stabilising Russia's security problems in central Europe. To that end the work of extinguishing the embers left over from the Polish revolt did not cease, and death sentences were continually carried out for participation in the revolt, and Poles who had fled abroad were condemned in their absence.

In central Europe it was important for Russia, because of the Polish situation and the liberalism in western Europe, to tighten her alliances with Austria and Prussia. This was achieved when talks were held at Münchengrätz between these three powers in September 1833, which resulted in an agreement in the traditional spirit of the Holy Alliance for intervention to suppress revolts in central Europe. The Münchengrätz system sought to reinforce the integrity of the post-1815 situation in the region and to emphasise the ability of the authoritarian-conservative system to act against western European powers and western ideas. It was also of relevance to the whole Russian security zone stretching from the Black Sea to Finland. Russian influence on the major political decisions of 1833 was seen extensively over the whole eastern half of Europe.[120]

We must examine separately how, in this new phase, Finnish society — the academic intellectuals, business circles and rural society — adapted to the conditions created by Russia's security policy.

Although the intellectuals had been passive spectators during the general European political transition of the years 1830–1, they had undoubtedly perceived that the nationalities were emerging more clearly than before in the overall framework of events. They had also experienced the extent to which there were possibilities of activating a national movement in Finland: once in the fate of Arwidsson, and secondly in the Polish revolt. It was recognised that a national awakening could not happen in such a way that the prevailing political system, with the emperor and his authority at its head, could be openly challenged. In Finnish conditions there were not the preconditions for a political fighting stand, emphasising the principles of nationalism and liberalism, against the Holy Alliance, as in continental Europe. Hence activity was steered away from extreme political positions and into a narrow path. The young academic intelligentsia who were leading the national awakening sought the support of the farming population. In the west it was historically the bourgeoisie who emerged as 'the third Estate', in the vanguard for change. But the Finnish bourgeoisie, largely Swedish-speaking, were not prepared, as a linguistic minority, for major political or social change, but supported the preservation of the *status quo*.[121] The Finnish nationalist movement, had similarities in its social foundation with the corresponding phenomena in the agrarian states of eastern and south-eastern Europe. In all these countries the intellectuals tried to develop national cultural interests. A politically active nation, on the other hand, was the characteristic phenomenon of the more advanced western half of Europe.

The cultural activity of the nationalist movement in Finland in the 1830s was being directed more strongly than before to seek out the internal sources of the nation's strength. The publication of the *Kalevala* in 1835 and the poetry of the young Runeberg accelerated this tendency. All this gave additional material for the search for a general Finnish identity. Thus the national self-confidence acquired a foundation originating in the nation itself. At the same time the idealisation of the common man acted, to some extent, as a counter-weight to traditional pride in status.[122]

The growth of attitudes of protest among the academic intellectuals in the 1830s and 1840s involved some kind of initial politicisation. At the same time they were splitting up and following different directions. One of these was the change of the national romantic tendency into a reform movement, whose central demand was to secure for the Finnish language the status of an official and cultural language. The emphasis on linguistic nationalism drew strength from the undeniable fact that, after the separation from Sweden, the language situation in Finland had been revolutionised. In the new situation the Finnish-speakers were the great majority in the Grand Duchy, forming perhaps seven-eighths of the whole population. The Finnish nationalists, or fennomans, wanted to build the future unity of the nation round the Finnish language. Because they were seeking reforms in favour of the country's Finnish-speaking people, and because most of them were farming people, the national movement so formed came to have the colouring of a social reform movement. Historical traditions and links with Sweden were to be rejected, as was the continuing dependence on Swedish culture. The writer J.V. Snellman saw the historical peculiarity of Finland as being that 'the national consciousness of the Finnish people is primarily repressed by a different power from the one that restricts its political independence'.[123]

The fennomans found themselves caught between two fires. In the first place their struggle was directed against Swedishness; the Swedish-speaking upper class was clearly an antagonist from the people's point of view, being close at hand, while the Russians, as strangers, were far away. The Russian language caused no problem in Finland — which was thus something of a special case in the field of European nationalism. The other tendency was expressed by those who were sympathetic to Sweden. In addition to old cultural traditions, consciousness of the difference in political conditions between Finland and Sweden also played a part. Liberal principles led to the idealisation of Swedish conditions by contrast with the reactionary conditions of their own country. *Aftonbladet* was the newspaper which these sympathisers sought to follow whenever possible. Student Scandinavianism, around which there grew up personal relationships and other contacts over the Gulf of Bothnia, was another impulse which turned sympathies towards Sweden in the 1840s.[124]

No open expressions of political dissatisfaction appeared in Finland in the 1830s and '40s, so powerful was the hold of the patriarchal-bureaucratic system and the personality of the emperor over the whole government. The intellectuals were well aware that there were no possibilities for the free exchange of opinions. The atmosphere prevailing in Finland was felt to be oppressive, particularly in comparison with Sweden. This realisation was heightened by observations made in journeys abroad. One then had to decide which was decisive, Finnish national feeling or a free political atmosphere. When J.V. Snellman returned to Finland from a long journey abroad, made in 1839–42, there followed a period of doubt, which, however, was very brief. In Sweden he had observed that there was little interest in Finland, and in Germany almost none. Snellman's pessimistic comment to one of his friends was that in Finland the intellectuals were as if preparing for their own funerals.[125] At the same time, he came to know wholly different political conditions abroad, from which he obtained valuable experience, and in Sweden in particular he became a debater of public affairs. His journey had started Snellman thinking in a new way and made him vigorously active. Concern about Finland's future was the dominant source of his thinking after he returned home. He seized especially on the place of small nations in historical development and began to look for materials to form a theory about their destiny. Because of his personal circumstances, he was forced to work in the remote town of Kuopio and from there to stimulate discussion of the country's national problems.

The poet J.L. Runeberg was cautious in his political attitudes and left no analysis of contemporary events.[126] However, when during the reign of Nicholas I he chose the events of the war of 1808 as the special topic of his poetry, this was in itself a political act. From this war, which had basically been a trial of strength between Sweden and Russia, he created 'Finland's war' and a battle for the liberty of the country. Taken as a whole it also meant that he stressed the country's historical bonds with Sweden and valued its defence. A line was drawn against Russia, though not provocatively. Runeberg's position in the Finland of his day was modest; he was the Latin teacher in Porvoo high school. In Sweden, on the other hand, he was made a member of the Order of the North Star, and the Swedish Academy proposed his election as a member. However, Oskar I intervened to prevent the nomination, which was seen as offensive to the Russian Emperor.[127]

The historical novels written by Zacharias Topelius presented the role of the Finns in the conflicts of the Swedish crown during the era of Sweden's greatness. Topelius was a eulogist of the monarchical ideal, emphasising a relationship of trust between ruler and subjects and the loyalty of the subjects. Unlike Runeberg, he took a stand on contemporary events. He was ostentatiously loyal to the Emperor and ready to praise the throne, and was accommodating towards the government in St Petersburg. The central administration of the country bestowed considerable marks of favour upon him.

The extreme political attitude in the 1840s was that taken by those academic intellectuals who speculated directly about the idea that Finland's political fate would change dramatically in the future. M.A. Castrén, who had undertaken extensive study trips among the peoples related to the Finns in central Russia, was of the opinion that Russia was seeking systematically to prevent all development towards freer conditions in Finland, and concluded from this that the Finns must begin to prepare a revolt against Russia. He meant by this an undertaking not for the present but for the future, nor was it to be any kind of separate Finnish popular insurrection either. According to him, it was to be linked with a favourable international crisis and would be realised as a general revolt against Russian domination, in which the non-Russian peoples from the Turks and the Tartars to the Finns would take part.[128] This kind of bold political vision, which was shared by some other intellectuals, could be expressed only to trusted friends.[129] Castrén described his vision of revolt in a letter to Snellman in 1844 which, for reasons of security, was not sent through the official post. When Castrén and other projectors of a radical view of Finland's future spoke of the danger from the east, they saw the country's original Swedish culture as a shield against Slavism. They held that a hurried break away from it, and an attempt to rely solely on the intellectual culture of the Finnish language, was weakly-founded and dangerous. They saw the finnicisation movement led by Snellman as needing time to develop in such a way that the country's future might be built upon it.

Political reaction as such was not a decisive factor for the business community, so much as the opportunities for engaging in economic activities and the future prospects generally. When Finland separated from Sweden, it had also begun to work free from that centralised economic system which had served the Swedish heartland and which correspondingly discriminated against Finland. The prospects for general economic development were poor in Finland in the post-1808 situation, however, although the peace that followed the Napoleonic wars was conducive to such development. The change in Finland's geographical position after 1808 influenced the direction of development. Whereas Finland had been on the periphery of Sweden, and its eastern region an underdeveloped backwater, it was now near to the Russian imperial capital and the westernmost part of the empire. In many respects it came to be one of the empire's most developed parts. The general conditions for economic enterprise were undoubtedly better in Finland than in Russia in the first half of the nineteenth century. Finland had its own state budget and its own tariff frontier, both with foreign countries and with Russia, in addition to which the tax revenues were wholly employed for the country's own benefit. All this was a cause for satisfaction. The country's dependence on the emperor was recognised in the Finnish business community, as was the danger of losing such aids to economic life as their own customs and law-making through political disturbances.

In the first half of the nineteenth century Finland was still largely an agrarian country, of whose population 90 per cent lived by agriculture, while industry was negligible.[130] For that reason maritime activity increased, and during the 1830s and '40s, the merchants of Oulu, Raahe, Kokkola, Pori and Turku came to own an abundance of merchant ships.[131] For its part, Russia perceived that Finland had a special role to play as the representative of maritime activity in the empire. Since maritime activity created capital it followed that, in the absence of real industry in the country, it promoted development in the economy as a whole. The low costs, especially in wages, influenced the success of Finnish entrepreneurs in this field,[132] and the state for its part received substantial tax revenue.

For the farmers at this time, there were serious economic problems. They had to pay the taxes and carry burdens, like road maintenance, the carriage of mail and maintenance of the stage-posting system. Income was meagre and years of bad harvest caused repeated disruption. At this stage one can scarcely speak of a rise in farmers' living standard, which in any case are difficult to determine.[133] But many reforms increased optimism about the future, and the long peace after 1808 added significantly to the feeling of security among the farmers; it was they who had personally experienced war and occupation during Swedish rule, but from the 1830s the number of those who had personal experience of war or of Russia as an enemy was diminishing. Thus some breaking of traditional ties with Sweden was obviously occurring, and at the same time the sailing of boats over the Gulf of Bothnia by Finnish farmers had decreased.

Political freedoms had not been essential to the farmers, and so the reign of Nicholas I did not seem to the farmers a period of reaction. The authorities hardly controlled their way of life, but they got little enlightenment either. For them priests were the intermediaries in public affairs, at a time when Finnish-language newspapers scarcely existed. However, from the 1840s the farmers were getting new spokesmen for themselves from the men of the finnicisation movement.

In its patriarchal management of affairs, the central administration of the country regarded itself as knowing the needs of the people, and the official picture of society which emerged in its statements and those of the church expressed harmony, without any conflict of interests. The patriarchal system also let it be understood that it could guard the common good without any extensive participation on the part of the population. Official circles sought in different ways to idealise prevailing conditions. Public discussion of society's defects was not regarded as consistent with the authority of the central administration. It was advisable for the newspapers to avoid publicising human misfortunes, illnesses or accidents. They sought carefully to protect security and contentment, according to the tradition of the system; what was new was that a need for social reform was acknowledged, even if it was assumed that its realisation would come by direction from above. It was dangerous to criticise existing conditions from the point of view of the subject, or make demands on the administration, and it was doubly dangerous to refer to foreign examples. When expressions of dissatisfaction in society did appear, an official attempt was made to explain them as arising from foreign revolutionary ideas or agitation from outside, which sought to disturb the patriarchal tranquillity of society.

The highest leadership of the country had sought, for its own political ends, to subsume culture, religion and the prevailing social system in a united, unbroken whole.[134] Such a procedure was not new in itself, but it was new that in Finnish conditions at that time this whole had come to be centred in religion to a remarkable extent.

6. *Familiarity with Finland's name abroad in the first half of the nineteenth century*

In new foreign maps Finland could now and then be distinguished from the Russian empire by the use of a different colour, an indication that Finland was a new territory in the empire, and perhaps an indication too that Finland had its own distinct nationality.[135] However, no image of an 'active' nationality was linked to the name of Finland during the first half of the nineteenth century. After its annexation to Russia, Finland was not connected with any politically significant event. Here the difference from Poland was very clear. In historical literature dealing with Russia or, exceptionally, with Finland only, there were some times general allusions to Finland's autonomy or to some separate factors which showed that the country had its own administration.

Travel writers on Finland usually described the country's natural phenomena.[136] Descriptions of Lapland had already appeared earlier, and especially in Britain there had been interest in the primitive conditions there.[137] Conditions in Lapland in fact became the general image of Finland abroad. Travel literature might also assess Finland's general level of development. Political assessments depended of course on the outlook of the writer. If he was conservative and a romantic, like the Frenchman Xavier Marmier, he could describe it as an advantage for Finland, at the beginning of the 1840s, that it had not yet experienced 'the phase before the great floods', or the influences of the revolution.[138] Anyone examining the conditions of the Russian empire critically would usually draw attention to the position of the non-Russian nationalities. Grievances would be exposed, and something positive said about the aspirations of the nationalities — the Finns among them.[139] But the name of Finland seldom appeared abroad in works of history and travel, and when it did, the circle of readers would have been a restricted one.

Political interest in Finland did not exist, at least not in Germany and France. The fear of Russia which appeared in Britain in the 1830s and 1840s emphasised that that country was continually striving to extend her empire. Writers usually pointed to the fate of Poland, and might also mention that Finland too was a conquered country.[140] Sweden was the only country in the first half of the nineteenth century where there appeared to be some political interest in Finland. But again only limited circles were involved. Psychologically it is understandable that the Swedes wanted to forget Finland; getting Norway as compensation had helped to calm feelings. But when a certain dissatisfaction with Norway appeared in Sweden, Finland came up again. The group in Sweden that was interested in Finland seems to have assumed unquestioningly that the Finns were dissatisfied with their new position, and wished to revert to the old one. Fennomania was by its nature alien to the Swedes. But in Sweden there could also be criticism of such a leading figure in Finland as Haartman, and claims that he was seeking to eliminate from the Finnish administration all 'Swedophiles'. Again Runeberg was seized on in Sweden and it might even be disputed which country had the better claim to him.[141]

The general picture of Finland, even among those Swedes who were interested in it, was muddled and influenced by prejudice. When Arwidsson and Ivar Hwasser were arguing about Finland's position at the end of the 1830s and the beginning of the 1840s, it was shown without any doubt that the Finns did not think about their own position in the same way as some Swedes did, but it was difficult for the latter to concede the point. There were many indications that the Finns, in their general thinking, were becoming isolated from their former mother-country.

V. The February Revolution in continental Europe, Finland in 1848 and the after-effects of the general European reaction

An extreme dualism had put its stamp on the general economic and social development of Europe in the period after 1815. The great lead of Britain in industrialisation in this period also affected the international political arena; it created generally favourable conditions for the strengthening of British sea-power, the accumulation of capital and the expansion of export trade. In contrast, there was the agrarian-dominated eastern half of Europe, of which Finland was a part. This difference in the level and rate of economic development of the different halves of Europe emphasised, as it continued, the deepening political differences between these 'two Europes'.

In France the bourgeoisie was in the process of dividing as a result of the development of events after the July Revolution; its wealthy element began to identify itself with the system represented by Louis Philippe, while the petty bourgeoisie was making demands for political liberalism and democracy. Social discontent also promoted political activity among the workers.[1] The strongly feudal features in Germany and elsewhere drove the bourgeoisie to unite in action against the privileged circles supporting absolutism, and to demand a greater role in society. Industrialisation in Germany and elsewhere in central Europe had progressed noticeably less than in western Europe, and from this it followed that the political and social radicalisation of the workers appeared primarily only in the western parts of Germany.[2]

1. Finnish society in the mid-1840s

The economic and social structure of Finnish society as a whole hardly changed in the first half of the nineteenth century.[3] Urbanisation increased little in this period: only 5–6 per cent of the country's population lived in towns and in only a few situated in southern Finland had the inhabitants risen above 10,000. There were few factories and only about 3 per cent of the working population were engaged in industry. The economic structure of the country appeared to be solidified; social mobility was a rare phenomenon.

Those engaged in seafaring and foreign trade, because of their occupation, came into contact with events abroad as the static section of Finnish society could not, and the coastal towns too obtained news about conditions and ways of life outside Finland in a manner denied to the rest. *Åbo Underrättelser*, which catered for seafaring and foreign trading circles, had for several years been reporting the essential occurrences in international economic development, such as the controversy in Britain over the corn laws. Contemporary political events such as the revolts in Spain, manifestations of nationalism in different countries, student unrest in Germany and even some early manifestations of the workers' movement were described so that readers had a general picture of the international situation and some notions of possible changes.[4] The wealthy burghers of the coastal towns recognised that, as entrepreneurs who were prospering economically, they were a privileged group, in that the central administration of the country did not try to control their foreign contacts. The attitudes of this group were dictated by their business interests; they did not engage in politics. Primarily it was questions of war and peace that interested them, and then only in so far as they affected the prospects for carrying on foreign trade.

Information also began to spread to Finland, as a result of increased trade, about conditions in St Petersburg and Russian daily life. Also the general horizon of the farmers in the coastal districts of southern Finland began to broaden with the coming of the 1840s. Those trading from their own boats, who had earlier sailed primarily to Sweden and Estonia, began trading with St Petersburg, and in some cases as far away as the southern Baltic.[5] In consequence the range of knowledge of the coastal farmers was enlarged and interest in public affairs increased. The nobility and upper classes of course came into contact with high-ranking Russians in St Petersburg and Helsinki, and these latter began to appear in Finland in the summer because the government had begun to put obstacles in the way of travelling to the resorts of continental Europe. Finns were also seeking careers as officers in Russia. Soldiering was the traditional career of a Finnish nobleman, but in the new conditions such a choice also reflected the attractions and opportunities a great empire offered to the upper classes.[6]

These contacts with the east meant that the traditional contrasts between Finland and Russia were in many respects withering away. The conduct of the upper classes drew criticism from the groups leading the national awakening, and the life-style they had adopted was seen as a dangerous indifference to the Finnish national consciousness. But those involved were a restricted group even if a conspicuous one. Because of this they constituted no real problem in a delicate phase of the development of national identity, even if this phenomenon perhaps delayed its comprehension in some upper-class circles.

Although Finnish society had remained socially static, it had begun to show signs of political grouping. The intellectuals understood better, and were more sensitive towards, the country's political conditions than before. They had many opportunities of following foreign events, even though the authorities had, among other things, seriously restricted their foreign travels. The intellectual circles, slight in themselves, felt that they were under special supervision by the country's central administration because they were regarded as the element that spread western ideas.

The finnicisation movement had been able to spread its ideas, even to accelerate discussion of public affairs, with the help of journals like Snellman's paper *Saima*, published in Kuopio from 1844, and subscribed to as far away as Helsinki, Turku and Viipuri. However, as the Finnish national movement changed from a national-romantic tendency to become political in its content and tone, the St Petersburg government's distrust was significantly strengthened. Snellman was regarded as a dangerous opponent of the prevailing system, and ranked with the revolutionaries of western Europe; in the mid-1840s, the Deputy Governor-General Thesleff and Provincial Governor von Kothen branded him as a communist.[7] Governor-General Menshikov regarded *Saima* as creating 'dissatisfaction with the authorities, the law, the orders of the government and existing conditions generally'.[8] When Snellman discussed public opinion in his paper and saw representative institutions and a political press as important factors in a developed society, the leaders of the regime saw this as revolutionary. *Saima* was suppressed in 1846. *Kanava*, which was published at the same time in Viipuri, also tried to arouse national consciousness and encourage discussion of the implementation of reforms. This paper was thought especially dangerous by the government because it was in Finnish and, in contrast with the Swedish-language *Saima*, was also read by members of the 'lower classes'.[9] As a Viipuri paper it also affected an area which was continuously under St Petersburg's watchful eye. *Kanava* too was suppressed in 1847 after appearing for two years.

The already middle-aged leaders of the fennomans had experienced many setbacks and very limited successes. The growing pessimism among them is exemplified in a review of the future written by Snellman in January 1848: 'Day by day our culture lags even further behind the culture of civilised Europe. . . . We were closer to it in 1809 than now. The further this gap widens, the smaller it becomes towards the east. . . . Our whole social position was in 1809 roughly the same as other nations. . . . Now we are the most remote and the last of all the European peoples, almost including the Turks.'[10] The young academics, who had only begun to participate in the 1840s, were by contrast optimistic in their outlook and ready to act in a new way.[11] This came out in the activity of the student corporations, which assumed a new tone with, for example, the founding of the Academic Literary Society in 1846, the purpose of which was to offer the possibility, rare in Helsinki at the time, of following the foreign press. The activity of these young men was essentially on behalf of the Finnish language, and not directed against the prevailing political system. A new feature in the finnicisation circles in the 1840s was the opening up of the linguistic-nationalist horizon towards the east, as they became conscious of the Finno-Ugrian family of languages. Those involved in the finnicisation movement emphasised that a necessary condition for its progress was contact between the academic intellectuals and the people. The enlightenment of the people was to be promoted and thus, national consciousness would be reinforced. An expression of this was the founding in 1847 of the newspaper *Suometar*.

New Scandinavianist contacts with Sweden also influenced the intellectual atmosphere. Their tone was anti-Russian and this prompted the authorities to prevent contacts with Sweden. While Finnish academic circles were well aware of this anti-Russian tone, they observed that in Sweden there were false impressions of conditions in Finland.

Clearer signs than before of knowledge of liberal ideas appeared in Finland. Everything which pointed towards political activity served indirectly to emphasise the need and significance of a liberal atmosphere. All economic reforms which involved a break from the system of mercantilist controls were also liberal-oriented, and the expanding foreign trade of the country brought liberalism in its return cargoes. On the whole, conditions in Finland in the later 1840s expressed political tranquillity, though not submission.

2. *The revolutionary wave in continental Europe, the attitude of Nicholas I and Finnish opinion*

The outbreak of revolution in Paris in February 1848 led swiftly to the abdication of Louis Philippe, proclamation of the Republic and the bringing into force of universal suffrage. The new revolution in France was more radical than the July Revolution and both political and social in character. It got support not only from the middle bourgeoisie but from the workers, and therefore took both liberal and socialist ideas as its intellectual slogans.

The disturbances spread in a few weeks from Paris to Berlin and Vienna and into Italy, and in one way or another to many other countries. In different parts of central Europe, liberal demands for the introduction of a constitution and basic political rights were accompanied by demands for the end of national oppression, in addition to which the idea of the unification of Germany and Italy was strengthened. The influence of these revolutionary events on the continent extended even to Scandinavia. In Denmark it led to the institution of a two-chamber system and universal suffrage, in Stockholm there was excitement, — and in Oslo liberal ideas were expressed at the same time as early signs of a workers' movement.[12]

When the news of the Paris revolution and the proclamation of the Republic reached St Petersburg, Nicholas ordered the breaking of diplomatic relations with France. Russia also began to concentrate large military detachments on the western border of the empire, in case the emperor should decide to start an intervention.[13] Once the wave of political changes reached Berlin and Vienna, the ideological bulwark once represented by those countries to Russian eyes lost its significance. From Vienna political disturbance even reached to Austrian Galicia, which raised the possibility of a new Polish insurrection.[14]

The outlook and mood of Nicholas I can be seen in his manifesto issued on 26 March. It was a thunderous demand to stand in defence of legitimism and the prevailing system. The Emperor announced that a 'destructive flood' was approaching the empire's frontiers and urged readiness to fight for 'the honour of Russia and the sanctity of its boundaries'. In the spirit of the Holy Alliance and Russian paternalism all available forces were to be gathered 'for the defence of religion, the Emperor and the fatherland'. He let it be clearly understood that in case of need he was ready to defend Russia and the position of the traditional system in central Europe with the help of his armies. At the same time, in the name of the empire's security, many precautionary measures were initiated on the whole western frontier zone from Finland in the north to Moldavia and Wallachia in the south. In June, Russia even occupied the two latter areas militarily. When it seemed that political disturbances were spreading from the continent to Denmark and even further north, the order was given from St Petersburg to close the frontier between Sweden and Finland. Passenger traffic between them was broken off and the postal service stopped.[16]

Finland's central administration was undoubtedly well aware that it was difficult to stop news about the revolutions from spreading into the country through the press; and international contact, e.g. in the area of foreign trade, had become so brisk over a couple of decades that it was difficult to erect effective lock gates on the country's borders in a crisis. In any case Finnish public interest in foreign affairs was clearly increasing, which had manifested itself, for instance, in the way that after the mid-1840s, some newspapers had begun to publish news about political events abroad on their own initiative. From the beginning of 1847, *Åbo Underrättelser* had given its readers clear indications that political crises were developing in various parts of the continent. Also the paper had later criticised *Finlands Allmänna Tidning's* foreign news coverage, which it regarded as seeking to hide the true political situation on the continent. As justification, *Åbo Underrättelser* published views from certain foreign newspapers about that situation.[17] From the beginning of 1848 *Borgå Tidning* and *Ilmarinen*, published in Vaasa, also printed political news from abroad.[18]

The central administration thought it important that the personal contacts of Finns with foreigners should be reduced to the minimum possible, once the February Revolution broke out. 'Political agitation' spread through the country in this way was naturally thought highly dangerous, because the authorities could not control it. For this reason they issued several prohibitions on Finns travelling abroad in the spring and summer of 1848. They were also effective, since the numbers travelling by ship between Turku and Stockholm was so reduced that several sailings were cancelled.[19] Menshikov had given notice in advance to leading officials that if revolution should break out in Stockholm, the Finnish frontier would be closed against Swedish citizens.[20]

After the outbreak of the February Revolution, the central administration of Finland concentrated political control on two particular groups: the young academic intellectuals and the 'lower class'. This involved no new activity but merely an intensification of existing controls. The news that in Vienna the students had taken part in the revolutionary events was a further shock to Nicholas, and the central administration in Finland accepted the possibility that political unrest could arise among the students in Helsinki. To prevent this the vice-chancellor, J. M. Nordenstam, issued appeals, and precautionary measures for keeping order were intensified. A prohibition was issued against joining secret societies — a clear reference to the continent of Europe.[21] In the control measures directed at the 'lower classes' the apprehensions created among the authorities by events in Paris were apparent. The order issued in May, which made the granting of entry permits to foreign apprentices, workmen and 'the lower orders of society generally' dependent on their prospective employer giving guarantees as to their habits of thought and behaviour was typical.[22] In the category of 'lower orders' Menshikov included farmers, control over whom in Viipuri province he regarded as important for the security of St Petersburg.[23]

While the revolutions on the continent caused the St Petersburg government and the administration in Finland to see new dangers, the former objects of their suspicions were not forgotten. They continued to see Snellman as a personification of revolutionary opinion in Finland. Even Menshikov called him a 'communist' in the spring of 1848, as other members of the administration had done earlier.[24] As a dangerous agitator who might cause political disturbances, they wanted to keep him far away from the centre of events. When he applied for a teaching post at Helsinki University in the spring of 1848, he was passed over in the final appointment. Since *Saima* had been suppressed he no longer had his own paper to edit either.

There were various reactions in Finnish society to the events on the continent. A great change had occurred among the intellectuals in that they now recognised political ideas and their general European dimension in a way they had not in 1830. Their political alertness was growing, and they wanted to break free from the isolation in which they had lived for decades. When news of the Paris revolution and its rapid spread to other countries reached Finland, the enthusiasm and joy among the intellectuals were unprecedented. They shared powerful optimism and a belief in progress.

The whole of Europe seemed to be facing profound changes. The young fennoman, S. G. Elmgren, believed that a worldwide struggle was taking place between the forces of light and of darkness.[25] Another young representative of this kind of thinking, Emil von Qvanten, saw the events as leading to 'a world revolution', compared to which 1789 had been only a modest beginning. According to him the course of history was directed by two great forces, the power of civilisation and the rights of nations, of which the latter was the more significant. Qvanten suffered disappointment when Poland did not follow the current revolutionary trend.[26] It was characteristic of the intellectuals, particularly the younger ones, to believe in progress as an absolute. At the same time they saw it as having its own internal laws and strength by which it would advance. This did not imply any view that the Finns themselves should in some way support the development of revolution; their role was as spectators of the great European drama.

In this attitude of the Finnish there was a kind of delayed ideological inheritance from the Enlightenment. Because the idea of progress was supreme, it was believed that 'the laws of history' would in the end come to affect Finland despite its peripheral position. The statement made decades later in the memoirs of the young liberal, August Schauman, illustrates such optimistic visions and sentiments: 'He who with the blazing heart of a youngster was able to live through the year 1848 — let him thank God'.[27] These views and moods appeared mainly among the young intellectuals attached to Helsinki University, where students numbered 400–500. The optimism of the older intellectuals was more restrained. They had lived through the long period of reaction, and well understood Finland's dependence on the empire. In a letter to Elias Lönnrot at the end of March, Snellman wrote that in the opening events of the French February Revolution there was an admirable calm and moderation. He described it as 'the revolution of human culture' and expressed the cautious wish that 'the unspoilt forces of the common people' would succeed in their important historical mission.[28]

The general attitude among the upper class to the revolutionary phenomena on the continent was plainly one of reserve, not to say insecurity. The attempts at change seemed turbulent and the course of events like an avalanche. In addition, Finland was no longer distant from these events, since there were even street demonstrations in Stockholm. Letters written by members of the upper class at the time indicate a clear desire to stay outside the events occurring in France and other countries.

When the February Revolution broke out, *Finlands Allmänna Tidning* had already lost its special position as reporter of events, which it had had almost twenty years earlier at the time of the July Revolution. For some weeks beforehand it had published the news that widespread political opposition had appeared in France, but early in March it seemed to be delaying publication of the decisive news that a new revolution in Paris had actually happened. In Helsinki, rumours of decisive events in Paris was already circulating, which could be confirmed from the official papers of St Petersburg.[30] In this situation, pressure grew in Finland to publish sensational news about the Paris revolution. When *Finlands Allmänna Tidning* finally did publish its own account of the revolution on 11 March, two other papers, *Helsingfors Tidningar* and *Borgå Tidningar*, did the same simultaneously.[31] Within the next few days, *Suometar*, *Åbo Underrättelser*, *Åbo Tidningar* and *Ilmarinen* also published it.[32] In *Finlands Allmänna Tidningar* it was coloured by a patriarchal-conservative tone; while Louis Philippe's abdication and the proclamation of the republic were noted, it emphasised that there had been extensive bloodshed, plundering and destruction in Paris.

The quantity of foreign political news had already been increasing in several newspapers in 1847 but the spring of 1848 brought a breakthrough in the communication of news in Finland. Suddenly foreign news became the dominant material in many Finnish newspapers. The situation in the country was also new from the point of view of St Petersburg. In the middle of March, when the first news of the revolution in Paris was being published in the Finnish papers,

Governor-General Menshikov, then in St Petersburg, issued two orders to the provincial governors in Finland. In one he commented that news had been appearing in the Finnish press 'for some time' containing criticism of the actions of the Senate. The second was linked directly to the publication of news about revolutionary events on the continent of Europe. He remarked that the press was only permitted to publish foreign political news which had previously appeared in the *Journal de St Petersbourg*, or was contained in those foreign newspapers admitted to the country by the censor. Newspapers were forbidden to express opinions of their own on foreign events.[33]

The Finnish authorities — at least to begin with — did not seem to exercise any specially effective control over the press; or they thought it appropriate to interpret the general instruction very loosely, since in fact the papers' choice of news remained free. Finland was a special case within the empire because of the relative size of its press. It was clearly seen in St Petersburg as expedient to loosen the hold slightly, so that the frustration of previous years had some means of escape. This was possible so long as nothing comparable with the continental upheavals happened in Finland.[34] Reporting on the revolutions was in fact very free in Finland during the following months, and the press acquired room to manoeuvre in quite a new way. No important political news from the continent was concealed; for example, at the beginning of April it was known from press reports that Metternich had been dismissed from his posts in Vienna. Right from the start, reliance on official papers in St Petersburg was rejected and Finnish papers began to draw their news straight from the west: they gave extensive reports of events in Paris, Berlin, Vienna and elsewhere as published in, for example, *Post-och Inrikes Tidning*, *Augsburger Allgemeine Zeitung*, *Journal des Débats* and *The Times*. However, the foreign news sources were often not specified, or the published news was said to be a summary from several foreign papers.

The Finnish newspapers did not generally comment on the revolutionary happenings abroad, but allowed the reader to draw his own conclusions. However, this rule was broken on some occasions in the spring of 1848. *Helsingfors Tidningar*, as early as the middle of March, ventured to advance some general assessments. It pointed out that the instigators of the 1789 revolution had been the 'Third Estate', the bourgeoisie, who had benefited from it, as well as from the July Revolution of 1830; now the 'Fourth Estate', the workers, seemed to be playing the most active part. Political revolutions, it said, were transient, whereas social ones would have an influence far into the future.[35] *Suometar* stated, on the basis of news received in the first week, that 'almost the whole of Europe has changed its shape as regards government'. At the beginning of April it gave its own impression of the reasons for the changes that had happened: 'As a man advances in civilisation, in the same proportion he progresses in his whole being, from a crude inadequate state to a better one, more suited to his mature civilisation. We see things happening like this in ordinary life, as well as for whole nations'.[36]

In spite of the reporting freedom adopted by the press, the country was at the same time 'calm', which may have delayed the censorship interfering with the press's content, although there was a clear instruction to this end given by Governor-General Menshikov in the middle of March. However at the beginning of May the supervisory board of the censorship sent instructions to its subordinate officials, which closely followed Menshikov's circular.[37] They also meant to ensure that it was obeyed; the papers now began to credit their sources of foreign news by name, which they had often omitted to do earlier in the year. Typical of the position of the Finnish press and the possibilities for reporting in this situation are some of its accounts of the workers' uprising in Paris in June 1848. *Finlands Allmänna Tidning* described it as 'a horrifying bloodbath' and singled out General Cavaignac's energetic measures for the restoration of order.[38] However, by contrast, *Åbo Underrättelser*, which credited as its sources certain Swedish and German newspapers, described the workers' revolt as 'a sad struggle, in which there is, however, also something magnificent, when it can be seen how little people care about all worldly things and, despising death, fight for their own ideal'.[39] *Helsingfors Tidningar* specifically emphasised — also citing certain foreign newspapers — the suppression of the workers' revolt, as essentially a bloody encounter between the skilful fighters on the barricades and the French regular troops.[40]

The Flower Day festival was celebrated near Helsinki on 13 May after a lapse of twelve years. The assembly was held in an atmosphere of national-romantic feeling and optimistic belief in progress. The historic coat-of-arms of Finland and Runeberg's song 'Our Country', which Fredrik Pacius had set to music, and which was performed for the first time, added to the enthusiasm of the festivities.

Fredrik Cygnaeus spoke of the occasion symbolising the coming of spring and awakening of nature, and in his speech he voiced the wish that a specifically Finnish way of life should be allowed to develop in a general human sense. Several papers afterwards reported the content of the speech and the emotion of the occasion.[41] Although there had been no desire to present a political challenge in the Flower Day festival, there was a reforming mood in the air, in many ways different from anything that had preceded it. It was obviously desired that Finland should in some way share in the positive aspects of general European developments. Yet at the same time, Finland must not be drawn into the avalanche of revolutionary events on the continent.

The intellectuals undoubtedly felt, despite their optimism about progress, that as a group they were both small and isolated compared with the rest of Finnish society. On the whole, both the burghers and the upper classes — excepting certain family connections of the intellectuals — stood apart from its manifestations. The intellectuals did not seek political participation, and they expressed themselves with remarkable restraint in all public declarations of their position. This self-discipline was not without a certain tension; it was visible, for example, when Topelius, in an article published in April in *Helsingfors Tidningar*, wrote that the most important thing of all was that tranquillity and order should be preserved in Finland.[42] He also criticised the undeveloped political consciousness of the Finns, and described the students as inclined to be swayed by whichever political winds happened to be blowing. The Northern Pohjanmaa student fraternity replied by passing an official motion of censure on him, and Topelius resigned from the fraternity.[43]

In any case the intellectuals were conscious of the political constraint surrounding them, even though they had not sought to present a political challenge. The authority of Nicholas I was embedded in peoples' consciousness and must have had a powerful influence. The Emperor's thunderous manifesto of 26 March was a reminder of the discipline and attitude of subordination demanded by the patriarchal system.[44] In Finland Europe's general political development was followed as if from an isolated seat in a theatre box, without any sign of mass unrest, even though new phenomena such as socialism were noted in the press.[45]

In addition to enthusiasm for the revolutionary events in Europe in the spring of 1848, there were also expressions of concern, particularly in the country's leading business circles. To them, revolution and the danger of war were closely linked, a traditional view in business circles ever since the long period of the French revolutionary and Napoleonic wars. The belligerence of Nicholas I's proclamation in the spring of 1848 made all who were involved in foreign trade cautious. In April they began to fear a possible war either between Russia and some of the western European states, or in a more restricted area of the continent. In the former case Finland itself might become directly involved, while in the latter case the indirect effects of war would be felt in the country's foreign trading. In any case the danger of an international crisis made Finnish business prepare against the supply of goods becoming difficult and prices rising.[46]

In May 1848, war did break out between Denmark and Prussia. Denmark began to blockade the northern German maritime cities, with which Prussia was in alliance. This made the continuation of Finnish trade with Lübeck and other German ports difficult. In addition Danish warships began to patrol the waters of the Sound, which thus also became an area of uncertainty for Finnish merchant ships.[47] With the situation in the Baltic coming to a head and with the possibility of a wider war, Finnish seafaring circles were extremely cautious, they were urged to cut down on traffic as far as possible to all those countries where there had been revolutionary disturbances, especially France, Germany and the Mediterranean area. At the same time it was emphasised that Britain was a politically stable country, with which it was safe to continue trade relations because, as well as everything else, she guaranteed the safety of merchant ships in the North Sea area with her own warships.[48] A noticeably smaller number of ships left Turku on foreign voyages in 1848 than in previous years.[49] In the

coastal towns of the Gulf of Bothnia, this period was one of economic insta-
bility. This was experienced in a slackening of international freight trade, a
tightening of credit, and reduction in shipbuilding.[50] Even Viipuri, whose trade
with the west had not been as significant as that of the towns of Pohjanmaa, was
forced to recognise a serious recession during 1848.[51]

The export of timber from Finland, especially to France, visibly diminished.
The same happened to the export of tar.[52] The share of exports in Finland's
economic life was still fairly small, but the economic uncertainties of the times
showed themselves in the rise in prices of foreign products.

There was little awareness in the farming community of the European events
of 1848 constituting a crucial transitional phase. However, certain information
may have been conveyed into their circles by the emperor's proclamations —
through the church — and it is likely to have spread a fear of war. The events
on the continent of Europe appeared to the Finnish farmer as remote. Ballads
spoke of the loyalty of the Finnish people — 'we do not deny the emperor,
breaking up the government'. How deeply the farmers echoed this sentiment is
a different matter.

3. *The spread of political reaction to Finland*

The political reaction to which the revolutionary events on the continent of
Europe gave birth in the latter half of 1848 did not leave Finland unaffected.
Nicholas I came to have a central position in restoring 'the old system'. His
counter-measures were, on the one hand, directed against liberalism and nationalism, while on the other their purpose was to re-erect a 'defensive wall' in
central Europe. For this reason, Nicholas gave military help to Austria in
suppressing the revolt which broke out in Hungary in 1849, and diplomatic
support to Prussia when its relations with Denmark returned to a peaceful foot-
ing.[53] In Finland, on the other hand, it was a question not of restoring the old
system, because no political disturbances had occurred in the country, but of
ensuring the continuity of the prevailing system with the help of various protective measures.

From the early summer of 1848 onwards, it began to be suspected by the
intellectuals in Finland that the revolutionary movement in Europe would not,
even indirectly, bring about any change to a freer tendency in the country's conditions. Fredrik Cygnaeus pessimistically compared Finland with a rocky
island, around which a severe storm raged by which it was wholly unaffected.[54]
People in Finland saw clear signs of a political change of direction on the continent, beginning when Cavaignac suppressed the workers' insurrection in Paris
and the victories of Austrian troops in Italy restored the princelings to their
former thrones.[55] By the end of July 1848, Snellman's attitude had changed
from the cautious optimism he had felt in the early spring to a deep pessimism.
In his opinion, Finland since 1809 had definitely lagged behind the European
development in general — a whole century behind. 'Intellectual ability which

does not wither here in Finland must be exceptional,' said Snellman, in a letter to Cygnaeus.[56]

In Helsinki University highly intensified political control was put into action by General Nordenstam from the autumn of 1848, and the next spring, a committee was set up to consider the reform of the University's statutes. Similar new rules for supervision and constraint were being carried out at the same time in Russian universities. C.G. Mannerheim was appointed chairman of the committee on the statutes. In his opinion, 'farmers and fennomans' were to be kept out of the University, for otherwise the way would be open to social mobility, which would shake the foundations of the present system. Mannerheim represented the attitude that 'there is a deeper morality prevailing among the upper classes'; his ideal was the social *status quo*, under which the upper social groups were permanently guaranteed their traditional leading place, and at the same time the rise of the 'working or bread-winning classes', giving them access to a position of influence in society, was prevented.[57]

A major change in the University world happened in 1852 when the student fraternities were abolished. In this way the authorities destroyed the traditional forums of discussion and sought to bind the students together with the teachers into faculties, which in the new situation acted under the control and guidance of a dean appointed by the chancellor. However, the number of students was not limited in Helsinki University, as had happened in Russia, and despite the changes in internal organisation and the intensified surveillance of the students, the University preserved its autonomous position, and did not come under the imperial ministry of education.[58]

The central administration of the country also instituted various measures of political control, with the aim of keeping a wide-ranging eye on Finnish society, especially its lower orders. This was carried out on traditional lines, in the sense that the leadership of the church was used as an important support. Governor-General Menshikov, the vice-chairman of the economic department of the Senate, von Haartman, Casimir von Kothen, who from 1844 had acted as governor of Viipuri province, and Edvard Bergenheim, who became archbishop of Turku in 1850, led this intensified political control.

Over the previous twenty years, Bergenheim had become known for systematically advocating attitudes of submission and obedience to worldly authority.[59] He considered it important to bring Finland closer to Russia, and his line of appeasement after 1848 may have been due in part to fear that the government in St Petersburg might otherwise strengthen the position of the Greek Orthodox church in Finland, as had happened in the 1840s in the Baltic provinces. The revolutionary events of 1848 in Europe were vigorously condemned by the Finnish church leadership, and in the proclamation of a day of prayer issued in December 1848, it lamented that in many European countries 'harmony, order and mutual trust had vanished, brother fought against brother and entire social classes, dominated by hate, acted against one another'.[60] The church leadership did not recognise political and social oppression as a cause of revolution, nor did it approve of new ideas of freedom. In the proclamation of another day of prayer in November 1849, 'pitiful ignorance, self-satisfaction and false dogmas' were stated as the reason why people were led astray from the right path. In the official view of the church leadership, the social position of the lower orders did involved no social problems which would have demanded solutions. 'The misfortunes of the period' were straightforwardly explained as caused by 'the love of wealth and luxury' leading people to revolution, while new needs only generated new discontents.

The attitude of the Finnish church was pointedly revealed, for example, in the circular sent by Bishop Ottelin to the clergy of Porvoo diocese in 1850. This obliged the clergy to come out against all rationalist theories, arguing that man himself is of divine worth and that the people have the right to criticise the actions of the authorities, and against egalitarianism and socialist or communist doctrines.[61] The church leaders described conditions in Finland as an exception to conditions in countries on the continent. Finland had been able to enjoy 'the fruits of loyalty, order and unity', and so had been able to live at peace. The industry and perception of the Finnish people were praised.

A new censorship decree came into force in 1850. It affected only the country's newspapers and publications in Finnish, and made it permissible to publish in Finnish only works of religious piety and concerning economic improvements. All reference to politics and foreign news was forbidden.[62] 'Lower class' disturbances — of which the insurrection of the Paris workers was the climax — had proved especially dangerous, and the fear of revolution had turned into a psychosis at high levels, where the emergence of the fenno-man movement in Finland was seen in this same general European context. In St Petersburg's eyes, the active role of the press in 1848 as a purveyor of foreign news — its vigilance and its many sources of information from abroad — had been unexpected, and the counter-measures regarded as appropriate, such as the new censorship decree, stemmed from this. Belief in the effectiveness of harsh prohibitions had not lessened.

Distrust of the lower orders was repeated after 1848 in the statements of Finland's leading civil servants in various contexts. Democracy was a disreput-able concept, representing mob rule, and as such was a major threat to the domi-nance of the upper-class élite. Forces dangerous to the existing system were seen as using this idea as their shield. Haartman emphasised how important were effective measures to prevent the spread of 'socialist and democratic ideas'.[63] Menshikov for his part criticised the 'communist spirit' of the times. A few years earlier one of Haartman's close assistants had already called the fennomans 'Jacobins in Finnish homespun'.[64] In these different contexts the fennoman movement was classed as subversive, while Snellman was still thought of as epitomising the popular agitator.

Within the overall plan for intensifying control in this period lay the question of the relevance of popular education. A committee was set up in 1851, whose composition — von Haartman as chairman, von Kothen and Bergenheim —

suggested that it was not concerned with solving pedagogic problems as much as how they could reinforce the maintenance of social 'discipline and order'. It was emphasised that 'confusion of thinking' and 'false directions', which had gained ascendancy in Europe, should be prevented in Finland. The growth of the country's population and the signs pointing towards industrialisation were seen as heralding the closer approach of such dangers. The committee also considered the question of intensifying police control in the countryside and the organisation of poor relief.[65]

The customs and postal services were also involved in the work of building an ideological 'protective wall' against the west. The customs service was given secret political surveillance duties by the Senate, concerning the inspection at ports of printed matter entering the country.[66] The postal service was to keep a close watch on post from Sweden, including newspapers, subscribed to in Finland. The number of copies of foreign, mostly Swedish, newspapers confiscated rose after the year of revolution at an unprecedented rate: in 1849, 317 and in 1850 490 issues.[67] Finland thus became more rigidly isolated from the west than at any time since 1808. This came at the same time as a growing need for the widening of the area of intellectual activity was appearing in Finnish society, not only among the intellectuals, but in other social strata. The tightening of the grip of political reaction was keenly felt among the academic intellectuals. The pessimism which was already apparent in Snellman in the summer of 1848 subsequently deepened. It appeared in his remark made in November the same year: 'We sit in our own graves, dead to the living life'.[68] Snellman doubted whether any progress would take place in Finland in his lifetime. It is typical of the period that, after being passed over for a professorship at Helsinki University, he was forced from 1849 to earn his living on moving back to the capital from Kuopio as a clerk in a Helsinki business firm. It also testifies to the reactionary atmosphere of the period that Topelius did not, as far as is known, write a single poem in the early 1850s.[69]

Russia as an empire had remained politically intact after the general European transition of 1848, unlike its allies Austria and Prussia. Although after the transitional period the old system was restored in those states as well, there was a certain degree of cooling off in the relations of the three great powers. Russia was forced to act alone in international politics more than before, while she also became more isolated from the others in her political philosophy than before.[70]

Russia only emphasised her position as the upholder of the old principles of the Holy Alliance when she carried out a military intervention in Hungary in 1849, and helped Austria to suppress the revolt led by Kossuth. At the same time feelings against Nicholas I were mounting in western Europe. This was also a consequence of a new phenomenon in the field of international relations, the emergence of a public opinion interested in foreign policy. The ideological contrast between east and west was also becoming more pronounced than before; besides Britain and France, Poland and Hungary, albeit 'invisibly', belonged to the western side.[71]

The great European crises, the July and February Revolutions, had afforded little intellectual stimulus to the development of Finland. In both, Finland had been on the one hand an onlooker but, on the other, forced to experience within her own borders the reactionary response generated in St Petersburg. However, thoughts and ideas from the period of the February Revolution did germinate in Finland. After the victory of reaction in the country, the difference from the west, above all from Sweden, seemed very pronounced. Among the intellectuals there was increasing interest in the free political debate on the other side of the Gulf of Bothnia. In these circumstances the intellectual response in Finland developed very slowly — only during 1849 — and it was roused not by the February Revolution itself but by the severity of counter-measures that followed it; in addition it took place on a very narrow base, being restricted merely to the circle of certain young intellectuals. The Russian military intervention to suppress the Hungarian revolt was the factor which aroused a response within the closed circles of the student corporations in Helsinki. The person of the emperor was not spared.[72] The young academics were experiencing a deep ideological transition. Since Russia had begun to emerge as the major opponent of the freedom movements in Europe, there was a desire to resist the political system in which Finland was an associate. When the Russians suppressed the national rising in Hungary, the tranquil view of the future began to change, and the question of how the Finnish people could be saved from the clutches of the autocrat rose over the horizon of these young people. This kind of response made the ground more fertile for the growth of liberal ideas in academic circles.

Nicholas I's general line of imperial policy had involved, as in the Polish revolt of 1830–1, ordering the Finnish Guard Battalion to take part in the military activity connected with the suppression of the Hungarian revolt, and reports of these events, following the official Russian communiqués, had been a central feature in the Finnish press for several months from the spring to the autumn of 1849.[73] In the end, the Guard Battalion was not involved in the actual suppression, but in spite of that it suffered considerable losses in the difficult conditions of the campaign.

Among the young intellectuals there was a gloomy and critical reaction to the duties assigned to the Guard Battalion. To most Finns who followed events, however, it was rather an unavoidable political obligation. This also appears in the services of thanksgiving, organised on orders from on high, on the theme of 'the success of our arms'.[74]

After the crisis of 1848, the authorities endeavoured effectively to detach Finland intellectually from the west, and to bring the country yet again under the umbrella of Russian security policy, with the obligations this involved. This took place during a long-continued period of peace and the extension of economic development in different fields. Peoples' views on prevailing conditions clearly reflected their social positions.

VI. The Crimean war and the Finnish question

1. *The outbreak of war and Finland's involvement in the international crisis*

Russia, from the spring of 1853, sought to secure a protective hold over Turkey, and Britain, supported by France, moved its fleet to protect Turkey's position against the Russian empire. Gradually this confrontation turned into open conflict. At the end of June Russia occupied Moldavia and Wallachia, and Turkey, relying on the western powers for support, declared war on Russia at the beginning of October. At the end of November, when the latter destroyed a Turkish naval squadron in the battle of Sinope, the relations of Russia and the western powers became severely strained.

Of the western powers, Britain was looking for an opportunity to strike a blow at Russia and weaken her position at sea. France was less interested in open conflict, but still supported Britain.[1] Broad circles in Britain wanted to give the approaching war the character of an ideological struggle between west and east;[2] there was a vigorous campaign on these lines in the press, pamphlets, and so on, and the country's political leaders felt pressure to seek a solution with Russia by force of arms. The ultimatum of the western powers to Russia at the end of February 1854 demanding her withdrawal from occupied Moldavia and Wallachia was followed within a month by a declaration of war. Before that Britain, France and Turkey had concluded a military alliance.

Britain sought a war on two fronts to prevent Russia concentrating her forces in the Crimea. The opening of a second theatre of war in the Baltic was also demanded in Britain by public opinion, which believed that a serious military blow could be delivered swiftly against Russia by threatening her capital, St Petersburg. France, on the other hand, was mainly interested in the struggle with Russia in south-eastern Europe, but because of her obligations as an ally, decided to take part in operations in the Baltic as well.[3]

After Russia occupied Moldavia and Wallachia at the end of June 1853, developments were followed with considerable anxiety in Finland, where people had got used to the long period of peace and had seen in it the surest guarantee of all economic progress, there were many signs which pointed to the coming of a crisis. In the autumn of 1853, for example, Russia brought part of her fleet into the shelter of Sveaborg, and the environs of Helsinki took on a 'militarised' appearance.[4] Prices also rose. Turkey was characterised among the Finns as a country on the verge of collapse, its people spoiled and debilitated, but in spite of that trying hopelessly to restore her lost greatness. In the Finnish press the picture given of the policy of Nicholas I was that it represented not only strength but also a will for peace.[5] The western powers were seen as clearly on the Turkish side, and for that reason there was fear of a situation in which Russia and Britain might become involved in war, with consequences for

Finland. Already in the summer of 1853, news was circulating in Helsinki that Britain had a naval squadron ready to be sent on a reconnaissance mission to the Baltic.[6]

In the early summer of 1853, *Finlands Allmänna Tidning* was still reporting that the international situation gave no cause for anxiety, but during the autumn the danger of a crisis was no longer concealed.[7] Also the writings of the Swedish newspapers, which were followed in Finland, pointed clearly to an intensification of the crisis. Events in the Balkans began to concern Finland tangibly when Turkey announced that she would hold all merchant and other ships flying the Russian flag which sailed through the Bosphorus from the middle of November.[8] Finland's Odessa trade, which had become considerable, was thus completely stopped.

Attention was soon being focussed on Finland as an area which could come within the sphere of possible military operations. For this reason much military and political attention was fastened on it in St Petersburg. Nothing comparable had happened at any time since the crisis years 1808–9. Nicholas I visited Helsinki in the middle of March 1854 to speed up preparations in the country and to show the Finns that the international crisis was serious; the declaration of war on Russia by the western powers came two weeks later. It was also desired to publicise the relations of trust between the ruler and his Finnish subjects in this exceptional situation. The Senate for its part made a gesture of loyalty on behalf of Finland during the visit; it announced that it would pay the costs of the gunboats ordered by the Russians from Finnish shipyards, and intended for the defence of the Finnish coasts.[9] Subsequently about forty of these small vessels were built.

When Nicholas I tried to influence Finnish political attitudes, his main aim was to root out possible sympathy towards Sweden and the tendency to speculate that a war might be coming, which could cause difficulties for Russia. There was much to encourage the circulation of rumours. Already in December 1853 there was a report in *The Times* that Admiral Napier had been appointed commander of the British naval squadron being sent to the Baltic. When the war was imminent, it began to be feared in Helsinki that the British fleet might bombard the city. This made people move out to the countryside in March-April 1854.[10] There were also rumours circulating that Sweden would join in the war on the western side.

For a long time already there had been signs that mobilisation measures would be introduced. At the end of December 1853 there was an order to establish a second Finnish naval squadron and men were enlisted to serve in it. From the turn of February-March 1854 Russian troops began to move into the country. The total number in Finland rose during the period of the war to nearly 70,000.[11] There was an attempt to speed up the still unfinished fortification works on Åland, which had been in progress over two decades. Sveaborg too was being prepared for defence. One of the three Russian naval squadrons in the Baltic made its base there.[12] In the middle of March, the Finnish Guards

Battalion was ordered to St Petersburg — not, however, to be sent on active service when war broke out, as at the time of the Polish and Hungarian revolts; it was left to carry out guard duties in the vicinity of Peterhof.

The Finnish administration and the government in St Petersburg kept an especially watchful eye on southern Pohjanmaa and Åland. The governors there and the crown bailiffs were instructed to note the political moods of the people, and official inspectors were ordered to go round these areas on special missions.[13] Vaasa became known among the higher officials as a city where the most varied war rumours circulated, including one of a coming attack on Finland from the direction of Sweden. Contacts over the Gulf of Bothnia, bearing news of western attitudes, were undeniably brisk. When Russian troops were brought into southern Pohjanmaa, the reaction of the farming population was powerfully hostile, reflecting the russophobia remaining in the area after 1808. The prevailing feelings in Vaasa in March 1854 were described in a report given by the provincial governor, Berndt Federley, as 'democratic'; there was not much wish for Turkey to lose the war. Federley therefore asked for the help of military police in case war broke out, to maintain order in the town.[14] The higher authorities do not seem to have trusted the governor of Vaasa province, and a new man was appointed to the post, Federley being transferred to a less responsible task as governor of Kuopio.[15]

In Åland the military and civil authorities began various measures in the spring of 1854, on the assumption that the archipelago would somehow be involved in military operations. Since communications with the mainland were expected to become difficult, a separate provisional administration was formed for Åland, within the framework of Turku and Pori province, under the command of Lieut.-Colonel V. Furuhjelm.[16]

The authorities regularly obtained information from the inhabitants of Åland on the movements of the western powers' warships in the adjacent waters. In addition their grain was stored in Bomarsund fortress for the use of the garrison. In March, the sheriffs made soundings among the population whether they might form volunteer forces for local defence. However, the response of the Ålanders proved very negative.[17] This may have been due to a desire to avoid any open commitment in a situation which might have led to the western powers occupying the whole of Åland backed by strong naval forces, and crushing all resistance. These feelings among the Ålanders made the situation problematical from the Russian point of view, since the main island of Åland might thus very easily come into the possession of the enemy. Because of this two battalions were sent from mainland Finland to the archipelago.

As war approached, the St Petersburg government also tried to take advantage of 'the union of throne and altar' to influence Finnish attitudes and feelings. Archbishop Bergenheim appealed to the clergy that in this critical situation they should express clearly 'the loyalty of subjects to the government given them by God'.[18] He went so far as to call for a declaration — following a manifesto issued by Nicholas I — that 'Russia's enemies are the enemies of God's people'.[19] As a counter-weight to the ideological war-cries of the western powers, the Russian side emphasised hostility to Turkey, in which, on religious grounds, the idea of a struggle against the pagans was included. This was undoubtedly a strong tradition even in Finland, as had been shown in the 1820s at the time of the Greek war of independence. However, Nicholas I added to this slogan something difficult to accept in Finland, namely a struggle for 'the Orthodox Church'.

However, the attempts to encourage hostility to Turkey when the western powers were the only actual enemies for Finland caused conflicts even within the church itself, as was shown by the pamphlet written by a priest, F.G. Hedberg, at the urging of Bergenheim. Hedberg tried to hold to the thesis that the Turks were the main enemy in the war, while Britain and France were ranked with the beast in the Book of Revelation. There was a sharply negative reaction to Hedberg's pamphlet, and a later attempt to get it published in Finnish proved difficult. The success of this attempt would have been important, because the influence of the pamphlet could then have reached the farming population. Among the intellectuals, the pamphlet was condemned, and it was said that he had sold his honour and his conscience to be used as political tools.[20] In the early phase of the war in the Black Sea area, services of thanksgiving were held in Finnish churches by order of the authorities.[21] However, in the proclamations of days of prayer later in the Crimean war, nothing appeared that was anti-Turkish.[22] It was merely deplored that half a century of peace had ended and that destruction had been inflicted by the enemy on the Finnish coasts.

Since there was an international crisis, in which rumours circulated in abundance, and peoples' ideas could clearly be turned in unexpected directions, it proved thoroughly dangerous for the country's central administration to obey the censorship decree of 1850 regarding the Finnish-language press. Political information was proving important for a wholly new reason. The authorities could not get by with mere prohibitions. The support of the press was now necessary to disseminate information and to calm public opinion. In the first place it was necessary to preserve confidence between the country's central administration and the mass of the people. The earlier apprehension of a crisis, and the actual existence of one were now shown to be completely different things; this caused the policy of censorship being followed to be radically changed shortly after it had come into force. Apart from *Finlands Allmänna Tidning*, only the country's Swedish-language papers had been allowed to report the deepening of the international crisis in the Black Sea area from the summer of 1853.[23] The big change came on 10 March 1854, when *Suometar* got permission to publish news of the war in the Balkans — just before the visit of Nicholas I to Helsinki; however it had to do this by following the reports in the paper *Russkiy Invalid*. Gradually *Suometar* began to examine the international situation, the relations of the western powers and Russia, and problems which particularly concerned Finland as well. A couple of weeks later, on 24 March, the country's other Finnish-language paper, the *Oulun Wiikko-Sanomat*, also began publishing news about the international situation in the same way.[24] Just then the news of the coming of the British fleet to the Baltic began to arrive, a situation likely to give rein to rumour and 'loose talk'.

The outbreak of war between Russia and the western powers brought a gloomy outlook for business in Finland. Finnish merchant ships had been freighting in the south, as was usual in winter, and their intention was to return home later in the spring, when the ice had gone. In this interim period during which the outbreak of war occurred, the shipowners were virtually out of touch with their far-away ships abroad. Some degree of panic was reflected by the fact that even before the declarations of war, they began to sell Finnish ships that were abroad for fear of seizure, often at knock-down prices. It is true that Britain had announced on 20 March that if war broke out, merchant ships sailing under the Russian flag would have the right to load up during a six-week period and then leave for home. In addition it was stated that Russian merchant ships intercepted at sea would have the right to continue their journeys after inspection, if they could show that they had loaded before the end of the stipulated period.[25] This announcement seemed to give Finnish merchantmen the possibility of returning home even at the beginning of May, when it could be expected that the ice situation would already have eased. However, the ships of the British squadron commanded by Admiral Napier began to seize Finnish merchantmen which they met in the southern Baltic in the latter half of April. News of this added to the panic. Thus as soon as the Crimean war had broken out, the Finnish merchant fleet suffered great losses — in all nearly half the country's merchant ships and nearly 60 per cent of their cargoes were lost.[26]

With the outbreak of war, Finland's trade with the west stopped, apart from the links with Sweden. However, even these links across the Gulf of Bothnia became difficult in the summer of 1854, as will be discussed later. The export of timber and tar was at a standstill, the consequences of which were visible both in the port towns and in the procurement areas. At the same time, because of import difficulties among other things, the prices of coffee, sugar and salt rose.[27] Attempts were made to compensate for the disruption of Finland's western sea communications by organising landward transits from continental Europe through Königsberg and St Petersburg, and correspondingly from Sweden through Haparanda.[28] Finland's foreign trade connections were now confined to two directions. Both in 1854 and 1855, imports from Russia formed over 60 per cent of the reduced total imports. At the same time Finland's exports to Sweden, having been around 4–8 per cent in the five last years of peace, rose exceptionally to nearly half of the total (1854, 35 per cent and 1855, 48 per cent). This included transit trade, for example to Germany.[29] However, the share of international exchange in the economic life of Finland was still relatively small, and so the reduction of foreign trade did not much affect people's daily lives. In addition, good grain harvests were secured both in 1854 and 1855, which reduced the sense of emergency in the country; just before the war Finland had experienced harvest failure.[30]

The war occasioned many precautionary measures in Finland. For example, the Bank of Finland moved its metal reserves from Helsinki to Hämeenlinna.[31] In spite of this it seems that the population did not quite believe that some areas of the country might become involved with military activity. Clearly the long peace led people to believe that existing conditions could not change. In the latter half of May 1854, when the British naval squadron carried out harassing attacks in the districts of Hanko and Tammisaari, people were surprised and confused. However, the thorough destruction of Raahe and Oulu, directed by Admiral Plumridge at the turn of May-June, was a real surprise. It may have been intended to support the blockade of the Russian coast, which had been effected slowly. Further, the traffic across the Gulf of Bothnia seemed to be the means which would be used to maintain trade between the Scandinavian countries and Russia in an emergency.

The British naval squadron had the initiative in the summer of 1854 and directed the western powers' military activity in the Baltic. In London there was clearly no particular respect for the Russian Baltic fleet, which at this time comprised twenty-seven ships of the line and numerous smaller vessel. On the other hand it seems that British naval circles already knew that the fortifications of Kronstadt were especially strong.[32] The disparity between Russia's naval and coast defences may have led to a degree of wishful thinking in Admiral Napier. However, an attack against St Petersburg proved to be an altogether too difficult task for the British squadron sent to the Baltic. From this time on, the southern coast of Finland became the main area of operations of the British squadron and the French one which joined it in the middle of June. When the British admiralty asked Napier what force would be necessary to capture Sveaborg, the admiral was forced to give an unequivocal answer: there was no such force in the Baltic. The operations of the western powers were then concentrated against Bomarsund; however, its capture required considerable help from land forces, according to Napier, and therefore a good number of French infantry were sent quickly to the aid of the western fleets.[33] In the middle of August 1854, Bomarsund was captured by the joint action of the sea and land forces of the western powers. After that the naval commander contemplated further operations, against either Sveaborg or Tallinn; these plans, however, were abandoned.[34] After the capture of Bomarsund the fortress was thoroughly destroyed and Åland was proclaimed 'free under the protection of the western powers'. When autumn came, the western naval squadrons and land forces withdrew from the Baltic theatre of operations.

2. *The attention given to the Finnish question abroad*

The general situation in the Baltic area was influenced by the declaration of neutrality issued by Sweden and Denmark on 2 January 1854. This permitted the same rights to the various belligerent parties, which meant that the Swedish

and Danish ports — with certain exceptions — were open to the warships of
the belligerents for their provisioning. This kind of neutrality promised advantages only to the western powers in the war, since the Russian ports were blockaded, and were thus cut off from communication with the Scandinavian
countries. Russia therefore regarded the declarations of neutrality as benefiting
the western powers only, and expressed her dissatisfaction in Stockholm and
Copenhagen.[35] To draw Sweden into the war on their side was in the interests of
the western powers, who believed that they could thus more easily strike at
Russia in the Baltic area, even if this would not yet be decisive. In Britain at the
outbreak of the war, the territorial weakening of Russia was contemplated, and
Lord Palmerston had put forward the idea of an independent Finland as well as
an independent Poland.[36]

This was the first war during which, with the aid of teams of war corres-
pondents, there was organised systematic reporting of events in the Baltic in the
western press.[37] It was also the first major war after the Napoleonic period,
which in itself created a great sensation. In the spring of 1854, extensive reviews
were published in British and French newspapers which sought to give the
readers basic information on the history and geography of the northern theatre
of war. A series of articles about the Baltic area, published in the *Journal
des Débats* in April 1854, was typical:[38] it emphasised among other things
that Finland had only been joined to Russia after 1808 and that in the Hamina
peace negotiations, Åland had been disputed between Russia and Sweden. The
western mood for a war of liberation against reactionary Russia showed itself in
the British press. It also offered much scope to wishful thinking, on the assumption that Russia would be given a decisive military blow. The *Daily News*,
which also hoped that Sweden would join the side of the western powers, saw in
the spring and summer of 1854 the possibility that a complete military and
political reorganisation of the whole Baltic area might arise, including the
detachment of Finland from Russia; it would be decided after the war whether
the country would become independent or be joined to Sweden.[39] *The Standard*
was also emphatically optimistic about the development of operations in the
Baltic. After the war the return of the territories of Finland, Poland and the
Crimea to their 'rightful owners' would be brought up.[40]

The Times differed from the generally optimistic tone adopted in the British
press towards the prospects of the western powers in the Baltic theatre: by mere
naval power they could not strike a decisive blow against Russia's powerful
fortifications, for which reason the achievements would clearly remain secondary for the western powers. *The Times* already proposed in the early summer of
1854 that part of the British naval force in the Baltic should be moved to the
Black Sea, the main theatre of war.[41]

The military events of the summer of 1854 reached the western press in small
fragments. The destruction of Oulu and Raahe and the capture of Bomarsund
received special attention in Britain, and with the defeat suffered by the British
at Kokkola, raised the question of whether this kind of warfare was appro-

priate.[42] *The Times* severely condemned the waging of war against undefended towns and emphasised that the property and stores which were destroyed, such as tar, pitch and timber, were not contraband, but Finnish goods intended for export and partly already paid for to be shipped to Britain. *The Times* remarked that prosecution of the war in this fashion against a nation known for its trading relations with Britain would exclude all possibilities of producing major political changes in Finland.[43] The destruction of the towns was also brought up in the House of Commons after a question put at the end of June. For the Admiralty there was an attempt to defend the conduct of Admiral Plumridge and it was alleged that the targets had been military.[44] The task of the French fleet in the Baltic was only to support the British naval action, but the commander of the French fleet also judged this action from a diplomatic point of view. Admiral Perceval-Deschênes' orders had emphasised that he should avoid taking open towns, and attacking places which were not militarily fortified.[45] For this reason, he regarded the activity of the British squadron on the coast of Finland as unsuccessful in so far as the aim was to detach Finland from Russia.

The capture of Bomarsund in the middle of August received exceptional publicity in western Europe and elsewhere. It was a clear military achievement and a demonstration of joint action by land and naval forces. But clearly it was also desired to make of it a 'great event', because up to then in the war against Russia nothing special had been achieved in either the Baltic or the Black Sea. Many papers published leading articles on Bomarsund, and long, detailed accounts of the different phases of the operation.[46] In London the significance of the capture of Bomarsund was hailed as a demonstration of successful joint action by the two allies, Britain and France.[47] But at first France had had reservations about the Baltic as a theatre of operations in the struggle against Russia. However the capture of Bomarsund won great publicity there. *Le Moniteur* acknowledged that the general strategic situation in the Baltic area had been greatly changed by the victory.[48] Napoleon III, who liked to be free with historical rhetoric in his communiqués, compared the achievement of the French troops at Bomarsund with that of Bonaparte's army in Egypt.[49]

The Finnish question made an appearance in the Swedish papers from the spring of 1854 in an explosive fashion. With the outbreak of the Crimean war, the idea of Sweden as a great power once more rose from the grave. The majority of the Swedish press took the position, from the spring-summer of 1854 onwards, that Finland should be returned to union with Sweden.[50] It was also maintained that the Finns were dissatisfied with life and conditions in their union with Russia. Hopes rose so swiftly that before anything decisive had happened the Swedes began to argue over whether, after its 'return', Finland was to be given a special position in the union, or whether it should be fully incorporated into Sweden.[51] But information did not travel quickly from Finland to Sweden over the Gulf of Bothnia, and it was also strongly selective, according to who were the senders and who the recipients. Anyway these ideas were built more on hopes than on facts, and the Swedes hardly recognised at all the powerful reactions in Finland because of the devastations by the British fleet.

In connection with the Finnish question Scandinavianist slogans were strongly in evidence in Sweden. However, there was also the question of Swedish national aspirations and the general strengthening of Sweden's position in northern Europe with a view to bringing Finland back again into union with Sweden.[52] King Oscar I was interested in Scandinavianism, but despite the general enthusiasm of the country's press, the king was cautious. When the Swedish press reported frequently in the early summer of 1854 that Finland wanted to revive the union, Oscar I reacted sceptically.[53] From the spring onwards he was in negotiations with representatives of Britain and France over the question of Sweden joining the war against Russia on the western side. Oscar's readiness for such negotiations was striking; however the conditions which he set for Sweden's participation in the war indicated caution. Offers of Åland were not at this stage sufficiently attractive. At the end of July 1854, the king set as conditions the formation of a broad European alliance — including Austria — against Russia, the incorporation of the whole of Finland with Sweden, and the obtaining of considerable military assistance. These far-reaching demands did not find acceptance with the western powers.[54]

The capture of Bomarsund in August received great attention in the Swedish press, unleashing anti-Russian feelings and hopes for the future of Finland. After taking Bomarsund the western powers decided to turn once more to Sweden, and they now proposed that Sweden should occupy Åland, which was in their possession. However, even in this new situation, Oscar did not wish to risk Sweden's neutrality, and his response to the offer was therefore negative.[55]

Interest in the military events around Finland appeared to some extent in the German press. The official foreign policy of Prussia was committed to cooperation with Russia, but public opinion there, as elsewhere in Germany, was divided between two tendencies, one conservative and friendly to Russia, and a liberal grouping sympathetic to the western powers.[56] The business circles of the north German cities, which had traditional trade relations with the Baltic area, including Finland, formed a special group on their own. The newspapers which represented them — among others the *Hamburger Correspondent* and *Lübecker Zeitung* — sought to give accurate information on events in the area after the entry of the western fleets into the Baltic. When these papers reported such events as the destruction of Oulu and Raahe, the military encounter before Kokkola and the capture of Bomarsund, their sources were remarkably varied; information was procured from Stockholm, St Petersburg and London.[57] These papers, however, only reported the war. They were not concerned with the political attitudes prevailing in Finland. Also, certain well-known German papers with a wide circulation, like the *Kölnische Zeitung* and the *Augsburger Allgemeine Zeitung*, reported the war in the Baltic extensively and likewise drew on a variety of sources. Furthermore, hostility to Russia and also a critical attitude towards Prussian foreign policy could be seen in these papers. They maintained, for example, that it was essential to bring about a political balance in Europe, to which end Russia had to be weakened. In these papers there was also an interest in looking for signs of anti-Russian political attitudes in Finland.[58]

3. Attitudes to the war in Finland

The restless early spring of 1854, characterised by rumour, political speculation and some apprehension while different emergency regulations came into force, was followed in April by a somewhat more tranquil phase. The situation in itself was unfamiliar, since for a whole generation the possibility of war had not appeared in this tangible way. The government in St Petersburg were taking the possibility of enemy attack seriously, with military preparations in Finland and on the south coast of the Gulf of Finland. However, no military participation in the defence of their country was demanded of the Finns themselves.

The devastation of Oulu and Raahe produced a powerful revulsion of opinion in Finland. The authorities clearly feared at the beginning that this kind of 'total war' would cause panic, and may therefore have held back the official news of it. *Finlands Allmänna Tidning* published an official account on 7 June, after which the news was published in the same form in the papers of southern Finland. *Åbo Underrättelser*, however, also published an account which differed from other papers, in which the damage inflicted by the British in Oulu and Raahe was described. The *Oulun Wiikko-Sanomat*, which was 'on the spot' in Pohjanmaa, published news of the damage two weeks later.[59] Reactions in Finland turned violently against Britain. *Helsingfors Tidningar* called Admiral Plumridge an arsonist and regarded the British methods of warfare as a kind of barbarism comparable with the behaviour of the Vikings. The logic of events moved the Finns to take an attitude towards the war.[60] *Åbo Underrättelser* and some other papers spoke cynically of the 'heroic deeds of the British'.[61] The previous political mood in Pohjanmaa, which St Petersburg regarded as an area of 'Swedish sentiment', was completely reversed. The burghers of the coastal towns generally, whose livelihood had received a severe blow, were deeply shocked — as too were the farmers of the area. Many later stories reflect this; the Crimean war was given the character of a British plundering expedition against the Finnish coast.[62] These events also had a broader significance in the development of attitudes in Finland. In Finnish eyes, Britain traditionally represented sea power and in that sense a potential threat. This had become clear already in the Armed Neutrality leagues concluded in 1780 and 1800, when Sweden and other states had tried to combat Britain's brusque methods against the merchant ships of non-belligerent countries. Thus the Finns had a suspicious, negative attitude to Britain, as representing armed force and strivings towards hegemony. These opening moves in the Crimean war stirred up real hatred of Britain, and at the same time caused loyalty to the Emperor to become more pronounced. In their crisis, the Finns looked to him for protection. In this way, what had failed to happen in the country during the adaptation to the new conditions after 1808 finally came to realisation. The change in attitudes affected the burghers and especially the farmers. The accounts that appeared later in folk tales of how the farmers carried 'the bloody glove of the British admiral' as war booty to St Petersburg were an expression of anti-British feeling appearing specifically among the farmers, and also of loyalty towards the emperor.[63]

There was little difference to be seen in the attitudes represented by the newspapers. *Helsingfors Tidningar* however had stressed that Finns must be unmistakably loyal in a war situation. On the other hand, *Morgonbladet*, edited by the liberal August Schauman, would have wished as little commitment as possible in the spring-summer of 1854: Finns would be wise to avoid either speaking of enemies or stressing loyalty. Then the news of the devastation of the towns in Pohjanmaa came like a thunder-clap in the midst of this discussion. *Helsingfors Tidningar* said that Finns could not be neutral when 'the blood of the fatherland is flowing'. *Morgonbladet* also joined in, even if conspicuously later than other papers, criticising the destruction the British had caused and asking ironically if this was the much-praised civilisation of the nineteenth century.[64]

August Schauman was plainly irritated because in his opinion, due to censorship, the debate had not been allowed to develop impartially and he had not been able to present all his arguments. In *Helsingfors Tidningar* Topelius, who had expressed strongly anti-Turkish views immediately after the fight at Tammisaari and even at that stage showed an antipathy towards the western powers, was liable to be held up by some as the representative of 'the Russian line' in Finland.[65] But in general anti-Turkish slogans did not arouse much response in Finland. The war in the Crimea was too remote and in the spring of 1854 in no way a concrete factor in the development of attitudes — unlike the war in the Baltic. This went under the name of 'the Englishmen's war' and in the country Plumridge was 'the arsonist admiral'. In south Finland on the other hand, because of subsequent events, it was called 'the Åland war'.

Stories of the movements of enemy warships off the coast of Finland were on the increase and were soon to be heard in every coastal parish — reflecting the fear generated by the war among the people. The tales spread from the coast far into the interior, where the danger was remote. British bombardments on the Finnish coast from northern Pohjanmaa to Koivisto were in any case a new kind of experience for the people, and when they had got used to the war a little, half-humorous stories began to appear. When, just at this time, it was noticed that the plaster had fallen off Leppävirta church, rumour had it that this was caused by the British bombardments on the coast.[66]

The government in St Petersburg used the new current of political opinion in Finland for their own purposes: the British landing attempt at Kokkola and its repulse became a 'major incident' of the war, and at the same time a symbol of Finnish loyalty to the empire. News of the fight at Kokkola was circulated through the official papers in St Petersburg even to foreign countries as well; when the attack was driven off by the united forces of the local population and the Russian troops who had come to the spot, it was pictured as demonstrating the brotherhood of arms of the Finns and the Russians. The Emperor ordered a portrait to be painted of the farmer Kankkonen, who had distinguished himself in the action, to be placed in the Governor-General's residence, as a symbol representing the will of the broad masses of the people to defend the country.[67] It was also decided to draw the Finns actively into the military defence of their own territory. This decision was made a couple of weeks after the battle at Kokkola, and Nicholas I issued a proclamation on 11/23 June, in which, referring to the destruction inflicted by the enemy on the Finnish coast, he ordered the calling up initially of two battalions of Finnish infantry and, in November that year, two more.[68] Because the new Finnish units were without any military training they had little practical value, at least at the beginning. However their significance was symbolic, reflecting the Finns' own participation in their country's defence and the general loyalty of the population to the empire.

The mobilisation of the militia battalions caused continuous movement in the western coastal districts from the summer of 1854 onwards, which undoubtedly had its own effect on Finnish attitudes in the subsequent phases of the war. 'The Finns now take care of things, protecting the fatherland and their Emperor', according to a new song which came into use in the militia battalions.[69] Thus the government in St Petersburg now regarded the Finnish people quite differently from what had happened in Poland after the revolt of 1831. Åland experienced a different kind of change from mainland Finland because of the operations of the summer of 1854; it became completely cut off from the rest of the country. Among the Ålanders sympathy towards the western powers appeared in various ways. For example, they did not seek to prevent the landing of British and French troops. At first, however, the atmosphere was unsettled, as the British made compulsory purchases on the islands and demanded that the Ålanders help them pilot their warships. But things became calmer after the capture of Bomarsund. As well as military operations having ended, the victors shared among the population the large stocks of grain from the fortress that had come into their possession. Communications with Sweden were restored and the Ålanders' trade could begin again — and, what was more, free of duty.[70]

When Bomarsund was taken, a special situation arose in Åland, since the occupiers issued a proclamation that the archipelago was 'free and under the protection of the western powers'. At the same time the inhabitants were given to understand that they would not need to pay taxes or other dues to the authorities of mainland Finland. Thus a kind of interregnum arose. While it lasted in the autumn of 1854, there were signs of disorder in Åland. When communications with Sweden were restored, political opinion there extended its influence to Åland; Swedish expeditions came to inspect the ruins of Bomarsund, and made propaganda for a return to Sweden. It was, however, 'private politics' and not in accord with the foreign policy of Oscar I.[71]

When the fleets of the western powers left the Åland area in the late autumn of 1854, communications between mainland Finland and the archipelago began to be partly restored; for example, the civil servants returned to their former posts. However, in the summer of 1855, when the British naval squadron returned to the Baltic, the blockade of Russian territory was resumed. In this phase the boundary between Åland and mainland Finland ran up to Kihti, which was patrolled by the British warships, and smuggling across this blockade line could not be prevented. For Åland, the summer of 1855 meant yet a new phase in the war, with trade relations between the archipelago and Sweden lively and free.

From the spring and summer of 1854 the loyalty which appeared in Finland was directed more to the Emperor than to Russia. In an emergency Finns sought security, and the ruler was the central figure in all important decision-making which concerned them. This attitude embraced both considerations of defence and Finnish national consciousness.

This general attitude, with slight variations, was broadly characteristic of Finnish society. There were individuals or groups — mainly in intellectual or upper-class circles — who deviated from it and who were Scandinavianists or liberals and therefore built their political hopes on the policies of the western powers and Sweden. They were dissidents, whom force of circumstances compelled to keep a low profile amid the powerful reaction caused by the destructive activities of the British navy. Although currently the enemy, Britain represented to them the kind of social development which they hoped would grow in Finland in the future. Russia, though currently representing military security, also stood for political and social reaction. These groups regarded the current war as an ideological confrontation of west and east. In these circles the foreign policy of Sweden, and above all the rumour that she would enter the war on the western side, were followed with keen, almost strained attention. However, this tendency was in no way organised in Finland. It was rather an almost invisible, yet recognised phenomenon of opposition-mindedness, directed against the central administration of Finland and the government in St Petersburg. The 'activity' of these groups remained at the level of wishful thinking, and did not develop into political action.[72] There were few signs of the emergency in Finland, apart from the considerable number of soldiers there. Because the western powers had blockaded the Finnish coast, shortages of some imported goods seemed natural, but the country's food supply was assured as far as cereals were concerned, and this meant some security in daily life.

The British squadron sent to the Baltic in the summer of 1855 was much smaller than that of the previous year, and France sent no fleet at all. This showed that the war was more than ever concentrated in the Crimean area. The British carried out some harassing activities on the south and west coasts of Finland, so that the country had to be on the alert. The only event resembling a proper military operation was when the British squadron bombarded Sveaborg at the beginning of August. From the beginning of 1855, when General F. Berg replaced P.E. Rokassovski, the acting Governor-General, who had proved to be a bad organiser, there had been an effort to strengthen the defences of Helsinki in particular. The bombardment of Sveaborg led to no real military consequences, but it set off rumours, and created for a time an apprehensive mood in the country.

Finlands Allmänna Tidning fed the Finns with official information on behalf of the country's central administration for the whole of the war, and the censorship authorities repeatedly emphasised that all the other newspapers must publish news of enemy activities in accordance with the information distributed in the official paper and not publish any of their own reports.[74] Considerably more information on the policies of the great powers and the international situation in Europe was gleaned from Swedish papers.[75] Because the tendency seemed to be in favour of Sweden's taking part in the war, for as long as they hoped for the re-union of Finland with Sweden, the censorship authorities confiscated many Swedish papers subscribed to in Finland. Because even in the emergency, there was contact between the countries, especially through Haparanda, Finnish officials could not prevent political information flowing into Finland from Sweden. The isolation from foreign countries was felt ever more clearly the longer the war went on. Also those engaged in foreign trade eagerly awaited the return of peacetime conditions so that they could begin to repair the great losses they had suffered in various ways early in the war. The burghers of the coastal towns especially felt themselves to be living in a state of oppressive idleness.

When Finns in small groups discussed questions of war and peace, those who followed affairs more extensively and watchfully tended to concentrate on the future of 'the Finnish way of life' within the Russian empire. These Finns were loyal in their general attitude, but felt the need — in the circumstances of the time — to render an account of the Finnish past and at the same time examine the prospects for the future. These people who debated matters more widely were to be found among the academic intellectuals, the upper classes and businessmen.[76] Their views of the future of Finland, which expresses deep concern but also involved optimism, were within certain narrow limits; the alternatives left outside those limits were on the one hand the Scandinavianist view that Finland should seek to break away from the connection with Russia, and on the other the idea, shunned now more than before, that Russia might win the war and everything would remain in Finland as before. Above all there were hopes of changes in Finland's internal conditions and generally the achievement of a freer range of political movement. The prolongation of the war added to such hopes, as in its own way was the news of the death of Nicholas I in March 1855, and of Alexander II acceding. The former ruler had been a figure of power and the embodiment of old-fashioned ideas, and now hopes for political change in Finland were fastened on the new emperor, about whose attitudes different ideas existed. Politically-conscious circles began to anticipate the outcome of the war, above all the possibility that Russia would be defeated. While this would mean a new kind of relative strength among the great powers of Europe, it was assumed — and hoped — that as a consequence, the general political atmosphere would change throughout the continent. In particular the visions of hope included a shift in which Finland would be able to break free from everything traditionally associated with the system of the Holy Alliance. In quiet discussions almost a new kind of Finnish world-picture was sketched out. Its starting-point was that the west represented altogether more advanced conditions, but that when the war ended reform activity could make a start in Russia. It was believed that the difference between Russia and western Europe could not remain as wide as before.

It was common to criticise the country's civil servants, and others too, on the grounds that they were following the Russian line, while one's own position could be called 'European'; it would be suggested hopefully that the end of the war would bring 'justice for all'. This often included the hope of an improvement in the position of small nations, to which Finland's destiny was linked. The criticism of the patriarchal and bureaucratic system included expectations of the inauguration of a constitutional system as well. In the view of the academic intellectuals, it was above all a question of achieving individual political liberty, and the opening of communications with foreign countries — also a new opportunity to realise the unfulfilled hopes of 1848.

4. *The Treaty of Paris of 1856 and the Finnish question in subsequent political discussions*

The capture of Sevastopol in September 1855 meant a clear shift in the war situation in favour of the western powers. Also Sweden seemed on the point of reconsidering her official policy: this appeared in the attitudes of Oscar I and not just in public opinion, which contained a strong and persistent element of nationalistic sentimentality.[77] In these circumstances negotiations were held between Sweden and the western powers, on the basis of the proposal made by the latter in the previous July that the inviolability of the Arctic Ocean coastline of Sweden-Norway be guaranteed. As a consequence of Oscar's counter-proposal, the negotiations had advanced to the point where the western powers were ready to conclude the so-called November Agreement, which extended the territorial guarantee they were offering to cover the entire territory of the Swedish-Norwegian union.[78]

The agreement of November 1855 meant that Sweden moved her line of neutrality a few points closer to the western powers. Oscar I was also prepared to make a decisive turn in foreign policy, and to bring Sweden into the war on the western side, supported by the activist spirit of public opinion. His readiness for this was shown dramatically when the French General Canrobert visited Stockholm just as the November Agreement was being concluded. The king gave him a proposed plan for a joint operation by Sweden and the western powers for the conquest of Finland.[79] Swedish public opinion, which did not know the precise content of the November Agreement but drew conclusions freely, began to express demands for the restoration of Sweden's external greatness. At the same time rumours circulated that the summer of 1856 would be the time of great military operations in the Baltic.[80]

The fall of Sevastopol figured as major news in the Finnish press, but apart from the official communiqués — including those published by the western powers — because of the censorship, it did not examine the changes it had caused in the international situation. The Finnish papers, at this point, did not contain any reporting of the political opinions and feelings being expressed in Sweden and elsewhere abroad. Russia's great military defeat in the Crimea undoubtedly gave further stimulus to enlightened circles in Finland to discuss the result of the war and the outlook for the future. Also in the autumn of 1855, discussions on the direction of Swedish foreign policy and the Finnish question, which had been carried on vigorously in Sweden from the spring and summer of 1854, began to project their influence across the Gulf of Bothnia. The transfer of the discussion to Finland in this late stage of the war was fuelled by two pamphlets published in Sweden on the position of Finland. The former fennoman Emil von Qvanten, who had moved to Sweden, had published under the pseudonym Peder Särkilax a pamphlet, *Fennomani och skandinavism*, which proposed that Sweden should join the war on the western side and liberate Finland from 'Russian slavery'.[82] He alleged that the Finns would receive a Swedish military force with joy if one landed. Qvanten emphasised at the same time that Finnish national consciousness had awakened, and that it was therefore important for Finland to receive an autonomous status in a Scandinavian union. The pamphlet *Det unga Finland*, by the editor of *Aftonbladet*, August Sohlman, agreed in some respects with Qvanten, but was also partly a reply to him.[83] Sohlman's starting point too was the hope that Finland, with Sweden's help, would be detached from Russia but he was not prepared to recommend any special status for Finland *vis-à-vis* Sweden. Specifically he did not accept that conditions in Finland favoured the building of a nation, and alleged that the Finns, who in his opinion were racially inferior, lacked the ability to create an independent culture from their own language; only a culture of Swedish origin could uphold in Finland the spiritual defences against Russianism. In the autumn of 1855 the Finnish censorship authorities ordered both these pamphlets to be confiscated,[84] but in spite of that they were circulated in Finland, and greatly sought-after, especially among the young intellectuals.

Political opinions and feelings could be expressed somewhat more freely in Finland at this stage. More clearly than before, opinions hostile to Russia and sympathetic to Sweden were in evidence. When the Swedish papers, in the spring and summer of 1855, had published 'letters from Finland' in which Scandinavianist political aspirations were expressed, it caused the Finnish authorities to increase their vigilance, especially over the young intellectuals. In official quarters, suspicions appeared that some secret organisation was working against loyalty to the empire.[85]

When, at the end of November 1855, a group of students gathered after a party and expressed political feelings sympathetic to the struggle of the western powers, the authorities seized eagerly on this so-called 'Töölö disturbance'.[86] There was no question of any organised opposition, though certainly an outburst of political opinions engendered by the Scandinavianist influences of the last phase of the war, and various rumours of a change in Swedish policy. This outburst occurred only within a very narrow circle of young intellectuals.

In November-December 1855 peace talks began to be speeded up by the western powers. They were considering a diplomatic initiative whereby Austria would present an ultimatum in St Petersburg on the pre-conditions for a peace negotiation, and would state that if Russia did not accept them, she would break off diplomatic relations and join the war on the side of the western powers. In the preliminary conditions sent to St Petersburg in early December, the completion of an international agreement for the demilitarisation of the Black Sea was central. In addition Britain had interests of her own which involved the demilitarisation of the Åland area.[87]

When the government in St Petersburg had to define its position on the ultimatum delivered by Austria in the middle of January 1856, it saw that the international situation had become considerably more difficult for Russia. It could be assumed that the number of her enemies would probably grow if the war continued. Among Alexander's advisers it was noted that not only Austria but Sweden too would possibly join the western side. It was thought that if the war continued, and these eventualities came to pass, Russia could possibly lose the Crimea, the Caucasus and Finland from her territory. This general assessment of the situation was the basis for Alexander II — closely following his advisers — to adopt the view that the preliminary conditions presented by Austria must be accepted and that Russia should begin talks on a peace treaty with the western powers in Paris.[88]

When the Crimean war appeared to be ending, Oscar I, whose schemes had been of a quite different tendency, was possessed by a kind of panic. He sought immediate diplomatic contact with Britain above all in order to get Sweden's interests introduced into the peace negotiations. However Sweden no longer had the same favourable position *vis-à-vis* the western powers as in August 1854, when the occupation of Åland was offered to her. Oscar now concentrated his hopes on Åland but for safety's sake presented Sweden's aims in the form of two alternatives.[89] The king proposed to the British government in the first place the hope that Åland could be joined to Sweden, but otherwise that it would be proclaimed a neutral area guaranteed by the western powers and Sweden, in addition to which the southern coast of Finland should be demilitarised from the west up to Sveaborg. Thus it could be ensured that Russia should not begin to construct a new fortress somewhere else in the northern Baltic area in place of

Bomarsund, and that she would lose her general military control of this area, while preserving a defensive zone on both sides of the sea passage to St Petersburg. However, Britain's objective for the Baltic in the Paris peace negotiation was limited only to the demilitarisation of Åland. The *status quo* after the destruction of the Bomarsund fortifications was to be confirmed with the aid of 'the European concert', that is by a separate international agreement, to be signed by a large number of states.[90]

The international agreement on Åland was signed in Paris at the same time as the general peace treaty in March 1856. According to it, Britain and France would be able to intervene in strategic questions in the Baltic area. At the same time the traditional aim of British policy — to hold open the sea route to the Baltic — was indirectly reinforced. Through the Crimean war, Russia had lost the position of dominance she had had in the Baltic area since 1815. However, Britain had not sought the kind of military solutions in the Baltic which would have restricted substantially the organisation of the defence of St Petersburg. By contrast the conditions to which Russia had to submit in the Black Sea, on the basis of the Treaty of Paris, went much further. In addition to a ban on fortifications, the maintenance of a fleet in this area was forbidden. Sweden for her part could regard the international agreement on Åland as advantageous in that the military threat to Stockholm was removed.

In Sweden the Crimean war and the Paris peace conclusively confirmed the view that the fate of Finland was decided 'for all time'. After a rapid rise, the idea of Sweden as a great power had as rapidly subsided. This fact meant also that the Finns who had moved to Stockholm, including J.J. Nordström and Emil von Qvanten, had to realise that their hopes were unfulfilled.[91] However, their activity on the Finnish question did not stop there. The conclusion of the Treaty of Paris brought to a climax in the Swedish press the bitter articles and accusations which had already begun a little earlier against the western powers that they had needlessly rushed to conclude peace with Russia, and were guilty of the fact that 'liberation of Finland' had not been accomplished.[92] The Finnish question also came up directly or indirectly in leading papers in the western countries when they examined the ending of the Crimean war; they also presented responses to the dissatisfaction felt in Stockholm. To the Swedish idea that Finland should have been joined to Sweden, *Le Constitutionel* remarked that the Finns themselves had not shown any desire for such a political change during the war.[93] *The Times* emphasised that there was undoubtedly greater significance for Sweden's international position in the November Agreement signed with the western powers, and the demilitarisation of Åland, than in detaching 'some province' from Russia.[94] *Le Siècle* affirmed that Britain would exercise military vigilance in the Baltic.[95]

The Crimean war had brought Finland great publicity abroad; the name of Finland achieved something of a breakthrough as its distinct identity *via-à-vis* the rest of the Russian empire began to be stressed. Conceptions of Finland as a national entity of its own also took root. On the other hand the provisions of the peace treaty did not directly concern Finland, except for the separate agreement on Åland. In spite of this, the indirect consequences of the Crimean war came to affect Finland's position in a remarkable way.

VII. The after-effects of the Crimean War and the wait for changes in Finland

1. *The return to peacetime conditions and the new vision of the future*

The Crimean war spelt a major defeat for Russia; above all, she had suffered a substantial blow as a great power. But the outcome of the war also affected the international system, since the alliance of the three conservative great powers, representing the tradition of the Holy Alliance, and renewed in 1833 at Münchengrätz, had been broken up. Austria had clearly turned against Russia; also, Austria and Prussia had drifted apart from one another. The consequence was that Russia was forced into an isolated position in international politics. She had lost that active role as the defender of the prevailing system in Europe, which she had played in 1848–9. At the same time she had been forced into the position of an onlooker, and although clearly dissatisfied with the new international situation, was still powerless to change it, at least for the time being.[1]

Russia's military defeat forced Alexander II to turn his attention to the internal reform of his empire. It had been disturbing that the Russian army had been defeated in the Crimea while defending the country against troops brought in from western Europe. Ruling circles were forced to seek the reasons for this in the backwardness of the country's internal conditions. As the war gave way to the post-war phase, schemes for great reforms were drawn up — and realised too in the fields of local government, communications and the peasant question. Results were seen when the *zemstvo* system came into force in the early 1860s and in the manifesto, issued in the spring of 1861, which abolished serfdom. The total reform programme also included the development of those non-Russian nationalities living on the western borders of the empire, having regard to their own aspirations and an interest in the organisation of their administration and conditions. The war led indirectly to changes occuring in Finland which she had not experienced as a result of the July and February revolutions. In Russia external defeat led to national self-criticism. 'It is better', Alexander II declared in 1856, àpropos serfdom, 'if we begin to abolish it from above rather than let the reform begin to realise itself from below'.

The peace was eagerly awaited in Finland, where many newspapers showed great diligence in reporting the preliminary soundings. The papers reported at the turn of January-February 1856 that Russia had accepted the first conditions for peace negotiations in Paris. In addition, *Oulun Wiikko-Sanomat* felt able to tell its readers on 9 February that the peace treaty would contain a clause forbidding the fortification of Åland.[2] The papers' room for manoeuvre had again widened, for they extensively reported foreign views on the peace treaty and on international developments in general. The Finnish press did not present any comments of their own, but they clearly hoped for a speedy conclusion of the peace treaty. Business also awaited the coming of peace and the restoration of overseas trade. The war had lasted so long that the shortage of goods was very apparent. Exporters had received enquiries, preparatory to placing orders, from abroad (some burghers of Oulu had even received them from Britain through intermediaries) and this caused them to make preparations, since the sailing season was approaching. The shortage of merchant ships, after the losses that had been endured, was recognised as a problem difficult to solve.[3]

News of the signing of the Treaty of Paris was published in the country's official paper on 4 April 1856, and as it quickly spread to the country through the other papers, satisfaction and enthusiasm were very obvious. Festivals were organised, services of thanksgiving held, and the sea ports were festooned with flags. Governor-General Berg issued an acknowledgment to the Finnish people of the loyalty it had shown and for fulfilling its duties during the two years of war: he particularly stressed the part played by the farmers, who had served in the militia battalions and assisted the supply of the military in the country.[4] A striking feature of the situation was that however enthusiastic the newspapers were about the coming of peace, they were still remarkably reserved when it came to expressing opinions about intention and hopes regarding the future of Finland. They had had plenty of time to experience censorship and other kinds of political control. Furthermore, the personnel of the central administration of the country had not been changed — which might have been interpreted as a change of direction.

As Finnish society moved from war to peace in the spring of 1856, a spiritual ferment was taking place. Both intellectuals and the business leaders may have thought that changes in conditions were inevitable. A new *Weltanschauung* was being shaped in these circles. First, they wanted to break the connections with a past marked by paternalistic supervision and control, and with the many kinds of restraint on political and economic development. It was also hoped that communications abroad would now be allowed to open up in a truly free way.

The Crimean war had given the St Petersburg government a remarkable experience of Finland which was to be significant for the future. The Finns had given proof of being loyal subjects, more than in mere words and reassuring newspaper statements. The Finns had spontaneously resisted when the enemy threatened, for example in June 1854 at Kokkola, before the area military commander had reached the spot with his troops. Above all, resistance had been offered to the enemy by people from different social levels, both burghers and farmers.

However, Åland was something of an exception and caused a special problem in St Petersburg, because the population there had had extensive contacts with western troops, and with Sweden. The Ålanders had first-hand experience of the conflict of the great powers and there had been many 'collaborators'; at the instigation of Finnish officials, many interrogations were carried out in the archipelago because of this.[5] On the initiative of Alexander II, however, an effective amnesty was given, and there were no legal proceedings. This created a calm political atmosphere in Åland — after the eventful years of the war.

During a visit to Helsinki in March 1856, Alexander II announced in a session of the Senate that various reforms would be prepared in Finland. When this news had the chance to spread and later in the spring was made public, it caused growing optimism about the future. Alexander had not, however, promised anything beyond that mentioned above which would have pointed to a change in the Finnish political system. Yet hopes of change did exist in the country. For example, Frans Ludvig Schauman hoped that the Finnish Diet would be summoned, and said as much at a festival in the autumn of 1856, held in Helsinki at the same time as the Emperor's coronation in Moscow. Such an expression of political aspirations from 'below' was a clear departure from the line of the traditional paternalistic system. With the characteristic caution of the time, the papers did not mention Schauman's speech. Later, Alexander expressed his displeasure that Schauman had raised such a matter.[6]

In the new post-war situation, Alexander regarded the non-Russian western borderlands of the empire to some extent as a unity. He recognised the necessity of reform in this area stretching from Poland to Finland, but he wanted to proceed with caution. The Polish question constituted a quite special problem for Alexander, for besides the after-effects of the revolt of 1830, Napoleon III had tried at the Paris peace conference to take up the question of the position of the Poles. From the Russian side, such international intervention in the affairs of Poland was sharply rejected; however, it was assumed unofficially that some reforms would be carried out there.[7] At this stage a new feature had appeared in the handling of the Polish question, in that leading circles among the Poles began to refer to Finland's autonomy when the political aspirations of their own country were raised. For example, at the time when Lithuanian and Polish leaders had been in touch with Alexander I before Napoleon's Russian campaign, the Lithuanians had referred to the autonomy achieved by Finland, at the same time hoping for a corresponding outcome for Lithuania (if Napoleon were defeated); by contrast the Poles, led by Czartoryski, based their arguments for their political existence only on Poland's own history.[8] After the revolt of 1830, when the Poles had lost their autonomy and were politically downtrodden, they began to take note of Finland, the only autonomous country in the Russian empire.

When Alexander II visited Warsaw in May 1856 he said in his speech to the leaders of the Polish aristocracy: 'You are as dear to me as the Finns, but the system which my father has brought into effect in your country is unchanged. All dreams must be rejected unconditionally. . . . The success of Poland is dependent on a full union with Holy Russia [*sa fusion absolue*]'.[9] In spite of this coldly straightforward rejection of the Poles' political aspirations, the Emperor was ready for economic and other kinds of reform to be prepared, but not to concede to the Poles their own 'political existence'. It can be deduced from the emperor's reply that the Poles had used the autonomy of Finland as an argument in support of their own aspirations, which made Alexander II generally very cautious regarding all political concessions in these western border areas of the empire. The Finnish question became linked with the Emperor's way of looking at the Polish question, and the latter in practice put a brake on his measures in Finland — though not on economic reforms, but on all that involved political changes in the country's status and conditions.

After the end of the Crimean war public discussion in Finland gathered speed. The statement, already mentioned, which was read into the minutes of the Senate by the Emperor in March 1856, regarding the preparation of reforms, was also a sign from above that discussion of such reform questions was permitted. The discussion concerned in the first instance specific questions about post-war reconstruction. In the spring of 1856 the Senate had set up a committee because of the heavy losses of the merchant fleet. This proposed that shipowners be given interest-free loans to speed up the building of ships; the proposal was adopted, with resulting benefits above all to the ports of the Gulf of Bothnia which had suffered the greatest losses (by contrast Viipuri, for example, had escaped with much less loss).[10] Hence a wholly new merchant fleet was quickly built in the country's own shipyards. The state also sought in other ways to speed up the return to normal, by removing the export duties on timber and tar for a specific period and by correspondingly reducing or abolishing certain import duties;[11] in addition a special fund was set up to support reconstruction.

No visible changes in Finland's economic structure took place after the end of the Crimean war, but reforms certainly did so, and thus strengthened the general belief in progress. The Saimaa canal was completed in 1856 and the railway between Helsinki and Hämeenlinna in 1858–62. The new Finnish customs tariff which came into force in 1859 meant a considerable step in the direction of free trade, very much in accord with the wishes of the country's business community. In the same year the decree on trade relations between Finland and Russia, enlarging the export quotas for Finnish products in many areas, promoted the growth of the export market in Russia for Finnish products.[12] True, there were also strains on economic life, like the severe harvest failure in northern Finland in 1856–7, repeated in 1862, but the effects were warded off primarily because the American civil war had meant exceptionally large tar exports which made it possible to buy grain abroad and lessen the effects of the failure.[13]

Economic liberalism and free trade ideas were also discussed by the press, stimulated by ideas received from Britain, whose economic debates had been followed in the Finnish papers since the 1840s. Sweden, where the development of industry was seen to be gathering speed, also aroused interest. *Åbo Underrättelser* and *Viborg* acted as flag-bearers for economic liberalism.[14] The Finnish business community was criticised for passivity, which was seen to be behind a lack of economic enterprise and long-term planning. The press recommended the limited company to the burghers of southern Finland as a suitable form of enterprise, already developed in the coastal towns of Pohjanmaa. In Viipuri business circles, for example, they were held to be very appropriate, because capital was thus accumulated more easily and at the same time risks were spread. The experiences gained and the losses suffered in the war had shown the business community that the pursuit of commerce was clearly dependent on international political developments. Demands were now made not just for an improvement in the conditions for the general exercise of foreign trade, but which reflected a fear of new international crises. One such demand, which originated from the coastal towns of Pohjanmaa at the end of the 1850s, was the wish of the burghers of Pietarsaari to have Finnish commercial agents in the important centres abroad,[15] to ensure that there would be Finns abroad to protect the country's trading interests in all circumstances and assist merchant ships to make contacts. The system had already been established in certain major Russian ports in the 1830s, and was now to be extended to serve Finland's trade with the west in the changed circumstances. Another proposal was for Finland to have her own flag. This proposal of 1862 came from shipping circles, also in the Pohjanmaa coastal towns, this time Oulu.[16]

2. *The fennomans and the liberals in the changed circumstances*

The exchange of political views was allowed to accelerate in Finland after the end of the Crimean war, albeit cautiously at first. This kind of activity had not happened in the country before. The harvest of foreign ideas shelved after 1848 was a motivating factor. At the same time the general opening of communications abroad allowed new influences to enter the country. Also, the Scandinavianist influence had found its way into Finland, particularly in the final phase of the war. Politicisation was getting under way, and although the intellectuals still played a central role, the expression of political views was spreading to different social strata. Fennomania was extending its influence as far as enlightened farmers and was also giving rise to a counter-movement among the Swedish-speaking intellectuals, supported by the upper class among others. At the same time, the student corporations were losing their previous special position as forums for political discussion.

The growth of the press enlarged interest in public affairs and continuously stimulated political discussion. At the same time the social structure of the newspaper readership had markedly changed by the end of the 1850s. The Finnish-language press had grown vigorously, its circulation increasing by 1860 to as much as the combined subscriptions of the Swedish-language papers. In addition to the intellectuals and Swedish-speaking upper class, an increasing number of Finnish-speaking farmers became newspaper-readers.[17] As the transmission of information reached new dimensions, public opinion began to emerge through the press.

The fennoman leaders concentrated on speeding up nationally distinct developments, and felt it important that they should make contact with the mass of the people. The liberals for their part stressed the Swedish origin of Finnish culture, and maintained that contacts with the other side of the Gulf of Bothnia were vital for preserving its vigour. In addition, they felt that there should be more internal political freedom. At first, the two tendencies differed only to the extent that they placed more emphasis on particular objectives. The basic problem was how the country's development could be most securely speeded up in the long term, while preserving Finland's identity in relation to Russia. The fennoman leaders began to emphasise that by adopting an attitude of loyalty to the new Emperor they could gain more flexibility regarding national development. Snellman, who was once more returning to public life, had demanded since the spring of 1856 that the Finns must dissociate themselves clearly from Sweden.[18] In the liberal-Scandinavianist camp, russophobia had strengthened under the influence of a broad wave of western European opinion and an inheritance from the war years. The criticism directed at Sweden by leading fennomans was not appreciated in these circles. In autumn 1856, replying to Snellman, the young C.G. Estlander suggested that contacts with Scandinavia had meant a great deal to the Finnish world outlook and the development of Finnish society. For Estlander it was important that contact between Finland and Sweden should continue.[19] On the other hand, the liberals did not believe that anything politically significant could be obtained from St Petersburg.

The discussion of Finland's position and of the national problems was stimulated at different levels of society as the country observed two significant historical celebrations: the seventh centenary of the coming of Christianity to Finland and the fiftieth anniversary of the Finnish war. Alexander II had given his consent to the former being celebrated as a jubilee; he had clearly hoped that it would be an event organised in the same 'union of throne and altar' spirit as the jubilee of the Augsburg Confession in 1830. The Emperor stated that the parallel tasks of his Finnish subjects were 'to fulfil their Christian and their national duties', while the duty of the clergy was 'to serve church and fatherland'.[20] In practice, however, the Christian celebrations offered an occasion for general analysis of Finland's relation to its past in a way that acquired a historical and political tone. The newspapers analysed the general significance and character of the coming of Christianity to Finland. *Suometar* thought the uniting of Finland to Sweden had been a linking of the country to free conditions and not to slavery. *Åbo Underrättelser* sought to maintain that the coming of Christianity to Finland had not involved any violence,[21] but *Litteraturblad* emphasised that the conversion carried out in Finland by the Swedes had been accomplished with the aid of the sword.[22]

Also in the spring of 1857, at a degree ceremony in Helsinki University in which guests from Sweden participated, strong expressions of Scandinavianism were expressed. The most striking was the speech of A.E. Nordenskiöld, which ended with a toast to 'the future of Finland, to an uncertain future'.[24] The authorities intervened and Nordenskiöld moved to Sweden. During the anniversary celebration for the war of 1808, which lasted from February 1858 till the latter half of the year, the Swedish- and Finnish-language press both wrote extensively on the events of that war. Above all, the Finns' share was recalled as a brave defence of their own country. Such events helped maintain an image of 'Finland's war', which Runeberg's tales of Vänrikki Stool had also fostered. That period had been, according to one paper, 'the golden age of our victories, our sorrow and our honour'. The anniversary was celebrated with particular attention in Pohjanmaa, where there were numerous battlefields of the 1808 war.[25] These memories brought to mind, in an appreciative way, the common history of Finland and Sweden. When this historical emotionalism was linked to the present, it often implied a reserved or ambivalent attitude to Russia.

At the beginning of 1858 Snellman proposed the adoption of a general political line in the post-Crimean war conditions. An article published in his *Litteraturblad* was an attack ostensibly directed at Nordström, Qvanten and other Finnish emigrants in Stockholm, whose activity did not, in Snellman's view, represent Finland's interests, and to whom he wanted to deny the right to act in the country's name.[26] However, it was also directed at those elements in Finland who continued to keep up contacts with Sweden and who spread false information about their own country with the aid of 'letters from Finland' in the newspapers there. Snellman wanted to refute the emigrants' criticism of conditions in Finland, and demanded that they should dissociate themselves from spiritual dependence on the other side of the Gulf of Bothnia. His aim was to arouse Finnish national consciousness and confidence in the future, and his severe demarcation line against Sweden was also more generally intended to affirm political loyalty to the Emperor and the empire. This attitude also proceeded from the fact that Finland had, within the framework of autonomy, quite different prospects for future development than it would have as part of Sweden. Snellman's stand, which was uncompromising in tone, came at a time when the historical significance of the relations of Finland and Sweden was being extensively examined in the country in connection with the two anniversaries. His aggressive article also speeded up the formation of a front against the fennomans. Many of his opponents regarded anyone who denied that Finland was politically downtrodden, at a time when, for example, there was severe censorship, as 'on Russia's side'. Snellman's stand even split the fennomans' own ranks: some wanted to emphasise the significance of contacts with Sweden and thought that in the prevailing conditions the finnicisation movement could not yet create a culture of its own to replace the traditional one.[27] While some young liberals were prepared to label Snellman a political tool of the government in St Petersburg, the young fennoman, Yrjö Koskinen, declared those of the Scandinavianist tendency to be 'aliens' in Finland. Koskinen also directed severe criticism towards Stockholm; he called Qvanten and other emigrants 'Finland's bastard offspring' in Sweden, and he stressed that over the centuries, Finland had paid its debt of gratitude to the other side of the Gulf of Bothnia 'in blood'. He also demanded that Sweden must concede to

Finland the right 'to be and remain of its own nationality', otherwise a 'cold mist' would come down between the two countries.[28]

The political confrontation also contained strong elements of social dualism. The fennomans sought contacts with farming society, whose spiritual enlightenment they held to be an important factor for the country's future. Their opponents for their part saw themselves as representatives of the élite, and as the enlightened aristocracy, also as keepers of tradition alongside the ignorant masses.

The traditional pillars of the prevailing system, the country's administration and the leaders of the Church and the University, had experienced a partial transformation in the circumstances of the Crimean war, the effect of which could be seen in the changed conditions.

The new Governor-General, Berg, based his actions on the loyalty which had appeared in Finland during the Crimean war. In the post-war conditions it caused him to look favourably on the fennomans in questions of supporting the Finnish language and culture. At the same time, in his general attitude which dated from the latter phase of the war, he was emphatically suspicious of the 'Swedish party'. He suspected that a secret society could be found within Helsinki University, which maintained contacts with Sweden; at the same time, he believed that Qvanten's agitation was having a powerful effect in Finland. In his opinion the Stockholm newspapers were 'revolutionary', and he favoured censorship; secret police methods too were not alien to him.[29] This in turn caused crises in the relationship of the Governor-General, the censorship authorities and the University.

The resignation of von Haartman and von Kothen from the Senate in 1858 meant important changes in the country's administration. Of these Haartman had been the personification of the paternal system; in his opinion the new phenomena of the post-Crimean era were 'raving constitutionalism' to which he was quite unreconciled.[30] Kothen too was a conservative offical. The appointment of Fabian Langenskiöld as chief of the finance department after Haartman meant change in many respects. He was a supporter of economic liberalism, which lent a new style both to financial decisions and to methods of procedure generally.[31] Langenskiöld also had contacts with the fennomans, for example with Snellman. The fact that the fennoman movement was favoured at a high level caused tensions in government circles. The Swedish-speaking civil servants at different levels of the administration, who were accustomed to relying on tradition, could see in this an attempt to overthrow existing conditions and adopt a dubious new general direction.

After the Crimean war, new political and social trends and outlooks appeared also in the upper levels of the Church, which was no longer a united pyramid directed from above. The archiepiscopal see of Turku, where the conservative Bergenheim was still the incumbent, lost some of its earlier controlling grip and became to some extent passive. Frans Ludwig Schauman, who in 1856 had boldly expressed the liberal aspiration for the summoning of a Diet, represented the new forces among the clergy. He came to have considerable influence in the Church leadership, first as a professor of theology and later (after 1865) as Bishop of Porvoo. Fennoman influences began to appear, even if somewhat slowly at the top levels; also, the integration of the revivalist movement into the state Church expressed the new tendency.

From 1856 a new spirit of the age showed itself in the proclamations issued for days of prayer.[32] These no longer concentrated, as throughout the previous period, on displaying loyalty to authority, but recognised that the problems of the peoples' earthly lives were important matters as well. This became clear, for example, when they began to praise the active and enterprising man who worked for development and progress; reconstruction work and repairing war damage and the consequences of the bad harvest were important, as well as reforms in the economic field. In the proclamation for the day of prayer issued in November 1856, it was explicitly stated that the demands of the times had changed, and even the relationship of the Emperor to Finnish society was depicted in a new way when this proclamation mentioned Alexander II sealing a union with the people of Finland. More than before, the Church began to examine its own existence apart from the state, as a distinct entity. Schauman belonged to those who saw the Church's independence as a priority. The preparation of a new Church ordinance stimulated the exchange of opinions within the church itself.[33] In the new phase, the Church leadership did not have the same hold on the country as before. Many changes, including the vigorous growth of the press, clearly meant that days of prayer had lost their earlier significance.

Changes occurred too in Helsinki University, where intellectual tendencies were present among the teaching staff. The fennomans were represented by Gabriel Rein, acting Rector at the end of the war, and Snellman and Fredrik Cygnaeus, who had become professors in 1856. There were also liberals. In the new situation the control of the Governor-General was concentrated on those with sympathies towards Scandinavianism. Among the young intellectuals there was much criticism of Snellman, above all on the ground that he had proposed breaking cultural ties with Sweden.[34]

For the government in St Petersburg the pillars of Finland's administration were no longer the leadership of the country's Lutheran Church and Helsinki University. The grip of patriarchalism on society had clearly weakened, and these institutions were also internally divided. However, attitudes in Finnish society had also changed, and this had changed the situation — as seen from St Petersburg — into one more favourable for the Empire's security. The experience of the Crimean war had caused suspicion of the Finn's political loyalty to diminish, and at the same time this suspicion was turned on different sections of Finnish society. The lower classes were clearly less distrusted, since their loyalty had been put to concrete proof. Instead, suspicion of certain liberal intellectual circles and of the Swedish-speaking upper classes had gained strength.

After the Crimean war, Alexander II adopted a clear policy of reform both in Russia and separately in Finland and Poland. However, he was restrained and cautious in changes affecting the political system. In Finland he avoided public discussion of reform and everything which had a political tone. In 1859 he ordered the administration to resolve which reforms in Finland could be realised by administrative action and which required the assistance of the Diet. Although in this way the Emperor indirectly acknowledged all the political institutions comprised in the country's autonomy, Governor-General Berg also directed that the question of the Diet could not be discussed in the newspapers. Caution at a high level over foreign influences was also demonstrated by Berg's order to the censorship authorities in 1860 that the press could only write of events connected with the national unification of Italy which 'were in accordance with the principles of a law-abiding people on morality and a sense of duty'.[36] The events in Italy were clearly seen as an alteration of the political system from below, because there had been national risings and national referendums.

After the experience of the Crimean war, the country's administration recognised the press as important and necessary for spreading information in society. Alongside *Finlands Allmänna Tidning*, an official Finnish-language newspaper, *Suomen Julkisia Sanomia*, was published from 1857. The press was not, however, recognised as a 'western' institution which could help to form political opinion in the country from below. A new factor of political conditions in Finland from the end of the 1850s was an awareness of the country's own constitutional laws. This was connected with endeavours to get the political life of Finland started up in a framework of greater local activity. For example, the debate in 1859–61 between J.P. Palmén and Snellman, in the course of which both were able to adjust their previously-held ideas on the country's constitution increased general interest in this subject.[37]

In such a political atmosphere, interpretations of the birth of Finland's autonomy also took shape. The Diet of Porvoo of 1809 was thus claimed to be the only Finnish Diet in which the Finns' own national role in the political transition of 1808–9 was emphasised.[38] Thus political consciousness was awakened by looking back into the past, but the real purpose was to serve the political objectives of the present. From the liberal point of view this was the true 'Finnish state', on which they wanted to build their hopes for the future. For the fennomans, the 'discovery' of the Porvoo Diet was also a counter-move against Qvanten and others in Sweden, who sought to deny the existence of Finland's special position. The administration did not try to prevent discussion of such themes associated with the country's history, but if some contemporary theme was in question, the censorship was soon watchful. This was a special problem for the liberals, who were thus compelled to estimate carefully what could be published. But it also proved to be a problem for Snellman, whose article entitled 'Nyåret 1861' did not get a publication permit in *Litteraturbladet*.[39] In it he examined the awakening of the national spirit in different parts of

Europe and the Finnish position in connection with Russia. He argued, as a condition of the political existence of every nation, for a 'representative system of government'; he hoped that Finland would be able to participate in such a development.

In March 1861, the Emperor announced that he was prepared to set up a special council in Poland to discuss reforms.[40] When at the same time hopes were expressed in Finland for the summoning of the country's Diet, Alexander II rejected such an idea. Instead he issued a manifesto in April 1861, whereby a 'committee' of forty-eight members was convened in Helsinki representing the different Estates. Alexander was clearly following similar policies in Poland and Finland. In Helsinki however a protest movement against the summoning of the committee came into being; it was said that the committee was 'against the constitution', because it was regarded as acquiring the functions belonging to the Diet. These negative reactions, which could not be published in the press because of the censorship, were a demonstration of the general awakening of consciousness about the constitution. The strength of the opposition — among other things they began to collect signatures for an address to the Emperor — was such that the Governor-General did not see how he could repress it. It was interesting that Alexander was prepared to review and define his position by giving an explanation in August of the same year, according to which the task of the committee, to meet in January 1862, was only to make proposals and prepare business. The actual decision-making in the question of reforms belonged to the Diet.[41] In starting up an opposition the liberal intellectuals had played a significant role, in contrast to Snellman, who had appeared cautious. Besides emphasising their own objectives, the liberals also sought revenge on Snellman, who had tried to put them into a politically untenable position in 1858 because of their contacts with Sweden.[42]

One contemporary realised that 1861 was the most significant year for Finland since its annexation to the Russian empire.[43] The exchange of opinions gathered speed in the newspapers when the censorship regulations were eased significantly at the end of that year; this process was no longer concentrated in Helsinki and Turku, but papers in Viipuri, Hämeenlinna, Pori, Vaasa, Kuopio and Oulu also took part. It was just at this time that public opinion truly made its appearance in the country.[44] External factors played their part in activating the exchange of political opinion in Finland. From the west, the discussion in Sweden about reforming the structure of the Diet, begun in the early 1860s, had a special effect, but in general the liberal-inspired 'new age' (*die neue Ära*) which had begun from the end of the 1850s in continental Europe also made itself felt. However, there were influences from the east as well. The manifesto on the abolition of serfdom, issued by the Emperor in the spring of 1861, gave birth to the idea that Russia too was changing fundamentally.

3. *Political interest in the Finnish question abroad*

It was apparent in different parts of Europe that the phenomena of nationalism and liberalism were reviving after a ten-year interval. Thus Moldavia and Wallachia proclaimed themselves an independent Romanian state in 1858, and in 1859 the unification of Italy began; this was at the same time as constitutional questions were coming to the fore in many countries. In such circumstances, interest in similar intellectual phenomena was awakened on the periphery of the continent as well.

To some extent Finland emerged internationally as a marginal case in relation to the general intellectual developments in Europe. The signs of opposition which arose over the question of the January Committee in 1861 aroused interest abroad because of their wider applicability, and they got some degree of attention in certain leading newspapers in France, Germany, Belgium and Britain. Generally, however, these papers only published the straight political news of this affair, and only in a few cases articles concerned with conditions in Finland generally. A stimulus to news of events in Finland may have been provided by certain Parisian papers, which had traditionally got news from Stockholm, where events in Finland were actively and regularly followed. News about Finland could pass into continental papers through many intermediaries, and could also be strongly coloured politically. Some 'letters to the editor' about Finland can also be found in *The Times*.[45] For example, the view expressed in the Paris paper *La Patrie* in the autumn of 1861 that 'the Finnish question' was getting the kind of attention in France which had earlier been directed at Poland and Hungary was typical of the period. At the same time it drew the straightforward conclusion that ideas of liberation were breaking out in different parts of the Russian empire.[46] Some foreign newspapers described opposition phenomena in Finland in great detail; for example, *Kölnische Zeitung*, reported that in electing members to the January Committee, the burghers of Helsinki and Vaasa had expressed a view on the constitutionality of the Committee's remit.[47]

In Sweden, interest in Finnish politics was continuously expressed, although the hope of Finland returning to a connection with the former mother-country had received a severe blow when the Crimean war ended. In the new period, however, only such papers as *Aftonbladet* and *Nya Dagligt Allehanda* increased their coverage of conditions in Finland. These two were bitter over the outcome of the war, but when Scandinavianist opinions and feelings were continuously appearing in Finland, they were enthusiastic. From 1857 these Stockholm papers published 'Letters from Finland' sent from Helsinki in which the country's rulers were criticised — such information not being publishable in the country itself because of the censorship. *Aftonbladet* and *Nya Dagligt Allehanda* acted as political safety valves for the Finnish liberals. Qvanten was active again at this time and collected the 'Letters from Finland' published in the papers as a series of pamphlets. The various writings published in the Stockholm papers on conditions in Finland undoubtedly caused quiet satisfaction among the Finnish liberals, whose type of thinking they supported. On the other hand they irritated both top officials in Finland and the leading fennomans. The latter considered that they gave a one-sided picture, in addition to which the government in St Petersburg felt a new distrust of the loyalty of the Finns. The political furore in Finland created by the summoning of the January Committee seemed only to stimulate the type of criticism of conditions in Finland appearing in *Aftonbladet* and *Nya Dagligt Allehanda*. *Aftonbladet* called it a kind of *coup d'état*, because the Diet was not assembled at the same time.[49] At this time a leaflet called '*Censur-Kalender*', edited by Qvanten, appeared in Stockholm, containing articles publication of which had been forbidden in Finland.[50]

At the beginning of the 1860s the Finnish question also interested the Polish émigrés active in Paris. It was in their political interest, and indirectly supported their own cause, to spread information on the discontents among the other non-Russian nationalities in the Russian empire. The Finnish case thus suited them as a propaganda weapon. The Polish emigrant leadership decided in December 1861 to establish their own liaison organisation for propaganda activity in Sweden, with Z. Jordan as its director. Jordan was in touch with Nordström, Qvanten and Nordenskiöld in Stockholm in the spring of 1862, and tried, with their assistance, to get information on the political situation in Finland.[51] When Jordan broached the question of a possible uprising there, the Finnish emigrants were somewhat unresponsive. On the other hand, they promised information to the Polish émigré leadership in Paris on conditions in Finland, to be circulated through their international press. These Finns regarded this kind of outlet as valuable in two respects: they could get publicity for the Finnish question in France, and perhaps in other continental countries; and they hoped, through the Paris newspapers, to influence the Swedish press and public opinion as well in its attitude towards Finland.[52]

In this way different channels of information spread knowledge of the Finnish question abroad. This information could have many kinds of colouring added to it: anti-Russian, Scandinavianist, or the wishful thinking of the Polish émigrés, and it followed from this that the news was not always reliable. In any case the Finnish question interested certain circles abroad, who followed politics. Such was the effect of the Crimean war.

VIII. The Polish revolt of 1863, the international crisis and the Finnish question

After the Crimean war Finland no longer constituted an irredentist issue in Swedish politics. This was the case both with official policy and among the majority of active political circles. The fact that some newspapers, like *Aftonbladet* and *Nya Dagligt Allehanda* still maintained a pronounced interest in Finland showed how difficult it was for certain Scandinavianist circles to accept the change that had caused the collapse of their political aspirations.

For Russia, Finland had strategic significance as long as it could be assumed that there was an invasion threat from Sweden; after the Crimean war this danger could be regarded as eliminated. The destruction among the coastal towns of the Gulf of Bothnia by the British had caused great material losses, but militarily it had not been a danger to Russia; also, the defence of Finland as a whole against an external attacker was not a problem for the defence of St Petersburg, because of the country's territorial depth.

Of events in Europe, the unification of Italy in 1859–61 and the image of Garibaldi achieved some popularity in Finland. Garibaldi was admired by both the fennomans and the liberals, and indeed some Finnish volunteers went to fight in Garibaldi's army.[1] At the same time the nationalist ideal began to have a real significance for Finnish people alive to events abroad. Typical of this was a synopsis of what had occurred in Europe during 1861 in the new provincial newspaper *Hämäläinen*: 'The consciousness of nationality in the world . . . is the real thrust of the present day, the real historical kick, which will bring mankind to new positions. Therefore the existence and situation of those states which have collected together many nationalities will become very difficult.'[2] This reference was clearly directed at Austria, but it could be read as referring also to Finland's position *vis-à-vis* Russia.

When civil war broke out in the United States in 1861, reports were published in Finnish newspapers describing the events, but political and ideological attitudes received little analysis: the Atlantic Ocean seemed a dividing factor, interest in such things being largely confined to Europe.[3] Finnish business circles, however, were conscious of the American civil war, since it caused disturbances at sea and dangers to international trade; the situation was looked at in the light of the experience of the Crimean war. The hope felt in the coastal towns of the Gulf of Bothnia of Finland getting its own trading flag was connected with this. At the same time it was hoped that the St Petersburg government would acknowledge Finland's own interests in the field of foreign trade by organising special commercial representation as well.

1. *The Polish revolt in the Finnish press*

When a new revolt broke out in Poland in January 1863, the danger of an international crisis loomed yet again. As seen in St Petersburg, many of the problems of 1830–1 were repeated. Russian policy sought above all to keep the suppression of the revolt and all measures connected with it as an internal affair of the empire. In this it was supported by Prussia, which also had Polish territory in its possession, and which was committed by the so-called Alvensleben convention to political and military solidarity with Russia.

Russian military activity in suppressing the Polish revolt and Prussia's supporting stand caused sharp reactions in western Europe, especially in France. Napoleon III's desire to act as the patron of liberation movements, and the anti-Russian character of British politics led to diplomatic intervention to achieve a conciliation in the Polish question. In the middle of April, France and Britain, with Austria and some other countries, informed St Petersburg of their opinion that the provisions of the international agreements of 1815 on the position of Poland were being violated, and they demanded that Russia put the agreements into effect.[5] This was a clear hint that Polish autonomy should be restored. However, the three great powers did not intend to initiate any kind of military intervention. In a second note delivered in St Petersburg in the middle of June, they defined their demands for the restoration of the special status of Poland in a specific six-point programme, which contained among other things summoning the Diet and ordering the use of Polish as an official language in the country's administration and schools.[6]

The outbreak of the revolt stimulated political activity among the Polish emigrants, especially in France but also in Britain and Sweden. They carried on a powerful propaganda campaign, and began to speculate on the possibility of a western military intervention on Poland's behalf, in which the role of Napoleon III was assumed to be critical.[7] In Sweden at this time, in addition to pro-Polish sentiments, there also appeared, mainly in circles around *Aftonbladet* and *Nya Dagligt Allehanda*, a political interest in what was happening — or was assumed to be happening — in Finland as well. In Finland, the revolt in Poland had not caused the same surprise as the first revolt. Finns were aware of the discontents which had surfaced in Poland since the beginning of the 1860s; they had been mentioned in the Finnish press,[8] and the Polish question had also been discussed in a few restricted circles.[9]

In the opening phase of the Polish revolt the Finnish newspapers, including *Helsingfors Tidningar*, *Suometar* and *Helsingfors Dagblad*, reported the revolt in accordance with the official Russian communiqués, which were published in the St Petersburg newspapers. According to these, the support for the revolt was narrowly-based and the rebels had acted in a bloodthirsty fashion; Russian officials and soldiers in Poland had experienced a kind of St Bartholomew massacre.[10] However, from the latter half of February Finnish newspapers began also to use foreign papers as sources of news on Poland, and to compare Russian and foreign sources with one another, criticising the content of the former. In this the Swedish newspapers were a ready help. Russian official news was seen as understating their own losses and exaggerating those of the Poles. *Helsingfors Tidningar* and *Helsingin Uutiset* may have been the first Finnish papers which, at the beginning of March, stated clearly that Russian reporting of the Polish revolt was unreliable, and in conflict with foreign news services.[11] A bold further step was taken when some Finnish papers began writing of Poland as waging a 'war of liberation', and referred to the earlier 'war of liberation' of 1830–1.[12] While the country's press had assumed for itself a very broad freedom in acquiring news, criticism of the Russian imperial army was difficult — and dangerous since it could involve *lèse-majesté*.

The interest of the Finns in the new Polish revolt was quite different from their passivity during the revolt of 1830–1. However they were not interested in the new revolt because the Poles had the same kind of autonomous status as Finland, but above all as an expression of the idea of nationalism. The attitude to the Polish revolt in its entirety constituted for the Finns a political-moral problem.[13] They were faced with two alternatives: should they demonstrate loyalty to the empire, and so think primarily of the inviolability of Finland's position, or was sympathy with an oppressed nation seeking freer conditions more important? Interest in Finland was also at this time directed to the general international situation, and to circumstances which pointed to crisis and danger of war. Such analysis began to have systematic features. The exchange of notes between the western powers and Russia on the Polish question was followed, as were the development of attitudes in different countries, and the different assessments of future international developments. The reaction in Finland to external events had become livelier, since the old time-lag was a thing of the past: news was received daily and foreign newspapers could be followed more easily.

From the end of April Russian troops were moved into Finland. This, besides causing the international situation to be followed more closely, caused a powerful wave of rumour, as in the opening phase of the Crimean war. The events of the crisis were far off, but the question was whether they might come closer and affect Finland in some way. In the spring of 1863, signs of a 'war of nerves' appeared in Finland. In Helsinki and many coastal towns there was a disturbed atmosphere, and in Åland, the Turku archipelago and some places on the coast there was even said to be panic.[14] On the coast of the Gulf of Bothnia, the terrifying memory of Admiral Plumridge once again became vivid.[15]

There was now a political press in Finland, although it was not entirely free. Nevertheless it published its own opinions on the international developments, and in some papers 'reviews of the week' and other summaries were published.

2. *The attitude of the liberals and Snellman in the international crisis*

The most influential groups in the formation of political opinion in the country were the intellectuals and the businessmen. But under the influence of their experiences of the Crimean war, other sections of Finnish society had also begun to react in a political way, especially over questions such as the country's status, and war and peace. It was now less difficult to distinguish who among the political groupings were the leaders, which were the newspapers which supported them, and who were the supporters. The supporters, however, were difficult to define; often it was a matter of a general attitude only, not of actively supporting any political aims. The liberals were led by a group of intellectuals, whose political attitudes had been moulded by the Crimean war and its consequences, and been influenced by Scandinavianism. The mouthpieces of this group were *Helsingfors Dagblad*, which dated from 1862, *Åbo Underrättelser*, and *Päivätär*, which began to appear in 1863.

The liberals represented a clear westward orientation, which seemed to free them in a remarkable way from political commitments, and led them to the view that Russia was 'remote' from Finland. Their purpose was above all to liberalise Finland's position in relation to Russia. Their endeavour to loosen the relationship between the two was shown, for example, when they began to speak of Finland's 'union' with Russia in connection with the international crisis of 1863. The liberals in different parts of Europe had, from the middle of the nineteenth century, been interested in international law, on which the development of an international system should be based.[16] This liberalism had a distinctly pacifist tone. In Finland too, liberal circles were interested in discussing such international questions: for example, a plan was put forward in the spring of 1863 by the young Leo Mechelin for an 'international league of diplomats', on the basis of whose arbitrations the maintenance of peace should be sought.[17]

The liberals believed that Finland's special status could be developed by swift bounds. At the beginning of 1863, *Helsingfors Dagblad* proposed a plan for establishing the country's own consuls abroad. Such hopes had been entertained since the end of the 1850s, when plans were put forward in Norway for Norwegian consuls as commercial representatives in important countries. In making this proposal the Finnish liberals were thinking of the problems that could arise if a new war broke out between the western powers and Russia. The postings of the consuls were planned in such a way that if the situation of the Crimean war period recurred, they would be situated in the countries hostile to Russia: in London, Marseilles, Constantinople, Alexandria and Quebec.[18] It would thus be a protective system for the country's foreign trade in the event of an international crisis. The liberals also contemplated a more general supervision of Finland's commercial interests abroad; this was reflected in the proposal to establish in Helsinki a special central institution, the '*konsulatdirektion*', to collect information from abroad and maintain contact with the consuls.[19] This institution was intended to function in the same way as the Swedish Board of Trade. These schemes corresponded with the hopes of business circles.

In the spring of 1863, the liberals proposed some very bold measures for the development of Finland's special political status; the international crisis was just then coming to a head. There were also contacts between the liberals and the Finnish emigrants in Stockholm. The latter criticised some liberals in Finland for being ready to publish their political dissatisfaction through anonymous 'letters from Finland' in the Stockholm press, while also being very cautious at home. *Helsingfors Dagblad* published an article on 15 April 1863 examining the case for Finnish neutrality. This article was a bold venture, but it was also unrealistic in two respects: first, the writer saw it as possible to rank the position of Finland with Switzerland and Belgium, both of which were neutral in their international arrangements. Secondly, it openly proposed that the initiative in proclaiming Finland neutral should be taken by the Swedish king, Karl XV.[20] These ideas took no heed of the true situation prevailing in the country; Russia had just begun to move in extra military forces to secure Finland so that Finland should not cause her any surprises in a new international crisis. *Åbo Underrättelser* published the same article complete two days later, to emphasise that such ideas were not supported by little groups only, but also by the 'majority of enlightened citizens'.[21]

These bold expressions of opinion put forward by the liberals related to a period when the outbreak of war between the western powers and Russia was thought to be possible. While the situation in itself prompted the liberals to publicise such schemes, speculation about the different alternative developments of the international situation was not unconnected with their behaviour. Privately they may have thought that if the western diplomatic intervention in the Polish question compelled Russia to make concessions in Poland, it could also lead to a wider reorganisation of the western, non-Russian areas of the empire. If on the other hand war were to break out between the western powers and Russia, and Russia should lose, then a programme for a change in the position of Finland had already been published in advance.

Neutrality was not at all a defined concept in the circumstances of the 1860s. Its content was primarily territorial demilitarisation, of which Åland provided a recent and near-at-hand example. In the Finnish case it was thus mainly a question of Russia's military withdrawal and Finland forming a 'separate islet' within the international system. The liberals were undoubtedly taking a risk with Russia, and started from the assumption that Russia, as a state that had lost a war, would be weak. They evidently wanted Sweden for her part to carry out certain diplomatic moves, as *Helsingfors Dagblad*'s dramatic appeal to Karl XV indicated. The liberals also wanted to ensure by one way or another that Finland should belong to the west.

The neutrality proposal for Finland published in *Helsingfors Dagblad* undoubtedly irritated the country's administration, and was noted in St Petersburg. The incident set the censorship authorities in motion because material had been made public which could be interpreted as a deviation from loyalty to the empire. As a natural consequence of this, *Helsingfors Dagblad* dropped all discussion of the question of neutrality for some time and returned only to the proposals about consulates.[22] *Åbo Underrättelser*, on the other hand, continued to discuss the idea of neutrality, and emphasised that it had the majority of enlightened citizens behind it. It explained too that there were examples in Europe of some parts of a country being proclaimed neutral; at issue was an objective which it was important and timely to achieve in a situation where war was possible and from the point of view of Finland's future generally. She would be protected from suddenly being drawn into war and would generally be assured of peaceful and undisturbed development. The paper was strikingly optimistic about the preservation of neutrality in wartime.[23] *Åbo Underrättelser* also thought it important for the realisation of its neutrality that Finland should have its own armed forces. These would be used only within the country's boundaries, and at the same time they would make the presence of Russian troops unnecessary. The paper was also critical of the use of the Finnish Guards Battalion to repress the earlier revolts in Poland and Hungary.[24]

In their basic political attitude, the fennomans differed from the liberals, in that they declared their loyalty to the empire, and sought to tranquillise public opinion against rumours of war. In addition, they criticised the 'belligerent opinions' published in certain Swedish papers, and the Finnish liberals in general. *Helsingfors Dagblad* was regarded as belonging to those who were stimulating 'war fever' in Finland; its declared aim of neutrality was held to be both impractical and disloyal. Opinions critical of the liberals were published in many papers.[25]

Snellman was nominated to the Senate in April 1863, by which means the fennomans had come into the position of a party of government, although criticism of him had appeared among them too.[26] They now had quite different prospects from before of getting their own aims realised within the country's administration. There began to appear in the attitude of the fennomans a sense of responsibility for the general conduct of business and for the course of events which characterises a party of government. An article of Snellman's, 'War or Peace' (*Krig eller fred*), published in *Litteraturblad* at the beginning of July, was important in forming political opinion. His approach was similar to that adopted by the Swedish foreign minister, C. Manderström, in the Swedish semi-official *Post och Inrikes-Tidningar* in April the same year.[27] Snellman's line was to sketch out a Finnish security policy to suit the prevailing international crisis. His starting point was the fennoman emphasis on loyalty to the Emperor; he condemned the speculation in Finland which the current situation had prompted, which included the hope of a drastic change in the country's position. To build on such a foundation was misleading; a war between Russia and Sweden would be dangerous precisely because Finland might again become divided territorially, which would be fatal to the nation's development. Russia would never — so Snellman believed — give up the whole of Finland. Snellman also criticised the view being expressed abroad that the Finns were dissatisfied with their lot; in a letter written about this time he wrote that it was important to impress Sweden above all, so that they would not build up false hopes there concerning Finland.[28] If this were successful, it would in turn influence France, where military intervention on behalf of Poland had been contemplated. The danger of Finland being drawn into a possible future war would thus be eliminated.

Snellman's 'War or Peace' article was clearly intended as an answer and a counter-move to the liberals' concept of neutrality; in it national aspirations and loyalty to the empire were fused. He feared that Poland's fate could befall Finland if war ever touched her territory. At the same time he assumed that Finland had the possibility of national development within the imperial framework. This opinion showed that his ideas had changed sharply since 1848. Snellman's caution sprang from his view that at the moment the best choice for Finland's development was a limited but externally secured independence. His article also expressed ideas which were important to St Petersburg — especially after the idea of Finnish neutrality had surfaced. The fact that he did not mince words undoubtedly had an effect in St Petersburg and his appointment to the Senate was a way of ruling Finland from St Petersburg, and at the same time ensuring that the country's policies were broadly based in the population.

Snellman's views in fact coincided with those of the patriarchal-conservative civil servants. Russia had changed, as had the attitude of its government towards Finland. Snellman viewed the future on two levels. First, the nation should not aspire to anything which could not at present be achieved and retained. When he spoke of 'the interests of the state', he meant that the Polish revolt was not to be handled as any kind of moral-political phenomenon. The attempt to protect Finland from war and crisis was also aimed at developing the 'large perspective', that is the strengthening of national consciousness and peaceful progress, and the aspirations for reform those elements contained within them. Snellman's becoming a senator had increased his sense of responsibility; the opposition man's commitment to ideology and partisan positions had to be left behind.

Snellman received strong support in the country's Finnish-language press, and the ideas and arguments contained in his article were repeated in many papers.[29] He clearly appealed particularly to the population of Pohjanmaa, and also to the business community there which had experienced the destruction of war only ten years earlier. Snellman saw himself as representing the majority of the Finnish people, while the liberals had declared that they spoke for the 'majority of enlightened citizens'. The difference was that Snellman's supporters were mostly far from Helsinki, in Pohjanmaa and the countryside generally, unlike those of the liberals in the towns, and in the province of Uusimaa. *Helsingfors Dagblad* defended itself against Snellman by returning to the idea of Finnish neutrality. The belief that Finland would be insulated from wars after the separation from Sweden had proved false; Finland was 'the area of the Russian empire that could be most easily damaged'. *Helsingfors Dagblad* maintained that Finland must above all avoid a 'war between brothers', i.e. against Sweden.[30] This paper admitted at the beginning of July that 'Finnish neutrality cannot be examined except as a question belonging to the future'. However it repeated its argument that a guarantee of the country's neutrality by the great powers must involve the interests both of Russia and of Sweden. However, it also wanted to emphasise Finland's 'international position', namely that the country was 'a sovereign state united to Russia'.[31] By this it did not mean full independence, but that Finland had her own interests to take care of on the international level too, which it called 'our foreign policy'. Giving due weight to these interests was seen as vital for the country's development.

Åbo Underrättelser had supported the line of *Helsingfors Dagblad* in the spring, but no longer took part in the debate in July. A little earlier it had met with difficulties from the censorship authorities, which may have prompted caution. At the beginning of September the ideas of the liberals' main paper received unexpected support from *Suometar*, which said that it wished Finland's position to be like those of Belgium and Switzerland, which would perhaps, make it possible, for the country to be freed from Russian troops and the upkeep of its own army.[32] The liberal *Päivätär*, which began to appear at the beginning of September, also hoped for 'a pacified status' for Finland as a perpetual right.[33]

The international crisis in 1863 set off a broad discussion in the country about a Finnish flag. This reflected the growth of national awareness, and a consciousness of the problems which emerged in the management of relations with foreign countries, particularly in times of crisis. Different proposals regarding a Finnish flag or a commercial ensign were initiated by intellectuals, the business community and the upper classes, argued on a theoretical basis, or from the viewpoint of trading interests. The various political views mentioned above concerning Finland's status had their part in this debate, which continued from spring to autumn in many of the country's papers. Most of the proposals took the Finnish coat of arms, inherited from the sixteenth century, as the starting-point, and resulted in a flag in red and yellow;[34] this was seen as representing the national tradition. *Helsingfors Dagblad* proposed a blue-yellow-red combination,[35] the same colours as the Swedish-Norwegian union flag: this undoubtedly concealed political sympathies for Scandinavia. Topelius, in *Helsingfors Tidningar*, put forward his own proposal for a Finnish flag of blue and white,[36] colours that were regarded as happily reflecting nature in Finland — the lakes in summer and the winter landscape. These two colours also, at the time, expressed loyalty to the empire, whose flag comprised both of them.

As was mentioned earlier, *Oulun Wiikko-Sanomat* had already discussed the flag question in 1862; it believed that Finland should get her own 'neutral flag' which, being distinct from others, would protect the country's merchant ships at sea in time of war.[37] In the discussions on the flag, a great number of proposals were advanced, even in provincial newspapers, criticism of the 'Dagblad flag' being clearly evident in them. The fennomans and the burghers of the Pohjanmaa towns thought it a 'dishonest' flag,[38] concealing a secret attempt to construct a political link between Finland and Sweden: by 'honesty' they meant that the country's own flag would clearly distinguish Finland as a nation of its own.

3. *Interest abroad in the Finnish question in connection with the Polish revolt*

In Sweden both press and public opinion took a strong stand for the Polish cause; but by contrast there appeared notably less anti-Russian opinion in the country generally, a factor influenced by the Crimean war.

Nya Dagligt Allehanda in its stern russophobia differed from many other papers. In April 1863 it published a series of articles on Swedish foreign policy, openly advanced the idea that Sweden should seek an alliance with the western powers, with the aim of beginning military action against Russia. The paper wanted Sweden to go back to the activist schemes which had been proposed at the time of the November 1855 agreement. These articles aroused great attention because of their extremism, and were answered in *Post och Inrikes-Tidningar* by the '*Krig eller fred*' article, which warned the Swedes against all 'politics of adventure'.[39] Its author was revealed as the country's then foreign minister, Manderström, and *Nya Dagligt Allehanda*'s belligerent articles, for his part, proved to be the work of a Finnish emigrant, Karl Wetterhoff. News of this spread through Stockholm's diplomatic channels to the foreign ministries of different countries.[40]

In the international crisis of 1863, *Nya Dagligt Allehanda* was the kind of general mouthpiece of the political emigrants in Sweden — Poles, Finns and some Russians. Even *Aftonbladet*, which had earlier expressed a similar line, criticised its habit of expressing uncompromising conclusions on the international situation as it affected Sweden. Over the Polish question, it did not approve the extremism of *Nya Dagligt Allehanda*, although it too felt strong sympathy towards the rebels.[41] This paper's russophobia and its relations with émigré circles also determined its attitude to the Finnish question. Despite the result of the Crimean war, it still hoped for a sharp turn in the country's political position. It was prone to see anti-Russian feeling among the Finns, to sustain its own political aspirations. It even reported at the end of May 1863 that the Finns were waiting for a chance of changing their rulers, and regarded a Swedish entry into their country with favour.[42] Both *Nya Dagligt Allehanda* and *Aftonbladet* gave great publicity to the visits to Sweden, in the spring of 1863, of the émigré politicians Konstantin Czartoryski, a Pole, and the exiled Russian revolutionary Mikhail Bakunin. Bakunin's visit caused a great sensation; he issued political statements, which covered the Finnish question: 'We offer our hand to Finland which, like the Poles, aims at freedom and independence.' He also emphasised that all enemies of the tsarist regime were his friends, and all its friends his enemies.[43] In Polish émigré circles they hoped for a second revolt which would ease the situation for them. Such aspirations were directed at Finland, concerning which they circulated political news corresponding more with their wishes than the facts. In relation to the Polish revolt, the 1862 agreement between the émigré agent Jordan and Qvanten had special significance. Qvanten acted in Stockholm on the executive of a Swedish organisation which supported Polish activity, besides which he acted as assistant to Bakunin.[44]

The Finnish question came up in the leading papers in France and Britain during the crisis of 1863, but only as a small item, since news of the Polish revolt dominated international politics from month to month. The idea of Finnish neutrality put forward by *Helsingfors Dagblad* in the middle of April was published in most of the significant papers in Paris and London, and for some months was the only important news on Finland.[45] In the situation of the time, it heightened speculation over a possible new direction in the course of events in northern Europe.

Among the leading British papers, *The Times* had taken a cautious attitude to the Polish revolt, while *The Morning Post* was very sympathetic to the aims of the Polish émigrés. The difference also showed in their attitudes to the Finnish question. *The Times* published little news on Finland and not a single article on the subject during the spring and summer, whereas *The Morning Post* gave more space to Finnish political news and published a leading article at the end of July on the feelings of the Finns. It reported that the Finns were politically oppressed and dissatisfied with their conditions, and that if war should break out and Sweden were involved, the Finns would not remain quiet.[46] This article may be explained by the close relations which *The Morning Post* had with the Polish émigrés.

The leading Parisian papers gave more attention to the Finnish question than did the British papers — which was linked to their greater activity in support of the Polish revolt. Furthermore, they got news through Stockholm, which also influenced their choice of news about Finland.[47] The *Journal des Débats*, for example, reported at the beginning of June that the Finns hoped for liberation from the Russian yoke, and that hostility towards those who ruled Russia was present among all levels of society.[48] It was typical that the article on Finland in *The Morning Post* was reported in several Parisian papers.[49] These papers also discussed the Russian troop movements into Finland[50] and carried reports from some Stockholm papers that Russia had begun to fortify Åland, contrary to the 1856 agreement.[51]

At the time of the Polish revolt the Finnish question was also discussed, at the diplomatic level. It was assumed that a general European war might result if France were to initiate a military intervention on behalf of the Poles. In such a situation it was suspected that Sweden might take the side of France, and use the opportunity to attack Finland.

The possibility of such an international crisis seems to have been discussed from March 1863 onwards at least among the diplomatic corps in Berlin. When the British envoy there thought it appropriate to examine such alternatives, Bismarck had held the assumptions put forward misleading, in so far as the information received by the Prussian foreign ministry from Stockholm did not justify the conclusion that Sweden was prepared to begin a war against Russia.[52] The British minister in Stockholm reported that dissatisfaction with Russia was a persistent characteristic of Finnish political sentiments,[53] while the French representative there described the situation rather as being that the country's inhabitants were not especially fond of Alexander, but had also made it clear that they did not want a return to union with Sweden.[54] In the reports of the French embassy in St Petersburg, attention was concentrated on the difference between Alexander's respective policies in Finland and Poland, but not on the political sentiments prevailing in Finland; they did not — at least in the opinion of the ambassador, Montebello — constitute a problem in the present international crisis. Britain did not recognise the existence of a 'Finnish question', but it still had an interest in Finland, since its trade relations there had developed continuously, and a consular representative had been stationed in Helsinki. The discussion over the Finnish flag interested the British foreign office, and the British consul in Helsinki reported Russian troops movements in Finland.[55]

For language reasons it was easy for the Swedish foreign ministry to follow the Finnish press, even if the resulting picture was liable to be one-sided because the Finnish-language part of the press got less attention. Sweden's chief consul in Helsinki also reported very carefully the movement of Russian troops into Finland in the summer of 1863, and the defence works which were being built in southern Finland.[56]

4. *Alexander II and the Russian 'shop-window' policy in Finland*

The diplomatic intervention of the western powers after the Polish revolt, and the resulting danger of war, led to extensive mobilisation in Russia, and from April onwards this involved Finland and the Baltic provinces. In all about 600,000 Russian troops were called to arms, including 120,000 in the Baltic area, and 33,000 in Finland.[57] Because the outcome of the Crimean war had been a new experience, the rulers of Russia wanted to avoid involvement in a second defeat, whether it should be a matter of the international crisis breaking out into a general armed conflict, or of diplomatic pressure. 'Russia's preparations will destroy allegations that she is weak', foreign minister Gorchakov told von Redern, the Prussian ambassador in St Petersburg, in April 1863.[58]

The attitude to Finland of the St Petersburg government when the Polish revolt broke out had been different from all earlier experiences, in that they tried to avoid political intervention and control in the country as far as possible — in spite of the fact that discussion of the Polish revolt and the international crisis in the Finnish press had become very free. Undoubtedly Finnish loyalty during the Crimean war played a part in this. It was undoubtedly a surprise for St Petersburg when *Helsingfors Dagblad* brought the political aspirations of the liberals for Finland's neutrality unequivocally into the open, appealing at the same time to the king of Sweden, and it caused embarrassment that the affair received attention abroad. St Petersburg also noted that the political activity of the

Finnish émigrés in Sweden was still vigorous and, besides, was linked to wide international contacts. The reports of the Russian ambassador in Stockholm gave detailed information about this.[59] Obviously the Third Section of the Russian interior ministry, which had the functions of a political police, had its own sources of information in Stockholm. The news that Bakunin had arrived in Stockholm in April 1863 also caused anxiety in St Petersburg.[60]

From the end of April political control in Finland increased. It was thought expedient to tighten the censorship, primarily because of the behaviour of the liberals. This control soon became evident as well, both in *Helsingfors Dagblad* and in *Åbo Underrättelser*,[61] and on the initiative of St Petersburg, with Minister-Secretary A. Armfelt and Governor-General Rokassovski as intermediaries, steps were taken in Finland to have special loyal addresses sent to the Emperor, as had happened in other parts of the empire.[62] The purpose of such measures was to counter the ideas of the liberals on Finnish neutrality, and foreign assertions that the Finns were dissatisfied and of questionable loyalty. Both the groups whose support for an address was sought, namely the teachers of Helsinki University and the burghers of the larger towns, took a negative attitude.[63] They did not want to deny their loyalty to the Emperor, but they thought that if addresses were sent to him, other things would follow. Above all they wanted to avoid in any way giving their approval to Russian measures to suppress the Polish revolt.[64] The sending of such addresses could easily be interpreted as expressing general confidence in Russian imperial policy. The liberal papers and the fennoman *Suometar* and *Helsingin Uutiset* were on the subject of the addresses. Snellman, however, took a stand in their support.[65] This not only reflected his new position and his caution, but perhaps was also an attempt to limit the numbers of Russian troops in Finland.

St Petersburg in fact failed to get addresses from Finland, but it did not react openly. It was announced in May that the Finnish Guards Battalion would not be used for duties in the empire, and would not even be sent to the annual training camp near St Petersburg,[66] but would be reserved for duties connected with the defence of Finland.

The crisis forced the Emperor to make concessions by which he sought to eliminate dangers from various directions, and to attach the Finns firmly to the 'imperial front'. It also forced from Alexander's policy the kind of solutions for Finland which were at least partly dictated by necessity. They also perhaps went further than the solutions which the government had intended to carry out in the immediate future. Their purpose was in any case to serve realistically such Russian interests as were involved in broad views of the future. Alexander II acted towards Finland as Alexander I had done in face of a different kind of threat.

At the same time as Alexander II rejected the second western diplomatic intervention in the Polish revolt he also, on 18 June 1863, made two important decisions on Finland. He ordered the summoning of the country's Diet for the first time since 1809 and issued a special decree on language, whereby Finnish was decreed the country's second official language alongside Swedish. These decisions on Finland were similar to some of those which, in their June note, the western powers had demanded should be carried out in Poland, but which Alexander had rejected.[67] Alexander's 'hard-line policy' on Poland was not only determined by the fact that a rebellion had been raised there; it was also an area of strategic importance to Russia. Finland was less important in the military sense, even if it was not insignificant, a circumstance which helped to create a 'soft-line policy' in that part of the empire. Finnish loyalty in the Crimean war was especially important, and with the threat of war and other dangers, the Emperor tried to build further on that foundation.

Alexander's decisions on Finland were designed to fulfil a variety of aims. Through them he sought to influence Finnish society down to the lowest levels, as in the language decree, which reflected a new phase in St Petersburg's attitude, to the finnicisation movement. An earlier international crisis had resulted in the 1850 censorship decree, which reflected a quite different attitude to the Finnish language. Alexander also sought to eliminate the danger of a 'second revolt' in the empire. This was intended as a blow not only against the Polish émigré propaganda, but also against speculation on the danger of war, generally in the west. A policy of concession in Finland aimed to knock the bottom out of the continuing activity of the Qvanten group in Stockholm. The same applied to Bakunin, who had sought to extend his activities to Finland — where copies of his secret publications and the paper *Kolokol* were found.[68]

The bloody image of Russian policy created by the suppression of the Polish revolt, and the anti-Russian feelings in the west were a great problem for Alexander, the more so since western diplomatic activity over the Polish question was continuing. By adopting a liberal line on Finland, he also wanted to make it a 'show window' to the west for a kind of Russian policy that was different from his policy on Poland.

The considerable significance of the Finnish question in overall Russian policy in the international crisis of 1863 is shown in the two visits which Alexander II made to Finland at this time. On the first one, he carried out an inspection at Parola camp of the Guards Battalion and the nine battalions of militia which had been called into service. This gesture had a political significance, since it sought to emphasise the relation of mutual trust between the Emperor and his Finnish subjects in the prevailing crisis. And the fact that Snellman, who had promoted the language manifesto, was presented to Alexander was closely associated with the image created by the Parola review. It was meant to demonstrate the atmosphere of loyalty and the gathering of the nation around the ruler in a politically new way. Since the battalions at Parola had been assembled from different parts of the country, the news of the inspection spread widely.[69]

Alexander's second Finnish visit was connected with the opening of the Diet on 15 September. The Finnish Diet was now, after more than half a century, once more a reality — in itself a major political change. Alexander wanted to follow clearly liberal solutions, as his speech opening the Diet showed. He said the constitutional system was one which 'the sentiments of the Finnish people favour and which has grown together with the country's laws and institutions'. Thus Alexander, an autocrat in Russia, recognised clearly Finland's own political and social traditions and the significance of public opinion in the country. In his speech he also sought to emphasise his belief in the political loyalty of the Finns. He hoped 'the Finnish Estates will show that free institutions cause no danger to the nation which, with the aid of common sense, is working to develop its conditions.'[70] He distinguished the Finns clearly from the rebellious Poles, and in this sense showed Finland off to the west. At the time of the opening of the Diet, a large parade was held in Helsinki, with about 20,000 men taking part, mainly crack Russian troops. Rumours had been circulating that major military manoeuvres would be organised in the vicinity, but these did not happen.[71] From a military point of view, the festivities had a clear imperial motive. Although Alexander had made significant concessions in Finland's internal affairs, the unyielding line of Russian policy for the empire as a whole was still emphasised. Foreign policy and military affairs were imperial questions.

5. *The beginning of the work of the Diet in Helsinki — Finnish and foreign viewpoints*

For the whole first half of the nineteenth century, politics in Finland had been of interest to small groups only, while society had been firmly directed from above. But now politics had become a matter for society at large. The development begun at the end of the Crimean war, manifested by a continuous expansion of the political press and public opinion, had led to a solution with effects seen on all sides, including the farming population. Politics and political activity had become acknowledged as a right. Different ideological tendencies and economic and social interests could now be expressed through the Diet. Autonomy, which up to then had primarily taken the form of independent administrative activity, began to be seen, through the activity of the Diet, as involving legislation and the making of various economic decisions. The four Estates represented Finnish society in different ways, but in their entirety only a part of it, perhaps a little over 30 per cent of the country's population. In spite of this they formed a national representative institution, whose representativeness was remarkable compared with the previous situation in which the Diet had no existence at all. The first of the Estates, the nobility, represented only a small group, but it included those accustomed to the handling of public affairs, like many of the country's leading civil servants, which gave it authority. The clerical estate to which, by the Diet ordinance of 1869, university and secondary-school teachers were entitled to elect representatives, gathered within itself social experience, especially in local government and public education; in addition it was significant as representing the educated element in society. The representatives of the Estate of burghers were elected by the wealthy elements in the urban population, from independent entrepreneurs to property-owners. The Estate of the farmers represented the wealthiest of that group, whose right to vote in Diet elections was regulated by their land-tax assessments. The power of the Emperor was preserved after 1863 as before, but his role appeared different from what it had been. The dynamic forces at work in society and the enterprise in economic activity weakened and limited the grip of patriarchalism, even if it was not altogether eliminated.

The political atmosphere in Helsinki at the time of the Diet's opening was enthusiastic: a new era was beginning, with the most varied possibilities of development. The Emperor was seen not as a ruler, but as the supporter of reforms and the guide of development. Alexander's 'speech from the throne' contributed to this, by making the institution of the Diet an event pointing to the future, and by promising reforms in different fields, including additional rights for the Diet.

The fennomans felt all this to be their special achievement since, led by Snellman, they had been emphasising that loyalty and confidence in the Emperor were the basis for progress in the country. *Helsingin Uutiset* called the Diet's meeting the 'birthday of national liberation'[72]; Finland was being 'raised into the society of nations'.[73] The Diet could not fail to have a powerful effect on the liberals too, although their attitude was not so unreservedly favourable since they did not really trust the promises that had been given. *Helsingfors Dagblad* declared, just before the opening: 'We are moving into a new period of our history, with fluctuations no one can foresee, but on which, however, the whole future fate of Finland will depend.'[74] It was a question of a clear commitment to a vision of Finland's political future and, for certain aspirations also, a break with the past. The spirit of constitutionalism and liberal principles were what finally gave the liberals the impetus to move ahead, in spite of what they had publicly proposed in the spring of the same year. The 'Finnish state' was the axiom on which they relied, believing it to be the starting-point for continuing changes in Finland's status, with constitutionalism its driving force. The commitment to constitutional political life pushed aside those hopeful visions which Scandinavianism had maintained until then, mainly among the liberals. The era during which, from 1809 onwards, small groups and individuals had been able to speculate in various contexts on the idea that major change could occur in the status of Finland, i.e. a 'return to the old way', or union with Sweden, had finally ended. Clearly the Finnish liberals, in the political atmosphere of the autumn of 1863, had not said everything that was in their minds.

In the British and French press, the meeting of the Finnish Diet in September 1863 was accorded the status of important political news. It was a novel development in the international crisis. Important British newspapers like *The Times* and *The Standard* published Alexander II's speech to the Finnish Diet, but

without comment.[75] British policy in relation to the international situation
had become very restrained from the spring of 1863, also over the Polish question; Britain was clearly stepping to the sidelines.[76] The calling of the Diet
was welcomed from the point of view of British political tradition; in so far as
there were some doubts regarding Russia's political motives, they were not
expressed.

The French press reacted rather differently. The official *Le Moniteur* published
Alexander's speech after a conspicuous delay, and was clearly irritated by the
unbending tone of Gorchakov's reply to the new French note on the Polish
question.[77] Openly critical views on Russian policy in general were published in
the other Parisian papers, together with news of Alexander's speech and the
meeting of the Finnish Diet. The influence of the Polish question was clear. The
Journal des Débats remarked that the Diet granted to Finland was a good omen
on the Russian side, but nothing more; it also stressed that its significance made
the Polish question a European problem, and what had happened in Helsinki
could not in any way mitigate Russia's conduct.[78] Also, the great parade of
Russian troops in Helsinki coinciding with the meeting of the Diet did not pass
unnoticed by some Parisian papers.[79]

The leading papers of Germany also discussed events in Finland in the autumn
of 1863. Polish events had been continuously to the fore, since they were close at
hand and Prussia had her own problems with her Polish minority. What was
written about Finland concerned Russian defence measures there, the meeting
of the Diet and Alexander's speech.[80] These items continued after the Diet
began work, and gave the impression that a significant change was taking place,
which truly gave expression to autonomy.[81]

In the Swedish press the meeting of the Diet was presented as a great event
leading to changes in the country's fortunes. Everything on the other side of the
Gulf of Bothnia which indicated a western European development was noted
with satisfaction;[82] this was natural for those circles which had given up all
political hope of Finland's return, after the end of the Crimean war, but on the
other hand *Aftonbladet* and *Nya Dagligt Allehanda* found it considerably more
difficult to accept the course of events. Alexander's behaviour in Helsinki was,
in the opinion of *Aftonbladet*, a carefully calculated playing of the liberal role.
This paper saw Alexander's conduct in Helsinki as greatly influenced by the
contemporary situation elsewhere in Europe; it was an attempt to conceal the
'Polish horrors' by liberal-sounding actions elsewhere in the empire.[83] *Nya
Dagligt Allehanda* described the events connected with the summoning of the
Finnish Diet as 'a unique performance in world history', when the mighty
autocrat of Russia appeared as a constitutional monarch in small, subordinate
Finland; Alexander's speech was 'a significant fact, which gives rise to great
joy', and if the promises were realised, it would lead to a genuinely constitutional form of government in Finland.[84] On Russian policy in Poland, the paper
affirmed that events in Helsinki were a ray of light, while elsewhere in Europe
'the unrestrained advance of barbarian executioners' proceeded. It made a wild

attack on Snellman, who, it maintained, had scorned the country's liberal opposition, and was now trying to claim the credit for what had happened in Finland. The fennoman newspapers *Helsingin Uutiset* and *Suometar* both reacted with scorn to these articles, and hoped that Finland could at last break free from submission to the tutelage of Sweden.[85] *Helsingfors Dagblad* and other liberal papers took no part in the caustic dialogue across the Gulf of Bothnia.

In Russia too they had begun to criticise the political development that had occurred in Finland. In the background was the strongly nationalist intellectual reactions produced in the empire by the Polish revolt — a tendency of which M.N. Katkov became the leading figure. In Katkov's view, Finland too was becoming a growing problem for the Russian empire; its political aspirations represented 'federalism', which sought to fragment the united Russian state. He did not approve of the summoning of the Finnish Diet.[86] However, in 1863 only a few articles on Finland appeared in Katkov's mouthpiece, *Moskovskiya Vedomosti*, mainly because the Russian censorship presented obstacles. In the articles which he did get published, irritation with *Helsingfors Dagblad* was expressed, because in the spring of 1863 it had advanced the idea of Finnish neutrality, and had alluded many times to Finland as a state.[87]

Helsingfors Dagblad and *Åbo Underrättelser* set themselves to rebuff Katkov's attacks on Finland. Both sides used a strident tone. The arguments of the liberals against Katkov were of two kinds. They began by claiming that he did not understand Finland's special status of Finland, and furthermore gave false information about it. They also pointed out that Katkov's views were representative of only a narrow circle among the Russians.[88]

Dissatisfaction with the interpretation of the Finnish liberals, that the relations of Finland and Russia were 'contractual' and to be classified as 'a genuine union', also appeared in the Russian foreign ministry, on whose initiative Minister-Secretary Armfelt arranged for an article on the Finland's status to be published in the *Journal de St Petersbourg* in January 1864.[89] In this article, which was semi-official, the views in *Helsingfors Dagblad* were 'political metaphysics'; Finland was a country united to the Russian empire, which had administrative autonomy, but which in 'political questions' was dependent on the empire. Alexander II also intervened in his closing speech to the Finnish Diet on 15 April 1864, referring to certain discussions in the Diet on Finland's status, in which 'errant ideas' about the relationship of the Grand Duchy to the empire had been expressed. It was in Finland's interest to try 'to strengthen, and in no way weaken her close ties with Russia'. From this, evidently, St Petersburg was dissatisfied over some debates in the Diet. Because of Finland's dependent position and the inviolability of the sovereign, it followed that no comment on the Emperor's speech was published in the Finnish press.[90] Alexander's warning stopped discussion of Finland's special status in the country's press for several years.

There was a kind of intellectual after-effect of the crucial year 1863 in Finland, concerned with western orientation, i.e. Scandinavianism and Sweden. The war of 1864 between Denmark and Prussia ended in a Danish defeat and the loss of Slesvig-Holstein. Here the fennomans criticised Denmark, which had based its policy on the assumption that in a crisis it would be helped by Sweden. *Suometar* said that the fate of Denmark was a lesson to those in Finland who had claimed that Sweden was prepared to help neighbouring countries in diffi-culties.[91] *Suometar* said that a nation should rely only on itself, and *Helsingfors Tidningar* that nations should aim only at what they could achieve by their own resources.[92] Hence the liberals' aspirations to develop Finland's special status in the spring of 1863, and all other far-reaching aspirations, had been utopias. Scandinavianism finally lost all its support in Finland after the defeat of Denmark. Finland was part of the Russian empire, not only because of Alexander II's proclamation, but because of the Finns' loyalty. From the autumn of 1864 Snellman assumed that progress lay ahead, but that all advances must be cautious. This was particularly so in connection with further develop-ments in autonomy, once the continuation of statutory meetings of the Diet was secured. Snellman was especially cautious on issues that could affect the powers of the sovereign, or infringe his authority.

In the new circumstances the liberals followed a policy of western constitu-tionalism, and in the autumn of 1863 had sought, by means of various petitions to the Diet, to get Finland's special status further strengthened. Katkov's attacks had clearly come as something of a shock to them, and caution could be seen in their attitudes, especially after the Emperor's speech delivered at the closing of the Diet in April 1864. At the same time, belief in a further develop-ment of the country's special status was clearly weakened, at least for a time.

The year of political transition coincided with a degree of economic insta-bility. The boom period, when the American civil war had boosted Finland's tar exports, had now weakened. Fear of war in the spring of 1863 had a fall in exports, and a price increase. The grain harvest was satisfactory, however, and prices dropped during the latter half of the year.[93]

The Finnish question, as a 'marginal case' of interest in international politics, was pushed to one side after the 1863 crisis. There had been specific views concerning Finland in foreign countries during that time of transition, but when it passed they almost disappeared. After 1863 news of Finland in the leading papers of Britain and the continent was infrequent.

After 1863 attitudes to Finland changed in Sweden to the extent that all Swedes recognised Finland as being part of the Russian empire. A new image began to take shape, in which the growing language struggle in Finland was an important ingredient. In the highest social echelons in both countries, there was a feeling that native Swedes and Finnish Swedes had a special relationship, akin to a great family.[94] In the period that followed, Runeberg, for example, could be placed in the vanguard of western culture against Slavonic influences in Finland; this was how it was expressed in the introduction to his collected works, published in Stockholm in 1873.[95]

In the view of St Petersburg, the Baltic had formed, in 1863–4, an area more or less free of military problems. Sweden had settled quietly in her place, after the wings of Scandinavianism had been finally clipped. Denmark had suffered military humiliation, and even Britain had not intervened in her favour. Prussia had grown in military strength, but she had no naval power. Since the dangers had thus become very slight, the Russian troops were mostly withdrawn from Finland from the beginning of 1864. Finland's strategic significance for Russia had also lost its urgency — and the country seemed politically reliable. It may be seen as one consequence of this change that the Finnish field battalions, with their low military value, were disbanded in 1867, and no new military units were established in their place. After this Finland was long a military vacuum, which could, however, easily and rapidly be filled, especially as the railway from Riihimäki to St Petersburg neared completion.

IX. The Franco-Prussian war and the Paris Commune; Finnish reaction to events in Europe

After the end of the Crimean war the pressure for change from the system of 1815 increased within the European international system. Nationalism was becoming important in international relations as a dynamic force operating across existing frontiers. Here the unification process in Italy and Germany in the 1860s gave a general character to developments in the western half of Europe, and brought about major changes. As historical phenomena, both movements were centripetal in character; while nationalism was a unifying factor, in each case the national phenomenon had a specific ideological content.

In the post-1863 period both Britain and Russia adopted a more passive role in European affairs. The centres of activity and the crises in the European international system had become concentrated in continental Europe, and after 1863–4 the Baltic was not involved in major events. The Franco-Prussian war of 1870–1 formed a new turning-point in the relations of the continental great powers. Prussia's victory over France was followed by the unification of Germany, a state which played a leading European role. France, in contrast to its earlier central role, was condemned, in consequence of its defeat, to an isolated position in high politics. The era of great changes in continental Europe ended with the Franco-Prussian war; only the Balkans remained as a separate area susceptible to future change.[1]

Another characteristic of this period was the continuing growth of industry in different countries, the extension of large-scale capitalism, and the growth in the importance of the banking system.[2] There was also a general expansion of communications. Economic development united the powers in quite a new way into a functioning entity. This in turn affected international relations, in which questions of investment, tariff policies, railways and all kinds of traffic became closely linked with diplomatic activity. Also, the international capital markets controlled from London and Paris began to influence Europe's whole economic development, extending even as far as the Russian empire.

The emergence of an organised labour movement was a consequence of this economic and social development. The founding of the German Social Democratic party in 1863 and the activity of the First International, founded the following year, underlined the demand for social change. The spectre of a social revolution raised by the workers' movement and its internationalism and new forms of action made of it a terrifying counter-force to the prevailing system — with a potential power which was hard to gauge. The new political-social ideas were to be given forceful expression in the Paris Commune of 1871. Its three-month-long activity and the phenomena associated with it — the overthrow of old traditions and acts of violence — formed a kind of terror-image of socialism, which the press spread across frontiers.

After the meeting of the Diet in the autumn of 1863, Finland had moved into a new period of internal development. This was reinforced by the Diet Act of 1869, which required the statutory summoning of the Diet every five years. During this period, a series of major reforms were enacted including the currency reform of 1863–5 (the introduction of the silver mark), the rural local government reform of 1865, the 1866 primary school law, the Diet Act of 1869, the church statute and the 1873 urban government reform.

From the mid-1860s there was a time of economic depression; 1865 was a year of crop failure, and the great famine of 1867–8 was not confined to Finland but spread widely over Europe from the Iberian peninsula to north Russia. After the 1865 crop failure, the Finns expected that the international market would be replenished, causing the price of grain to fall. On both counts they were mistaken: uncertainty prevailed in continental Europe in the wake of the war of 1866 between Prussia and Austria; this caused stockpiling of grain against emergencies, and then a strong demand followed because of the extent of the harvest failure. At the same time, Finland's export prices were falling.[3] This situation shook confidence in the power of the state, and Snellman had to resign from the Senate. He also had to endure partisan attacks from the country's Swedish-speakers.

The great crop failure of 1867, in which over 100,000 Finns died of hunger and other consequences, hastened reforms in agriculture, for example the development of dairy farming, which made butter an important export item. It also influenced the general outlook: there developed a greater mobility and a shift in the farming community from a subsistence to an exchange economy.

Economic activity was increasing in many ways and the shock of these bad years was one factor speeding it up. At the same time, the religious idea of Providence as an all-embracing force extending even to the everyday life of the individual began to lose its force. The fact that Finland had hitherto been relatively isolated from foreign countries was now felt to be harmful since it slowed down general development: 'A closer association among the peoples', said *Uusi Suometar* at the beginning of 1870, 'is now the necessary condition of all progress, whether on the spiritual or the material level.'[4] The breaking of the dominance of agriculture was clearly under way from the end of the 1860s. The growth in the demand for timber in the world markets hastened the birth of the timber processing industry. However the industrialisation thus set in motion was limited to a narrow sector. The structural change in the economy took place two decades later than in Sweden, but once begun it accelerated more rapidly.[5]

The development of industry in Finland was influenced by very different factors. Besides the increase in the international demand for timber, the development of prices was generally favourable to the sellers, since transport costs were reduced as steamships became more general in freight traffic. Certain spontaneous factors, like the abolition of mercantilist restrictions, also played a part.[6]

The timber processing centres attracted new concentrations of population, but the social consequences of industrialisation extended far from the centres of industry. The rural population of great areas of the interior took part in cutting, hauling and floating of timber; thus people who had previously lived static lives came at certain seasons of the year to be mobile. Peoples' traditional attitudes began to change and information circulated more freely.

Finland's timber industry started the process of integrating the country into the economic development of western Europe. Exports grew, purchasing power became greater, and there were consequences in the organisation of everyday life. For Finland to have her own currency at a time when it was sorting out its economic relations with other countries was important. Another new feature was the raising of loans for the purposes of the Finnish state on the international money market. Finland also began to feel the effects of international economic recessions. The first such was experienced after several boom years in the mid-1870s, when the experience of social insecurity acquired a new dimension. With the money economy spreading even into the lumber camps, money became the new social yardstick to measure the difference between rich and poor. The new phenomena were criticised — based not on any ideology but on concrete experience of life. The causes of the market phenomena, which were the focus of the criticism, led back to the continental countries, but the socialist ideologies born there with the development of industry had not extended their influence to peripheral Finland.[7]

In the 1870s and 1880s, Finland became a uniform territorial entity in a way quite different from before. Pohjanmaa came to be integrated with southern Finland, especially after the railway had been extended from Hämeenlinna first to Tampere and thence to Vaasa at the beginning of the 1880s. Eastern Finland had lagged behind the western parts of the country in many respects, culturally as well as economically, but the opening of the Saimaa Canal meant that large areas in the east of the country ceased being permanently backward areas. The importance of Viipuri grew as a port for the inland regions. At the same time, St Petersburg exercised a permanent influence on the economic development of eastern Finland.

The centre of gravity of the economic life of the country was shifting to southern Finland. Helsinki, as the capital, had its own magnetism, and Turku was the centre of perhaps the wealthiest part of the country. The significance of Pori grew as it came to be an important centre of the timber trade and Rauma became important for shipping.

The country's press had grown significantly over a long period, even if at the end of the 1860s — in the midst of economic difficulties — some Finnish-language journalistic enterprises had come to grief.[8] The proportion of foreign news in the Finnish press, both Swedish- and Finnish-language, had been increasing all the time.

A certain 'world picture' was taking shape in Finland, among some sections of society; the intellectual divisions which were forming in the country gave it its definition. In addition international cultural tendencies and foreign trade connections were influencing the Finnish outlook on Europe.[9] Interest in France had originated among the upper class at the end of the eighteenth century; this represented the so-called Gustavian cultural tradition. On the other hand, interest in Germany appeared in fennoman circles, especially from the mid-nineteenth century onwards. Snellman's Hegelianism had expressed such an orientation. The intellectual debate, coloured by this philosophy, which went on in Germany in the 1850s and 1860s as the nation sought a common expression and unifying ideals, reflected in a similar debate among the fennomans, within their narrower framework. In contrast to France and Germany, Britain remained somewhat excluded from the Finns' intellectual and cultural interests: this was true of both the Swedish-speaking upper class and the leaders of the finnicisation movement. In some areas, influences from Britain had certainly been absorbed, for example economic liberalism and Darwinism; yet British culture was generally, little known in Finland. Contact with Britain and knowledge of English were largely limited to those who had commercial dealings with western Europe, or were engaged in seaborne trade.

There was awareness among the farmers of the generally advanced condition of western Europe on the basis of both newspapers and trade contacts.[10] There was a similar conception of Sweden, with which trade relations from the west coast still persisted. At the other extreme, in the eyes of farming circles, was Turkey. With the backwardness of their conditions of life and their baseness, the Turks represented, as they had done in the past, the prototype of the pagan — a view supported in Finland by the Lutheran tradition. The political occurrences abroad which interested the Finns above all were connected with the advance of nationalism. Increasingly, what the papers reported dealt with the political systems of the various countries, and efforts to change them. On the other hand the social problems which went with the growth of industry, and such new developments as the workers' movement, did not yet arouse interest in the 1860s; in Finland there was no politically conscious social element that was sufficiently receptive. Such happenings as the founding of the Social Democratic party in Germany in 1863 and the founding congress of the International in London the next year do not seem to have been picked up by the Finnish press at this stage, even as small news items. Although distance had ceased to act as an isolating and delaying factor in the transmission of influences, the general level of development was still, in many areas of Finland, so far from that in the developed western countries only the upper levels of society were receptive to them on any significant scale.

The government in St Petersburg thought that such major political events on the continent of Europe in the 1860s as the war between Prussia and Austria in 1866 did not cause such changes in the international system as would have made a major reassessment necessary. On the other hand, St Petersburg began to see in the ideas representing social revolution — whether appearing as socialism or anarchism — a threat of a wholly new kind. Ideas of social revolution which emphasised the principles of internationalism were seen as especially dangerous in that they moved freely across state frontiers. These dangers had a particular topicality in Russian government circles when an attempt was made to assassinate Alexander II in 1866. One of the consequences was a new conservative trend in education policy. School discipline was tightened and subjects dealing with current affairs were replaced in favour of classical languages, etc. [11]

Echoes of the change of direction in Russian internal politics, due to the perceived threat of social revolution, [12] were soon seen in Finland too. In 1869 Adlerberg, the Governor-General, began to enforce the new education system which had been in preparation for a long time. The overall purpose of the school system was once more to maintain social obedience, i.e. a return to the bureaucratic-conservative views of the popular education committee of 1851. The decree setting up a Finnish education department was approved in 1869, its task to ensure that 'a right idea of the duties of the subject and respect for authority' was given. It was striking how, in the field of cultural administration, the role of the Governor-General was especially emphasised; he was to nominate the leading members of the new education department. [13] General von Kothen was recalled once again, this time as director of the department. The appointment of an army general to take charge of Finnish education clearly expressed the reactionary mood in St Petersburg, in a situation where they feared foreign revolutionary propaganda spreading inside the country's borders. Kothen's particular role as guardian of law and order is shown by his simultaneous appointment as vice-chancellor of Helsinki University. Direct in his methods, Kothen was interested in bringing Finland and Russia closer together. Therefore he favoured the extension of the teaching of Russian in the country at the expense of Finnish. In addition he clearly wanted to guide the Finnish élite into state service, as had been done earlier with the Baltic Germans.

This was also a difficult time for the Finnish church, as the new church ordinance was submitted to the sovereign for confirmation. The relation of 'throne and altar' in Finland became somewhat looser than before as a result of this ordinance. The Lutheran church came to form a unit of its own, while the handling of its business would be carried on at a lower level, more 'democratically,' than before. [14] However the Diet, as the legislative body, still had authority over it, and the position of the Emperor remained unchanged, in that he could still exercise a veto. But he could not, as before, influence the undertaking of business within the church.

Alexander II thus generally maintained the liberal line in Finland, and this prompted gratitude among many fennoman leaders. In their view, at a time when reaction was in the ascendant in Russia, there had been a 'battle for the Emperor's soul' — and for Finland the great danger had passed. It also meant that the line of development begun in 1863 could still be followed successfully.

After the international crisis of 1863, the Finnish press followed the major events in continental Europe attentively, although the danger of war had clearly receded.[15] Prussia's attack on Denmark in 1864 in order to annexe Schleswig-Holstein, was condemned in the leading Finnish papers. Both *Helsingfors Dagblad* and *Suometar* criticised Prussian militarism, and the latter stressed that 'German nationalism had turned into a mockery and a derision of the nationalist aspirations of our century.[16] *Helsingfors Tidningar* joined in the same line of criticism, saying that 'Prussia . . . is a military state best represented by bayonets'.[17] However, Snellman deviated from this line of thought when he emphasised that Germany was a land of culture, within which national solidarity worked as an important intellectual force.[18] With the setting up of the North German Confederation, which brought the unification of Germany an important step nearer, the position of the leading Finnish papers began to change gradually into one more favourable to Prussia,[19] and criticism began to be directed at Austria, which was seen as a backward state and an obstacle to national development.[20] The change which occurred affected both fennomans and liberals; among the fennomans there was even a certain urge to defend the policy of Prussia and an admiration of things German.[21]

The attitudes of the leading papers to the German question were principally ideological; only a few also noted the consequences which the victory of Prussia could have for the international system. *Helsingfors Dagblad* was one such exception. In its opinion the traditional continental balance of power was being upset at the expense of France; this paper was clearly pro-French in its attitudes.[22] The fennoman Yrjö Koskinen also assumed that the strengthening of Germany's position was a fact, but in *Kirjallinen Kuukausilehti* he drew attention to the change which had occurred from the Russian point of view. Prussia was seen as eager for conquests and nationally arrogant and he described Bismarck as a dishonest diplomat.[23]

After the Franco-Prussian war broke out in August 1870, the events of that war occupied centre-stage in the Finnish press for the next six months. Although Finland was in the position of a complete outsider *vis-à-vis* the war, it took a strong stand towards the belligerent parties. France had declared war on Prussia, and was thus ostensibly the aggressor, but, the leading liberal papers, *Helsingfors Dagblad* and *Åbo Underrättelser*, were clearly sympathetic to the French side,[24] an attitude which was probably common to the country's leading Swedish-speaking circles. France had occupied a central place as a great power in Europe, and Napoleon III had succeeded in creating an image of himself as the advocate of the idea of liberation. By contrast Bismarck was hated among liberals — a general European phenomenon since the period of constitutional crisis in Prussia at the beginning of the 1860s. Attitudes were also influenced by the cultural ties of Finland's Swedish-speakers with France. In addition, sympathy for France was strong in Sweden, and the press there mostly came to its defence.

Uusi Suometar, on the contrary, stood openly on the Prussian side from the

beginning of the war. To the fennomans nationalism had become more important than before; its realisation, irrespective of the means employed, was a value
and achievement in itself. *Uusi Suometar* virtually acted as Bismarck's advocate,
and at the same criticised France.[25] It found itself somewhat isolated in the early
phase of the war, because the provincial papers on both sides of the language line
took a stand generally sympathetic to France. It is typical of reporting in Finnish
papers at this time that France, although she originated the war, was not generally criticised, except by *Uusi Suometar*. *Åbo Underrättelser* even saw Bismarck's
diplomatic activity as being a precisely calculated influence behind the outbreak
of war.[26]

When the battle of Sedan ended in the defeat of France, feelings in the Finnish
papers ran high. *Uusi Suometar* commended Germany for having 'brilliantly
repelled' France's rash aggression;[27] the paper's followers were 'truly enrap-
tured' by the victory.[28] The commitment of *Helsingfors Dagblad* and some other
papers to France had been so strong that they reacted to the battle of Sedan with
both astonishment and bitterness. They criticised Prussia in a number of ways
— for example, accusing her of treating prisoners badly and alleging that her
methods of warfare were barbaric. *Åbo Underrättelser* in February 1871 even
announced it was launching a collection in Finland because of the pitiful state of
France.[29] *Uusi Suometar* also enthused over the formation of a united German
empire, which resulted from the war. The paper emphasised that 'the German
people . . . have contributed enormously to the civilisation of Europe'.[30] Only
in a few exceptional cases did the Finnish press consider the general political
consequences of the Franco-Prussian war; but these were the same, already
ingrained attitudes which had been expressed over the outcome of Prussia's war
of 1866 against Austria. In *Kirjallinen Kuukausilehti* Yrjö Koskinen repeated the
view he had expressed after the previous war that Prussia's victory upset the
European balance of power. To this he now added that the Germans despised
the small nationalities.[31] *Helsingfors Dagblad* also repeated its earlier view that
Prussia's victory had endangered the European balance of power.[32]

The interest aroused by the Franco-Prussian war was rapidly pushed to one side
by news of the revolutionary Paris Commune, set up at the beginning of 1871.
This became the central topic in the Finnish papers from March until June.[33]

The Paris Commune was depicted as mob-rule and as a social revolution
directed against all social values which were regarded as fundamental in Finland,
from the upper classes to the farmers: the sanctity of property, religion, personal
integrity and the family. The acts of violence and bloodshed which occurred
were generally ranked with the activities of socialism and the International. The
Finnish press as a whole reacted sharply to the Commune, and both liberals and
fennomans adopted the same severely negative attitude.

Åbo Underrättelser pictured the International as a new 'contemporary great
power';[34] socialism was seeking the overthrow of peace and morality, said *Uusi
Suometar*, which re-stated that discipline, order and respect for the law were

central social values.[35] In the Finnish press there were few exceptions to this kind of conservative reaction. *Helsingfors Dagblad*, however, expressed its doubts that 'the fear of communism' would be used for the establishment of a new Holy Alliance in Europe.[36] A change in Finnish political attitudes can be seen in that where earlier the threat had been perceived as being 'from above' — from the autocracy — the new threat was arising 'from below', from within society itself.

By the mid-1870s a theoretical kind of literary discussion of socialism had begun among the leaders of Finnish society, concentrating on how the spread of this idea could be stopped. Academic support was obtained from the so-called *Kathedersozialismus* (desk socialism), which in spite of its name represented an anti-socialist trend among academic intellectuals in Germany. By this stage some small signs had appeared in Finland of labour unrest, such as the strikes of printers and coachmen in Helsinki in 1872.[37] Yrjö Koskinen's article 'The case of the workers', published in 1874 stimulated the discussion among the Finnish élite. Although it was stressed that socialism must be prevented from coming to Finland, the substance of the ideology was thoroughly analysed and comparisons were made between it and economic liberalism.[38]

The exchange of opinions about socialism was further accelerated in Finland in 1877 when the German Diet passed the special so-called 'socialist laws,' banning the activity of the labour movement. Finnish evaluations of socialism cited the assassination attempts on the Kaiser and cases of arson, which the German conservatives had blamed on the socialists;[39] at this point Snellman joined the discussion and sharply criticised socialism ideologically.[40] In general it was thought that the passing of the socialist laws in Germany had been inevitable; only *Helsingfors Dagblad* dissented.[41]

The discussion about resisting the ideas of social revolution was fuelled at the end of the 1870s by events in another quarter, namely Russia, where several new assassination attempts had been made on the Emperor. In this connection, it became a habit to couple together the ideas of socialism and anarchism. Characteristically, the Finnish papers, when discussing the assassination attempts, referred to 'our Emperor'. Thus socialism and anarchism were regarded as being forces which were a danger to Finland's autonomy, and to the preservation of the relationship of Finland and Russia.[42]

The leaders of the church also took part in this discussion. The proclamation of a day of prayer in November 1871 stated that the actions of the Paris Commune were a clear divergence from 'God's order',[43] and would reduce the whole structure of society to a state of disintegration. New ideas — those concerning liberty, equality, fraternity and common ownership — were said in the proclamation to be essentially misleading, and would, if carried out, herald a new kind of slavery and the rule of human passions. The church also condemned the use of force in promoting social change. The church leaders, from the period after the Crimean war, had had to reorient their general social attitudes and, for example, recognise the importance of the individual in solving everyday problems. From the beginning of the 1860s, the Finnish church, which in many ways was fixed within the image of an agrarian society and its basic values, and was generally conservative in its traditions, saw before it a new challenge.

The Franco-Prussian war also affected Finland's foreign trading relations and hence her economic development. When the French fleet came into the Baltic at the beginning of the war and cruised as far as the vicinity of Danzig, the Baltic became hazardous for the merchant ships of non-belligerent countries to navigate. Finland's international trade had expanded well beyond before its pre-Crimean war level, and therefore suffered — both in exports and imports. Shipowners were cautious in view of their experiences in earlier crises. Exports of butter, which had only developed in the latter 1860s, noticeably contracted because of the Franco-Prussian war, thus making some Finnish farmers aware of the war.[44] However these negative effects on Finland's trade with the west were partly alleviated by the improved prospects of further trade with the east which occurred at the same time: the Riihimäki-St Petersburg railway came into use in 1870.[45] However this could not compensate for the reduction of timber exports to the west.

Defeated France paid the large war indemnities to Germany with unexpected speed — within two years. Because of this Germany acquired a large amount of capital, which sought investment outlets beyond the country's borders, including 'virgin territories' such as Finland.[46] In the early 1870s entirely new and exceptional features of entrepreneurial activity appeared in the economic life of Finland. There was a lively market in the sale and purchase of forests, as felling rights were leased: contemporaries called it 'forest madness'.[47] This in turn enriched those farmers who were the other party to the bargain. Employment opportunities were improved, and those who worked as lumberjacks in the forests or in other related jobs got good wages. This happened at a time when the Finnish countryside was just changing from a subsistence to a money economy. Money, suddenly plentiful, was spent freely and uninhibitedly in these conditions. Finland was seeing for the first time a kind of 'culture of conspicuous consumption'.[48] When a forest sale had been made, it was said afterwards that 'the farmers drank champagne and the loggers schnapps'.

In the mid-1870s, however, the boom period in Finland collapsed. In the background was the international slump of 1873, with origins that were not in Britain, as in all previous slumps, but in Germany. It was also the first international slump with effects that were apparent in Finland. The depression extended from the new centres of timber processing in different coastal districts to the lumber camps of the interior. The effects were felt the more harshly because the countryside had recently tasted a money economy. In addition there was a local slump in 1876 when, the iron industry of eastern Finland got into difficulties and some furnaces were forced to go bankrupt.

X. The Russo-Turkish war and Finland's involvement in the shadow of the international crisis

The results of the major reforms realised in the 1860s and the development of industry and internal reform of agriculture in Finland began to be apparent in many areas. Finnish society was changing: it was, on the one hand, clearly modernising and, on the other, acquiring more nationally distinctive features. The primary school system had spread widely in its first ten years of activity, and this promised to raise the general cultural level in the country. In economic development, remarkable results had been achieved as well, as shown, for example, by the exhibition of Finnish industry, held in Helsinki in the summer of 1876. Industrial development had, after many initial difficulties, gathered speed in the country. All this implied a changing of attitudes in Finnish society. There was satisfaction with the economic development, the atmosphere of progress created by the reforms and an increased political flexibility. In addition, the country was enjoying a secure period of peace. Because of the change in attitudes which had happened in the two decades after the Crimean war, the new generation was clearly different from its predecessor. From political dependence it had moved into a new situation where quite new opportunities were emerging.

Even in this new phase, however, there were two clearly recognised limitations on the exchange of political opinion. One concerned Finland's foreign relations — when, for example, the question of setting up her own official representative organs abroad was raised. The other concerned the development of the Finnish political system; here it was easy to clash with the prerogatives and sovereign integrity of the Emperor. These facts made the Finns cautious in approaching the boundaries of their political freedom of movement. For a long time the experiences acquired under Finnish conditions still served as a warning to the leaders in their political activity.[1]

This change was also seen in the relationship of the Finns to Alexander II. In the general consciousness his name was identified with the realisation of reforms, and he was perceived as the central factor in the favourable developments that had taken place. Both the clergy and the country's administration were engaged in propaganda which fixed the image of the Emperor among the people as a 'noble', 'just' and 'merciful' ruler. The Emperor was, alongside the constitution, a kind of guarantee of security in Finnish politics. This conception embraced a consciousness of his power and influence on the course of events.[2] Such an attitude of loyalty towards the Emperor was particularly strong among the country's Finnish-speaking population. The fennoman political line had been influential in this direction. The name of Alexander was associated further with the language manifesto, and the development of the status, and increasing influence, of the Finnish-speaking population.

For the Swedish-speakers, loyalty to the ruler along with the constitution expressed one essential part of the country's autonomous system. Their attitude to the Emperor was based on the country's constitution; his prerogatives were recognised, but it was thought that political activity could not be built around his person as such. Although the Swedish-speakers were often socially conservative, the Scandinavian respect for the principles of legality was important to them. For the liberals among them, Finland's autonomy was incorporated above all in the possibility of following a political line of their own.

1. *Russia's involvement in war from the Finnish viewpoint*

The next major international crisis in Europe was in the Balkans. Although obviously further removed from Finland geographically than the Franco-Prussian war had been, the Balkan question belonged traditionally to the central interests of Russian foreign policy, and when Alexander II and his advisers laid down a line in connection with it or made major decisions, Finland's dependence on the empire was also brought into focus.

The revolt which broke out in Serbia in 1875 was discussed in the leading Finnish papers as an important item. Even in Finland the Balkans were recognised as an area of major historical contradictions, where an extensive international crisis could break out. The religious confrontations there also aroused interest in the Finnish press, but the destinies of its nationalities — particularly the Serbs — and their prospects of breaking away from Turkish power, were considered more important. An anti-Turkish mood also appeared in the papers, which carried news of the Finnish volunteers serving in the Serbian army.[3]

When a wider international crisis was forecast in connection with events in the Balkans, it was thought possible that Russia and Britain would go to war again: in Finland's past experience, the danger that this represented for her were clearly perceived. In the summer of 1876, Finnish business circles began turning their attention to the problems the country would face if such a war should break out; the coastline of Finland could be blockaded in the spring of 1877, and trade with the west completely cut off. Therefore in the autumn of 1876 they began to store foreign produce and procure raw materials from abroad; on the other hand, 1877 proved to be a good year for timber exports, demand for which was stimulated by the fear of a general European war. Exports of butter also rose. The danger of war caused many kinds of speculation in Finland; one sign of the emergency was a rise in prices. However, when Russia's relations with Britain were not broken off in the spring of 1877, there were difficulties over reversing the economic precautions. It was difficult to sell the accumulated stocks and release the capital thus tied up for other uses.[4]

When Russia carried out a partial mobilisation early in 1877, it was indicated that major decisions were at hand in the empire's foreign policy. In January that year the Finnish Diet met, and since an international crisis was impending, the question was raised — on the initiative of the leading fennoman, Agathon Meurman — of whether they should send an address of loyalty to the Emperor and the empire.[5] When they began to discuss the question more closely, a political split appeared between the fennomans and the liberals; it appeared again in the discussion of certain other similar questions at the beginning of 1877. The characteristic political caution of the fennomans and the need to state their loyalty to the Emperor clearly emerged in this connection. Meurman himself expressed this viewpoint by emphasising that the Finnish people, 'living their own national life, stand faithfully at Russia's side, in enjoyment of the advantages which flow from the union with her, and bearing the attendant hardships'.[6] Snellman's view was basically the same: he thought that Finland's national development had advanced remarkably in the reign of Alexander II, that the country had obtained many advantages in international relations from Russia's position as a great power, so that in any crisis for the empire she ought to 'do something' for Russia.[7]

The liberals, on the other hand, wanted to remain as distant as possible from Russian foreign policy, and to endeavour to follow a certain isolationism. *Helsingfors Dagblad* voiced again the liberals' old slogan of the 'union relationship' of Finland with the empire, meaning that Finland had room to manoeuvre *vis-à-vis* Russian foreign policy as well as that of other states. The principle of neutrality expressed by the liberals in the international crisis of 1863 seemed to be still alive. The liberals wanted to avoid acknowledging the aims of Russian foreign policy, or taking responsibility for it in any way. Most important of all for them was the preservation of peace.[8] The proposed address did not lead to the result which the fennomans had hoped for. The Estate of the nobility and that of the burghers, among which the liberal outlook had great influence, did not support it. However, similar questions arose again in the next few months, when the international situation underwent a decisive change. At the end of April 1877, when Russia went to war with Turkey, the general political atmosphere in the empire was ultra-nationalistic and in favour of an offensive war. Russia's major decision was of course reflected in Finland, though this could not hide the fact that a different spirit and a different policy line prevailed there, and continued to do so.

When war broke out, the fennomans were prepared to give strong support. 'There has never been a ruler', *Uusi Suometar* declared, 'who unsheathed his sword in a better or juster cause than that for which Alexander II has called his people to fight.'[9] The paper depicted the Turks as pagans, representing 'blind stubbornness' and 'extreme violence'. In the eyes of the fennomans, Russia's war aims in the Balkans, acquired a highly idealised colouring; *Uusi Suometar* had weeded out from them anything that pointed to political interests and Pan-Slavist ideals. The 'noble prince' had gone into battle 'on behalf of freedom and humanity'; it was a question of saving the Christians of the Ottoman

empire from misery and persecution. Thus with a religiously coloured turkophobia they concealed the fact that Russia was waging a war of aggression.
They repeated the words of the official proclamation that the Emperor had been
'compelled to draw his sword reluctantly'. Snellman thought it fitting to point
out that the Emperor had taken a stand in support of the interests of small
nations in the Balkans.[10]

It was not easy for the Finnish liberals to express dissent against the war. In
their view, the outbreak of a major war in the Balkans was a crucial event which
also demonstrated the failure of diplomatic conciliation. They hoped the war
could be limited to the Balkans, and that Finland would remain outside the
danger zone; in any case her foreign trade had already begun to suffer from the
uncertain situation.[11] *Helsingfors Dagblad*, in describing the war in the Balkans,
maintained that it was a matter of the conflicting interests of the great powers,
a different line from that of *Uusi Suometar*. All enthusiasm about participation was foreign to the liberals' leading newspaper; it did not want to take a
stand against Turkey, nor did it advance any religious view on the causes of the
war.

These differences in attitude were also expressed in the Diet when the war
started. Meurman's attempt in this new phase to secure some kind of common
expression of opinion and rapprochement with the Emperor from the Estates
did not succeed.[12] The consequence was that only two Estates reacted to the outbreak of war; Meurman delivered a speech in the Estate of the farmers, which
wished the Emperor good fortune, and the clergy read a prayer of intercession
for the sovereign. By contrast nothing happened with the nobles and the
burghers. The differences were also apparent in the exchanges of view over J. I.
Berg's proposal in the Diet for a grant of money for medical supplies for the
Balkan theatre of war.[13] This was in no way a humanitarian initiative, but an
indirect form of political approval for the war. Berg's proposal stated that
Russia was defending 'the honour of the empire and the liberation of co-
religionists from a yoke of tyranny'. As well as Meurman, Snellman spoke in the
Diet in favour of the proposal, saying that Finland must support the war in
some way.[14]

The liberals showed restraint during these discussions, indicating their
general reluctance to take any kind of stance in support of Russia's campaign in
the Balkans, or to assume responsibility for it. However, in the prevailing situation, they were compelled to consider carefully in what form such an attitude
might be expressed. *Åbo Underrättelser* was critical of Berg's proposal claiming
that the Finnish Diet could not easily make decisions other than those concerned
with the country's own interests; 'a gift to another nation' went beyond the
Diet's competence.[15] *Helsingfors Dagblad* proposed that in this connection the
country should act quite separately. It hoped that the Finnish Red Cross, which
was set up in the spring of 1877, might mount a humanitarian initiative in the
theatre of war.[16] After a lengthy debate, in which the conflicts were resolved,
the discussion of the Berg's proposal ended with the Diet approving the

grant. While its opponents were able to accuse the supporters of Berg's proposal of grovelling to the Russians, they did not dare to take the demonstrative line that which would have been necessary had they been prepared to reject the making of the grant. The sum in question was later assessed as an extraordinary poll tax.[17]

At the beginning of September 1877, Alexander II decided to send the Finnish Guards Battalion, with the other units of the Guard, to the Balkan theatre of war. For Finland this naturally added a new dimension to the war. Not even the liberals questioned the order to the Battalion, which Leo Mechelin, for example, noted as a necessity arising from the circumstances.[18] Dependence on Russia clearly strengthened once war broke out, and when Russia suffered setbacks, people in Finland wanted to avoid straining relations. The ceremonies in Helsinki marking the departure of the Guards Battalion for the war on 3 September were carefully linked both to Russia's official war aims in the Balkans and also — in what was considered an appropriate manner — to Finland's military tradition. Making the official address to the Battalion, Senator Molander stressed the sacrifice of life and blood 'for the highest interests of humanity', and State Counsellor R. Furuhjelm declared that the Battalion was leaving to fight for 'the honour and faith of the fatherland' and for 'our co-religionists against the traditional enemy'.[19] The Battalion's departure received great publicity in the whole of the Finnish press.[20] Because of the Battalion's participation, the war in the Balkans was closely followed in Finland. Accounts of the battles appeared in the newspapers, and 'letters' were published about the Battalion's fortunes and experiences. The latter was of special interest among the farming population, which had provided its manpower. Since at the same time some 400 – 500 Finns were serving as officers in the Russian army, this affected the political attitudes of the upper class as well.[21]

Because of this general interest in the Turkish war, newspaper circulation rose, particularly that of the Finnish-language ones; *Uusi Suometar* doubled its print-run during the war years.[22] The great interest in events in the Balkans among the farmers also meant that the religious aspect was given prominence. Lutheranism contained a historical tradition of turkophobia, as expressed in Luther's book of homilies, though this had little effect on the Finnish clergy at the time of the Turkish war. By contrast, for the farming community the struggle against the 'heathen' Turks acquired an ideological character. Popular war poetry also became very popular in Finland at this time. In it were political features like loyalty to the sovereign, a Christian-coloured turkophobia and even an anti-British attitude. It also expressed a certain spirit of brotherhood in arms between Finns and Russians. The war poetry was sarcastic in tone and remarkably naive.[23] Being in Finnish, it found a response especially among the farming community; and it was not simply war propaganda, since its circulation was not directed by the authorities. However it undoubtedly influenced the attitudes of ordinary people, and increased interest in the war. While the military achievements of 'our side' were emphasised, recognition was also given to the courage of the enemy, especially of Osman Pasha, who defended Plevna.[24]

2. *The military service law and Finland*

In January 1877 the Diet was presented with a proposal for introducing military service in Finland. This had long been in preparation at committee level, and its consideration was taking place now in the shadow of the Turkish war.

For St Petersburg the military significance of Finland had once again increased. The threat of war from Sweden had disappeared, but the military threat that was assumed to exist in the rise of a united Germany was a new problem. In Russian government circles the significance in this respect of the Franco-Prussian war was grasped only slowly; when this happened, Finland too, as a virtual military vacuum, became a new and urgent problem. When St Petersburg decided in favour of a separate Finnish army, this was politically an interesting act. It demonstrated anew that the Finns were regarded as loyal, in which context they were clearly differentiated from the Poles, who had lost their own army after the revolt of 1830. Although the war minister, Milyutin, was not prepared for Finland to have her own army, he was compelled to accept the decision which the Emperor supported.[25]

During the debates in the Finnish Diet on the military service law, some political problems of importance for the Finns came up. These concerned above all the question of how the Finnish army's role should be specified. According to the Emperor's proposition it would be 'the defence of the throne and the empire', but this definition contained no geographical limitations, and therefore it aroused suspicions among the Finns. Russia was an empire stretching across two continents, and with multifarious interests. These debates in the Diet were enlivened particularly by the circumstances of the autumn of 1877. By then, the Guards Battalion had already been ordered to the Balkans, and at the end of October news was received of the heavy casualties it had suffered at the battle of Gornyi Dubnyak.[26] Even before that, in September, Leo Mechelin had expressed the blunt opinion that Finnish soldiers had no desire to die 'under the bullets of the Khirgiz and Chinese', or to fight for the remote areas of the Russian empire.[27] The Diet began to reach a general consensus that the role of the Finnish army must be clearly limited. Although the proposed military service law was a constitutional law — and as such a matter for the Emperor's initiative alone — the committee considering it undertook to make amendments ensuring that the future role of the country's army was 'defence of the fatherland and the throne'. Although even this definition did not completely restrict the role of the army to within the country's own borders, it did clearly emphasise the priority of this role. 'Defence of the throne' could be regarded as meaning primarily a duty to defend St Petersburg as well.[28]

In the Diet debates on the military service law, the fennomans and the liberals reached a common policy. Only a few Swedish-speaking members of the Estate of nobles, who differed from them, would have preferred a decision in favour of an army of paid professionals. When the liberals, led by Mechelin, decided to support an army based on compulsory military service, they undoubtedly hoped that they would thus be freed from having Russian troops in Finland as well; 'our own army' had been a liberal objective in the crisis of 1863 precisely for this reason.[29] Snellman held similar views; when he talked of the duty of the Finns, he undoubtedly kept in mind the fact that the military vacuum constituted by Finland would be filled by the country's own army, not one of strangers. However Snellman did not make a major issue out of defining the role of the Finnish army; he would have been prepared, out of caution, to approve the Emperor's proposal because he believed that in practice the Finnish army would operate primarily in defence of Finland.[30] The army, on the basis of the military service law, was to consist only of infantry — rifle battalions — to which some cavalry units were later added. Because of this structure, its tasks were limited to 'local defence'; because it possessed no artillery, for example, leading political circles recognised as obvious that on the outbreak of a war Russian heavy equipment and supporting troops would be moved into the country.[31]

The Finnish army was to have its own commander, a major-general, who would be in charge of its training. For operational planning, the army was subordinated to the St Petersburg military district. The defence of the south coast of Finland and of its fortifications would be in the hands of the Russians, as before, and was integrated into the broad system of fortifications defending St Petersburg.

3. *The Balkan war, the Congress of Berlin and the Finnish press*

From 1876, as the crisis in the Balkans grew, the St Petersburg government followed carefully the criticism directed at its policy from abroad. The Finnish censorship authorities also scrutinised the foreign newspapers entering the country. If any of them contained criticism of Russian foreign policy or critical opinions on conditions inside the empire, or anything which could be regarded as insulting to the Russian army, the copies were confiscated. In 1877 this policy mainly affected such Swedish papers as *Stockholms Dagblad*, *Nya Dagligt Allehanda* and *Fäderneslandet*, and exceptionally some German papers as well.[32]

The Swedish press did not discuss the Finnish question separately in connection with the international crisis caused by the Turkish war. Such matters as Finnish political attitudes, or the despatch of the Guards Battalion and its casualties in the Balkans, received no special attention in the country's leading newspapers; interest in the Finland's status in relation to Russia had ceased. Instead, the desire which had appeared from the 1860s onwards to preserve a 'cultural bridge' between Finland and Sweden was seen when the death of Runeberg in May 1877 was given major attention in Sweden. In the midst of the war in Europe, the Swedish press examined Finnish cultural life and the internal contradictions that were appearing in it.[33]

In this period, the debate on the military service law was the only truly political issue which figured in the reports from the foreign consuls in Helsinki. On the other hand, nothing occurring in Finland was considered of sufficient political significance to figure in the reports of the foreign ambassadors in St Petersburg to their foreign ministries.

The division of attitudes that had appeared in Finland in the opening phase of the Turkish war was overshadowed in the summer and autumn of 1877 by the attention given to the great events of the war. Some of the differing views beneath the surface became public even in this phase: whereas the fennomans gave Balkan events the character of a war of religion and depicted the Turks as loathsome and cruel,[34] *Helsingfors Dagblad* noted in October that 'Finland has not a single enemy among the nations.'[35] This, in its context, was a deliberate and bold observation that Finland should remain outside great power conflicts.

By the late autumn of 1877 the Turkish war had begun to pose a problem for Finland, distant though it was from the actual theatre of war. The heavy casualties of the Finnish Guards Battalion created a mood of uncertainty and pessimism, and the war began to be felt indirectly in many ways. After the exceptionally favourable conditions which developed for Finland's exports to the west at the beginning of the war, a slump occurred. Falling prices in foreign markets affected exports of both timber and butter. Timber processing plants reduced production, causing unemployment and finally a serious depression in the trade. Finland's merchant shipping also did badly in the international freight markets; much capacity went unused, or it had to accept low freight rates.[36] Even Finland's traditional exports to Russia began to run into difficulties: the war caused disruptions in the economic life of the empire both in production and in demand; in addition, the fall in the rate for the rouble caused further difficulties for Finland's eastern trade.

Thus the disturbance in Finland's economic life which occurred in 1877–8 was caused by the growing difficulties of her trade both with the west and the east.[37] The budget of the Finnish state also suffered; customs revenue was reduced, and the emergency with its special measures meant extra expenditure. The country also became drawn into the Russian war economy: various orders for the needs of the imperial armed forces were executed in Finland, including torpedo-boats, artillery equipment, ammunition and transport wagons and a variety of other military supplies.[39] This created something of a war boom, which helped to compensate for the diminution of peacetime exports to the east.

The decision made during the Turkish war to take the Finnish mark off silver and tie it to the gold standard and the French franc in itself led to greater stability and a step forward for the country's economic life.[40] Finland now had not only its own currency but its own monetary standard. Russia thereby conceded a considerable independence to Finland in this area.

After the conquest of Plevna at the beginning of December 1877, hopes were high in Finland that peace would come quickly. When this did not happen, the resulting disappointment was seen in the changed tone of the leading papers at the turn of the year. They began to take a more critical attitude to the Turkish war. *Hufvudstadsbladet* wrote of the 'terrible demon of war', and *Uusi Suometar* called the war a 'bloody performance' which, furthermore, seemed to be spreading.[41] *Åbo Underrättelser* saw the war as causing a 'barbarising' of habits of thought, both among the belligerent nations and those who followed the war at a distance.[42] The realistic way of thinking that this denoted was gaining ground in Finland. Yet at the closing of the Diet in late January 1878, when there was still no news of the war ending, the different Estates emphasised their general sympathy towards its aims and tried to give an impression of an 'official front' in Finland corresponding to the expectations of the empire. In their greetings addressed to the Emperor, the Estates repeatedly referred to the 'lofty and noble aims' of the war being waged by Russia and the 'honourable victories' achieved by its gallant armies. The spokesman for the Estate of farmers referred to the 'modest sacrifice' which Finland had been able to make 'for the great aims' of the war. References were also made to 'oppressed co-religionists' and the 'war of liberation' in the Balkans. However, at the same time the hope that peace would be re-established was clearly expressed.[43]

The peace signed at the beginning of March 1878 between Russia and Turkey at San Stefano did not, however, seem to have stabilised the international situation. Britain and Austria opposed the peace treaty, fearing Russian domination in the Balkans. Thus a new state of tension arose, which made a fresh outbreak of war between Britain and Russia seem possible. In Finland it was feared that a situation like that of the Crimean war, with all the local destruction that accompanied it, would be repeated. In the spring of 1878, work began on building fortifications on the coast of southern Finland. At the same time, St Petersburg asked the Senate whether, in the absence as yet of a conscript army, they should use troops mobilised through the territorial system or paid professionals for the defence of Finland. The Senate preferred the latter, which it believed could be effected swiftly.[44]

In this new situation *Helsingfors Dagblad* urged that Finland's interest lay in standing aside from the empire's problems in the Balkans; and war between Britain and Russia would certainly cause major losses to her merchant fleet.[45] It would be politically fatal for Finland to become identified with Russia in a war between two great powers. The basic outlook of the Finnish liberals was strongly western-oriented. The fennoman paper *Uusi Suometar*, by contrast, set itself to defend the treaty of San Stefano. It also repeatedly criticised Britain, accusing her of a 'policy of adventure' in The Balkans. However, it was not blind to the danger which a war between Russia and Britain would pose to Finland: there might even be attacks on the coastal towns, but it was to be hoped, that a critical world opinion would restrain Britain.[47]

In the spring of 1878, a plan was launched in Russia to equip merchant vessels as auxiliary cruisers if war should break out between Russia and Britain; but *Helsingfors Dagblad* and leading businessmen in the larger Finnish towns took a firm stand against such schemes, which were regarded as contravening the rules controlling war at sea, agreed at Paris in 1856. It was further emphasised that if such methods were used in war, British retaliation would hit Finland's merchant fleet particularly hard. The fennomans, on the other hand, sought to sympathise with the Russian proposals and directed their criticism against Britain. Snellman wrote strongly in *Morgonbladet*, accusing Britain of defending piracy and saying that, compared to her, 'the other sea-powers are civilised and humane'. A vehement press war arose between *Helsingfors Dagblad* and *Morgonbladet* on this question, with *Åbo Underrättelser* supporting the former and *Uusi Suometar* standing completely aloof from the conflict.[48] When the Senate had to clarify its position, it followed the line represented by the liberals and business circles; in other words, it took a negative stand on the use of auxiliary cruisers.[49] This happened at the time when Russia was already on the point of conceding that the terms of San Stefano should be reviewed which caused the danger of war to recede over the horizon.

The tense situation in the Balkans created by the treaty of San Stefano led, on Bismarck's initiative, to the assembling of the Congress of Berlin in the middle of June 1878, with the object of resolving the conflicts between the great powers — primarily Britain and Russia. For Russia the main problem was what concessions it needed to make to ensure genuine peace in Europe. For Finland, hopes were pinned on a single issue — the necessity that war between Britain and Russia should be avoided, because of the particular dangers it would spell for Finland.

The Finnish papers reported the Berlin negotiations extensively, and carefully explained the attitudes of the different parties taking part and the points of view they advanced; at the same time they refrained from expressing their own opinions on the great powers.[50] The preservation of the peace was a dominant Finnish interest, and in this liberals, fennomans and the country's business community all shared the same aspirations. When the Congress ended in a compromise, and Russia was forced to make considerable withdrawals in the Balkans, the reactions in St Petersburg were clearly negative and exasperated, and there was criticism of Bismarck and his role as a mediator. In Finland, on the other hand, reactions to the outcome of the Congress were quite different. The country's leading papers were satisfied, and even enthusiastic, over the compromise solution that had been reached; 'world peace is guaranteed' was a typical statement in the Finnish press. With peace thus assured, industrial and commercial development in Finland would again be able to proceed with confidence.[51] In the view of the Finnish papers, Bismarck was the man who had saved peace. It had been customary to see him as the supreme embodiment of power politics, but he appeared now in a wholly different light, and all the criticism directed against him in St Petersburg was antipathetic to the Finnish newspapers.

When the international crisis that had followed the Turkish war had truly ended, the Finns could more easily assess the developments of the years 1877–8. This was true above all of the liberals, who had tried throughout to avoid involvement in the backwash from the empire's foreign policy. It was notable in itself that when *Helsingfors Dagblad* examined the international situation in the light of the Berlin decisions, it saw the treaty of San Stefano as one-sided; the Congress of Berlin was trying to annul 'the hegemony of the Russians and other Slavs' in the Balkans. However, it regarded the solution adopted as full of problems, in the sense that there were great difficulties in reconciling the principles of nationalism and great power interests in the Balkans.[52] It was characteristic of the liberals' position that for the paper the most significant achievement was that through peaceful negotiation a new round of war had been avoided. *Åbo Underrättelser* drew attention to the praise which the Finnish participation in the war had attracted, and the enhanced prestige of the Finns because of it. However, the paper wanted to emphasise that the Turkish war could not attain the same status in the eyes of the Finns themselves as the war of 1808, since it had not been a struggle for the fatherland.[53]

When the Emperor confirmed the military service law in December 1878, it was a sufficiently notable occurrence to revive discussion of the subject in the country's press. *Uusi Suometar* saw the creation of its own army as itself a significant achievement for Finland; but it also stressed that the army's role was limited to the defence of Finland and of the throne. The paper regarded this as an achievement, because the Finns had for centuries had to pour out their blood 'for the interests of strangers' in different parts of Europe. *Oulun Wiikko-Sanomat* also belonged to those who saw the positive significance of the solution achieved: 'Finland now really enters the ranks of the nations', it remarked.[54] Liberal circles reacted — retrospectively — to the military service law with reservations, once the emergency of the Turkish war was past. *Åbo Underrättelser* remarked that only the future would show what effect the establishment of a conscript army would have upon the country's destiny.[55] *Hufvudstadsbladet* noted that once Finland had an army, she would be vulnerable to becoming involved in international conflicts.[56]

But for the liberals the law's coming into force also spelled hope. For example, *Helsingfors Dagblad* hoped that in future only Finnish troops would be stationed around Helsinki;[57] and *Åbo Underrättelser*'s hopes went still further, since it assumed that Russian troops could now be wholly withdrawn from the country.[58] As has already been shown, leading fennomans assumed that if an international crisis broke out, Finland's small conscript army could not protect the integrity of Finland's territory alone.

The Finnish church, as one of the country's central institutions, had inevitably become involved in the course of great events during the Turkish war. It sympathised with the official slogans of the war, and in a proclamation of a day of prayer in October 1877 its leaders had spoken of the Turkish empire as 'the hereditary enemy of Christendom'. But in the same proclamation, they also deplored the difficulties and disturbance which the war had caused in Finland's economic life. When, in the spring of 1878, the outbreak of a new war between Britain and Russia was avoided, the church leaders saw this as salvation from a great peril. Yet the church made no allusion — at least in the proclamation of a day of prayer issued in the autumn of 1878 — to the fact that the peace of Europe had been assured at the Congress of Berlin by the joint action of the great powers.[60] Possibly, because such a conclusion was politically a sensitive matter in St Petersburg, the church leaders wanted to avoid expressing points of view which could have caused irritation there.

Although the 'official front' in Finland expressed satisfaction, the political leaders were aware that the country's position contained major problems for the future. Among the fennoman leaders there was fear and uncertainty that after Alexander II, the country might experience bad times. Meurman had suggested this when the military service law was being debated. Attacks on Finland's autonomy, which appeared in the Russian press at the end of the 1870s, had been noted with concern in Helsinki. There was thus an awareness that the foundations of Finland's special political status were, in the last resort, weak. Some Finnish political leaders, including Snellman, began to fear possible changes in the Russian political system: if the autocracy were changed into some kind of popular representative system, it would become possible for new, unknown forces to intervene as of right in Finland's affairs. The reaction to this uncertain situation was also seen in a pamphlet which a Finnish émigré, Colonel Becker, published in Paris in the spring of 1880, entitled 'Independent and neutral Finland' (*La Finlande independante et neutre*); it contained a scheme for the country's political future. Snellman vehemently attacked Becker as a political adventurer;[61] he seems to have feared that Becker's publication would lead St Petersburg to draw unfavourable conclusions concerning the country's loyalty.

When advance information arrived in Finland of a plan, being prepared in St Petersburg, for a national representative institution for Russia, which also made provision for Finland to send representatives to a parliament of the empire, this was seen as a grave threat to the country's status.[62] Alexander II was assassinated in 1881, however, and the plan fell through. When Alexander III ascended the throne, Snellman presented greetings to the new sovereign which contained obvious apprehensions over the future; Finland asked of the new Emperor his 'mighty protection'.[63] Thus there was fear of a crisis approaching in the relations between Russia and Finland.

XI. Change and signs of crisis in Russo-Finnish relations in the early 1880s

The period of intensified conflicts between the great powers, which began with the Congress of Berlin, speeded up the formation of alliances. Germany and Austria concluded an alliance in 1879, to which Italy later adhered to form the Triple Alliance. Because of the fear born of the rise of Germany, there was a drawing together between France and Russia, despite the great difference in their political systems, and in 1891–4 the so-called Dual Alliance was concluded.

The competition among the great powers was on the one hand of a purely political character — they reacted sensitively to matters of prestige — and on the other hand they competed for foreign trade and in other areas of the economy. The growth of industry and the development of communications strengthened national power resources. The return to protective tariffs also worked indirectly in the same direction. A vigorous rearmament and the new kinds of national rivalry it generated came to colour the system of international relationships of the great European powers as they moved into the twentieth century.

The development of the international situation naturally influenced the internal development of the great powers.[1] This appeared in various centripetal tendencies, e.g. a general improvement of administration, the extension — and standardisation — of educational systems, the development of internal communications and an enhanced significance for the armed forces. The great-power-centered international system also meant pressure on minority nationalities within the state frontiers: the nationalist trend sought to eliminate all 'deviations' which could cause difficulties for the central government in times of crisis.

Each of the great powers tried to appear outwardly as a unified national entity, thus emphasising its own political capacity and authority. These aims appeared in other than purely political contexts. For example, in the years before the First World War, the great powers began to resist actively the appearance of non-sovereign nations as separate national teams in the Olympic games. Also, in the last decades of the nineteenth century, the imperialist aims of the great powers were involved in the development of the international system. The European 'balance of power' was enlarged by means of territorial conquests and division into spheres of interest worldwide, first in the 1880s in Africa and then in the 1890s in east Asia. In this phase, the development of liberal ideals of international law — in contrast with the middle of the century — was no longer a considerable factor in international politics. A counter-force to many of these developments was the rising socialist workers' movement, support for which was continually broadening within the general European framework. The

Second International was founded as an international coordinating institution of the socialists in 1889. In peacetime conditions other social groups also expressed the characteristic pacifism of the workers' movement. This atmosphere, relying on cultural optimism, was in sharp conflict with the actual development of international politics.

The field of action of the international system had thus broadened in many ways, and the intensity of the influences on it greatly increased at the same time. The general extension of parliamentary democracy and of the multi-party system in the western half of Europe brought new participants into politics and stimulated political activity in a quite new way, even in relation to questions of foreign policy. At the same time the number of political problems increased and the process of resolving them was fraught with additional complexities. Russia too had begun to display the influence of the press and public opinion in the field of foreign policy and other corresponding issues, even if on a narrow political foundation.

1. *The peculiarity of Finnish national development*

The development of Finland in the final decades of the nineteenth century was diverging greatly from everything associated with the Russian empire. Continuing industrialisation extended Finland's economic integration with the west even if at the same time the country's trade with Russia increased. However, the development of Finnish exports to the east was halted in 1885 when Russia raised the tariffs on products imported from Finland. This acted as a restraint for a while, but western trade expanded correspondingly at the same time. As well as her trade with Britain, Finland's trading relations with Germany also began to be considerably extended from the 1870s; imports in particular increased, which included both industrial products and grain. The framework which the timber processing industry had created for Finnish production became more pronounced, and at the same time, surrounded by her own tariff walls, Finland and her economy were recognised in foreign business circles as an entity of their own.

The explosive expansion of Finland's cultural life in the 1880s emphasised for its part the country's national characteristics. This dynamic development affected specifically the Finnish-language side of cultural life; among the Swedish-speakers development had in many respects come to a halt.

The political division into fennomans and svecomans (an opposition grouping to the former started in the 1870s) stamped the general character of Finnish public life in the century's last decades. The svecoman ideological tendency and the birth of a Swedish party represented the adoption of a defensive position by the hitherto politically dominant minority language group. A.O. Freudenthal put forward the idea that Finland's Swedish-speakers belonged to a different race from the Finnish-speakers, and in the manner of August Sohlman, he also regarded the Swedish-speakers as representing a superior race. At the same time a politically élitist outlook began to be stressed, which saw in the fennomans a striving for power for the masses. For example, for V.M. von Born the mere preservation of Swedishness meant little other than the preservation of the status of a superior social class. C.G. Estlander and R.A. Wrede also argued that no concessions could be made over the franchise, because the majority in society would strike a blow at the linguistic minority.[2] The general aim of the Swedish-language minority was to preserve existing conditions unchanged. In the Diet of 1885, Wrede legalistically maintained that in elections for the Estate of burghers, it would be possible to adopt sharply different weightings of votes on the basis of wealth, an extreme obligarchic view with no counterpart among conservative circles in any of the other Scandinavian countries. The background to Wrede's move was that in the Diet the Estates of the nobles and the burghers supported the Swedish-speakers, who feared that a change in the franchise for the Estate of burghers could change the existing state of 'balance' between the language parties in favour of the fennomans. Finland's Swedish-speakers felt that they continued to receive influences from Sweden which gave them spiritual vitality; they wanted to be Swedish. The Scandinavian countries' tradition of freedom and of a society based on law represented the ideological inheritance which they cherished. At the same time they sought to interpret this tradition so that it could serve as a protective shield for their linguistic and social status.[3] Liberalism also influenced Finland's Swedish-speakers. A liberal atmosphere was an established general factor among them, being seen *inter alia*, as respect for the principle of political debate and for certain other libertarian concepts. And there were corresponding influences in the cultural liberalism of the Swedish-speakers: all this expressed the western tendencies among the country's language minority, whose conservatism it mitigated.

Swedishness in Finland as a whole represented an attitude of opposition to the prevailing system in Russia, to its culture and to Slavism. Because of this, the language minority in Finland — or at least a considerable section of it — waged a defensive battle on two fronts, against the east and against the fennomans. Among the Swedish-speakers it was generally considered that the finnicisation movement as a whole weakened the nation's spiritual defences against the Russian empire.

Among the fennomans the attitude towards their more advanced neighbour, Sweden, showed signs of a national inferiority complex, as they tried to create their own Finnish-language culture. Generally in their relations with Sweden, the fennomans sought to denigrate the idea of the historical 'debt of gratitude' as Yrjö Koskinen did in the mid-1870s.[4] In continuing the struggle for the Finnish language, the fennoman side had begun to hold to everything which was regarded as strongly representing Finnish traditions. This circumstance, added to the fact that the backbone of the finnicisation movement consisted of the clergy and the country's economically prospering farmers, led to a generally conservative attitude gaining ground among the fennomans. In their attitude to the reception of international influences, there was also an introspective tendency:

they considered that patriarchalism was well adapted as a model for running society in Finnish conditions, and for solving social problems.

During the 1880s, two groups represented a reaction against conservatism, and against the way that the language struggle sucked up strength and diverted attention from the questions of political and social reform. In cultural questions, moderate and liberal-minded Finnish-speakers belonged to the *Valvoja* circle, from which new leadership material was later to emerge for the Finnish party; and the Young Finland circle formed in the later 1880s consisted of young literary intellectuals, interested in political liberalism, who wanted to 'open windows to Europe'. It was not only a question of receptiveness to foreign ideas of political and social reform, but a general interest in cultural liberalism and the doctrines about the outlook on the world and on life associated with it.[5]

Among Finland's relations with foreign countries, those with Germany were constantly being extended. This occurred in the area of academic culture, learning and university education, and in technology: a rapidly industrialising Germany could offer many new commodities and technical expertise generally. Young people looking for forms of specialised advanced training which their homeland could not provide might go to study engineering in Dresden or veterinary science in Hanover. Also, the contacts of representatives of the Finnish church with Luther's homeland had become frequent from the middle of the century. The foreign links of the country's businessmen were extending to the north German ports from Hamburg to Stettin, and to the industrial centres in the west of Germany.

In the 1880s there arose new kinds of association with France. Contacts were sought particularly with the 'new France' born after the destruction of the Second Empire. Artists and writers discovered the realist school in Paris and its different manifestations. Representatives of the younger intellectuals, who looked at problems from the liberal and radical points of view, were interested in democracy, parliamentarianism, the women's question, religious freedom and other new issues, and wanted to consider them from the Finnish angle. The so-called cultural struggle in France between the state and the Catholic church stimulated general debate on the church's position and duties. The Dreyfus case was followed attentively in the Finnish press, and the young intellectuals generally supported Dreyfus.[6] The circle in which French influences were accepted in Finland was thus partly new and socially different from previous ones. At the same time admiration for traditional French culture was losing ground, as Swedishness was losing strength in the country. Among the young liberal intellectuals, apprehension was expressed that before long 'rusting and rigidity' would set in in Finnish cultural life. 'Europeanism' the systematic slogan in these circles, represented a demand for development in different fields and a kind of cosmopolitanism.

Contacts between Finland and Russia were forever expanding in the later nineteenth century. The number of Finns permanently resident in the growing metropolis of St Petersburg had grown by the beginning of the 1880s to well over 20,000, which was as many as lived in the largest Finnish towns of the time. The various Finnish artisans who lived there were acquiring additional professional skills, and as trading relations expanded, there were Finns serving as various kinds of commercial representative in St Petersburg and the other major cities of the empire. The former were skilled workers of the petty bourgeois class, while the latter belonged to the upper classes of Finnish society in Russia, which also included officers, engineers *et al*. The number of Finnish officers serving in the Russian armed forces varied from the mid-nineteenth century to the outbreak of the First World War from around 700 in any year to under 400.[7] During the last decades of the century, cultural influences too were received in Finland from Russia. The influence of realism in Finnish literature came from the east as well as the west, and in addition Tolstoyism was influential in Finnish intellectual life.[8] It should not be forgotten that St Petersburg was a cosmopolitan society through which continental cultural influences could be transmitted to Finland. By that route — to mention just one example — the first information on Pestalozzi's educational ideas is thought to have been obtained somewhat earlier.

2. *The German threat as seen by the Imperial authorities*

After the Congress of Berlin, relations between Germany and Russia began to cool and the St Petersburg government considered the possibility that if a general European war should break out, Germany might be Russia's enemy.

From 1882 several military committees were at work in St Petersburg, considering the effect of the changed general situation on Russia's military position. Their main task was to consider the danger of the attack threatened from Germany. It was felt that the main thrust of such an attack would come from Poland, but then the enemy might carry out landings from the Baltic. The area of Courland was held to be especially dangerous, because from there the enemy could attack St Petersburg from a much shorter distance than through Poland. The Finnish direction came up only as a third possibility, and it was not thought necessary to draft a plan for the defence of Finland as a whole, but only for the south coast. Above all it was considered necessary that the fortifications of Sveaborg and Viipuri should be strong, because together with Kronstadt they formed a support zone for the Russian fleet to repel a possible attack from the direction of the northern Baltic.

In the Russian General Staff's mobilisation plans for 1888, the contribution of the Russian troops to the defence of the south coast of Finland was contemplated as two infantry divisions and two artillery brigades.[9] These forces would be deployed in the fortified areas already mentioned, Hanko and Tammisaari, and the Turku area. Åland was left out, and there were no extensive military plans for the west coast facing the Gulf of Bothnia, Sweden not being considered an enemy. The joint manoeuvres of Russian and Finnish troops, organised at Tsarskoe Selo in the later 1880s, were part of a design to increase the military preparedness of the southern coast of Finland.

3. *The rise of Russian nationalism and the Finnish question*

The government in St Petersburg began to examine the Finnish question in the last decades of the nineteenth century within a new and different general framework. Major changes had taken place in the administration of the empire during the century; the days when the sovereign himself, assisted by a few advisers, had handled the major business of the empire, and imperial rescripts had announced the decisions, were long past. In the greatly expanded Russian administrative machine, the preparation of business and its discussion ran along their own well-established bureaucratic rails, and this affected the content of the Emperor's final decisions.[10]

The rise of nationalism in Russia affected intellectual attitudes towards Finland's autonomy. The intellectual slogans of that nationalism sought on the one hand to put Russia in a central position, and on the other to declare all that was particularly Russian as opposite to what was western. They did not accept that the basis of evaluation should be the degree to which conditions were advanced in the west, but instead the question of where to discover 'the essence of life'; in the latter respect it was said that Russia was in advance of the west.[11]

In various connections the autocratic system of government was included in Russian nationalism, and was said to be part of Russian tradition; according to this interpretation, liberalism represented a doctrine of the west, alien to Russia. In an autocratic empire, it was felt that the privileges of the non-Russian nationalities constituted a deviation; there was a strongly negative reaction against them in Russian nationalist circles, which demanded the removal of such 'abnormalities'.[12] The accession of Alexander III to the throne had speeded up the russification policy in the non-Russian areas from the Baltic provinces to the Caucasus. Evidence of this change was seen in the fact that Katkov, whose ideas Alexander II had not accepted, now belonged to the Emperor's entourage, together with Pobedonostsev, the procurator of the Holy Synod.[13] The Baltic provinces were involved by geography with Russia's communications with Europe, and with her strategic interests in central Europe. At a time when the relations of Russia and Germany were cooling, apprehensions were aroused in St Petersburg over how the Baltic Germans would behave towards Russia in a possible international conflict.[14]

Finland constituted a clear geographical entity and was not nationally divided like the Baltic provinces. When, on taking his oath as sovereign, Alexander III acknowledged Finnish autonomy, he was following the tradition established by his father; but new factors were developing which began to affect the relations of Finland and Russia. In the final decades of the nineteenth century, Finland possessed a feature which did not go unnoticed by Russian governing circles, and frequently aroused irritation: after the failure of the revolt of 1863, Poland had remained nationally dormant, whereas Finnish society had developed in the most diverse fields — like an avalanche, as many thought. When foreigners noted that Finland was a western country, it was a challenge to the Russians. The special character of Finland's administration was also continuously being accentuated. The country had acquired even more of the features of a sovereign state; as well as its own constitution, administration and tariff barriers, it had its own currency, postage stamps, etc. Many Russians might wonder at Finland in this respect and even think of it as an independent country.[15] Others again thought of Finland as 'abroad', unlike, say, Riga and its environs.

The so-called Afghan crisis, which developed between Britain and Russia in 1885 as a dispute over the limits of the spheres of influence of the respective powers is interesting in view of the above from two angles.

The Russian nationalist press reacted strongly when *Helsingfors Dagblad* brought out the liberal call of twenty years earlier for Finnish neutrality in case war should break out, emphasising the separate position of the country's army in the empire. The Russian press, led by *Novoye Vremya* and *Moskovskiya Vedomosti*, attacked Finland's special status more extensively and vehemently than ever before. Because of what was being written in certain Finnish newspapers, the Governor-General, Heiden, gave a warning to the Finnish press — on the basis of hints received from St Petersburg — on the treatment of 'sensitive matters'. In addition he received the right to suspend newspapers, either wholly or for a stipulated period, when they 'wrongly interpreted the relation of Finland to the empire'.[16]

When the Afghan crisis was finally resolved, the subsequent reckoning in St Petersburg had a strongly self-critical character. Questions and doubts were raised as to whether Russia had the capacity for vigorous action should a war with a great power break out. Further, the Russian public finances had just now shown weakness, with a fall in the rouble exchange rate. Among Alexander III's entourage, ideas based on the experiences gained in the crisis of 1885 tended towards the unification of the Russian empire to strengthen the empire's capacity for international action. At the same time it was recognised in St Petersburg that Russia was without allies.[17] Since government circles were adopting a more definite line of conservative nationalism than before, they also began — on ideological grounds — to regard Russianness and the Greek Orthodox religion as a guarantee of the population's greater reliability and goodwill. An indirect conclusion from this was that all other nationalities and beliefs in the empire were seen as showing 'weaknesses' and being factors of political uncertainty. The rise of nationalism as the guiding factor in Russian policy also meant that in the management of Finnish-Russian relations the cosmopolitan atmosphere, which from the early decades of the nineteenth century had been a distinct protection for Finland's special status, was thrust aside.

The general modernisation of Russia, due to industrialisation and other

circumstances, also produced the aim of integrating Finland into the empire —
a tendency that was also present in the other European great powers. At the
same time it was clearly shown that Russia's backwardness had long been a safeguard of Finland's special status. Since the attitude of Russia's political leaders
to Finland's special status was changing, the contentment of the Finns was no
longer considered as nearly so important a factor as earlier. The new ruling
circles in St Petersburg, in contrast to their predecessors, made it clear that as
they saw the danger of attack from Germany increasing, they were prepared to
impose their will on the Finns. This raises the question of whether they thought
that in the new situation the political dissatisfaction of the Finns was less of a
danger than it had been, or merely assumed that there would be time to
'assimilate' the Finns effectively before any international conflict broke out.
The straightforward view that every advance made by Russian nationalism in
the non-Russian areas meant a strengthening of the empire may also have been a
basic assumption in St Petersburg. Thus the demands of nationalism and the
empire's military interests seemed to be tending in the same direction.

4. *Finland and the policy of russification in the early 1890s*

When Alexander III came to the throne in 1881 there were some changes in the
Finnish administration, notably in the channels of communication to the
government in St Petersburg. The changes of personnel in the posts of Minister-
Secretary and Governor-General were a demonstration of this. The importance
of the former as a kind of advocate for Finland in St Petersburg and as a
diplomatic observer was clearly weakening.[18] During the time when
Rehbinder, A. Armfelt and Stjernwall-Walleen had held office as Minister-
Secretary, a qualification for the post had been a good knowledge of Finnish law
and conditions. By contrast, the new incumbent T. Bruun (1881–8) came from
the background of Old Finland and, unlike his predecessors, had made his career
in the Russian civil service. To an administrator of Bruun's type, the feeling for
the fatherland which Finns had was a very indistinct idea, and the practices of
the Finnish constitution and the spirit of autonomy were alien. Working in the
Russian administrative machine had accustomed him to adapt to the spirit of the
autocratic system. Bruun's successor was General J.C. Ehrnrooth (1888–91),
one of whose previous posts had been that of military commander in Bulgaria.
He was a straightforward and efficient soldier; for him, like his successors W.C.
von Daehn (1891–8) and V.N. Procopé (1898–9), the interests of the Russian
empire and acting 'in accordance with the trust given by the Emperor', were
paramount considerations.

A corresponding change, in the direction of identifying the interests of the
empire more closely than previously with the work of the Governor General,
was personified by Fyodor Heiden. His period of office (1881–97) coincided
with a general change in the relations of Finland and Russia. In the mid-1880s,
there developed a series of legal questions which gave rise to differences between

the ruling circles in the two countries. One question related to the revived project to codify Finnish law: Heiden transferred the work of the committee considering this question to a mixed Finnish-Russian committee. In this connection Russian concepts began to be advanced which sought to deny the constitutional basis of Finnish autonomy and reduce it to a local autonomy. Another point of difference was raised by the revised Finnish criminal law. St Petersburg demanded changes so that it should become consolidated with the criminal law of the empire. As differences were emphasised in this fashion, the dispute began to widen and intensify. Some leading groups of Finnish liberals wanted to take the discussion of Finland's special constitutional status into the international forum and so get support for their own views; this was the objective of Leo Mechelin's work on the constitutional and legal status of Finland, published in French in 1886 and in German in 1889.[19]

Finnish interpretations of the country's special status, which were based on a western conception of law and a strong constitutionalist ideology, provoked irritation among the Russians; this was especially so in the case of the discussion, which occurred from time to time in liberal circles, of a 'union' relationship between Finland and Russia, and of Finland as 'a state', and the desire which surfaced in some Finnish circles to emphasise that Finland had 'freedom of manoeuvre' in the international crises which involved Russia. In such contexts the Russians accused the Finns of 'separatism'. K. Ordin's book *The Conquest of Finland*, published in 1887, was intended as a systematic reply to the interpretations advanced by the Finns. Its dominant idea was that in the autocratically-governed Russian empire there could not be such a peculiar, constitutionally-governed part. Finland had, according to Ordin, only 'local autonomy'. Several Russian constitutional experts explained that Finland, with its own constitution, was logically irreconcilable with the state-structure of the empire.[20] Thus at the end of the 1880s, pressure from various directions was turned against the special political status of Finland; however, there were restraints which blocked or delayed the final breaking of the dam. Finland's autonomy had been clearly recognised by St Petersburg, especially in the actions of Alexander II. The loyalty of Finland was also a fact; no revolt had occurred there as in Poland. Finland was not, from the military point of view, such a vital area as Poland or the Baltic provinces, but still, it was not insignificant.

Endeavours towards russification began to emerge clearly around 1890. As an autonomous country, Finland at this stage formed an ever more prominent anomaly after the assimilation policy carried out in Poland and the Baltic provinces. On the basis of initiatives originating in St Petersburg, the question was raised of uniting the Finnish postal system, currency and customs tariff with the corresponding Russian systems. Imperial centralisation was however realised only for the Finnish postal system which, in a special manifesto of 1890, was united with that of Russia, and the distinctive Finnish stamps, in use since 1856, were withdrawn. In Finland not only the decision itself, but also the fact that it had been implemented by decree in the form of a rescript issued by the Emperor, were regarded with suspicion. The event showed on what a weak basis Finland's special political status rested. The reorganisation of the postal system had been wholly prepared in St Petersburg, the system for the handling of Finnish affairs had been thrust aside and the Emperor had in Finnish eyes deliberately broken the laws of the constitution. Business leaders in Finland now feared that the Russian rouble, which had proved unstable in the international market, would come into use in the country in place of the Finnish gold mark. Moreover, if the tariff barriers between Finland and Russia were abolished, this would mean, besides the shrinking of autonomy, a loss to the budget of the important and continuously increasing customs revenue, which had helped to finance many reforms and economic projects in the country. However the abolition of the tariff barriers was clearly opposed in Russia as well, because it was thought that without them Finnish industry could become a dangerous competitor to its nascent Russian counterpart.

At the beginning of the 1890s, certain Russian newspapers began a long press campaign against Finnish autonomy. *Moskovskiya Vedomosti* and *Novoye Vremya*, which led it, were important lobbyists for nationalism, and had contacts with the most influential circles in the empire.[22] The intensity of the campaign is shown by the fact that in 1890 there was, on average, a leading article in *Moskovskiya Vedomosti* on the special status of Finland every week. The paper's Helsinki correspondent, Yakubov, acted as a kind of 'political watch-dog' who took up the various occurences in which he regarded the Finnish administration as overlooking the interests of the empire. The liberal *Novosti* and *Vestnik Evropy* mostly endorsed the Finns' own view of their special status. They, like Russian liberals generally, regarded Finland as a valuable 'peninsula of liberalism' in the empire. However, the stand taken by these papers in defence of the Finns only seemed to increase the irritation among the Russian nationalists.

During this Russo-Finnish press war, the activity on the Finnish side is shown by the fact that during the five-year period 1890–4 there were about 700–800 articles in *Hufvudstadsbladet* and *Nya Pressen* which referred to Finland's special political status.[23] Of these, about half were translations of articles in the Russian press. The Finnish press appeared united at the time of the conflict, although *Uusi Suometar* was more restrained in its polemics than the other papers in Helsinki. The Russian papers for their part held *Nya Pressen* as the most active defender of Finland's special status. One argument used by *Moskovskiya Vedomosti* in the conflict was that the broad mass of the people in Finland were not opposed to the Russification policy; opposition to it was only 'the separatism of the masters'.

At the beginning of the 1890s, the Finns lived within their own political traditions, concentrating on the development — and defence — of their autonomy, and on the internal reform of Finnish society. The crises which arose in Finland's relations with Russia at this time were felt primarily by the governing élite in Finland and by those accustomed to following politics systematically. By contrast, the crisis does not seem to have been felt at all in the farming community for instance. The uncertainty and insecurity of the country's political leaders over the questions of Finland's special political status had already been increased. On the Finnish question the wind in Russia had clearly turned, but there were still many incalculable factors involved in the situation. The view of Leo Mechelin moved somewhere between pessimism and mild optimism, as he explained in a letter to a Swedish friend in December 1893: 'I have not lost hope that if we still behave realistically and moderately, we shall get through the difficult crisis without shipwreck'.[24] This statement shows that the basing of political activity on the constitution and Finland's separate development had largely lost credibility. The political leaders now began to react very cautiously to all changes, fearing all the time that the special political status of the country might become subject to change: they must therefore be content with the lesser evil when it proved difficult to achieve improvements. It was not possible, for example, to think of developing the Finnish tariff structure when there was a danger that the country might lose its own customs system entirely. A defensive kind of national conservatism was thus forming among the Finnish political leaders, as they feared that relations with the east would deteriorate further.

5. *The name of Finland abroad and attempts to establish a Finnish information service*

The signs of crisis which occurred around 1890 in the relations of Finland and Russia also attracted attention in the foreign press. The preceding twenty-five years and more, a time of great internal reforms in the country, had seen no occurrences dramatic enough to arouse attention abroad as major political news. Also, Finland's relations with the Russian empire had caused no friction, so this too did not merit consideration outside the empire's borders.

In Germany, by the 1890s, both in official foreign policy and in public opinion, there had appeared signs of anti-Russian feeling which resulted in attention being given to the internal weaknesses of the Russian empire, such as the position of the non-Russian nationalities.[25] In addition the Russification policy begun in the Baltic provinces in the 1880s, directed as it was against the German part of the population among others, had occasioned wide discussion in the German press. The German opposition groups, both liberal and social democrat, felt uncommitted regarding their country's official foreign policy. They wanted to criticise freely the internal conditions of Russia, in which they saw much that was reactionary, and the oppressive measures against the non-Russian nationalities. In addition the general attitude of the German social democrats was traditionally anti-Russian, drawing inspiration from Karl Marx's views on Russia.[26]

France's new alignment in foreign policy, built on its alliance with Russia, had its opponents whose views were most strongly coloured by the general ideological conflict between tsarist Russia and republican France.[27] Those circles in France which were hostile to tsarism, when criticising Russian conditions, gladly seized on evidence of oppression of the nationalities. Since Poland, a perennial object of sympathy in France, had vanished from the picture after the 1863 revolt, the Finnish question was the kind to which liberal circles could give their attention.

In the early 1890s, interest in Finland was also felt in Britain, where changes were taking place in the general direction of political concern. A period of two decades was coming to an end, in which Britain's political attention had been concentrated primarily in two directions — towards Europe, to those changes which followed the rise of Germany, and towards the realisation of the colonial policies being carried out in Africa.[28] Now interest in Britain was turning back to the development of Europe in a more general way. The question of Irish home rule added to the general interest felt among British liberals in autonomy, of which Finland showed one of the few examples in Europe.

For more than two decades Swedish interest had been concentrated mainly on Finland's cultural life and the development of the language struggle. Now there started up in Sweden a discussion of the 'Russian threat'. The ending of the Reinsurance Treaty between Germany and Russia in 1890, the postal manifesto in Finland and other events lent credence to the idea that changes of a destabilising nature were to be expected in eastern Europe. This prompted the question in Sweden of whether the country's armed forces should be developed and strengthened. At the beginning of the 1890s in Sweden, the Finnish question was discussed in the press and elsewhere, and fear was expressed that the Russian hold on Finland might be strengthened, which would lead to the Scandinavian tradition in Finnish public life, and cultural relations and other contacts between Sweden and Finland being diminished.[29]

The writings which appeared in the foreign press at the beginning of the 1890s about its special political status often provoked dissatisfaction and even concern in Finland. From these writings it was very clear that information on Finland's political circumstances was often inadequate and not infrequently erroneous. The conclusions about Finland's future were often pessimistic. Crises in Russian-Finnish relations were often described as a step towards the full russification of the country; the matter was presented thus in *Le Matin*.[30]

Among Finnish political circles the idea arose — apparently for the first time — that an information service should be established abroad, to be administered unofficially.[31] Finland had already tried to achieve international recognition in certain fields; for example, she had taken part in international exhibitions to promote her industrial and agricultural exports, though not without difficulty. She had not been allowed by St Petersburg to exhibit at the Paris world fair in 1878 in a separate section, but despite this had succeeded to some extent in creating an image of the country abroad — its culture and people — as the two gold medals obtained at the Paris fair showed.[32] Finland did however manage to appear in a section of her own at the 1889 Paris world fair. Such international achievements undoubtedly fostered Finnish national consciousness at a delicate stage in its emergence. All such activity was helped by the fact that Finns had begun travelling abroad in greater numbers, creating commercial and cultural contacts. From around 1890 tourism had expanded considerably in Europe; travel literature increased at the same time and there were now works dealing exclusively with Finland.[33]

In this period of national development, and with signs that a political crisis was appearing, publicity about Finland abroad — if so exacting a term can be used — was clearly perceived by the country's leaders as an important matter. It is difficult to follow the development of this phenomenon in detail, though some indication of what was attempted can be seen in the publication in 1894 of a work in English, French, German and Swedish called *Finland in the Nineteenth Century*. Its authors were a group of the country's foremost men, from Mechelin to Topelius, and its purpose was to give well-informed foreigners a well-founded overall presentation of Finland, the development of its special political status, and the country's cultural and economic life. By the standards of the age, this work received considerable publicity in several countries. In addition, its publication stimulated writing about Finland in foreign newspapers and periodicals,[34] which because of its solid content, its appreciative attitude to the country, and recognition of the high level of culture, gave great satisfaction to Finnish political circles.

XII. The February Manifesto (1899), the crisis in Russo-Finnish relations and its international repercussions

In the course of the nineteenth century the security and loyalty of Finland came to form complementary aspects of her relations with Russia. Finnish politicians were unwilling to take changes in their country's position seriously. When difficulties appeared, they tried to find ground for optimism by constantly wishing for a return to the times of Alexander II and taking refuge in the image of the ruler which he had created.

From the 1860s Finland's different political groups had worked along the same lines in carrying out the major reforms, and had been united in emphasising the importance of the Diet, but from the 1880s questions of the position of the Finnish language had divided the Diet sharply in two. At the same time the political division of fennomans and svecomans had spread from south Finland into Pohjanmaa. This also isolated the language groups from one another in daily life. As there was a powerful belief among the Swedish-speakers that they represented the country's élite, so the Finnish-speakers had begun in increasing numbers, as the strong numerical majority, to demand the exclusive right to express what was in the minds of the Finnish people. Surrounding the language struggle there was thus a strong aura of power struggle, and the relations between the language groups were coloured accordingly.

Finnish society in turn was divided socially into two, the upper class and the common people, not only on the basis of social position and wealth, but also by education and family tradition. Beside the predominantly Swedish-speaking upper class a new Finnish-speaking educated class was emerging; often with its roots in farming society, it had studied at the Finnish-language secondary schools set up in different parts of the country from the 1870s. The 1890s saw a powerful awakening in the rural areas.[1]

At the same time Finnish society was undergoing broad social change, due particularly to the development of industry and, after the famine of 1867, a major increase in population. In 1892–4, there was a depression which had wide social consequences, including unemployment leading to social discontent. From this there developed a proletarian consciousness and open hatred of the bosses. Socialist ideas from continental Europe found a receptive soil. When in the mid-1890s, strike movements broke out, for example in the building trade, both the country's Swedish- and Finnish-language newspapers reacted in a sharply negative way, and when labour was recruited from St Petersburg to break them, there was no special discussion in the press.

1. *The general aims of Russian policy and the February Manifesto*

The beginning of the 1890s saw broad repercussions from certain changes that had occurred in Russia's international position. The military alliance concluded with France gave security against Germany, but indirectly provided more room for manoeuvre politically within the borders of the empire. This affected the position of the non-Russian nationalities, including Finland. The Russian General Staff began to show more interest than before in the Baltic. The fact that Germany was developing her fleet and building the Kiel canal was thought to make a concentration of German naval forces in the Baltic a possibility: hence the need to pay attention to the future naval operations of the assumed enemy. It was believed that the Germans could use the areas of Courland and the Gulf of Riga for landings preparatory to attacks on St Petersburg. To counter this danger naval bases were built at Libau and Windau, under the protection of which units of the Russian Baltic fleet could be stationed.[2] The Russians also gave renewed attention to the organisation of defence in the Gulf of Finland. The war minister P.S. Vannovsky proposed to Alexander III in August 1891 that the Finnish army and conscription system should be brought more into line with the system of the empire.[3] On this point he followed the same line as his predecessor, General D.A. Milyutin, who had not approved of the separate conscription system in Finland at the end of the 1870s. In 1893, the French military attaché in St Petersburg noted the increasing military significance of the Finnish question in the context of a possible war between Germany and Russia. He was familiar with the political attacks against the special status of Finland at this time in the Russian press, and saw them as possibly having significant consequences. In any case, he thought that 'submission to discipline and respect for lawful authority' were characteristics of the Finns, as was an unconditional loyalty to the empire.[4]

International political developments were followed in Finland too, most of all the formation of alliances between the great powers. However, the Finnish way of looking at international politics was deeply coloured by domestic considerations; illegality and oppression of small countries were given special attention. They talked of illegality in the same breath as they talked of all power politics. The cases of Bulgaria, Ireland and Portugal were regarded as clear examples of the distresses of small nations.[5] The general attitude of the Finnish newspapers to the international situation was pacifist, and with it there often went hopes of smoothing out the conflicts between the great powers. The most significant political occurrence of 1891 was thought to be the rapprochement of France and Russia, the outward sign of which — the visit to Kronstadt in that year of a French naval squadron — was widely noted in the Finnish press.[6] In the development which led to the Dual Alliance, France was often depicted in the Finnish press as the active partner, which was trying to 'fawn' upon St Petersburg and upon those Russians, primarily the nationalists, who spoke in favour of a military alliance. The alliance of France and Russia was further regarded as strange because of the ideological contradictions between them, and on that basis it was liable to be characterised as 'ambiguous'. Typically, *Uusi Suometar* regarded France as morally degenerate, and thus of questionable value as Russia's ally. *Päivälehti*, on the other hand, criticised the countries of the Triple Alliance, stressing German militarism and describing Austria-Hungary and Italy as burdened by heavy military expenditure.[7]

The examination of international political developments in the Finnish papers was superficial to the extent that they do not seem to have discussed the possible consequences of the Franco-Russian alliance and its indirect effects on, for example, Finland's relations with Russia. The traditional nineteenth-century attitude appeared when war broke out between Turkey and Greece in 1897, and turkophobia was again strongly in evidence. This was the last noteworthy appearance of an 'anti-pagan' stance in Finland.[8]

In the 1890s, the government in St Petersburg continued, as ever, to distrust Finland's Swedish-speakers; the roots of this feeling went back to the Crimean war, and the international crisis of 1863. The svecomans were clearly seen as supporters of Westernism who were ready to react against everything that was Russian or Slav. The government based its assessment of the fennomans on different criteria. In the 1830s it had begun to 'tolerate' this intellectual move- ment; it was seen then as estranging the Finns from their historical and spiritual ties to Sweden. Of course St Petersburg did not approve of the fennoman ideal as such, but were prepared to use it for their own purposes, seeking to keep it as a purely cultural tendency, while hindering it from becoming politicised. The Crimean war and the transition of 1863, when the attitude of the fennomans concerning loyalty had emerged, led to a clear change of position towards them in St Petersburg: thereafter the fennomans were preferred to the svecomans. At the same time, there was a strengthening of conservatism and patriarchalism within the fennoman movement, which appeared to guarantee security against western revolutionary ideas spreading into the Finnish borderlands.

From the 1880s, governing circles in Russia began to regard with suspicion the 'young Finn' group of the fennomans, which was detaching itself as a distinct political entity. Its democratic programme were feared as constituting a basis for a dangerous political mass movement. In addition, like the svecomans, the young Finns' leaders were strong adherents of the country's autonomy. The Emperor's entourage sought to use the older fennomans, whose leader was Yrjö Koskinen, as a tool for weakening the influence of the svecomans. Thus Finnish- speakers were favoured in official appointments and Swedish-speakers were passed over. The arrival of Heiden as Governor-General in 1881 had also meant that the nature of official contacts with Finnish political circles at this top level changed, and Yrjö Koskinen, who became a senator in 1882, was accorded a more prominent position.

Behind the great change, of which the new attitude to Finland emanating from Russia was a symptom, there were three main factors, as has been shown earlier: the modernisation of Finnish society in a western direction, and its obvious differentiation from the empire; the rise of Russian nationalism, in connection with which the russification taking place in other parts of the empire made Finland a source of irritation; and thirdly the development of international politics, which emphasised the importance of thinking about straightforward military preparedness, and pushed aside more flexible political procedures. At the same time, the growing international tension freed Russia to act on the Finnish question.

The high-level changes of personnel after the accession of Nicholas II as Emperor in 1894 set in motion practical measures in relation to Finland's special status. After General Vannovsky, the energetic General Kuropatkin became minister of war in 1898, and at the same time the offices of Governor-General of Finland and Minister-Secretary were vacant, following the resignations of Heiden and von Daehn in 1897. The key figure in russification policy in Finland was General Bobrikov, who had held many important military posts, *inter alia* as chief of staff to the St Petersburg military district, and had also been a member of the military committees set up in the early 1880s to consider Russia's military position in the light of the danger threatening from Germany. So far as is known, Bobrikov was already hostile to Finnish autonomy, which in his opinion was an anomaly *vis-à-vis* the unity of the empire, and had expressed his opinion on 'breaking up' the special status of Finland and 'the eradication of separatism' there.

In June 1898 Bobrikov was actually given the special task of drawing up an overall russification programme for Finland, and when the programme was presented to Nicholas II on 29 August 1898, he was nominated as Finland's new Governor-General. Bobrikov was an advocate of the traditional Russian system and a nationalist, with a strongly anti-western attitude. Military considerations weighed heavily in his outlook.

In the programme drawn up by Bobrikov, the whole nineteenth-century relationship of Finland and Russia came under severe criticism. Finland was regarded as forming 'a border area which up to now has remained foreign . . . to Russia'. Russia's prestige demanded that Finland should gradually be transformed into a 'Russian borderland'. It was intended to undertake measures in different fields 'to reduce Finnish separatism': the assimilation of the Finnish armed forces into those of Russia, the definition of the basis of the fundamental constitutional law, the adoption of the Russian language in public offices and as a subject of study in schools, the abolition of Finland's separate currency and customs system, the bringing of Helsinki University under supervision and subjecting school textbooks to inspection.[10] As soon as Bobrikov was nominated, *Novoye Vremya* hastened to announce that it expected energetic measures from him. The invitation already given by the Emperor for the meeting of the Diet in January 1899, to consider a new proposal for an imperial military service law, was the practical inauguration of this new Russian policy on Finland.[11]

When the Diet met at the beginning of 1899, it soon became clear that the

Finnish Estates would insist on their own interpretation of the country's constitution, and would reject the imperial proposal to change the military service law. In Nicholas II's entourage this had possibly been anticipated, and therefore preparations for a general redefinition of the basis of Finland's special status were quickly started, for which a secret committee was established. The counter-stroke of the Russian leadership was the manifesto signed by Nicholas II on 15 February. Its aim was to set limits to the peculiar development of Finland and secure a stronger supervisory grip on the country. This so-called February Manifesto laid down the framework for imperial legislation, i.e. for the handling of legislation concerning Finland and Russia jointly, or 'Russian interests in Finland'. Appealing to the 'basic principle' which it enshrined, the Manifesto also directed that the proposal before the Diet for a new military service law and certain other matters would be transferred for consideration to the Russian State Council; the function of the Finnish Diet would be to make comments on the legislation only.

A difficult political problem arose in Finland over the publication of the February Manifesto. Bobrikov may have threatened severe counter-measures if the Senate held this up;[12] however this did not happen. The question of publication was resolved in the Senate, although the votes on the issue were tied, which enabled the chairman to decide the content of the resolution.

After the February Manifesto, the discussion of the military service law went ahead; by contrast, new imperial decisions in the spirit of the Russification policy followed slowly, clearly influenced by the reactions from Finnish society. Among the significant later measures were the language manifesto of 1900, concerning the use of Russian in the higher levels of the country's administration and as a major subject of study in secondary schools, further limitations on the right of freedom of association and public assembly, and the suppression of some newspapers, most notably *Nya Pressen*; in addition Eero Erkko was forced to resign as chief editor of the young Finns' *Päivälehti*.[13]

After the Manifesto the question of political methods of action in the new situation came to absorb much discussion and energy in Finland. In addition to the work of the Diet, attempts were made to find new dimensions of activity, such as the collection of signatures for the so-called Great Address in the spring of 1899: it was thought that when the Emperor saw the opinion of the whole, loyal Finnish people, he could not break the country's constitution. The collection of signatures for the Address was undoubtedly well organised throughout the whole country, but there were other reasons for its success. The February Manifesto had deeply disturbed public opinion, and here the country's press acted the part of instructor. The general social awakening of the countryside was an influence in the background. The result was something unprecedented in Finnish circumstances; the Address got over 522,000 signatures.

As the vote in the Senate on the publication of the February Manifesto had already shown, a new kind of political division was appearing in Finnish political circles. It was thought that they must decide first what methods of action should be adopted towards those Russian measures which were held to be illegal. This was connected to another major question, namely what were they aiming for, and how far did they intend to go in St Petersburg on the Finnish question, and were Russia's interests mainly military, or were there wider aims, such as a general russification in Finland.[14] In the new political groupings which arose in the transitional period, which lasted from the publication of the February Manifesto to the end of 1900, even the language barriers came to be broken. It was firmly believed that the Manifesto was part of a russification policy deliberately framed in St Petersburg, which might lead to the complete destruction of Finland's special status. The problem was seen as basically a legal one, to be answered by the methods of legal struggle. Passive resistance was regarded as the appropriate tactic, and this brought together two very different political groups: on the one hand the Swedish party, whose political outlook was strongly conservative and oligarchic, but for whom legality and the preservation of existing conditions were highly important, and on the other hand the young Finns, who in the mid-1890s had broken away as a political group of their own to demand reforms in accordance with liberal and democratic principles. The workers' movement, which had organised as an independent party in 1899 (first called the Finnish Workers' party and from 1903 the Social Democratic party) also joined the passive resistance group. It saw Bobrikov's activity, not only as directed against Finland's constitutional rights, but as socially reactionary. Since it sought to limit all political activity in the country, it might also curb the activity of the workers' movement and make the realisation of its aims difficult.

The alternative to passive resistance was the so-called appeasement policy, which assumed that Russian aims in Finland were limited, and that what was happening was a temporary disturbance in the relations between Finland and Russia. Harmony was to be restored by making 'realistic' concessions. The older people in the Finnish party, led by Yrjö Koskinen, believed that by negotiation and 'bridge-building' a compromise could be found. Their position was founded on an attitude of loyalty traditionally represented by the fennomans, although their previous activity as the party of government caused them to emphasise responsible behaviour in all circumstances. The respective emergence of a passive resistance and an appeasement line acutely divided the academic intellectuals, their Finnish-speaking part splitting in two. The new situation in the country also created a personal dilemma for those holding government posts, who had to decide whether an order from above was in accordance with, or contrary to, the Finnish constitution and how they should act if it was contrary. A civil servant who refused to carry out an order could face dismissal. Hence K.J. Ståhlberg was relieved of his post as minute-secretary to the Senate in 1903 on a matter of principle, and P.E. Svinhufvud was dismissed in the same year from the office of associate judge of the Turku Court of Appeal. However, this happened to only relatively few officials, and many yielded to circumstances, which on various grounds they sought to interpret as *force majeure*.[15]

The clergy and the farmers' leaders had close connections with the fenno-mans, and in particular with their conservative tendency, within which old Finn ideas were growing. At the same time the clergy were reacting strongly against cultural liberalism and the criticism of the church and religion connected with it,[16] and this influenced the political line which the clergy adopted. The farmers, especially the wealthier section represented in the Diet, tended to be conservative and traditionalist.

At the time of the February Manifesto, the Finnish clergy's position was unique in that nowhere else in Europe did the clergy still constitute an Estate in a Diet; hence it was forced to take a stand on the major political issues of the time. The archbishop, Gustaf Johansson, on a number of occasions before his elevation in 1899, had stressed the importance of constitutionalism. But his attitude changed after a conversation with Nicholas II which led him to conclude that Finland's autonomy would be left undisturbed once certain changes, regarded by St Petersburg as necessary, had been carried out. After this the archbishop held it to be important that the church should conduct itself with political caution. He was also convinced that the measures which the Russians had carried out against the Lutheran church in the Baltic provinces had been provoked by the clergy there interfering in politics. Johansson gave his view in pastoral letters to the clergy, a considerable majority of whom elected to follow the old Finn line of appeasement.

2. *The Finnish information service abroad and foreign reactions to the February Manifesto*

After the February Manifesto, Finnish political leaders had tried in various ways to get into contact with St Petersburg, but with little success.[17] At the same time, the leading passive resistance groups wanted to 'internationalise' the crisis between Finland and Russia; they wanted to generate discussion abroad on what was a just interpretation of the country's autonomous status. They did not seek to appeal to governments but to experts in constitutional law in the different countries. Because the latter were outside normal politics, it was hoped that by their neutrality they could influence the Russian Emperor and his entourage. It was not the intention of these passive resistance circles to abandon loyalty to the Russian empire, or to build up hopes that there would be external diplomatic intervention on Finland's behalf. Primarily, then, they espoused the view, which had remained alive in Finnish liberal circles since the 1860s, that enlightened European opinion was a significant factor which could even influence the fates of nations. The optimum aim of the Finns was to produce such expressions of international opinion as would prevent the measures against Finland's autonomy from being put into effect by Russia.

For the first time a large group of Finns were active abroad for a political purpose. It consisted mainly of older academic intellectuals, especially Swedish-speakers, who varied contacts in several countries. There was no organised leadership of Finnish activity abroad; however, a working group in Helsinki led by Leo Mechelin (*Kommittén för utländsk propaganda*) held meetings in Helsinki. This was a liaison organisation, which endeavoured to develop the propaganda activity abroad. A difficulty was that those involved had no official status, nor even any official credentials.[18] Moreover, the fact that the Finnish Senate had published the February Manifesto made activity abroad that was directed against that manifesto difficult. One noteworthy example of Finnish activity abroad was the so-called Cultural Address, for which the names of foreign scholars and other cultural personalities were collected, and which it was intended to deliver to Nicholas II as an international protest at the infringement of the Finnish constitution. This was the common product of the sympathy felt towards Finland, mainly in academic circles, and the influence of leading Finnish academics.[19]

The unofficial Finnish information service, set up in the aftermath of the February Manifesto, constituted a kind of orientation to the west. Hopes were focused upon Britain and France, where it was believed support would be found for Finland's autonomy. German constitutional lawyers on the other hand tended to base their thinking on the authority of the sovereign. The renowned jurist Georg Jellinek had put forward the idea some years earlier that Finland was not a state but a part of a state (*Staatsfragment*), a view unfavourable for the defence of the country's autonomy. There were very few German signatories of the Cultural Address.[20] No significant opinions appeared in Germany seeking to deny Russia's sovereign rights in Finland, and on the whole the publication of the February Manifesto attracted little attention there. In so far as it was referred to at all, it was usually in the context of the new military service law, and how the aim of tsarist policy, powerfully implemented by Bobrikov, was to safeguard Russian military interests in Finland.[21] The only exceptions to this general indifference were found among liberal and democratic circles not committed to Germany's official policy. The liberal *Vossische Zeitung*, which valued all constitutionalism, judged that the February Manifesto was having a paralysing effect on the Finns.[22] The social democratic *Vorwärts* drew the extreme conclusion that Finland's autonomy had received its death blow; later it spoke of the Manifesto as 'an attempted assassination by the tsar' directed against Finland.[23]

In Britain the events in Finland interested some small groups, and the affair also received limited coverage in the press. *The Times* discussed the fate of Finland's autonomy in an editorial in March 1899. The paper observed a contradiction in Russia's policy, due to its having begun to undermine Finland's autonomy at the very time that Russia was working to bring about an international conference for the peaceful resolution of conflicts. Finland, a highly-developed country, had suffered the fate of Poland through no fault of its own.[24] The liberal *Daily Chronicle* criticised Russian policy severely; it thought that a *coup d'etat* had taken place in Finland and, like *The Times*, saw a contradiction in

Russian policy.[25] There were also signs in British papers of the Finns' own activity; for example *The Times* published a letter from J.N. Reuter.[26] The readiness of the leading papers in France to discuss the crisis in the relations between Finland and Russia seemed once again, as in the 1890s, to reflect indirectly their attitude towards French official foreign policy and the alliance with Russia. However, France was a country where traditionally, justice was an important element in political thinking, and it was also of some significance that the relationship of a great power and a small one was the question at issue. Typically, *Le Matin* remained cool on the Finnish question, but *Le Temps* published a leading article expressing sympathy for Finland and criticising Nicholas II. The Finnish Diet, according to the paper, had been changed into 'an advisory Zemstvo'.[27] *Journal des Débats*, which published the views of both parties on Finland's autonomy side by side, said that the Finns represented a western point of view.[28]

Sweden was the only foreign country in 1899 where the Finnish question received broad coverage, and where public opinion was deeply engaged on the subject. Extensive writing in the Swedish papers on Finland's status had already begun in the autumn of 1898, when Bobrikov's appointment as Governor-General was announced, and when it began to be clear that a new russification programme was being worked out. If Sweden had ceased to be a problem for Russia, there was no doubt that Russia was becoming a serious problem for Sweden. Events in Finland were seen from Stockholm as reflecting Russia's military policy. Sweden was especially concerned at Russia's attempt to obtain a dominant hold over Finland and was seemingly taking a step towards the west. However, the Swedish papers also showed a clear sympathy for Finland. Old cultural ties and principles of justice had not lost their power, and in the situation of 1899 they acquired an enhanced position. This wave of sympathy did not extend only to the Swedish-speakers, but to the whole Finnish people, which was defending its political rights and protecting its culture. Russia's policy in Finland was criticised with special severity in Sweden by *Nya Dagligt Allehanda* and *Aftonbladet*. The February Manifesto was frequently described as an 'annexation', with the purpose of supplanting the country's constitution.[29]

However, alongside the main tendency of the Swedish press there was also another attitude to events in Finland, expressed by certain influential circles involved in the country's official foreign policy. Harald Hjärne gave vent to this kind of thinking in articles in *Svenska Dagbladet* in 1899. He did not approve of moralising declarations in the field of foreign policy, and demanded that feelings should be put aside, especially in a small country; in discussing the Finnish question, criticism of Nicholas II should be avoided. Hjärne's views attracted a lot of attention.[30]

The Cultural Address, signed by over 1,000 influential people, among them many jurists from different countries, was a remarkable expression of international opinion. The Paris world fair of 1900 also had political significance in spreading an image of Finland round the world. The Finnish pavilion, designed by Eliel Saarinen and for which Aksel Gallen-Kallela painted frescoes on themes from the Kalevala, tried above all to depict a country that was culturally and economically developed, a country of western culture which was threatened from the east.

In the spring of 1899, Finnish political circles were optimistic about the significance for the future of the propaganda being launched abroad in defence of the country's autonomy. When the Hague Peace Conference assembled, later in 1899, the Cultural Address clearly helped to nurture the belief that it would be possible in the Conference itself to engineer declarations of protest against the promoter, Russia, because of her infringement of Finnish autonomy.[31] However the inner circle, led by Mechelin, was well aware of the difficulties which faced Finnish propaganda abroad. At a time when the Boer war was attracting keen attention in Europe, and when the conflicts of the great powers were abundantly in evidence, Mechelin did not think it opportune to present the problems of Finland's autonomy internationally.[32] The success of the early phase of foreign activity soon changed, as opportunities were exhausted, although publications about Finland continued to appear in English, French and German. Quantitatively they had undoubtedly achieved much,[33] but over the effect of this activity, there was disappointment.

The crisis in the relations of Finland and Russia created by the February Manifesto attracted considerable attention in the reports of the foreign diplomatic representatives in St Petersburg. Also the consuls of Britain, France, Germany, Austria-Hungary and Sweden in Helsinki made detailed reports,[34] in which two features predominated. On the one hand the Manifesto was seen as portending a major change for Finland's autonomy and giving rise to pessimism. On the other hand the reports often criticised the political behaviour of the Finns, and being written by representatives of great powers, were often sympathetic towards the actions of another great power. This was especially true of Russia's efforts to obtain the solution she wanted for her military interests in Finland; this aim was generally regarded as an essential element in the February Manifesto. The Finns' own political outlook, especially over its autonomy, was thought of as characteristically self-centered and isolated from the broader sweep of events. The French ambassador in St Petersburg, for example, observed that it was a series of political follies committed by the Finns themselves which had led to the February Manifesto. In the view of the foreign representatives in St Petersburg, the Finnish question posed a considerable problem for Russian policy, and had caused annoyance in Russia, because the Finns had internationalised the question of their autonomy. Later, however, as Bobrikov's activity continued, criticism of Russian policy also appeared in the diplomatic reports. Russian attempts to unite Finland to the empire by strong ties were seen to be leading to the creation of a 'second Poland' in the vicinity of St Petersburg.

The publicity secured abroad for the Finnish question after the February Manifesto was clearly felt in St Petersburg as a disturbance of international relations, although there had been no question of any kind of international crisis. The Russian foreign ministry sent out material to embassies in St Petersburg, in which they sought to explain Russian policy in Finland, and to refute the western interpretations of Finnish autonomy. Also V.M. Plehve, one of the Emperor's closest advisers, was given the task of organising counter-propaganda abroad against that put out by the Finns. Some extensive Russian statements on the status of Finland appeared in major western languages after 1899.[35]

Nicholas II also discussed the criticisms which had been expressed abroad of Russian actions against Finland's autonomy with the British ambassador. The Emperor said that he approved of British action in South Africa and expressed the hope that Britain would reciprocate over Russian actions in Finland. This proposal of the Emperor for mutual non-intervention was clearly intended to deter the British government from taking up the Finnish cause. Anyway, the government in St Petersburg was trying to put a stop to the international discussion on the status of Finland.

3. *The Finnish political crisis and Finnish émigrés in Sweden*

By 1901 the constitutionalist group had reached a point where it had to begin re-assessing the situation. On the one hand it was clear that the activity abroad had not achieved its objectives, and indeed, after the early success, had clearly failed. On the other hand, the situation in the domestic political forum was in many ways puzzling, with the Finnish political leadership sharply split two ways in its attitude to St Petersburg.

The leadership of this group also had problems of their own concerning the organisation of passive resistance. The support given to the Address had undoubtedly been quite unprecedented in Finnish circumstances, but it had been primarily a demonstration of initial reactions to the February Manifesto. It remained an open question how ready those broad sections of the population in town and country who were excluded from participation in the Diet, but who formed 70 per cent or more of the adult population, to support passive resistance.

This was linked to another question, to which the constitutionalists also had to pay attention. Bobrikov's oppressive measures in the first two years after the February Manifesto had primarily affected only the leading groups in Finnish society. The ordinary people, on the whole, were not affected by them. However, political perspectives began to change when the new 'imperial' military service law was about to come into force, and service in Russian military units was to be expected. The leaders of the constitutionalists faced the question of how passive resistance activities could be organised over the whole country, and how the mass of the people could be drawn into them. For this purpose a secret conference of the leaders of the constitutionalists was held in the autumn of 1901.

The aim was to create an active group in every parish in the country which should organise passive resistance as needed. The attitude of the clergy was of vital importance, and to ensure broad support it was thought important that the working class should participate in this kind of united demonstration. At the conferences of the constitutionalist leaders held in November 1902, it was decided that contacts must be established with the workers' movement:[36] the existence of severe social problems in the country was recognised in Mechelin's entourage, but it was hoped that they would not be an obstacle to creating this kind of joint action. They wanted to be sure of support from the workers' movement, although it still represented a very modest factor. As an organised force at the end of 1902 there were over forty workers' associations in the country with a membership of a little over 8,000:[37] it was recognised as a political force of increasing strength. By involving the workers it was hoped to balance the situation caused by part of the Finnish-speakers having shifted to the appeasement line.

The so-called conscription strikes, organised in 1902–4 in connection with the call-up for military service, were nationwide, organised passive resistance, supported by the Young Finns, the Swedish party and representatives of the workers' movement with the aid of their own organisations. Opinion was divided over reactions to the call-up. Both secular authority and the church leadership were active in ensuring that the clergy read out the call-up announcement in churches; of about 500 clergy, only some seventy refused to do so. The latter were mainly from Swedish-speaking areas, especially Uusimaa, where there was a strong tradition of passive resistance.[38] Passionate debate over participation in the call-up also went on among the students of Helsinki University, where the Young Finns and Old Finns disputed whether passive resistance or appeasement should be followed.[39]

Another facet of Bobrikov's oppressive policy, felt more widely by the people, was the limitation on the freedom of association and public assembly. This was noticed in the workers' movement when the founding of new workers' associations became more difficult, and particularly in 1903 when, because of the uncertain conditions, the planned workers' party congress had to be held in the remote parish of Forssa. The peak of Bobrikov's activity was the so-called dictatorship decree, which came into force in 1903. This gave the Governor-General very wide powers during three years to carry out policies of centralisation and russification, including the right to limit general civil liberties, and a wholly new authority to banish from Finland, abroad or to Russia, persons whom he regarded as harmful to 'political order and general tranquillity'. This new policy was directed and carried out directly from Helsinki. Bobrikov sought by his expulsion orders to break the backbone of the passive resistance. Among others Mechelin, von Born, Jonas Castrén, Eero Erkko and Eugen Wolff were exiled abroad, and Wrede, Ernst Estlander and Emil Schybergson to Russia. It was clearly intended that these measures should have an intimidating effect lasting into the future. Probably Bobrikov also aimed to prevent the attitude of passive resistance finding a response among ordinary people. It seems that to prevent mass resistance, carefully calculated rumours were set in motion among the rural poor by the Governor-General's entourage at the time of the conscription strikes to the effect that there would be schemes for carrying out a distribution of land in Finland.

Finnish political leaders thus found their scope far action narrowing. A policy based on the constitution and the 'word' of the Emperor seemed in every way to have lost its foundation. They had tried extensive passive resistance, and succeeded to the extent that many had refused the call-up. Certainly the resistance associated with the call-up had enormously increased political consciousness in the country, but on the other hand the attempts of the appeasers to build a bridge with the ruling circles in St Petersburg had remained fruitless. Political activity in the country was in many respects coming to a stop, writing about politics in the newspapers was meeting ever more obstacles and limitations, and pessimism was gaining ground. Relations between those who stood for passive resistance and appeasement were also becoming more tense. The appeasers, who had members in the Senate, were increasingly labelled as tools of the 'Bobrikov system'; and despite their efforts they had not succeeded in winning approval in St Petersburg through their conciliatory stance. In some circles the prominent supporters of appeasement were called the 'Russkies'.

Those exiled abroad generally established themselves in Stockholm, from where the situation in Finland could be followed and contact maintained with the homeland. Erkko was an exception who travelled from Stockholm to the United States. The mood among the political émigrés was gloomy; in their new circumstances opportunities for engaging in political activity were few, and there was the additional difficulty of settling in Swedish society and finding employment. The émigrés and their moods were felt to be a definite problem among the leaders of the constitutionalists in Helsinki; they wanted to ensure, in the autumn of 1903, that no decisions on political activity should be made in Stockholm before they had been given their approval from Helsinki.[40] In their new foreign environment, the émigrés were tied by the conditional nature of their residence permits; the Swedish authorities kept an eye on their political activities and did not want them to put a strain on the country's policy of neutrality in relations with Russia.

Some of the émigrés came to the conclusion that the fate of Finland's autonomy had been finally settled, and that the possibilities of returning home were non-existent. Schemes were evolved for founding a 'new Finland' in a safe environment somewhere overseas. Konni Zilliacus planned a colony for Finns in Canada and Erkko was enthusiastic about a similar scheme in Cuba. Reuter, some years earlier, had been in touch with the British colonial secretary, Joseph Chamberlain, to explore such possibilities as the British might offer.[41] However, political activity gradually gained momentum among the Finnish émigrés in Sweden. The underground paper, *Fria Ord*, which had been edited and published for some years under the leadership of Konni Zilliacus and Arvid Neovius, became an uncensored channel for political news from Sweden to the homeland, and a special distribution network was created in Finland for its circulation. The print-run of *Fria Ord* was small, although it was also published in Finnish with the title *Vapaita Sanoja*,[42] but had greater significance in spreading news and shaping opinion than the size of its print indicated, because copies passed from hand to hand.

A bold attempt to get the opinions of the passive resistance leaders published in Sweden — by-passing the Finnish censor — was Axel Lille's endeavour to buy *Stockholms Tidningen* into Finnish ownership. But the Swedish government intervened and prevented any permanent change in the paper's ownership from taking place.[43] Here was demonstrated the cautious attitude of Swedish officialdom to the political activity of the Finnish émigrés in Stockholm. When Erkko got to the United States he started a paper called *Amerikan Kaiku* whose purpose, besides the circulation of news about political conditions in Finland among the Finnish emigrants, was to try to spread uncensored information to the homeland. By the beginning of 1904, however, officials at home had already blocked this endeavour.[44] Erkko also busied himself with founding a special Finland Fund in the United States to support propaganda activity on Finland's behalf.

XIII. The Russo-Japanese war and the political crisis in the Empire and Finland

1. *Russia's defeats in the war and the new political activism in Finland*

War broke out at the beginning of 1904 between Russia and Japan. This war and the defeats suffered by the Russians had an important influence on the development of political attitudes and feelings, both in Finland and among the émigrés in Sweden.

As early as the beginning of 1904 Mechelin in Stockholm seems to have had the idea that the Japanese war could lead to major internal changes in Russia.[1] Political wishful thinking was easily provoked among the exiles, who knew that their fate depended on the course of the war. The Finns abroad had better sources of information on the course of events in east Asia than those at home, because news published in Finland was based on official Russian communiqués. In Finland too the course of the Japanese war was soon seen as the kind of event which could liberate the country from political oppression, if Russia's rulers got into real difficulties because of their losses. When news of major Russian defeats in the war began to filter through to Finland, expectations rose.

Since 1899, the Finns had experienced the pressure of a great power being exerted on their own small nation. There was no recognition either of its development as a nation or of the people's loyalty. Development seemed to be halted in every way, because social reform too had become unrealisable. The period of oppression had wiped out nearly all the loyalty towards the Emperor and the empire which had taken root during the nineteenth century, and malicious satisfaction, expressed in jokes and popular songs, was felt at the defeats inflicted on Russia's army and navy by the Japanese.[2] *Fria Ord* in Stockholm was unrestrained in its criticism of Nicholas II and his advisers.[3] Although Japan had hitherto been completely unknown to the Finnish people, and although the Japanese did not belong to the white race, their soldiers became heroes in the eyes of the Finns. In them Finland's oppressor had found an opponent stronger than itself, an opponent who was punishing him mercilessly.[4]

While the Russian defeats continued, Governor-General Bobrikov was murdered in Helsinki in June 1904. The news spread like wild fire round the country. The Senate condemned the killing in a communication it sent to the Emperor; indeed its position was difficult, since the feeling which had sprung up in the country had forced the Old Finns, as the government party, into a more isolated position than before. The newspapers published the news of Bobrikov's death in accordance with the official hand-outs; they tried to avoid taking a position — including that of condemning the killing.[5] There were many who regarded Eugen Schauman's act as justified, and saw a tyrant receiving his just reward. People had come to regard Bobrikov as an enemy of

Finland. However, there were apprehensions that the Russian policy of oppression in the country would only grow in severity.

The Finnish émigrés in Stockholm and elsewhere saw the event from a different environment, free of political restrictions. For them, revenge had been accomplished and death had struck down a villain.[6] *Fria Ord* summarised Bobrikov's murder as follows:[7] 'When oppression and injustice have become blinded by their superficial victories, and have exceeded all restraint, they thereby come to give strength to the forces of freedom, and this has generally led to the defeat of the oppressors. The more inhuman the oppressors, the more blind are they to this logic of history, but instead they are intoxicated by the sweetness of power and calculations of their own advantage. However, the revenge they conjure forth becomes the more violent, and the condemnation which falls on them, and the rejoicing at their downfall, are the more unanimous.'

Bobrikov's murder was given much attention in the foreign press as well. According to the *Kölnische Zeitung*, it demonstrated how powerful had been the hatred aroused among the Finns against Russian use of power over them and the bringing of the country close to the empire. The political murder of a dictator in the land of 'discipline and good behaviour' was, in the opinion of *Vossische Zeitung*, a sad commentary on the Russian style of government.[9] *Vorwärts* was even more severe; it stated that for years a barbarous despotism had prevailed in Finland, and expressed its hope — a little dramatically — that Japan would help the Finns in their resistance.[10]

The British press regretted the resort to violence that had happened in Finland, but did not regard it as surprising. *The Times* took a clear stand, and regarded Bobrikov as a representative of tyranny and his murder as a demonstration of the general development of political feeling in Finland.[11] Criticism of Russia's Finnish policy was not lacking in some leading French papers too: the *Journal des Débats* thought that the Russification policy had deeply offended Finnish national consciousness.[12] In several of the leading Stockholm papers, the assessment was that something of this sort had been expected to happen in Finland for some time.

At the end of the summer of 1904, a few months after Bobrikov's murder it seemed that a distinct relaxation of Russia's Finland policy was taking place. The new Governor-General, Obolenski, eased the censorship to some extent, some banishments were cancelled, and the controversial military call-up was withdrawn. In addition the Diet was summoned; however, the dictatorship decree remained in force. The changes which occurred were undoubtedly connected with the defeats Russia had suffered from Japan and the deteriorating position of the empire's political leadership.

The political activity of the Finnish émigrés, while gathering momentum in Sweden, was also beginning to split; their proposed forms of action differed in aim and content. This was seen above all in the difference between the views of Konni Zilliacus and Leo Mechelin. For Finland's cause, Zilliacus was ready for close collaboration with the different opposition parties in the empire, including the various groups in the workers' movement, and the Poles, to work for changes in the entire political system. To this end, even extreme methods would not be shunned. However, the aim set by Zilliacus for the status of Finland was not clear. He certainly maintained that the country must be secured a freer status, but this aim was given slightly different emphasis in different contexts, and it even included complete independence. Zilliacus was a Finnish cosmopolitan who had outstanding ability to maintain contacts with the various Russian opposition groups. As a social radical he had no inhibitions on this score, and he succeeded in winning their confidence.[13] Mechelin and his circle wanted, on the other hand, to keep the Finnish question as a separate issue, without involving it in the activities of the resistance groups in the Russian empire. The aim was to restore Finland to the pre-Bobrikov situation. Mechelin felt some interest in attempts at democratisation in Russia and in possible future changes coming by that route. He had contact with Russian liberals, but their internal disunity diminished its importance.[14]

The optimism created by the Japanese war, and the feeling that major internal changes might be in the offing in Russia, led to plans for holding a joint conference of the different opposition groups, Russian, Polish and Finnish, in Paris in the autumn of 1904. Zilliacus was an important force in initiating the collaboration, and was to become the chairman of the Paris meeting. However, Mechelin and his supporters, while prepared for close collaboration with the other opposition groups, thought that with Obolenski as Governor-General the situation in Finland was perhaps changing for the better. Mechelin and many others had no confidence in the Russian opposition groups, which stood for social revolution. In Mechelin's view the situation of Finland could only be aggravated by the Finns participating in the Paris conference; hence a waiting game was appropriate, since the Diet had been summoned. It would be unwise to sign any kind of joint proclamation of the opposition groups in Paris, and to examine the issues involved in Russia's conduct of the war publicly. Mechelin also did not support the establishment of a standing coordinating agency among the opposition groups.[15] The Paris conference clearly aroused little optimism within the main group of Finnish émigrés. Fewer people participated in the conference than expected; some Russian workers' groups did not take part at all. In addition it proved difficult for the different participants — Russian, Polish and Finnish — to agree what the future status of the non-Russian nationalities in Russia was to be. Zilliacus on the other hand did not allow political caution to influence him when decisions had to be made at the Paris conference. He signed all the resolutions 'on behalf of Finland' and approved the setting up of the standing coordinating agency.[16]

Zilliacus' political activity also had other dimensions. He had contacts with the Poles, and tried through his own international contacts to persuade Polish soldiers serving in the Russian army in Manchuria to refuse to fight against Japan; in this he may have had some success.[17] The culmination was Zilliacus' secret contact in the spring of 1904 with the Japanese military attaché in Stockholm, Colonel M. Akashi, with whose aid he got an arms consignment sent to Finland.[18] Such activity served Japan's aims of weakening Russia and encouraging revolt in the empire's western border areas, as did the corresponding help given by the Japanese attaché in Paris to the Polish opposition group led by Pilsudski. For Zilliacus, this kind of activity meant a clear break with the passive resistance line and the dropping of all restraint in the struggle for Finland's rights.

As the Russo-Japanese war had changed feelings in Finland, so passive resistance began to gain momentum. The political group supporting it was enlarging its previous support, but it was also suffering internal division. The workers' movement, which was now pushing its way to the forefront, brought a radical spirit to the passive resistance, alongside the conservative Swedish party and the liberal Young Finns. The socialists began to use methods of action that were quite novel in Finnish circumstances, as the mass demonstrations staged in different parts of the country from the summer of 1904 showed. Whereas, after the February Manifesto, the Finns had hoped for intellectual support from the west, in the new situation they were looking to Russian opposition elements whose international staging routes ran through Finland.[19]

At the end of January 1905, after the Russian surrender at Port Arthur, a great demonstration was organised in St Petersburg against the Emperor which, because of the counter-measures of the police, acquired the name 'Bloody Sunday'. The demonstrations spread rapidly to the western, non-Russian parts of the empire, and when the police tried to suppress organised demonstrations in Helsinki and Turku, there was violence on both sides.[20] A second mass demonstration was organised in Helsinki at the beginning of April 1905 at the time of the Russian defeat at the battle of Mukden; this demonstration was also used by the workers' leaders to protest against illegality and arbitrary police power.

The changed political atmosphere began to be seen at the beginning of 1905 both in the energetic activity of the workers' movement and in the changed attitude of the bourgeois parties to the development of the Finnish political system. Universal suffrage, which had been a slogan of the workers' movement since it was founded, later received backing from various groups in the Young Finn party. The Old Finn party put forward the same demand at its party congress in June 1905. The changed atmosphere affected even some parts of the Swedish party: Wrede announced in the summer of 1905 that he would support a two-chamber system in which one chamber could be elected by universal and equal suffrage.[21] This was a considerable change from the opinions which he had expressed in the mid-1880s about the franchise and methods of election to the Estate of burghers. It was also realised that since the country's official Diet was built on a narrow basis of support, a democratically-inspired popular activism might thrust it aside.

A group had broken away from the bourgeois constitutionalists at the end of 1904 to form the 'Finnish active resistance party'. This group, which was closely linked to the activities of Konni Zilliacus, was prepared for collaboration with the workers' movement, since it was interested in using the power of the masses, and, in contrast to the constitutionalists, approved of the use of methods of violence. This circumstance caused the bourgeois constitutionalists to renounce contacts with the activists. The latter built their political plans on the assumption that revolution would soon break out in Russia. In their programme adopted in November 1904, it was emphasised that the only way Finland's autonomy could secure adequate guarantees was by 'agreement' with a democratically-governed Russia. At a new conference of the opposition groups of the Russian empire, held in Geneva in the spring of 1905, the changing of the Russian political system was the central topic.[22] The Mechelin group took no part at all in these discussions, but Zilliacus was a very active participant.

Finnish society as a whole, in its political attitudes and feelings, was radically different during the Russo-Japanese war from a generation earlier during the Turkish war. The mood of 1904–5 — malicious satisfaction at the military defeats of the Russian armies and the political setbacks of tsarism — had started in the major towns of southern Finland and then spread to the rest of the country. Since the reaction had spread to the countryside, the feelings of the farming population developed in an anti-Russian direction. The smuggling of rifles on the Pohjanmaa coast in the autumn of 1905, carried out by Zilliacus, spread rumours and influenced thinking in that part of the country too. If such attitudes were the dominant trend, then the appeasers — at least the ones who were in some way committed to Bobrikov and the Senate's policy, or were civil servants involved in implementing his policy — remained outside it. This is a general assessment of the mood prevailing in the country and not a more precise charting of attitudes. The Old Finn party had examined its former position by the autumn of 1905: it was no longer content to demand that the application of the February Manifesto be limited to only a few matters, but demanded the abolition of the emergency regulations in their entirety.

However, Finland came to have its own particular links with the Russo-Japanese war in 1904–5. Many of the Finns serving as officers in the Russian army were ordered to their units, which campaigned in Asia against the Japanese.[23] Among them were General Oscar Gripenberg at the senior level and Lieutenant-Colonel C.G. Mannerheim, representing a younger generation. All these Finnish officers obviously influenced the attitudes of their own families, and perhaps wider circles in their homeland. It was a bond which kept certain milieux in Finland loyal to the empire and discreet in expressing any opinions against the prevailing political conditions. Finland was also involved with the economy of Russia at war. Since 1901 Russia had ordered from Finland torpedo-firing destroyers from Crichton's yard in Turku, and large consignments of ammunition from Kone ja Silta Oy in Helsinki. When the Japanese war broke out, orders for ammunition and other war materials came in abundance to the Finnish metal industry. In addition Russia urgently ordered various small war-ships, but mostly the vessels were only completed in 1906, when the war had ended.[24] The exports of Finnish metal industries to Russia grew to such an extent during the Japanese war, and even after it that they far outstripped former peacetime exports. The war boom increased Finnish exports to Russia in other fields also, for example, textiles.[25] Employment and wages therefore rose in these industries.[26]

2. *Political disturbances in the Russian empire, the 1905 general strike in Finland, and political changes*

At the end of October 1905 a general strike broke out in St Petersburg and Moscow, and spread to Finland. In the avalanche of events the working class movement represented the active spearhead, organising the general strike com-mittee in Helsinki as a kind of provisional 'authority' in the country. The strike was also joined in the capital by students. However, only when the bourgeois constitutionalists joined in did it become a true general strike and a display of national strength.[27] These events did not, however, lead to the kind of violence which occurred at the same time in the Baltic provinces. There discontent was directed at Russian political oppression, and at the peculiar social position of the German upper class. In the industrial area of Riga and its surroundings, the workers mounted mass demonstrations, and in Livonia and Courland the agricultural labourers had organised extensive strikes from the summer of 1905, which resulted in the burningdown of the German-owned manor houses.[28]

The growing tension, and at the same time the importance of Russian imperial interests in the Baltic provinces, is reflected by the fact that this area was declared in a state of siege in the late summer of 1905, and Russian troops, including Cossacks, were brought in. In Finland, by comparison, the adminis-tration had relaxed its grip, giving the political opposition more room for manoeuvre. Whereas the general strike in St Petersburg and Moscow began on 28 October, that in Finland did so on the 30th. In the interval Russian troops were moved from Finland to St Petersburg to protect the imperial system; about 6,000 troops probably remained in Finland.[29]

The Finnish bourgeois constitutionalists and the workers' movement jointly strove for the measures of oppression to be ended and the restoration of legal conditions; the resignation of the Old Finn Senate, the Minister-Secretary and the 'Bobrikov' civil servants; and the reform of the Diet on the basis of universal and equal suffrage. However, differences soon began to appear over the choice of means. The workers' movement represented a new force in the events that were changing the nation, while the bourgeois constitutionalists saw them-selves as the country's traditional élite; it was typical that the delegations from each of the parties supporting the general strike presented the same demands to the Governor-General separately. Obolenski promised to transmit the demands to the Emperor, and to request his own resignation. The Old Finn senators also promised to resign.[30]

The split on the strike front began to be deepened with the publication in Tampere on 1 November of the 'Red Proclamation'. This document, inspired by the Tampere workers' movement, sought to speed up the course of events, and set more far-reaching objectives. According to the Tampere proclamation, it was by no means self-evident that Finland belonged to Russia on the basis of her traditional autonomy. The demand in the proclamation for the summoning of a national constituent assembly and the election of a provisional government meant major changes in the country's internal political structure. The Proclamation was given a social tone by its condemnation of the existing 'class society' and the aims of 'the propertied class'.[31]

Thus the workers' movement had brought additional aims to the general strike beyond the restoration of constitutionalism. But the situation remained in the control of the leading bourgeois constitutionalists, who saw on the one hand the danger that the workers would go their own way, and on the other that because the general strikes in St Petersburg and Moscow had ended on the day the Finnish strike began, the favourable conditions with which they started might slip out of the Finns' hands. They also, through Obolenski and by other channels, had contacts with St Petersburg, whereas the workers' leaders were inexperienced in politics, and seemed bogged down in meetings and in holding the great mass of the people together. Its members were clearly isolated, and lacked precise information on how events were developing in St Petersburg and in Russia generally.

In this situation, the bourgeois constitutionalist leaders and the Old Finns who supported them tried to get the Emperor's approval in St Petersburg for their own programme, and to put an early end to the general strike. Obolenski, who saw that it would be difficult to preserve order if the general strike should go on, was also prepared to support them. At this point the Emperor had already issued a manifesto according to which the Duma would become the legislative body, and the general strikes in Russia were over. By contrast the central strike committee in Helsinki, endorsing the Tampere Proclamation, had begun preparing for the election of a provisional government for the country. Since the bourgeois constitutionalists had refused to take part in it, the socialists were forced to try and fill the list of candidates solely from their own ranks.[32]

When Nicholas II and his advisers came to assess the Finnish situation, the general strike there was seen as expressing the national will and the strength of the desire for autonomy. Thus the situation was quite different from the Baltic provinces and Poland, where internal divisions had been dominant. Also Finland's developed character as a 'Scandinavian society' had emerged in many ways in contrast with the semi-feudal Baltic provinces and Poland. Furthermore, Finland — almost a vacuum in military terms — presented Russia with a security problem, since the Finnish general strike had extended its influence to within a few miles of the imperial capital, and all communications with Finland were cut off. In this situation Nicholas II made concessions in order to end the strike quickly. He signed a manifesto on 4 November, which was published in Finland the next day, based on a draft of Mechelin's representing the views of the bourgeois constitutionalists. It declared the illegal orders issued since 1899 to be suspended (Mechelin's draft had demanded their cancellation); and a promise was given to reform the Diet on the basis of universal and equal suffrage.[33]

The November Manifesto was a major concession made exclusively to Finland; nothing like it was offered to the other western, non-Russian border areas of the empire. In Poland the Catholic church got some small privileges, but in the Baltic provinces there was straightforward military repression, in which thousands of lives were lost.[34] The general effect of the November Manifesto in Finland was liberating. The country had obtained freedom to express political opinions, such as had never been experienced before. All this was accomplished very suddenly. In political circles there were different ideas about what had really happened. The ordinary man interpreted the retreat of tsarist power as a victory for passive resistance, and the result of an unyielding defence of what was right — by an unarmed people. In all this, the favourable political circumstances were ignored, and the significance of the Finns' own role was exaggerated.[35]

In 1905, a new 'alternative Russia' had risen above the horizon. In Finland it was especially admired, in the workers' movement because it had fought against tsarist power, shown a love of freedom, and had suffered a great deal. They felt gratitude towards the representatives of this 'alternative Russia' and believed that it would support them in the future too in defending Finnish rights. On the other hand the Russian workers' movement, especially its internal divisions, was little known to the Finnish socialists.

The prospects for the political future of Finland after the general strike were seen in different ways in the different political groups. The Young Finn, P.E. Svinhufvud, felt that Finland's liberties had been greatly extended. But at the same time political passions had also flared up, and there was an intensification of the conflict between the parties.[36] Konni Zilliacus, like many other émigrés, returned home after the general strike, and at the end of November, he seems to have felt that Finland's internal situation was especially serious. There was opposition between the workers' movement, which demanded a single-chamber system, and the country's older constitutionalist circles which favoured a two-chamber system, and assumed that the composition of the second chamber would be determined in accordance with their class interests. The constitutionalists, according to Zilliacus, were short-sighted and were aggravating the country's internal situation: within the Finnish working class movement, the beginning of a new revolution in Russia could at any time set off new political disturbances, and then, Zilliacus believed, the bourgeois constitutionalists led by Mechelin would be thrust aside in Finland, the country would

be proclaimed a republic, and the socialists would form a provisional government, of which the final phase of the November general strike had already given
indications.[37]

The general strike created an avalanche of new ideas and points of view; there
was debate and argument over all the hitherto accepted 'sacred values', and new
forms of social activity began to spring up, not concerned with politics alone,
but in the professions, sport and other fields. On the one hand quite new forces
were trying to break out, and on the other traditional groups were trying to
adapt to a changing society.

This transition period had put the position of the clergy in Finnish society in
the balance in many ways. They were discriminated against politically in the
new era, because the majority of them had represented appeasement in the years
of oppression. Clearly they felt relief that their activity as a political Estate was
ending; they recognised the necessity of abolishing the division into Estates in
the reform of the Diet, beyond this they were uncertain.[38] Aside from this, the
clergy had become the target of severe criticism from the rising workers' movement. The socialists described them as representing social reaction and they
strongly attacked both the church and religion. The clergy, for their part, felt
anxious and uncertain because traditional values had become threatened in
society. Not only had the old conception of authority and of a patriarchal order
been put to the test, but the political activation of the mass of the people and the
rise of socialism were seen as a major danger to sacred values.

The great politicisation of 1905–6 affected the countryside as well as the
towns, especially those elements which had not been entitled to vote for the
Estate of farmers. The party founded in 1906, the Agrarian Union (*Maalaisliitto*),
whose supporters came primarily from Pohjanmaa and Karelia, was an indication of the changes taking place in the countryside. Another sign of change
was the political organisation begun among the tenants and other landless
people.

The Diet reforms enfranchised the broad mass of the nation, and which
diminished the importance of the élite groups which had flourished throughout
the previous century. The academics were still prominent, but they were no
longer to dominate public life as before. They had divided primarily into supporters of the older bourgeois parties, the Old and the Young Finns and the
Swedish party, but a small group of academics, during the general strikes, had
also joined the workers' movement around 1905. Those who joined did not,
however, form a distinct intellectual group within the Social Democratic party,
but adapted and merged into the totality of the rest of the movement. Several of
them soon came to occupy leading positions in the party. In other respects
'student politics' were becoming centred on language and cultural issues,
strongly coloured by nationalist ideology.[39]

Business had enjoyed 'good times' in the period after the Japanese war, which
had seemed a time of promising prospects. The political unrest in the country

was seen primarily as a routine disturbance. Industrial production in the country was growing, as were trade relations with the west and Russia. On the whole, the business community did not take a public stand on Finland's problems in the empire, and remained 'neutral' on political questions. It did, however, take a stand on social questions, often of a patriarchal-conservative kind.

In the new phase it was the Old Finn and the Swedish parties which above all suffered political reverses. The whole political atmosphere of the country had, after November 1905, turned against the line of appeasement which the Old Finns had represented since 1899, though the leaders of the discredited party seemed to have the ability to develop a new image. They even made moves towards the socialists, proposing that on the basis of the provisional constitution a national constituent assembly could be summoned. The new programme of the Old Finn party also emphasised social reforms.[40]

The country's Swedish-speaking minority and its leaders also faced difficult problems. The traditional dominance of the Swedish-speakers in the Diet, which was based on their majority position achieved in two of the Estates, was lost for ever, and their minority political status was suddenly revealed. The radical slogans of the workers' movement were directed against the Swedish-speaking upper classes, and there was a new danger of 'majority oppression' from the finnicisation movement. The Swedish-speakers also had reason to fear the loss of their previous positions and influence in the country's cultural life. The Swedish party's change of name in 1906 to a 'people's party' (*Svenska folkpartiet*) was only an outward adaptation to the new situation.

The birth of the workers' movement in Finland was a very late occurrence by general European standards. However, by those same standards the rate of increase of the Social Democratic party was also exceptionally rapid. The number of workers' associations rose tenfold from 1904 to the autumn of 1906, from about 100 to over 1,000. The confidence in the power of the masses, which had appeared in the general strike, acted as an inspiration. A Marxist programme had been adopted by the party in 1903, when it was still very small, but at the end of 1906, when its membership had grown to more than 120,000 — with a considerable bias towards the rural areas — a structured party organisation with a central leadership and regional levels was created. In this respect too the development of the Social Democratic party now began to compare with that of the continental workers' movement. The exceptional support won by the cooperative movement and the slow growth and development of trade unionism gave the overall development of the workers' movement in Finland an additional peculiar character; as an illustration of the major change within it, those who had been members before the general strike were often called — irrespective of their age — the 'elders'.[41]

The general strike fixed the idea in the workers' movement that the masses are the locomotive of history. This kind of political thrust from below was new in Finland, and it aroused optimism in the movement for the future: they set as their target a new democratically elected parliament. But the sudden ending of the general strike had left the movement — above all the leaders — with a strong feeling of frustration: 'The workers did not get anything for themselves, the bosses got everything' was an experience which was also to leave its mark. As a result, the workers' movement detached itself from bourgeois circles more clearly than before. One special feature which followed the general strike was the founding of Red Guards within the workers' movement. From the spring of 1906 onwards, as a factor of political pressure, the Red Guards, with their violent methods of action, represented a potential revolutionary force in Finland.[42]

The Leo Mechelin constitutionalist Senate appointed at the beginning of December 1905 drew a firm line against the supporters of appeasement, who were left to carry the burden of history. The new Senate was made up of Young Finns and Swedish party men, and one socialist, J.K. Kari although the Social Democratic party did not officially recognise him as its representative. The aim of the Mechelin Senate was a peaceful return to legality in the country, and the secure achievement of reform of the Diet. In addition the Senate sought to keep Finland isolated from the ferment of Russian internal politics, which it feared might in some way influence Finland's internal conditions. The Emperor gave the Estates the task of terminating their own existence.

The extra-parliamentary pressure of the workers' movement and the activism of the Red Guard helped to shape the course of events. The conservative Diet of Estates approved not only the introduction of universal suffrage, but also a single-chamber system. Their aim was to calm the country politically. The unanimous stand on the question of reform adopted by the Diet bound Nicholas II to confirm a radical reform which differed markedly from, for example, the institution of the Duma. The Emperor confirmed the new constitutional law for Finland, which included the reform of parliament, on 20 July 1906, at the same time as ordering the Russian Duma to be dissolved and the numbers entitled to vote to be considerably reduced in the new elections.[43]

Soon after this, in July-August 1906, a revolt broke out among the Russian garrison of Sveaborg, which was part of a broader plan of revolt among revolutionary military elements in the armed forces. It may however have broken out spontaneously, and earlier than planned. The Sveaborg revolt was a problem both to the Mechelin Senate and the Social Democratic party. The Senate had acted with caution, in that it had not granted asylum in Finland to Russian revolutionary refugees, in the fear that Russia could thus easily be induced to intervene in Finland's internal affairs. In addition the Senate believed that political terrorism might easily spread from Russia into Finland.

Faced with the news of the revolt in Sveaborg, the Finnish workers' movement was at a kind of crossroads. The Social Democratic party leadership judged the situation to be very critical, because it was afraid that Red Guard activists might wholly disregard the party organisation in making their political decisions. A number of leading figures therefore sought to dissociate the party from the revolt. When the commander of the Red Guard, Johan Kock, decided in spite of this to participate, it was the decision of one man;[44] it was also the peak of Red Guard activism. The consequence was that armed detachments of workers went to Sveaborg to help the rebels, while in Helsinki, on Kock's orders, a general strike was proclaimed to prevent the organising of measures to counter the revolt. Towards the end of the revolt, there was an armed clash in Hakaniemi Square between Red Guards and members of the Defence Guard, which represented bourgeois elements. This was an unprecedented event in Finland. The Hakaniemi skirmish, in which there were casualties on both sides, ended when a Russian Cossack detachment arrived on the scene and emptied the square.[45] Russian troops loyal to the Emperor quickly suppressed the Sveaborg revolt. When, shortly afterwards, the Senate suppressed the Red Guard, the relief in bourgeois circles was considerable. Feelings in the workers' movement fluctuated between a sense of defeat and a certain relief.[46]

When, soon after this avalanche of events, the party congress of the Social Democrats met at Oulu, the radicals and moderates in the workers' movement came into collision. The failure of the Sveaborg revolt worked to the advantage of the moderates, who had throughout built their political hopes on parliamentary reform. Valpas, a moderate, expressed mistrust of Russian policy: 'Russian policy has always been one of giving to one part of the empire some kind of concessions to pacify it at the same time as, in another part, it carries out repressions. We know that Finland got privileges at the time of the Polish revolt, but that things went badly for Poland. . . When the bureaucracy gets one part of the empire crushed, it can pounce upon another. When, for example, it carries out a 'pacification' in the Caucasus, it may give us privileges, but at another moment it could instead select us for oppression and give some kind of privileges to the Caucasus.'[47]

The swift and surprising development of events in Finland that flowed from the general strike seemed now to be turning towards a peaceful course. All except the country's Swedish-speaking upper classes felt that the institution of the single-chamber parliament offered new hope for the future. It was typical of contemporary political views in Finland that, while universal suffrage was held to be an essential part of democracy, it was not clearly recognised that the overall framework of the country's political system — above all the powers of the different organs of state — had been retained unaltered. The new parliament would have no more powers than its predecessor, while the sovereign still had an unlimited veto over the decisions of the Finnish parliament.

In the results of the first parliamentary elections held in March 1907, the Social Democrats won eighty seats out of 200. The Swedish party, which had had the key position in the Diet of Estates, had only twenty-four seats in the new parliament. The result of the elections as a whole was a disappointment for the bourgeois constitutionalists, since the Young Finns got only twenty-seven seats, but the Old Finns got fifty-nine. On the basis of the election results the

Mechelin Senate was a minority government, but the bourgeois parties supporting it formed, together with the Social Democrats, a considerable majority.

3. *The Finnish question abroad*

The revolutionary disturbances in Russia in October-November 1905 attracted
close attention in Europe and evoked very different kinds of reaction. The
Finnish question and its distinctive features did not remain unnoticed in connection with the major events.

In France many leading papers examined the unrest in Russia with great
anxiety. They feared that if Russia fell into the grip of anarchy, this might
weaken her significance as France's ally and could bring about changes in the
international system. French government circles, remembering the fate of the
Dual Alliance, concentrated their hopes on Russia's new prime minister,
Witte, and hoped that he would be able to carry out reforms in the empire and
restore the authority of the state.[48] Events in Finland were described with
restraint, but the internal conflicts between the bourgeoisie and the workers'
movement in the country were noted.[49] *Le Temps* explained that Finland knew
how to make skilful use of the internal crisis in the empire, and make 'her own
revolution' as a consequence of which the restoration of autonomy might
succeed.[50]

The French socialists looked at events in Russia in 1905 from a sharply
different viewpoint from that of the circles supporting the country's official
policy. The articles by Jean Jaurès published in *L'Humanité* expressed enthusiasm for everything which pointed to the advance of democracy in Russia. It
was believed that a clear turn in this direction would strengthen democracy in
Europe generally. Jaurès especially believed that internal changes in Russia
would put the authoritarian system in Germany to the test and could lead to its
overthrow. Such a development would also affect international politics and
would strengthen the prospects of preserving peace.[51] The French socialists also
supposed that the replacement of the authoritarian system would generally ease
the position of the non-Russian nationalities in Russia. Already in the summer
of 1905, Jaurès had put forward the view in *L'Humanité* that if revolution
should break out in Russia, the empire could then move from a centralised
system of government to a federal one. Thus Poland too would get her
autonomy back and Finland's autonomous rights would be restored and further
extended.[52] *L'Humanité* thought in November 1905 that Finland, by virtue of
the peaceful way events had developed, was able to profit from the situation in
Russia. There had not been violence as in the Baltic provinces, and Russian
troops had not intervened. Finland had been able to break free from subjection
to dictatorship and return to the conditions preceding the February Manifesto.[53]

Leading British papers expressed their satisfaction with everything which
pointed to a change in the Russian political system in a 'European' direction. In
the western border areas of the empire, Finland received most attention in the

British press, and after that Poland. *The Times* and many other papers pointed out that Finland had made a 'peaceful revolution', as distinct from all the rest of the Russian empire; the restoration of Finland's autonomy was arousing enthusiasm 'in the whole civilised world'. At the same time it praised the Finns as a nation which, through its culture, educational system and political conditions, was on the level of the most developed nations in Europe.[54] *The Morning Post* pictured the Finns as a nation that loved peace and freedom, and had been forced by Bobrikov's methods to abandon passive resistance. There were thus quite special reasons for the general strike, but the political situation too had become especially favourable.[55] *The Daily Telegraph* too thought that the Finns had suffered cruel oppression and had therefore taken the first opportunity to break free from it. According to the *Manchester Guardian*, Finland was the only part of the Russian empire which had profited from the political transition of 1905. The country had regained its freedom calmly.[57]

In Germany, government circles, despite Russia's defeats in the Japanese war, did not want to create difficulties for Nicholas II and his advisers, because the aim in Berlin was closer relations between the two countries. The attitude of many Germans to the western, non-Russian areas of the empire was conditioned by their special emotional concern with the Baltic provinces, where the violent side of the political disturbances was directed against the German inhabitants, many of whom fled to Germany as refugees. The Germans recognised the nationalist background to the mass movement in the Baltic provinces, but the phenomenon as a whole was interpreted as a social revolution.

As seen from Germany, events in Finland were peripheral, though some attention was devoted to them, because they differed from events in the Baltic provinces. A typical comment in the German press was that the Finnish general strike had not caused bloodshed or loss of life.[58] The internal political divisions in Finland were noted, but as the *Hamburger Correspondent* remarked, the country was able to show vigilance and act as a nation. The struggle for the constitution had been slow to yield results, but it had matured the people politically.[59] *Vorwärts* pointed out that the Finnish workers' movement could control the situation in the country,[60] which implied an obvious criticism of the disturbances in the other border areas of Russia.

The revolutionary events of 1905 received great attention in the Swedish press. Interest in Finnish affairs had been lively since the February Manifesto, and it had increased as the great wave of changes approached. The leading bourgeois and social democratic papers depicted the calm political behaviour of the Finns in the midst of revolutionary events; *Stockholms Dagblad* declared that Finland had freed herself from the bonds of coercion without a formal revolt.[61] The Finns were depicted as champions of legal order, even though they had finally accepted the futility of passive resistance.[62] *Social-Demokraten* thought that the behaviour of the Finns had been impressive, and their restraint had forced the Emperor to draw back. No rash attempts had been made by the Finns to detach their country from the Russian empire.[63] The restoration of legal conditions and stability was hoped for; conservatives feared that a revolutionary tendency might take control in Finland.[64]

The Sveaborg revolt was recognised as part of the wider revolutionary uprising against the tsarist regime. In the news about it published in Britain and Germany, the internal conflicts in Finland, the emergence of the Red Guard, and the Hakaniemi skirmish were also noted. In the Swedish papers there was controversy about the significance and background of these occurrences.[65] The reform of the Finnish Diet also aroused interest abroad. The single-chamber system in itself was a remarkable innovation, but universal suffrage had been extended to include women; it was remarkable that progress in any part of the Russian empire should have been carried so far.

It was therefore natural that there was foreign interest in the first elections to the single-chamber parliament in Finland, held in the spring of 1907. The most interest was aroused by the large number of seats gained by the social democrats; in no European country, not even in Germany, did the socialists in parliament comprise so large a proportion as 40 per cent. This result was felt to be the more surprising because to foreign eyes the Finnish social structure was 'east European', i.e. there was relatively little industry and the country was predominantly agrarian.[66] In consequence, the foreign press began to look at the peculiarities of Finland's internal conditions.

Finland was at this time a kind of base for the Russian opposition, whose freedom of action was limited everywhere else in the empire. Thus the Russian Bolshevik party held a secret party congress in Tampere in December 1905. It has been said that 'St Petersburg simply breathed through Finland'.[67] The Russian liberals had previously regarded Finland as a western peninsula within the borders of the empire; now the country offered the Russian workers' movement opportunities for action and refuge.

XIV. Russia's international position and policy towards Finland after 1908

1. The position of Russia after the Japanese war

Defeat in the war with Japan had generally weakened Russia's military position in the Baltic area. The land forces moved to the east Asian theatre of war from those areas were defeated, and the Baltic fleet was completely destroyed at the naval battle of Tsushima. In addition political disturbances in Poland, the Baltic provinces and Finland had given rise to difficult security problems for the empire.

The dubious state of the Russian armed forces after the transitional period of 1905 is illustrated by the fact that the French military attaché in St Petersburg, who usually had at his disposal highly confidential and detailed information about the Russian forces, and about any plans that might be afoot, was now receiving no detailed information. The attaché concluded that Russia had little value to France as a military ally against the central powers in the next few years.[1]

The Russian General Staff regarded the military reorganisation it had in hand as needing so much time that only by the spring of 1909 or the spring of 1910 could the new plan be realised. Even then exceptionally large purchases of weapons and supplies had to be made, in accordance with the planned timetable.[2] The operational plans of the Russian General Staff differed from the pre-1905 system in that now the whole military disposition on the western frontier of the empire for a possible mobilisation would be strongly deployed in depth, not for the beginning of an offensive but with a view to defence. This was the situation in Poland and the Baltic provinces. Since Russia had lost her whole Baltic fleet, it was considered more probable than before that on the outbreak of a war, the enemy would try a landing in the region of Libau.[3] In addition to Germany, Sweden too was considered a potential enemy.

The change in the overall military situation caused major changes too in the military plans that concerned Finland, and the appreciations on which they were based. Since Russia had little naval strength, it was thought possible that the enemy could make a successful landing in the Hanko area, and that Russia would then be forced to give up part of Finland and organise her main line of defence on the line of the Kymi river. If the enemy should succeed in advancing even further, a landing at Koivisto was thought a possibility. The old, traditional fortified 'gateway' system on the Gulf of Finland was considerably modified, and the defence of St Petersburg was now to be based in the first instance on the fortified triangle Koivisto- Kronstadt — Yhinmäki. Later, in 1909–11, a regrouping of the Russian defensive system was made in the area of the Gulf of Finland, as the general equipment programme and the building of the Baltic fleet began to be realised. This meant that the planned main line of defence was advanced so that in the 'gateway' system the fortified triangle Porkkala-Naissaari-Paltiski formed an important new element. For the land forces the main line of defence north of the Gulf of Finland was moved from Kymijoki to the level of Lohja. When they next sought to move the Russian defence line on the Gulf of Finland forward, Hankoniemi and the northern point of Hiiumaa came to be the new zone of the gateway system formed by the planned line of fortifications. In this phase they also began to fortify the island of Örö, to the west of Hanko, while the Åland archipelago began to attract more attention in the General Staff in St Petersburg as a support zone. The fact that, under the new naval building programme, Russia would in the years ahead possess large, dreadnought-type battleships as well began to influence the review of the defensive system on the south coast of Finland.[4]

After 1905 Russia and the Triple Alliance still remained at odds. The activity of Austria was apparent in the Balkans when she annexed Bosnia and Herzegovina in 1908, and caused an international crisis. This ended in the spring of 1909 because Germany's stiff attitude forced Russia into a diplomatic retreat. German attempts to get influence in Turkey constituted a new source of tension between Russia and Germany. By contrast a rapprochement was taking place in the relations of Russia and Britain. Fear of Germany, which was caused above all by the rapid growth of the German navy, had induced Britain to conclude an alliance with France in 1904 (the Entente Cordiale), and in 1907 to make an agreement with Russia over their differences in Asia over Persia and Afghanistan. Britain and Russia were thereafter on friendly terms, although there was no actual treaty of alliance between them. Russia also acquired from the British navy the counterweight she had wanted against German naval forces in the Baltic.[5]

The balance between the great powers in Europe had come to the fore in international politics, and the colonial question was forced, temporarily at least, into second place. Russia tried to free herself from the limitations on her sovereignty in the Baltic area which the Paris agreement of 1856 on the demilitarisation of Åland had created. In these endeavours she reached an understanding with Germany in the summer and autumn of 1907, but when in the spring of 1908 an agreement on the Baltic area was signed by the four powers concerned (Russia, Germany, Denmark and Sweden), it did not include any terms that were clearly slanted in Russia's favour.[6] At the same time the military position of the Danish Sound in an international crisis had been discussed, and Germany had pressed Denmark into military collaboration. When a new defence plan was adopted in Denmark in 1909, the defence of Copenhagen against a seaborne attack was given priority. This meant that Britain and her navy were regarded as the enemy.[7]

2. Stolypin's policy and Finland

Finland constituted a special problem for St Petersburg after the Bobrikov period and subsequent events, and its importance further increased with Russia's military difficulties. Finland had displayed in the general strike a united national will, which would make it unlikely that an internal split could be created. In addition, St Petersburg had for a limited time been cut off from communication with Finland. Earlier, ruling circles in Russia had spoken of separatist phenomena in Finland, but now they feared the possibility of outright revolt. Earlier the distrust of the government in St Petersburg was directed at Finland's Swedish-speaking population, but now the wide extent of support for the country's workers' movement was the main cause for alarm, especially in view of recent events in Russia. Finland was seen as an area which Russian opposition elements could use to their advantage. The Sveaborg revolt was regarded by the Russian General Staff as especially dangerous, compared with other similar incidents at that time, in that it had occurred within the St Petersburg defensive zone and some Russian officers had taken part in it. In addition, some Finnish elements had been involved.[8]

The key person in the exercise of Russian policy in Finland was P.A. Stolypin, who was appointed prime minister in 1906. On his initiative, both the securing of the empire's interests in Finland and the strengthening of control over Finland's administration and internal conditions were raised once more. Stolypin tried to advance cautiously and by degrees in his Finnish policy, and to avoid direct measures such as those resorted to by Bobrikov. When Russia's military 'pacification policy' in the Baltic provinces was brought to a conclusion, he raised the organisation of imperial legislation concerning Finland. When he spoke in the Duma of the position of Finland on 18 May 1908, he emphasised the aim of his government to suppress all revolutionary endeavours and to establish order throughout the empire. He also stressed Russia's military interests, and explained that the imperial legislation in Finland did not require the consent of the country's own parliament. By bringing up military considerations, Stolypin could obviously influence the attitude of liberals in the Duma in any matter under discussion, with the result that only a section of the liberals, led by Paul Milyukov, opposed the system of imperial legislation concerning Finland. The workers' movement was no longer represented in the Duma at this stage, since the groups entitled to vote in elections had been reduced.

On 2 June 1908 the Emperor confirmed the special minute of the Council of Ministers, in which the procedure for the handling of Finnish business concerning 'Russian interests' was laid down. The Council of Ministers was to examine all administrative and legislative business concerning Finland and, before the business was submitted it to the Emperor for confirmation, to decide whether it involved Russian interests. The consequence was that the Russian Council of Ministers was put in the position of the supreme organ of government in Finland, as the Norwegian minister in St Petersburg noted.[9] What had been decided was the general principles of the new system; what was not yet revealed was how actively the Russian government would interfere in

Finland's internal affairs.

The next stage occurred when a draft law was put before the Duma and the Imperial Council in 1910, spelling out in detail the categories of state business for which it was considered that imperial legislation was necessary. This proposal, signed by Stolypin, also included a clause whereby Finland was expected to elect two members to the Imperial Council and four to the Duma. Stolypin's proposal stated that the Finnish parliament's task was to give an opinion, but not to participate in the actual decision-making. Parliament however refused to give the mere opinion asked for, because it could not in its view give up the general power of decision belonging to it under the constitution. This draft on imperial legislation was before the Duma and the Imperial Council for final consideration in June 1910, Stolypin emphasising again that the question of imperial legislation did not fall within the decision-making competence of the Finnish parliament, whereas Milyukov and other liberals defended the traditional basis of Finland's autonomy. Nicholas II signed the law in June and ordered it to be enforced in Finland.

The deliberate caution characteristic of Stolypin's policy was seen over the question of the Finnish army. In 1909 it was decreed that Finland should pay an annual contribution towards the costs of defence as compensation for conscription not being applied in the country. This decision showed that the Finns were considered politically unreliable. It was no longer felt appropriate to leave the task of providing covering forces for the coast defences of the Gulf of Finland to military units made up of Finns. Clearly in making this decision the Russians had assumed that the coastal fortifications of the Gulf of Finland could be manned with stronger Russian forces, which would also act as covering troops in case of need. Stolypin's policy had the ulterior motive of securing a controlling grip on Finland's administration and political life. In November 1909, General F.A. Seyn, head of chancellery to the Governor-General in Bobrikov's time, was himself appointed Governor-General. At the same time, in various parts of Finland, provincial governors were dismissed, the police were brought under Russian control, and the position of the gendarmes was strengthened.

Changes began to occur from 1908 in the composition of the Senate, which implied a major political turning-point. Mechelin's constitutionalist Senate resigned in the spring of that year, and was replaced by a government composed of representatives of both the constitutionalist bourgeois parties and the Old Finns. However, disputes developed in the new Senate and in the spring of 1909 the constitutionalist senators resigned, to be followed in the autumn of that year by the Old Finns. The new Senate, in which General W. Markov acted as vice-chairman, was largely composed of high-ranking Finnish officers who had served in Russia. Finland's supreme administration had thus become 'russified', so among the country's political institutions only parliament now remained genuinely representative of Finnish political opinion. In its composition, however, it was representative of the people in quite a different sense from the old

Diet. From 1908 the Finnish parliament was dissolved prematurely several years in succession, and because of this the country was forced to hold new elections very frequently.

The new deterioration in the relations of Finland and Russia in 1908–9 caused a powerful political reaction in the country. In parliament, the press and general political discussion, the disappointment and bitterness caused by the measures of Russian state power were expressed. The constitutional conditions restored by the November Manifesto of 1905 were shown to have been only a passing interlude. The Finns thought they had been loyal to the empire, but they now realised that in spite of this Finland's autonomy, which had been established precisely in order to win over their loyalty and confidence, was not respected in St Petersburg. A sense of impotence and pessimism were evident in the advocates of passive resistance, from the Young Finns to the socialists. At the same time the former appeasers were forced to recognise that the bottom had fallen out of their compromise attempts and model solutions.

Hence the fundamental differences in attitude to Russian policies of oppression had largely disappeared among the Finns after 1899; however, the division between bourgeois circles and the workers' movement was greater, and personal relations between their representatives worse than ever. The working class was affected not only by the lack of parliamentary reforms, but more generally by oppressive working conditions in industry and agriculture.

The prevailing political crisis seemed to the Finns a confrontation between a large and a small country, in which the right of the stronger prevailed. At the same time as they recognised their own lack of power to act, they felt that the Finnish sense of justice had been deeply offended, a state of affairs that was continuing. In this new phase attitudes to the Russian policy of oppression sharpened, and also changed. Whereas before, resentment had been mainly directed against the system of oppression, it was now turned more against Russia and the Russians in their entirety. The support given in the Duma for Stolypin's Finnish policy,[10] and the fact that the experience in 1905 of an 'alternative Russia' had quietly disappeared from the picture, and that the Russian workers' movement had now been driven underground, affected the attitudes both of the bourgeois constitutionalists and the workers' movement. The difficulty of finding any political way out accounted for this negative attitude.

Although the situation in the country made radical gestures dangerous, in their thoughts and observations Finns could move across the boundary of traditional loyalty and, in so doing, burn their boats.

3. Finnish attitudes to international politics

When the second period of oppression began in 1908, there also occurred a quiet Finnish re-orientation towards a wider international arena. Finnish contacts abroad had both intensified and widened in scope, especially in trade and cultural relations. To this were added many intellectual influences, all this adding up to the western contribution to the development of Finland. At the same time, however, there had remained an obvious remoteness from international politics.

In the background was the recent experience that the threat to Finland's autonomy prior to 1905 had not aroused any significant public outcry abroad. In the period after 1899 the Finns had also been compelled to recognise that liberalism and democracy had no decisive influence in international relations, an impression only reinforced when the new period of oppression began. The phase which began in 1908 was much more favourable to Russia internationally than the period after 1899, and for Finland the second period of oppression was even less favourable than the earlier one. When the Finnish question was before the Duma in May 1908, it was overshadowed by contemporary international events. Several visiting rulers attracted major attention. The Swedish king, Gustav V, visited St Petersburg in May 1908, and in June the British king, Edward VII, met Nicholas II off Tallinn, to be followed a month later by the French president Fallières. Finns who followed affairs had to observe that Finland had been pushed under the wheels of major forces.

It was characteristic of Finland that international politics aroused little interest; the subject was followed primarily through the press, in other words superficially. There was also an incapacity to analyse high politics in depth. Finns were not familiar with the real power-relationships of the major states, which were perhaps a sensitive matter to discuss. They traditionally fastened on to the ideological aspects of international politics; their attitude to war, being influenced by the pacifist strain in constitutionalist ideology, was negative.

At the turn of the century, there was interest in the Boer war (1899–1902), the Boers being pictured by the Finns in emotional terms as brave soldiers, brought up in primitive conditions, who were defending their territory against the well-equipped British.[11] Their struggle could also be seen specifically as one between the great and the small, to which the Finns' own relations with Russia offered an obvious comparison.

The Russo-Japanese war aroused exceptional interest in Finland, but this arose not from the crisis itself but from the general desire to settle accounts with Russia and the political system she represented. Another event of this time, the break-up of the union of Sweden and Norway, attracted little interest despite its geographical proximity. The reason was primarily that the reports of the break-up of the union were over-shadowed in the Finnish papers by the sharpening crisis in Finland's relations with Russia, which finally erupted into the general strike. Among the country's Swedish-speakers, who did take an interest, there appeared a division of opinions. Most of them were 'on the Swedish side', following old cultural traditions, but some members of Swedish-language literary circles, who had had contacts with Norway as far back as the 1880s, were sympathetic to Norway.[12] The country's Finnish-speakers, in so far as they followed the matter at all, had no difficulty in identifying with Norway's right of self-determination.

The Bosnian crisis of 1908–9 earned considerable attention in the Finnish papers. This was not treated in isolation, as such events had often been in the past, but the press tried to relate it to the European great power relationships as a whole. The Finnish newspapers saw clearly that the great powers had their own interests and that these were decisive. *Helsingin Sanomat* was critical of Austria, which was regarded as having unscrupulously violated the Berlin agreement of 1878 by annexing Bosnia and Herzegovina to her territory. This was stressed too in *Nya Pressen*.[13] *Uusi Suometar* by contrast sympathised with Austria's action and held Serbia to be the major threat to peace. It tried to explain that the Austrian measures did not really mean any change in the Balkan situation, any more than Bulgaria's proclamation of its independence at the same time.[14] *Työmies* differed from all the rest by also criticising the policy being followed by Russia in the Balkans. Russia had not been any 'liberator' or 'defender' of small nations there, but a power which pushed countries along the path of military adventure.[15]

Certain differences were observable in the attitude of the Finnish press to the Moroccan crisis which broke out in the summer of 1911. In *Helsingin Sanomat* and *Uusi Suometar* this conflict, caused by a German naval demonstration in Agadir harbour, was noted in the news columns, but not with the status of a major international event.[16] By contrast the leading Swedish-language papers, influenced by the Swedish press, ascribed much more significance to it, and quoted the opinions of the major European newspapers on the subject.[17] Different cities — London, Paris, Berlin, Vienna as well as St Petersburg — were the sources of information for the Finnish press on international affairs. At the time of the Bosnian crisis, and later during the Balkan wars of 1912–13, *Uusi Suometar*, for example, relied heavily on Berlin, so that the current interests of the Triple Alliance could not fail to leave their mark. London was often the source for *Helsingin Sanomat*, which also tended to stress the point of view of the western powers. It seems that the leading Finnish papers paid little attention to the way these sources might colour or select the news. Independent commentary on international events in the Finnish papers was, as already indicated, rare. It was not a question of censorship or of self-censorship, but of the unfamiliarity. Rudolf Holsti in *Helsingin Sanomat* and G. Mattson in *Dagens Tidning* were exceptions to the rule with their articles in which they tried to interpret international politics. Since the country had no foreign policy of its own, it did not have agencies abroad which might have directed attention to international politics, and influenced those circles actively interested in politics.

The alienation from the methods of the Russian workers' movement which had appeared among the Finnish socialists had clearly gained impetus from the Sveaborg revolt. In 1911, when the Social Democratic party congress was stressing the struggle against tsarist rule, it was seen as appropriate to remark that 'it is not at all necessary to involve our struggle with the struggle of the Russian proletariat, which would be dangerous for our workers' movement'.[18]

The world-picture formed up to then in the Finnish workers' movement was clearly centred on Germany and continental Europe. Finnish socialist circles held the great names of the German workers' movement, August Bebel and Karl Kautsky, in high esteem. In the years after the general strike, most of the many translations of socialist literature published in Finland were of German origin.[19]

Tsarist rule in Russia was seen by the Finnish socialists as so powerful that there could be no real confidence in the potential of the workers' movement there. During the events of 1905–6, the leaders of the different leftist parties in Russia had remained virtually unknown to the Finns.[20]

In the view of the Finnish workers' movement, any major social change would be launched from Germany. The emphasis on internationalism got further justification from the feeling of impotence into which the Finnish workers' movement felt it had been thrust. Moreover, the Finnish socialists' own links abroad were still very slight in practice.

4. *The second period of oppression and the attitude to Finland abroad*

The development of international relations in Europe caused a lessening of interest outside Finland in the country's autonomy and its efforts to defend its special political status. A change of attitude was noticeable in the leading British papers after 1905; indeed British attitudes to Russia in general were changing, and the two countries drew much closer together after 1907. In Britain many thought that the Russian political system had become more western, with the Duma becoming a national representative body. Stolypin was seen not as a reactionary but as a conservative reformer, whose aim was the internal strengthening of Russia. According to this view, affairs in Russia were moving 'towards improvement'.

In Britain, Russian policy in Finland was clearly understood because that country had similar problems, especially in relation to the Irish. The involvement of the Duma in decision-making was another factor which eased understanding. The change which had occurred was noted in all the important British papers, starting with *The Times* which began in 1908–9 to regard Stolypin as the representative of a constitutional system.[21] It gave considerable coverage to Stolypin's speech on the Finnish question in the Duma in May 1908. The *Manchester Guardian* gave great significance to his remark that it was wrong to suppose that the Duma would have supported the policies of oppressing small nations pursued by Bobrikov and the autocracy. Further the paper showed interest in the enforcement of imperial legislation that Finland could in some way be represented in the Russian Duma and the Imperial Council.[22] The Russian government's aim was seen as being the extension of imperial control in Finland, but at the same time *The Morning Post* thought the attitude of the Finnish parliament was inflexible.[23] It was not understood in Britain why Finland could not send representatives to the Duma.

In the French papers, anything connected with the relations of the great powers in Europe, especially those of France with Russia and Britain, was given prominence. They also touched on matters of interest to France concerning the Baltic area, like the construction plans for the Russian navy and the strategic prospects this opened up.[24] There were also rumours in the Paris papers of Russian intentions to fortify Åland.[25]

By contrast, the handling of the Finnish question in the Russian Duma was a minor item; *Le Temps* and *Journal des Débats* had brief and sympathetic references to Stolypin's speech.[26] The few articles in the French papers on the Russian attitude to Finland were by writers either sympathetic to the Finnish side or unconnected with official French foreign policy.[27] Finland seldom made an appearance in the leading German political newspapers. The social democratic *Vorwärts* took a distinctly anti-Russian line, in contrast to the papers which supported the country's official foreign policy. It used the term 'June coup' of the Emperor's confirmation of the law concerning imperial legislation in Finland in 1910.[28]

The Swedish press was especially sensitive to everything connected with Russian military preparations in Finland, including Åland.[29] However, there was no extensive discussion of the new phase of oppression in Finland such as there had been in 1899.[30] The sharpening of conflict between the great powers and the possibility of open crisis, made the Swedish press emphasise Sweden's policy of neutrality towards all the great powers, including Russia. The visit of Gustav V to St Petersburg at a critical time, May 1908, muted any tendency to criticise Russia's Finnish policy.

Thus it was not in the interests of any foreign power to raise the Finnish question internationally. Support for Finnish autonomy was an expendable issue in Europe; and Russia's position in the post-1905 political constellation was favourable. In this respect, the Russian initiative on Finland in 1908 was a carefully executed manoeuvre.

The foreign propaganda activity of the Finns on behalf of their rights after 1908 was very insignificant compared with that of the post-1899 period. J.N. Reuter continued to be the agent in Britain while Adolf Törngren was active in France. The Finns themselves could no longer get any real momentum into this propaganda activity, largely because of the swing in opinion towards Russia among influential circles in Britain and France. From about 1910 there was open disappointment in Finland that their countrymen had not succeeded in developing contacts with western newspapers. However, they did succeed, despite great difficulties, in getting some public international support for Finland. Typical of this was the resolution in favour of her autonomous rights presented at a conference of international lawyers in London in 1910; this resolution was intended to influence the debate on the Finnish question then in progress in the Duma, but it was published only after the debate had already ended.[31] A new development was the raising of the issue of Finland's autonomy at the conference of the Socialist International in Copenhagen in 1910. The Finnish socialists had managed to activate the French socialists in particular over this issue — the latter, led by Jaurès, had become severe critics of tsarist rule after 1905, and were interested in the fate of all the oppressed nationalities in the Russian empire. The congress of the International approved the resolution condemning the violations of Finland's autonomy, and the oppression of the Finns by the tsarist regime.[32]

The Russians also began to run a very active information service with the aim of defending Russian policy on Finland. This was a tacit admission that the Finnish propaganda after 1899 had been a nuisance to them. The Russians evidently assumed that the Finnish international activity of the 1899 period would be repeated. After 1908, with the active connivance of the Russian government, numerous books, collections of documents and articles dealing with Russian policy in Finland were published in the major European languages. Typically, General Borodkin had, by the end of 1911, published four books on Finland and its history, most notably a work defending Russia's current policy called *Finland, a Russian borderland*; this appeared in English, French and German.[33] In publications of this kind Russian military interests were stressed — arguments which generally found favour in the policies of the great powers. Finland was described as having 'local autonomy'.

Before 1914 the Finns were widely recognised in Europe as a nationality, but a less well-known one than, for example, the Poles and Hungarians. Geographically Finland formed a distinct entity. The barriers between the different language-groups were indeed sharp, but Finland was not nationally divided like the Baltic provinces. The image of Finland abroad was liable to be somewhat uneven, due to the generally limited knowledge of the country. Seen from a political viewpoint, the long, duration of Finland's autonomy indicated developed conditions, as did the existence of universal suffrage in parliamentary elections, and the social rights of women. The image of Finland formed by foreigners often included its high cultural level; this may have been influenced by the culture of the country's Swedish-speakers, and brilliant men like Runeberg, but it was also well-known that literacy was general in the country and popular culture relatively high.

In contrast, however, there also existed an image of Finland as a primitive country, where nature was exceptionally beautiful but the climate harsh; so there were certain stereotyped characteristics typical of such an environment. The people living in these primitive conditions were thought of as industrious and honest, retaining a pristine freshness in their human relations: industrialism, urbanisation and other factors had not been able to spoil them. This foreign view of the Finn might also have included a touch of supercilious social romanticism. In western and central Europe the Finns were also compared with the Slavs, the general view was often strongly negative. In the Olympic Games Finland made an unquestioned impact, especially in the Stockholm Olympics of 1912, when — thanks to Hannes Kohlemainen and others — she 'ran her name on to the world map'.[34]

XV. The outbreak of world war in 1914, Russia at war, and the Finnish question

1. *Russia and Finland as an interdependent system*

From 1910 onwards, military considerations came more to the fore in the Russian attitude to Finland. Conservative-nationalist policies also continued to have a powerful influence.

On both sides of the Gulf of Finland the Russians sought to push the 'portcullis' system westward from the immediate environment of St Petersburg: the outer 'gate' was being built at this stage at the level of Hanko and the northern tip of Hiiumaa, but the coastal areas between Hanko and Åland were also discussed in the Russian military planning covering Finland. Movement in this extensive area of archipelago posed a particular problem in any crisis situation. The differences of opinion arising out of these questions surfaced in a strike of Finnish pilots in 1912 to resist the reorganisation of the pilot system in Finland. The Russian authorities broke the strike by bringing Russian pilots from the Caspian Sea to replace the Finns.

The importance of the military preparations on the south coast of Finland was ultimately bound up with the major problem of whether, in the event of war, Germany would direct her main attack against Russia or against France. Although Russia had by degrees moved her main defence line forward in the Gulf of Finland, it was feared in St Petersburg that, as the execution of the plans was still incomplete, Germany could attempt a landing, with strong naval forces, as deeply in the rear of the main defence line as Koivisto.

To repel this danger the Russians had begun in 1909 to build the fortification of Ino.[1] In 1911, a plan (later shelved) was published for attaching certain parts of the western Karelian Isthmus to the region of St Petersburg. This proposal was obviously inspired by military considerations. The general emphasis in St Petersburg on the military importance of the south coast of Finland may also be reflected by the fact that by 1912 the Russian military command was stressing the unreliability of the Finns and thus the need to get a firmer grip on the administration of Finland.[2]

A desire to fight for autonomy had appeared in Finland in 1908, but thereafter the Finns began to feel uncertain and pessimistic about the future. This pessimism can be seen in the growing passivity in party activity, and in the low turn-out in parliamentary elections (around 50–65 per cent). From 1912 onwards, rumours appeared that Russia would seek an even firmer administrative grip on Finland than before.[3] Whereas Russian imperial policy sought very systematically to 'russify' the Finnish administration, it put no serious obstacles in the way of the activity of the political parties in the country. In addition the Finnish press could launch strong criticisms of the policy of oppression, and even of the

Russian Council of Ministers — though not the sovereign. Obviously the authorities in St Petersburg were trying to prevent political reactions from the broad mass of the people from appearing, as in 1899 and 1905.[4]

Around 1910, the Finnish party newspapers adopted different attitudes towards Russian policy. *Uusi Suometar* wrote in its political reviews of the 'disappointment', the 'depressing measures' which had been experienced, and of attempts to 'ward off misfortunes'. The position of the appeasers had clearly changed since the first period of oppression, while the bourgeois constitutionalists took a sharply critical stand. *Helsingin Sanomat* criticised the much-increased 'measures of oppression', against which it urged action, and saw the danger of 'new night-frosts' ahead.[5] *Hufvudstadsbladet*, which took a stance as a defender of western values, feared that Finland's culture and legal system would be destroyed and that there would be an attempt to implant Russian social conditions in the country. *Dagens Tidning* spoke, in a review of the year 1913, of Finland's 'history of martyrdom'.[6] *Työmies*, with its intemperate use of political language, spoke of the 'oppressive measures of professional Russians', 'Russian strangulation', and 'Russian oppression'.[7]

Finland's leading newspapers were aware that after 1911 the international situation in Europe had clearly become critical. In *Helsingin Sanomat*'s retrospective survey of international developments in 1913, it stressed that the 'most threatening problem for the peace of Europe' had not broken out into open conflict;[8] *Uusi Suometar* noted too that the greatest achievement of the policies of the great powers in 1913 had been the avoidance of war.[9] *Hufvudstadsbladet* had already, two years in succession, spoken of a world war having been prevented.[10] *Työmies* stressed the 'dangers of imperialism' and the significance of the struggle against it.[11] These papers proceeded from different basic assumptions in their attitudes to the great powers. When *Helsingin Sanomat* discussed the foreign policy of Britain and France, it called these countries the 'western European democracies', whereas Russia and Germany were 'the world's conservative great powers';[12] however, *Uusi Suometar* did not seem to make a distinction between the powers. *Hufvudstadsbladet* regretted that the 'two leading cultural nations of Europe', Germany and France, had allowed events to lead so near to the catastrophe of a world war in 1911.[13] *Työmies* did not distinguish between great powers, but regarded them all as representing 'imperialism'.[14]

Although from the beginning of the decade these leading newspapers in Finland made clear references to the danger of a major war, Finnish society as a whole was far more concerned with the country's internal conditions. Finland lived — whether consciously or unconsciously — under the 'umbrella' of the Russian empire, and because peace had prevailed for more than half a century, most people did not seriously contemplate war as a serious possibility. Further there had been no major political changes in the Baltic area, nor any changes of boundaries, for a long time. The peaceful coexistence of Germany and Russia seemed so well established that it was difficult for contemporaries to envisage any alternative.

2. *The outbreak of the world war as observed from Finland*

The assassination of the heir to the Habsburg empire at the end of June 1914 was a sensational event which claimed the status of a major news item in the Finnish press, but no indications appeared in the leading papers of the possibility of a general European war. However, the events at the end of July 1914 when the Serbian crisis developed into a war, and Russia and the other European great powers suddenly began general mobilisation, saw a rapid change in the situation.

The military preparations of the Russian empire quickly extended to Finland. They first of all concerned the control of sea traffic, but on the evening of 30 July general mobilisation was announced and on the following day, 31 July, the territory of Finland too was proclaimed to be in a state of war. The commander of the St Petersburg military district was given supreme authority in Finland 'for the preservation of public order and social tranquillity'. Despite all the international crises that had occurred, the outbreak of the world war came as a great surprise. The first popular reaction was panic; people took refuge in the countryside as rumours spread that a German attack on Helsinki could be expected.

Once the world war had broken out, Finland's trade relations with Germany and western Europe were severed. At the same time, trade with Sweden became especially important because it was hoped that by that route contacts could be maintained with other countries, including Britain. Finland's trading relations to the east were also made difficult at first because of the choking of the railways caused by mobilisation, and the stopping of sea traffic in the Gulf of Finland. The exports of the timber industry stopped, and many plants like the Gutzeit and Halla factories at Kotka entirely ceased activity. The textile industry too was soon in difficulties when the arrival of foreign raw materials dried up; because of this, extensive unemployment began to appear in some industries. The authorities also had to consider the problems of food supply. Russia had decreed increases in the tariffs on foreign grain imports to Finland just before the outbreak of war; however, soon after that, communications with Germany, whose imports had led to the decisions being made, were broken. No immediate grain shortage appeared in the country, but as a precaution plans were made for the procurement of Russian grain for Finland.

The proclamation of a state of war in Finland was a security measure of the Russian military command; its purpose, in addition to emphasising to the people that an emergency existed, was to promote solidarity with the empire. The military authorities thus acquired special powers, on the basis of which they could regulate all political activity in Finland by emergency measures, and reduce the citizens' basic political rights.

Once the outbreak of the world war was a fact, Finnish society was in a state of expectation. At the beginning there was a fear the German operations would extend to Finland — conjectures were circulating of a German landing around Hanko. In addition, Finns were afraid that the Russian military authorities would interfere in the country's political life.

In the emergency there were no official organs in the country to express the views of the Finns. Parliament was not in session, and the Senate because of its composition could not represent the people. For the politicians the situation was difficult: obviously they wanted to avoid binding expressions of opinion. In this situation the newspapers, which represented continuity, were forced to express attitudes. This being so, Finnish society in the opening phase of the war — from the academics and church leaders to farmers and industrial workers, embracing all the political parties — was outwardly shrouded in a somewhat diffuse loyalty.

Uusi Suometar went furthest among the leading papers in emphasising loyalty. It thought that Finland should take part in Red Cross activity and generally in organising medical care on the Russian front against the Central Powers. *Uusi Suometar* supported the sending of Finnish volunteers to join the ranks of the Russian army.[15] The social democratic papers urged the responsibility of the workers to maintain order in the country. The leadership of the workers' movement was in a state of alarm; it feared that the military authorities would altogether forbid the activities of their organisations. The country's trade union organisation anticipated this possibility when, on 31 July, it forbade its members to go on strike or take part in demonstrations, even urging its member-unions to consider ending the payment of dues. In this way it sought to keep a few steps ahead so that a suppression of the trade union movement would not come as a surprise to its members. It was also decided to act in this way at the level of the individual unions, as a decision by the executive of the Printers' Union on the ending of membership dues and certain benefits in early August showed.[16]

Germany was commonly branded as guilty of causing the outbreak of the world war. Thus the church paper *Kotimaa*, stated that the war had evidently been planned in Germany for a long time, and for years war fever had been fanned in peoples' minds.[17] *Työmies* too criticised Germany and accused the German workers' movement of having done nothing to oppose the launching of a 'war of aggression'. While the social democratic papers generally explained the war as the fault of the capitalist system, they were also prepared to concede that socialists should participate in government in France and Belgium to support national defence.[18] Being forced to acknowledge that the international workers' movement was powerless to prevent the war, the workers' newspapers indirectly demonstrated loyalty to the empire and at the same time recognised, in a way, that their country belonged to the Entente as a whole. When the Germans advanced rapidly through Belgium into France, their method of waging war was criticised severely in very many Finnish newspapers. *Uusi Suometar* condemned them as 'worse than the Vandals' and *Kansan Lehti* as adopting the 'politics of bandits', while *Ilkka* carried details of German cruelties.[19]

The western-oriented *Helsingin Sanomat* adopted a somewhat different position. It remarked, with some irony, that Russian policy in the Balkans had
supported and was still supporting the national aspirations of small nations,
whereas in Finland it had acted in the opposite direction. It also dared to say that
the proclamation in Finland of a state of war was in some respects contrary to
the country's constitution. Likewise *Helsingin Sanomat* criticised Russian policy
towards Finland in general, and stated its belief that the Russian accusations
against the Finns for supposed disloyalty in the years of peace had been
fabricated; in the paper's opinion Russia herself would have to recognise this in
the new emergency.[20] At the same time *Helsingin Sanomat* stressed that the
Finnish people remained loyal.

Kansan Tahto, published in Oulu, differed from the other social democratic
newspapers in not accepting the view that Germany was to be regarded unquestioningly as the aggressor and initiator of the war.[21] In addition the paper
maintained that it was vitally important for the German social democrats that
their country should not be defeated in the war. *Kansan Tahto* also posed a
dramatic question: if Finland had been an independent state, how would its
workers' movement have behaved in a general European war? The answer was
that it would have had to make preparations to preserve the country's territorial
integrity. The paper reacted sympathetically to Germany and refused to accept
the allegations by Russian war propaganda of the 'vandalism' of the Germans.
It was explained that the existing war situation did not require that 'we should
regard people proclaimed as our enemies as devils'.[22] When Governor-General
Seyn suppressed *Kansan Tahto* two days after the appearance of this article, the
reason was clear.

On the outbreak of earlier international crises, the political leadership in Russia
had thought it appropriate to ensure the loyalty of the Finns by showing benevo-
lence towards the country's autonomy, and by expressions of goodwill. This
had been usual in the nineteenth century, and only the outbreak of the war with
Japan really formed an exception.

It could have been assumed that with the outbreak of a truly major war in
Europe in the summer of 1914, the tsarist power would have taken a lesson from
its earlier experiences of the Finns, especially since in the first moments of the
great war the Finns showed obvious signs of their readiness to adopt an attitude
of loyalty. However, Russia's only measure in this period was to proclaim
Finland in a state of war; no measures were taken this time to guide the feelings
of the Finns in a positive direction — and there was no compromise whatever
on the basic cause of tension, the Russification policy.

Imperial Russia and Finland drifted into this greatest — and final — international crisis of the period of autonomy with their positions and attitudes so
firmly fixed by the events of the previous decade and a half that the outbreak of
the crisis in itself could not change any of their essential features. Changes could

come primarily from only two directions: from actions by the enemies of the tsarist power within Russia, or the operations of the external enemies of the Russian empire in the world war. Whether the Finns, even in their wilder dreams, could foresee these possibilities in the emergency of August 1914 was another matter.

XVI. The end of an era

Autonomous Finland, as a part of the Russian empire, had on the whole experienced international crises and great power politics from a great distance. Only the Crimean war, which had brought military operations to Finland's coasts, was an exception to this. Otherwise the country was able to live for over a century secure from external dangers. This had made possible a concentration on the work of construction inside the country. However, there was another side to an existence sheltered from outside; the Russian Emperor had given the Finns a defined room to manoeuvre, which was not a constant, and was not even always self-evident. Thus, Finland's communications abroad were controlled by the censor, by passport regulations and other means, especially in the first half of the period of autonomy, a situation which had meant considerable isolation from the rest of Europe. After the middle of the nineteenth century, however, Finland's outside communications were gradually extended and eased.

Foreign, and especially western influences began more and more to change the direction of Finland's social development, linking the country to the modernising developments of western Europe and thus at the same time increasing her distance from Russia with her old-fashioned attitudes. This divergent direction in social development and the widening of the Finns' room for manoeuvre in the latter half of the nineteenth century created — in the long run — the starting points for the conflict of Finland and Russia at the turn of the century.

International politics, especially everything relating to power politics, remained alien to the Finns for the whole period of autonomy. This was influenced first by lack of knowledge but also by the characteristic emphasis on constitutionalism in the country's politics and the common conception of justice. The nineteenth century was a great formative stage for Finnish national identity, and the examination of political problems therefore remained strongly fennocentric. The expansion of the nationalist ideal significantly affected the general political and cultural advance in the country, but by its very nature it limited the extension of the practice of observation to the international political level. A realistic, all-round analysis of international crises could only rarely be seen in Finland: Snellman's conduct in 1863 was an example of this.

For the whole period of autonomy, Finland's special status was influenced by Russian security policy, above all the assessment in St Petersburg of the country's strategic significance. This essentially defined Finland's political room for manoeuvre. Here three phases can be distinguished: the beginning of autonomy, when such flexibility was restricted; the period beginning in 1860, when freedom of political activity was expanded; and the last decades of autonomy when St Petersburg made a powerful attempt to reduce that freedom. In the first phase, at the beginning of the nineteenth century, the aim of leading circles in Finland was to propagate confidence in St Petersburg, and in this they largely succeeded. The second phase was characterised by confidence on both sides and by the endeavour of Russia's ruling circles to make the Finns satisfied with their status and conditions. When mutual confidence showed signs of cracking from the end of the 1880s, Russia finally adopted a policy in Finland aimed at imperial unification. The preservation of mutual confidence and the contentment of the Finns were no longer essential aims.

Finland was also able to expand and develop contacts with the west in the second quarter of the nineteenth century. From the 1860s, with growing industrialisation, Finland began to be integrated commercially and economically with the west, but at the same time her trade with Russia was always growing, and in other fields too contacts with the east were increased. International crises were reflected in Finland's economic life as exceptional periods of either boom or depression, in which foreign trading relations were either interrupted or reduced. Much depended on the position of Russia in each international crisis; if Russia was involved, Finland's trade with the west was liable to be seriously disturbed, as during the Crimean war. At the same time, however, her trade with the east had considerable possibilities of growth in these exceptional situations. From the Turkish war onwards, Finland became closely involved with Russia's war economy as an important procurement area.

Great changes had taken place in the political roles of Finland's different social groups in the period of autonomy. In the strongly patriarchal conditions of the first half of the century the church leadership, together with the country's administration, had primary responsibility as mediators of opinion to the people. As society modernised and political conditions were liberalised, the press, the Diet, political parties, and various societies and social movements now had a place in the changing overall picture of society.

The church was a channel of influence from the first half of the century, as a transmitter to the people of announcements and political ideals from the Finnish and St Petersburg governments. It had no great problems in this special role as long as the basic aim of Russia's policy in Finland was the maintenance and strengthening of mutual confidence. With the subsequent sharp change in Russian policy, the church came under the conflicting pressures of the demands of obedience and nationalist attitudes. A situation developed in the first years of the twentieth century in connection with the call-up which pointed towards deadlock. By August 1914, the church was already isolated from the main flow of events.

The reactions to international crises of the intellectuals, and in later phases the farmers and industrial workers, were relatively spontaneous and free from restraints. The intellectuals in the first half of the nineteenth century had been quick to react to the various international crises; they also occupied an important position as the intermediaries for intellectual influences from foreign countries. When the constellation of political factors in Finland began to separate in the 1860s, the intellectuals no longer appeared as a distinct group; their influence was seen subsequently within the different parties, as promoters of ideas and in various leading positions. Extreme examples of the political activity of intellectuals in the early twentieth century were the handling of the foreign propaganda on behalf of Finland's rights, a central role in émigré politics, and their share in the work of the activist and workers' movements.

The influence of the business community, which had been strengthening its position in public affairs, especially since the 1840s, followed an opposite line of development to that of the church. The interest in politics of the commercial and industrial bourgeoisie began to show itself especially after the Crimean war. This section of society then found itself in a unique position insofar as international crises, and the sharp change in Russia's Finnish policy at the turn of the century, did not upset its essential interests; on the contrary the growing orders for the Russian war economy in times of crisis, and the quantitative expansion of eastern trade in general, could offer promising economic prospects. For this reason those involved in the interests of trade and industry, especially in the final phase of the autonomy period, formed a distinct grouping when the political interests of the nation were discussed.

The farming population had adapted slowly to the new association with the empire after 1808. However, by the time of Alexander II it had already adopted unrestrained worship of the sovereign — the shift from king to emperor had been accomplished — and after 1899 it shed these attitudes only slowly. Also the knowledge of international crises had reached the farmers later than others.

The late birth of the workers' movement in Finland coincided with the period of diminishing political-social influence of the church. The influence of each was clearly limited to certain spheres of the country's social life. Certain factors in the peculiar conditions of Finland's autonomy were to hinder the attempts to secure radical reforms by the workers' movement, and other reformist elements, from the end of the nineteenth century. As early as the 1880s, certain political circles had begun to express doubts about the wisdom of change, which might weaken Finland's special status. Alongside the general conservatism which showed signs of growing yet more entrenched in the finnicisation movement the Svecoman movement also tended to oppose social change.

It is strange that the tsarist regime, despite its generally conservative nature, its means of applying political pressure and its prohibitions, allowed the workers' movement to organise in Finland very freely — although at the same time the workers' movement sharply criticised the St Petersburg government and although its support was expanding with explosive speed. The workers' movement reacted against Russia's policy mainly on the same grounds as the groups in the country which emphasised constitutionalism, with the addition that the socialists stressed that tsarist power was not only nationally dangerous, but represented social reaction. Whatever the general development in Finland, there always remained the deep division between the workers' movement and the other political groups.

Autonomous Finland had to face a powerful wave of reaction from Russia at the beginning of the twentieth century, directed not only against the country's self-government, but against all that separate development which, from the 1860s, had in many ways estranged Finland from Russia in everyday life. At the same time, because of general technological development and the improvement of transport and communications, Finland had come closer to the flash-points of Europe's high politics.

In August 1914 Finnish society experienced the outbreak of world war in Europe more or less undivided internally; but Finland was hidden from outside view in the totality of the Russian empire, and escaped the attention which was generally concentrated on the great theatres of war on the continent.

Paradoxically, the desire and readiness for greater political and national liberty had grown continuously and significantly throughout the entire period of Finland's autonomy. This was to come to a head in national sovereignty in the latter stages of the war, but for the time being, Finland was politically subdued as the clouds of war rolled over Europe.

Sources

Foreign materials

Foreign diplomatic correspondence while it illustrates the foreign policy objectives of the state in question and its general position, also contains very diverse observations of interest from the point of view of this study, whether the observer's view of Finland is from St Petersburg or Stockholm. Alliances between the great powers greatly assisted in the procuring of secret information on the spot. In this context, the relations of Russia and Austria in the years 1815–54 may be cited. The same phenomenon appears in the relations of France and Russia at the time of the Dual Alliance, and even a little earlier; for example, the French military attaché in St Petersburg could transmit copies of the Russian mobilisation plans to his superiors on the French General Staff.

The Swedish consuls in Finland had the great advantage in not experiencing much of a language barrier. The information-gathering duties of other consuls in Helsinki generally extended to essential political events in Finland.

In the information procured by the military attachés in St Petersburg there is a clear difference between the representative of a great and a small power. The Swedish military representative, for example, did not seem to have access to very significant sources of information, on the basis of the available material, and their military observations were often very superficial or related to politics.

Finnish materials

The material relating to the leadership and the élite is good, and there is extensive documentation for the administration in Finland. Within the latter, two groups are especially prominent. The documents of the Governor-General's department reveal the aims of the administration, and archive material left behind by the censorship authorities throws much light on the practices of political supervision. In addition there are many private archives left by the country's civil servants.

The attitudes of the church leaders are illustrated by the circular letters of the cathedral chapters and the proclamations for days of prayer. Indirect conclusions regarding the attitudes of leading clergymen are possible, for example, from the patronage policy of the emperors. It is more difficult to draw conclusions about the ordinary clergy, and to ascertain how far the instructions of the leaders — apart from the official proclamations — were actually carried out.

The documentation for the academic intellectuals is good, and includes private letters, privately printed writings etc. While the opinions and views of the intellectuals are important in many phases, it is necessary to guard against exaggerating their applicability to Finnish society as a whole.

Any survey of the business community must take into account their position in society and prospects for pursuing their livelihoods, and the changes which occurred in this respect. This analysis is supported by extensive research in economic history. Business circles also give clear expression to political-social attitudes, which appear in the columns of some papers, like *Åbo Underrättelser*, *Oulun Wiikko-Sanomat*, and *Wiborg* from the beginning of the nineteenth century, and later in many other papers.

Newspapers for the farming interest are difficult to find, except in the final phase of our period. One is forced to draw conclusions about the farmers from their prospects for pursuing their livelihoods, and something can be deduced from measures of the administration directed at the farmers. Ballads and similar material from periods of crisis mainly reflect the attitudes of the more advanced elements among the farmers. The letters sent to various newspapers from the last decades of the nineteenth century also offer material originating in the farming community.

As for the industrial workers, in the latter half of the nineteenth century conclusions can only be very general, based on economic conditions and the like. When a workers' movement comes into the picture and its representation grows, especially after 1905, the documentation — from party and other corresponding materials — is extensive.

As regards the Finnish press, certain questions are repeated at different phases of the study; what the papers write about foreign countries and what they do not; what are their sources of information (St Petersburg or direct from abroad); what is the role of the censorship and what are the ways of circumventing it. Borrowing from foreign newspapers is important when it is difficult or impossible for the press to put forward opinions of their own.

In some respects the Swedish press constituted a special case for Finland. In some periods the 'Letters from Finland' published in the Stockholm newspapers express certain tendencies in Finnish opinion. However, they were a safety valve, and as such easily give a misleading picture of opinion as a whole.

Private correspondence is a valuable source, but is mainly limited to depicting the attitudes of the academic intellectuals and the upper class. The researcher must also question the degree to which the letters he is using are representative. For example, have some letters from 1808–12 been destroyed later, out of fear of political discrimination when political developments had taken on an irreversible direction? The same question can also apply to the letters and documents for the years 1854–63, and 1899–1916.

I have also interviewed people who, despite the distance in time, were still able to convey personal impressions or experiences of the time before 1914.

I would like to thank the following people who have provided references to source materials, commented on them, or offered some valuable points of view on the subject of my research: Professor Sven Andersson, Dr. J.O. Andersson, Dr. Michael Branch (London), Dr. William Copeland, Lieutenant-General Ermei Kanninen, Dr. Yrjö Kaukiainen, Väinö Liukkonen, Professor W.R. Mead (London), Professor R. Palmgren, Carl Ramsdahl, Lieutenant-Colonel Helge Seppälä, Dr. Arvo Soininen, Professor Ilmar Talve, and Lieutenant-General Tauno Viljanen.

Notes

Chapter I

1. Odhner II 1896, pp. 7, 12, 30; Gerhard 1933, pp. 9–13, 225–9, 241–2; Jägerskiöld 1957, pp. 124–31, 268–72: Malcolm-Smith 1937, pp. 224–9; Middleton 1947, pp. 21–3; Holborn 1962, pp. 379–80; Horn 1967, pp. 206, 207 221–3, 250, 251, 261–4.
2. Paloposki 1967, pp. 93–6; Alanen 1964, pp. 151–4, 256–8, 654–8; Pohjolan-Pirhonen 1970, pp. 562–3; Jutikkala-Pirinen 1973, pp. 175, 181–6; Renvall 1962, pp. 445–7.
3. Pohjolan-Pirhonen 1970, pp. 561–3, 677; Renvall 1962, pp. 439–40; Alma Söderhjelm I 1920, pp. 174–86, II 1924, pp. 133–205; *H.G. Porthans brev till M. Calonius*, I, pp. 53, 85, 91, 94, 104, 167, 232, 259, 278, 306; Haltsonen 1937, pp. 290–3.

Chapter II

1. Lobanov-Rostovsky 1947, pp. 160–4; Middleton 1947, pp. 25–30; Renouvin IV 1954, pp. 209–14.
2. Osmonsalo 1947, pp. 41–3, 63–80.
3. For the initial stages of the war of 1808 and the Russian aims, see Osmonsalo 1947, pp. 95–104; Tommila 1962, pp. 16–18; Käiväräinen 1965, pp. 172–3.
4. For the Russian proclamations 16/28 March 1808 and 20 March/1 April, see Osmonsalo 1947, pp. 162–3; Tommila 1962, p. 18; *Journal du Nord* 1808, XI(March).
5. Julku 1956, pp. 137–41.
6. *The Times* reported on 6, 14 and 23 July 1808 the counter-attack of the Swedish army on the basis of news received from Stockholm. The victory at Lapua, for example, was described as 'this brilliant affair'. The paper also got information about the war in Finland through Holland (see *The Times*, 12 August 1808). According to *The Times*, that war ended unexpectedly, and on 5 September it reported, 'The fighting in Finland seems to have ended.'
7. *Journal du Nord* 1808, XIII, XXIX, XXXIII, XXXV (April–September) — these were dominated by reports on the war in Finland; *Le Moniteur* 29 August 1808.
8. Osmonsalo 1947, p. 390.
9. Von Rauch 1953, pp. 39–45.
10. Hornborg 1963, p. 178.
11. Osmonsalo 1947, pp. 398–9.
12. Vuorela 1976, pp. 26–7.
13. Lempiäinen 1973, pp. 12–19.
14. Carl von Bonsdorff 1912, pp. 31–3, 72, 112–14.
15. Details of Russian pacification policy in Tommila 1962, pp. 40–3; L.G. von Bonsdorff 1929, pp. 201–7.
16. On traditional attitudes see Tarkiainen 1974, pp. 42–5, 68–72.
17. Ruutu 1965, pp. 145–6.
18. E.g. Mannerheim's letter to Rehbinder 23 February 1820 (Rehbinder's collected correspondence 7/VA).

19. Vuorela 1976, pp. 27–8; Mikko Juva 1966, pp. 13–15.
20. After 1 June 1808 there is a considerable gap in the circulars of Bishop Tengström, and the next signature does not appear before 25 July (*Åbo domkapitel: Circulärbrev* III 1808–12); also Mikko Juva 1966, pp. 18–19.
21. Vuorela 1976, pp. 30–1.
22. Anthoni I 1923, pp. 91–2.
23. Halila 1962, p. 520.
24. Osmonsalo 1947, pp. 249, 255.
25. It was typical of conditions in southern Finland from the spring of 1808 that the country's only newspaper, *Åbo Tidning* contained no news of the continuing war in Pohjanmaa; areas occupied by the Russians were mentioned on 13 April. Only after 2 July did the paper publish news of the war in Pohjanmaa, and then concentrated on reporting the renewed victories of the Russian troops. *Åbo Tidning* used the term 'troops' of the Russian forces, and 'the Swedes' of their opponents.
26. Hornborg 1955, pp. 115–16.
27. Osmonsalo 1947, p. 226; Tommila 1962, pp. 41–2.
28. Osmonsalo 1947, pp. 211, 212, 221–3, 248–50.
29. E.g. Carl von Bonsdorff 1918, p. 97.
30. Lindström 1905, p. 231.
31. Ryan 1959, pp. 443–5, 452, 463–6.
32. Lindström 1905, p. 232; Pohjanpalo 1965, p. 43.
33. Osmonsalo 1947, pp. 432, 436; Halila 1962, pp. 469–71.
34. Tommila 1962, p. 31; Korhonen 1963, pp. 31–2; Jussila 1969, p. 20; Mikko Juva 1966, p. 32.
35. Halila 1962, pp. 509, 530.
36. Lobanov-Rostovsky 1947, p. 172; Carlsson-Höjer 1954, pp. 128–30.
37. Lindström 1905, pp. 70–80; Joustela 1963, pp. 32, 33.
38. Woodward 1965, p. 78.
39. Apunen 1970, pp. 18, 47.
40. *Åbo Allmänna Tidning* discussed foreign events from 4 January 1810, when it carried reports on Spain and on the war between France and Austria and the subsequent peace treaty. There was a certain anti-British tendency; the paper published a speech by Napoleon mentioning that Sweden 'together with her ally Britain' had lost 'her most beautiful and important' territory to Russia (*ÅAT*, 4, 9, 11 January 1810).
41. Carl von Bonsdorff 1918, pp. 104–5; Tommila 1962, p. 48.
42. Carl von Bonsdorff 1918, pp. 107–9, 116; Pohjolan-Pirhonen 1973, pp. 237–45.
43. On the problems of migrating to Finland, see Blomstedt 1965, pp. 245–53; Carl von Bonsdorff 1918, pp. 60–2.
44. Tommila 1963, p. 117; Carl von Bonsdorff 1918, pp. 59, 60.
45. Halila 1962, pp. 528, 529.
46. For example, Carl von Bonsdorff 1918, pp. 43–5.
47. Tommila 1962, pp. 62–71, 91–5.

Chapter III

1. Tommila 1962, p. 291; also Birke 1960, pp. 14, 17; Shukow VI 1969, pp. 110, 111.
2. Carlsson-Höjer 1954, p. 16.

3. Lobanov-Rostovsky 1947, p. 207; Tommila 1962, pp. 288, 297–304.
4. Carlsson-Höjer 1954, pp. 167–70; Tommila 1962, pp. 367–72.
5. *Ibid.*, pp. 333, 334; Korhonen 1963, pp. 187, 188.
6. Alexander's decisions of 5 August and 13 August 1812. Halila 1962, pp. 547, 548. In the appeal of Governor-General Steinheil to the Finnish people there was stress on the dangers of the international situation 'to the Russian empire, your own father-land, the whole of the Nordic countries and mankind in general'. At the same time there was reference to the fight of the Spanish people for their independence, to the patriotism of the Russian people, and the wisdom of Karl Johan (*ÅAT* 27 August 1812).
7. Blomstedt 1963 pp. 363–5.
8. 'Till Finlands Innevånare af En Finsk Medborgare' (Supplement to *ÅAT* 29 August 1812); 'Till Stor-Furstendömet Finlands Invånare' (Supplement to *ÅAT* 17 September 1812).
9. The first bulletins on the outbreak of war (dated 25 June) appeared in *Åbo Allmänna Tidning* on 23 July 1812. On 22, 24, 26 September the paper published extensive bulletins on the war between Russia and France, signed by Generals Barclay de Tolly and Kutuzov. That of 26 September concerned the battle of Borodino. The paper reported on 15 October and 14 and 19 November that the theatre of war had moved to Moscow and its surroundings, and on 24 November that Napoleon's troops had begun to withdraw from Moscow. The first announcement of the heavy French losses appeared on 28 November, followed by the announcement on 1 December that Napoleon and his troops had begun a general withdrawal (*ÅAT* 23 July, 22, 24, 26 September, 15 October, 14, 19, 24, 28 November, 1 December 1812).
10. Apunen 1970, p. 19.
11. Circular letter of Turku cathedral Chapter 'Älskade medborgare i Christo', signed by Tengström 12 August 1812 (*Åbo domkapitel: Circulärbref* III 1808–12); also Anthoni I 1923, p. 120; Carl von Bonsdorff 1918, p. 230.
12. Tengström's circular letter, 12 August.
13. Seitkari 1939, p. 91.
14. For example, Hornborg 1965, p. 197.
15. Mardal 1957, pp. xiii–xiv.
16. Kaukamaa 1941, pp. 48–55; Pohjanpalo, 1965, p. 45.
17. For example, *ÅAT* 23 January, 4 May, 11 September, 18, 30 September, 7, 12, 21 October, 4, 9, 13 November 1813.
18. Alexander's proclamations 30 November 1812 o.s, and 25 December 1812 o.s. (*ÅAT* 23 January, 13, 18 February 1813).
19. *ÅAT* 2 July 1814, report of thanksgiving service in St Petersburg for the restoration of peace.
20. *ÅAT* 17 May 1814, report of thanksgiving festival in Turku for the entry of Russian troops into Paris; *ÅAT* 19 July, report of service of thanksgiving and festival in Turku.
21. Tengström's circular letter to the parishes of Turku diocese with the enclosed model prayer of 11 December 1812 (*Åbo domkapitel: Circulärbref* III 1802–12).
22. Report to be read from the pulpits on the battle of Leipzig, 16–19 October 1813 (*Åbo domkapitel: Circulärbref* IV 1813–18); also *ÅAT* report of 25 November 1813 of celebrations organised in Turku for the victory at Leipzig, and the prayer of

thanksgiving (*ÅAT* 25, 27 November 1813).

23. Tengström's circular letter to the parishes of Turku diocese of 4 May 1814 (*Åbo domkapitel: Circulärbref* IV 1813–18).

24. *ÅAT* 17 May 1814.

25. *ÅAT* 19 July 1814 report of the thanksgiving festival in Turku. Also Carl von Bonsdorff 1918, p. 231.

26. Tengström's circular letter to the parishes of Turku diocese of 13 July 1814 (*Åbo domkapitel: Circulärbref* IV 1813–18).

27. S.S. Uvorov, *Kejsaren Alexander och Buonaparte* (Åbo 1814) and *Berättelse om Paris' intagande* (Åbo 1814).

28. Uvorov 1814, pp. 23, 25.

29. Speech by Professor J.F. Vallenius in Turku in the summer of 1814, Heikel 1897, p. 7.

30. For the first expressions of emperor-worship directed at Alexander see the poem by Franz Mikael Franzén at the festival of Turku Academy in the spring of 1809 *ÅAT* 5 April 1809); Alhoniemi 1969, p. 61; Carl von Bonsdorff 1918, pp. 219, 220.

31. Rein 1918, p. 33.

32. See the tales originating from Napoleon's Russian campaign (Folk poetry archives/SKS).

33. Tommila 1962; p. 429.

34. *Ibid.*

Chapter IV

1. Rauhala 1915, pp. 99, 100, 107.

2. *Ibid.*, p. 106; Korhonen 1963, pp. 153–5.

3. *Ibid.*, pp. 191–200.

4. *Ibid.*, pp. 156–8.

5. *Ibid.*, pp. 200, 201.

6. Paasivirta 1968, p. 13.

7. *ÅAT*, 10, 15, 17, 19, 22 November 1814 and 7, 30 March 1815, 4, 6, April 1815.

8. *Ibid.*, 7 April, 29 September, 24 October, 5, 12 December 1818.

9. Castrén 1951, p. 37.

10. *Ibid.*, p. 38.

11. Nurmio 1934, p. 63 (supplement); Tommila 1963, p. 327.

12. Nurmio 1934, p. 129.

13. Danielsson-Kalmari 1914, pp. 3–12, 35; Korhonen 1963, p. 311.

14. Rehbinder's Memorandum to Alexander (copy in Frosterus collection/VA): 'L'esprit des paysans dans le Gouvernement de Wasa est mauvais.' Rehbinder gave as explanation the battles of 1808 in this area, and the fact that there were no nobility there. For Alexander's journey in Finland, see Pohjolan-Pirhonen 1973,pp. 305–13.

15. Mannerheim 1922, p. 102.

16. Proclamations of a day of prayer 7 October 1818, 16 September 1819 (*Samling af Placater III* 1817–1820, pp. 223–5, 483–6).

17. Vuorela 1976, pp. 54–8, 63.

18. *Ibid.*, pp. 136, 137.

19. *FAT* 22 April 1830.

20. Ruuth 1952, pp. 38, 39, 46, 47, 106, 107 (supplement: Bishop Molander's speech); *FAT* 29 June 1830. In Bishop Molander's speech credit was given to the Russian forces that had fought in Persia and the Balkans, and to Zakrevski as 'father of the country'.
21. L.G. von Bonsdorff 1946, pp. 122–6.
22. Korhonen 1963, pp. 294–6.
23. Examples of this in local history writings around the country.
24. For a general characterisation of the beginning of the national awakening, see Ruutu 1956, pp. 93–6; Mikko Juva 1962, pp. 364–5; Palmgren 1948, p. 73.
25. E.g. Castrén 1944, pp. 234–45, 302–5.
26. Korhonen 1963, pp. 191–204.
27. 'The awakening of the national spirit' as the aim of Arwidsson, Castrén 1951, pp. 264–73.
28. Korhonen 1963, pp. 356–62.
29. Ruutu 1955, p. 167.
30. On events in Spain see *FAT* 17, 21, 28 April, 5, 12, 15, 31 May, 19, 23 June, 16 August 1820.
31. On events in Naples see *FAT* 14, 18, 25 August 1820.
32. *TWS* 30 September, 18 November 1820 contained a few short reports on the events in southern Europe. 'In most states there have been at this time sometimes greater, sometimes lesser revolts and disturbances' (*TWS* 30 September 1820).
33. *FAT* 18, 27 October, 1 November 1821.
34. *TWS* 30 June, 8 September, 3, 10, 24 November 1821 and 9 February, 27 April 1822.
35. Krusius-Ahrenberg 1946, p. 270.
36. Luther's homily was written at the end of the 1520s, when the Turkish army was before Vienna and there was great fear in western Europe.
37. R.W. Seton-Watson 1968, pp. 75, 76.
38. *TWS* 17 February 1821.
39. Renouvin V 1954, pp. 101, 102; Lobanov-Rostovsky 1954, pp. 14, 15.
40. *TWS* 27 April, 22 June 1822.
41. Nurmio 1934, p. 188.
42. *TWS* 18 January 1823.
43. Seton-Watson 1968, p. 76.
44. *FAT* from 1823 passim.
45. Nurmio 1934, pp. 195–200.
46. *Ibid.*, p. 201.
47. *Ibid.*, p. 202.
48. Gardberg 1924, pp. 13–14, 22.
49. Korhonen 1963, pp. 375–8; Paasivirta 1968, pp. 13–14.
50. The decisions on land-grants in Viipuri province and the access of Greek Orthodox to offices in Finland see Hornborg 1965, p. 200; Halila 1962, p. 564.
51. Nurmio 1934, pp. 326–30.
52. Joustela 1963, p. 62.
53. Riassanovsky 1963, p. 367; Leslie 1964, p. 185; Grünwald 1946 pp. 116–18.
54. Renouvin V 1954, p. 64.
55. *FAT* 30 August 1830: the announcement that Zakrevski had travelled to St Petersburg on 29 August.

56. Circular letter of Russian Foreign Ministry to diplomatic corps, 4/16 August 1830; report of Austrian ambassador to St Petersburg to Metternich of 4/16 August (*HHStA Russland* III, 89).

57. Circular letter of the censorship authority to the Governors, 16 February 1830; correspondence occasioned by checking of libraries and monthly memoranda on confiscated newspapers. (SYH/EA1).

58. *FAT* 24 August 1830. The paper had earlier reported on political unrest in Paris on 14, 17 August.

59. *FAT* 26, 28, 31 August, 2, 7, 9, 16, 18 September 1830. All news items gave Paris as their source, except the previously-mentioned item dated 24 August and a small news item on 31 August from St Petersburg.

60. *FAT* 25, 28, 30 September 1830.

61. Tommila 1960, p. 83.

62. Nurmio 1934, according to the supplement p. 63, the number of Swedish papers subscribed to in Finland in 1829 was about 450 subscriptions (no statistics for 1830); according to Tommila 1963, p. 106, the number of copies of Swedish papers confiscated in 1830 was 17 in all.

63. *HT* 8 September 1830; *TWS* 25 September 1830; *ÅU* 23 November 1830.

64. J.A. Ehrenström's letters of 22, 30 August, 27 September to J.Fr. Aminoff (Riilahti collection 10/VA).

65. Proclamation of day of prayer 6 December 1830 (*Samling af Placater 1830*, pp. 133, 134).

66. *OWS* 24 September 1829, account of the Peace of Adrianople. Also *OWS* 24, 31 July, 7, 14, 21 August 1830 concerning the French landing in Algeria etc.

67. *OWS* 4, 11 September 1830.

68. *Ibid.*, 9, 16 October 1830.

69. *Loc.cit.*

70. Leslie 1956 pp. 150–156, 178–93.

71. Höjer III 1960, pp. 244–7; Göransson 1937, pp. 68–73.

72. Krusius-Ahrenberg 1946, pp. 301–13.

73. Rehbinder's letter to Walleen in December 1830, cited in Aulis Alanen 1960, p. 284.

74. Lillja 1948, pp. 360, 361.

75. Foreign minister Nesselrode's circular letter of 11/23 December 1830 to Russian embassies abroad. — Copy: the report of the Austrian ambassador in Petersburg to Metternich, 11/23 December 1830. — 'The Emperor must, by firm measures bring his deceived and criminal subjects to their obligations . . . [the Emperor] will not spare effort or sacrifice . . .'

76. *FAT* 16 December 1830, 3 January 1831; *HT* 15 December 1830, 12 January 1831; *TWS* 5, 12 March 1831.

77. E.g. *FAT* 10, 11, 12, January, 9, 22 February, 14, 28 March, 13, 21, 30 April, 4 May, 25 July, 3, 15 August, 29 September, 3, 10, 12 October 1831; *TWS* 22 March, 23 April, 14, 21, 28 May, 25 June, 2 July, 5 November 1831.

78. Ehrenström's letters of 23 January, 25 March 1831 to Aminoff.

79. SYH/EA1, 1831.

80. Tommila 1963, p. 106.

81. On the confiscation of German newspapers see previous note.

82. For example, *HT* 5 February, 7 May, 8 October, 21 December 1831.

83. Ehrenström's letters of 6, 16 January, 30 March 1831 to Aminoff.
84. C.G. Mannerheim's letter of 6 March 1831 to A. Blomqvist (cited Krusius-Ahrenberg 1946, p. 297).
85. Controversy over the so-called Polish toast, see Krusius-Ahrenberg 1946, pp. 338–42; Klinge I 1967, pp. 17, 18.
86. On the Helsinki burghers, see Waris 1951, pp. 36, 46–52.
87. The escape route of the Polish refugees ran through the non-Russian border areas to Sweden.
88. J.J. Nervander's letter of 12 October 1831 to Snellman (Havu 1945, p. 41).
89. Fredrik Cygnaeus' poem was published in Mellin's calendar *Vinterblommor*; he used the completely new pseudonym 'Rudolf'.
90. Proclamation of a day of prayer 12 December 1831 (*Samling af Placater 1831*, p. 178).
91. See Major Arvellan's speech in Viipuri when the Guards Battalion left for the Turkish war (*Östra Finland* 7 September 1877).
92. *HT* 24 November 1831.
93. Salminen 1963, p. 18.
94. For example *FAT* 16, 18, 23, 25, 30 November, 2, 7 December 1830 and so on. On the threat of cholera see also Lillja 1948, pp. 378–94.
95. Renouvin V 1954, pp. 78–80; R.W. Seton-Watson 1968, pp. 151, 152; Petrie 1946, pp. 197–99.
96. Strang 1961, pp. 117–20; Droz 1952, pp. 314–16; Henry 1945, pp. 12–18.
97. Osmonsalo 1949, pp. 119, 122; Pohjolan-Pirhonen 1973, pp. 462–3.
98. Seitkari 1939, p. 94.
99. Schiemann III 1919, pp. 282, 283.
100. Seitkari 1939, p. 97; Gallén 1961, pp. 198, 199.
101. Seitkari 1939, p. 97.
102. Gallen 1961, p. 199.
103. Bolsover 1948, pp. 333, 334.
104. Krusius-Ahrenberg 1946, p. 346.
105. Rauhala I 1915, p. 221; Klinge I 1967, p. 29.
106. Tommila 1963, p. 106.
107. SYH 1831–4; reports of inspections, interrogations etc.
108. Joustela 1963 pp. 63–6, 97–9; Paasivirta 1968, p. 21.
109. Joustela 1963, pp. 352, 353 (table) and 363 (figure); Hautala III 1975, pp. 227–9.
110. Osmonsalo 1949, pp. 157–9.
111. Jussila 1969, pp. 204–6.
112. Rauhala I 1915, pp. 245–51.
113. Takolander I 1926, pp. 290, 291; Ruuth 1953, pp. 124, 125.
114. Osmonsalo I 1939, p. 28.
115. *Ibid.*, pp. 25–9; Ruuth 1945, p. 307; Ruutu 1967, pp. 109–12.
116. Monas 1961, pp. 152–66.
117. Klinge I 1967, pp. 24, 31, 34.
118. Schiemann III 1919, p. 231.
119. *FAT* 13 June 1833: this announcement was published in Warsaw already on 23 April. *FAT* 17 October 1833 announced that, after returning from the Münchengrätz negotiations, Nicholas I had turned down the invitation of the inhabitants of Warsaw to visit the city, 'until they have by their conduct shown

that they deserve such a mark of goodwill from the Emperor'. On the Münchengrätz negotiations see also *Helsingfors Morgonblad* 21, 24 September 1833.

120. Riassanovsky 1963, pp. 370, 371; Leslie 1964, pp. 198, 199; Renouvin V 1954, p. 80.
121. On the general features of the nationalist movement see Lemberg I 1964, pp. 175–85.
122. Ruutu 1956, p. 95.
123. Snellman's letter of 1 October 1844 to M.A. Castrén (*Kootut teokset XII*, p. 117).
124. Klinge I 1967, pp. 84–9.
125. Snellman's letter of 1840 (n.d) to Fredrik Cygnaeus (*Kootut teokset XII*, pp. 133–4).
126. Viljanen II 1948, p. 303.
127. Brydolf 1943, pp. 113–15, 159–66.
128. M.A. Castrén's letter of 18 October 1844 to Snellman. (*Kootut teokset XII*, p. 118).
129. For example J.J. Nervander and August Ahlqvist had dreams of Finnish independence. Kohtamäki 1956, pp. 46–9, 221; Havu 1945, p. 239.
130. On the development of Finnish trade to foreign countries and to Russia, see Joustela 1963, p. 363 (tables).
131. Pohjanpalo 1965, pp. 48, 49.
132. Kaukamaa 1941, p. 15.
133. Schybergson 1973, pp. 164, 165.
134. On the different definitions of 'a united culture' see Mikko Juva 1950, p. 46.
135. Finland began to appear in foreign maps, coloured differently within the frontiers of the Russian empire, from the 1860s. It was common in European maps at the end of the century for Finland's special to be emphasised by a separate colour.
136. Von Gerschau 1821, pp. 340–51; Golovine 1845, p. 357.
137. Paasivirta 1962, pp. 31–3.
138. Marmier 1843, pp. 18, 53, 312.
139. Cadot 1967, passim, and as examples of the travel literature of the time: Fr.W. von Schubert, *Reise durch Schweden, Norrwegen, Lappland, Finnland und Ingermanland in den Jahren 1817, 1818 und 1820*, Leipzig 1823; G.M. Jones, *Travels in Norway, Sweden, Finland, Russia and Turkey*, London 1827; John Barrow, *Excursions in the north of Europe*, London 1835.
140. Gleason 1950, pp. 134, 138–9.
141. Brydolf 1943, pp. 60–2, 75–80, 273–80; Junnila 1972, pp. 120–36.

Chapter V

1. Droz 1967, pp. 250–4.
2. Koht 1948, pp. 10–25.
3. Manninen 1976, pp. 16, 23, 81.
4. *Åbo Underrättelser* 1841–46 passim, and Gardberg 1924, pp. 51–2.
5. Kaukiainen 1970, pp. 243–6.
6. Screen 1976, pp. 256–9.
7. von Kothen's letter of 20 April 1846 to the censorship authorities. (copy in Lagerborg 1953, p. 274).
8. Nurmio 1947, p. 90.
9. Kohtamäki 1959, pp. 199–207.

10. Snellman's letter of 6 January 1848 to J.J. Tengström (*Kootut teokset XII*, pp. 330–2).

11. Waris 1939, pp. 142–3; Schauman I 1922, p. 232; Klinge I 1967, pp. 87, 104, 117–18, 126.

12. Stadelmann 1970, pp. 32–3, 39–41, 54–7.

13. Riassanovsky 1963, p. 371.

14. Freeborn 1966, p. 85; Lobanov-Rostovsky 1954, pp. 117–18.

15. Nicholas I's manifesto of 14/26 March 1848 (*FAT* 3 April 1848).

16. The political situation in Sweden and Denmark as a cause for concern in St Petersburg: Foreign minister Nesselrode's letters of 31 March, 20 May 1848 to ambassador von Meyensdorff (*Lettres et papiers de Nesselrode VII*, pp. 76, 81, 92, 116). The frontier between Finland and Sweden was closed from March 20 1848, and the post held back.

17. *ÅU* 19 January 1848, *Året 1847*, and in addition 12, 22 January, 22 February 1848.

18. *Borgå Tidning* 8, 12, 15, 26 January, 2, 5 February 1848; *Ilmarinen* 19, 22, 26, 29 January, 2, 5 February 1848.

19. Nurmio 1947, p. 75.

20. *Ibid.*, p. 74.

21. The order issued on 20 March 1848 forbade membership of secret societies (*Samling af Placater XII* 1847–48, p. 89).

22. Order of the Senate issued on 15 May 1848. — Samling af Placater XII, pp. 96–7. 'Factory- and mineworkers' are spoken of as objects of surveillance.

23. Rein I 1928, p. 469.

24. *Ibid.*, p. 470.

25. See Elmgren's notes, pp. 588, 589.

26. Letter of Emil von Qvanten of March 1848 (apparently) to B.O. Schauman (*Kansanvalistusseuran Kalenteri 1953*, pp. 133–4); also Qvanten's letter of 11 May 1848 to Schauman (*B.O. Schauman collection/HYK*).

27. Schauman I 1922, p. 254.

28. Snellman's letter of 28 March 1848 to Elias Lönnrot (*Kootut teokset XII*, p. 221).

29. *FAT* 15 February, 3, 8, 9 March 1848.

30. Schauman I 1922, p. 268; Gunnar Castren 1945, pp. 300–1; Mikko Juva 1950, p. 76.

31. *Finlands Allmänna Tidning* of 10 March 1848 did not contain any news of the events in Paris (*FAT* 11 March 1848; *HT* 11 March 1848, *Borgå Tidning* 11 March 1848).

32. *ÅU* 15 March 1848 (referring to *FAT*); *Åbo Tidningar* 15 March 1848 (does not mention the source of the news); *Ilmarinen* 15 March 1848 (according to foreign papers received through St Petersburg); *Suometar* 17 March 1848.

33. See Menshikov's memorandum of 3/15 March 1848 to the provincial Governors (KKK, 1848–65/n. 266); Menshikov's memorandum of 3/15 March 1848 to the Governor of Turku and Pori province and of 6/18 March to the Governor of Uusimaa province (SYH 1/KD 30/122 1848).

34. Nicholas I was especially afraid of peasant disturbances in Poland, the Baltic provinces and the Ukraine (Nifontow 1954, pp. 247–50, 271–5). Menshikov was given the task of acting as chairman of the Russian censorship committee in St Petersburg (Nifontow 1954, pp. 258, 261). On the censorship instructions issued in Russia to the press there, see Monas, p. 239.

35. *HT* 15 March 1848.

36. *Suometar* 17 March 1848, 7 April 1848.
37. See the censorship authority's circular of 2 May 1848 to the censorship committee (SYH 1848), also Tommila 1963, p. 93.
38. *FAT* 11 July 1848.
39. *ÅU* 11 July 1848.
40. *HT* 15 July 1848.
41. *HT* 17 May 1848; *Suometar* 19 May 1848; *Morgonbladet* 18 May 1848; also C.G. Voivolin's letter of 17 May to Antero Varelius (Vareliuksen kokoelma/SKS).
42. *HT* 1 April Från Helsingfors (written by Z. Topelius).
43. Gunnar Suolahti 1933, p. 147.
44. Besides *Finlands Allmänna Tidning* (see note 15), it seems that no other paper published the Emperor's manifesto.
45. *ÅU* 12 May 1848, and 16, 19, 23, 26 May 1848; *Morgonbladet* 3 July 1848, and 6, 10 July 1848; further *Morgonbladet* 28 September 1848 and 2, 5, 9, 12, 16 October 1848; also *Litteraturblad* 1848 n.9/September.
46. *HT* 29 April 1848.
47. On the danger of war, se *ÅU* 2, 9 May 1848; *HT* 17 May 1848; *Ilmarinen* 10, 13, 24 May 1848.
48. See note 46.
49. Nikula 1972, p. 303.
50. Kaukamaa 1941, pp. 27–8; Hautala III 1975, p. 165; Saarinen 1972, p. 33.
51. The trade of Viipuri too declined in 1848 according to newspaper reports.
52. Lähteenoja 1939, p. 169; Alma Söderhjelm 1911, p. 217; Hautala III 1975, p. 213. The Bank of Finland also felt the pressure of the international situation, see Pipping I 1961, p. 531.
53. Riassanovsky 1963, pp. 371–2; Renouvin V 1954, p. 207.
54. Fredrik Cygnaeus' letter (sometime in the early summer of 1848) to Otto Furuhjelm; Nevander 1900, p. 207.
55. R. Polon's letter of 5 August 1848 to August Ahlqvist (Ahlqvist collection/SKS).
56. Snellman's letter of 29 July 1848 to Fredrik Cygnaeus (*Kootut teokset XII*, pp. 143–4).
57. Waris 1939, pp. 74–5.
58. Monas 1961, pp. 245–6; Heikel 1940, pp. 508–11; Ruutu 1939, pp. 3–6.
59. V.T.R (osenqvist): Edvard Bergenheim (*Kansallinen Elämäkerrasto I*, pp. 219–20).
60. Proclamations for a day of prayer 4 December 1848, 26 November 1849 (*Samling af Placater XII*, 1847–8, pp. 306–7, XIII 1849–50, pp. 184–6).
61. Menshikov's memorandum of 14/26 April 1850 to Bergenheim (Osmonsalo 1939, p. 97; supplement VI, 4); Bishop Ottelin's memorandum (n.d.) 1850 to the clergy of Porvoo diocese (KKK, 1850/n.56).
62. On the actual state of the Swedish-language papers after the enforcement of the censorship decree of 1850, see Gardberg 1924, pp. 70–2.
63. Nurmio 1947, p. 299.
64. *Ibid.*, p. 251.
65. Halila I 1949, pp. 194–7.
66. Osmonsalo 1939 A, p. 200.
67. Nurmio 1947, pp. 75, 81–3; Tommila 1963, p. 106.
68. Snellman's letter of 27 November 1848 to Fredrik Cygnaeus (*Kootut teokset XII*, pp. 149–51).

69. Gunnar Castrén 1918, pp. 240–1.
70. Schiemann IV 1919, pp. 220–2; Renouvin V 1954, pp. 214–17; Hugh Seton-Watson 1967, p. 316.
71. Droz 1952, p. 367; Andersson 1967, p. 15; Leslie 1964, pp. 298–9.
72. Teperi 1959, pp. 230–2, 237–40, 248–9; Klinge I 1967, p. 188; also Rein 1918, p. 53.
73. For example, *Suometar* 16 March, 27 April, 11, 18 May, 15 June, 20, 27 July, 24 August, 12 October 1849; *ÅU* 3, 17, 20 July, 7, 14, 17, 21, 28, 31 August, 14, 18 September 1849.
74. Ottelin's circular of 19 September 1849 to the clergy of Porvoo diocese (*Borgå domkapitel: Circulärbref 1830–1870*, pp. 210–11); circular letter of Turku Chapter of 19 September 1849 to the clergy of the archdiocese (*Åbo domkapitel: Circulärbref XI 1846–1850*). In the message of thanksgiving, ordered by the Senate to be read out in the churches on 12 September, it was emphasised that 'peace and contentment are likely always to remain prevalent in our country'.

Chapter VI

1. Henry 1945, p. 181.
2. Martin 1924, pp. 224–9.
3. Renouvin V 1954, pp. 292–3; Martin 1924, pp. 231–2.
4. *HT* 30 November 1853 (Leopoldiner bref 36).
5. *HT* 7 January 1854.
6. Elmgren: *Päiväkirja* 3 July 1853.
7. *FAT* 7, 17 June, 4, 17 October 1853.
8. *HT* 14 December 1853.
9. Rauhala I 1915, p. 325; also *FAT* 17 March 1854.
10. Elmgren: *Päiväkirja* 24 March 1854.
11. On the number of Russian troops in Finland and Baltic area, see Tarle II 1950, pp. 41–2; Lobanov-Rostovsky 1954, p. 165; Hugh Seton-Watson 1967, p. 324. Also foreign minister Nesselrode's letter of 26 April (o.s) 1854 to ambassador Meyensdorff (*Lettres et papiers de Nesselrode* XI, p. 56). Report of the French ambassador to Stockholm of 3 July 1854 to the foreign ministry (AAEF 326/Suède).
12. On preparations in Finland see Borodkin 1905, p. 12; from the times of the Crimean War *US* 21 August 1914; Seitkari 1939, p. 98.
13. See Alexander Wulffert's reports of 3 March and 6 April (?) 1854 on a tour of inspection in Pohjanmaa and Åland (KKK/*salaiset aktit* n.370/1854).
14. See Berndt Federley's memorandum of 26 February/10 March 1854 to Rokassovsky (KKK/*salaiset aktit* n.370/1854).
15. See Federley's memorandum of 26 March/7 April 1854 to Rokassovsky (KKK/*salaiset aktit* n.370/1854).
16. On the temporary administrative arrangements in Åland, see *Åbo och Björneborgs läns länstyrelse; Brefdiarium; Expédition de Bomarsund* 1854/SHAF G12b1. Also *FAT* 20 March 1854.
17. See the letters of the sheriffs of Eckerö, Saltvik and Pålböle of 1 April 1854 to the crown bailiff C.O. Lignell and letters from different parts of Åland to Lt.-Col. Furuhjelm (*Expédition de Bomarsund* 1854).
18. Bergenheim's circular of 22 March 1854 to the clergy of Turku archdiocese (copy:

Finska Förhållanden II, p. 45). Also bishop Ottelin's circular letter of 29 March 1854 to the clergy of Porvoo diocese (C.G. Ottelin collection/VA).

19. The following form of prayer was used in Kuopio archdiocese in the spring of 1854: 'Strike down the courage of the hereditary foes of Christendom . . . their supporters' evil intent' (*Kuopio domkapitel: Circulärbref* I 1851–6).

20. Murtorinne 1965, pp. 19–20; Elmgren: *Päiväkirja* 7 March, 25 June 1855.

21. Elmgren: *Päiväkirja* 23 December 1853.

22. Proclamations of days of prayer of 27 November 1854, 20 November 1855. (*Samling af Placater XV* 1853–5, pp. 165, 326, 327). Also Bergenheim's memorandum to the clergy of Turku archdiocese (copy: *Finska Förhållanden* II, pp. 48–9).

23. On news about the situation in the Balkans, see for example *ÅU* 2, 19 July, 12 August 1853, on military events between Turkey and Russia see *ÅU* from 11 November 1853.

24. *Suometar* 10 March 1854 and the Extra of 10 March; *OWS* 24 March and 1 April; 8 April.

25. *FAT* 13, 25 April 1854.

26. Nikula 1948, pp. 223, 248. Also *FAT* 18 March, 10, 18, 19 April, 4 May 1854; *OWS* 4, 24 March, 1, 22 April, 6 May 1854; *AU* 14, 25 March 1854; *Suometar* 31 March 1854.

27. Tigerstedt II 1952, p. 69; also *OWS* 11 March 1854.

28. The business correspondence of the leading commercial houses in Oulu (G. & C. Bergbom and J.V. Snellman G:son) during the Crimean war illustrates the practical problems for Finland's foreign trade which was concentrated in two directions (G. & C. Bergbom business archives 1854–5, and J.V. Snellman G:son business archives 1854–5/OMA). Also Tigerstedt II 1952, pp. 76–80.

29. Joustela 1963, pp. 352–3 (table: Distribution of Finland's foreign trade 1840–65).

30. Soininen 1974, p. 194 (table).

31. Pipping I 1961, p. 280.

32. Borodkin 1905, p. 6; Woodward 1965, pp. 101–3; Barlett 1963, pp. 104–6, 335.

33. Admiral Napier's report of 30 May 1854 to the British admiralty (*Russian War 1854*, p. 59). 'It is impossible to attack Sveaborg and Helsinki from the sea or from the land.' After this Napier, who had been informed that French troops were coming as his anxiliaries, began to prepare for an attack on Bomarsund. Napier 24 July 1854 to the admiralty (*Russian War 1854*, pp. 90–1).

34. After the capture of Bomarsund a new plan of attack was put forward either on Sveaborg or Reval, but Napier reported it was impossible with the forces at his disposal (Napier 28 August to the Admiralty; *Russian War* 1854, p. 109).

35. Jansson 1961, pp. 78–80.

36. R.W. Seton-Watson 1968, p. 326.

37. Paasivirta 1969, pp. 13–14.

38. *Journal des Débats* 19 April 1854 and 27 April 1854.

39. *The Daily News* 7 June 1854 leading article.

40. *The Standard* 5 June 1854 leading article.

41. *The Times* 22 June 1854 leading article.

42. Paasivirta 1969, p. 14.

43. *The Times* 24 June 1854 leading article; 1 July 1854 leading article.

44. Milner Gibson tabled a question in the House of Commons on 29 June 1854 on the

events in the Gulf of Bothnia, and the answer of the navy minister James Graham, explaining that the destruction had been for military purposes, clearly relied for its information on Napier's report sent on 18 June (*Russian War 1854*, p. 63).

45. De Bazoucourt 1858, p. 237; Admiral Parceval's report of 18 June 1854 to the French navy ministry. (AMF/BB 4710). In it Admiral Plumridge's conduct of the war was severely criticised.

46. *The Times* 21 August 1854 leading article; *Daily News* 18 August 1854; 21 August 1854; *The Globe* 23 August 1854 leading article; *Le Constitutionel* 19 August 1854 leading article; *Journal des Débats* 25 August 1854 leading article; *La Presse* 21 August 1854 leading article. News of the capture of Bomarsund was received in Helsinki 29 August 1854 (*FAT* 29 August 1854).

47. *Morning Post* 21 August 1854 leading article; *The Times* 21 August 1854 leading article.

48. *Le Moniteur* 20 August 1854.

49. Napoleon III's proclamation (*Journal des Débats* 22 August 1854).

50. On statements in the Swedish papers, see Eriksson 1939, pp. 168–75; C.M. Runeberg 1941, p. 108, 119–28, 148–52.

51. Jansson 1961, p. 92.

52. Holmberg 1946, pp. 231, 234–6.

53. Jansson 1961, pp. 91–4.

54. *Ibid.*, pp. 93–8.

55. *Russian War 1854* p. 110; Jansson 1961, p. 99.

56. Friese 1931, pp. 47–50.

57. *Hamburger Correspondent* 15, 17, 19, 21, 22 June 1854, 18, 24, 25 August 1854; *Lübecker Zeitung* 31 May, 14 June, 21, 25, 30 August 1854; *Hamburger Nachrichten* 14, 19, 22, 23 June 1854.

58. *Kölnische Zeitung* 7 June 1854; *Augsburqer Allgemeine Zeitung* 16 June 1854 leading article and 28 July 1854.

59. *FAT* 7 June 1854; *Morgonbladet* 8 June 1854; *ÅU* 9 June 1854, *OWS* 17 June 1854 (there was no mention of the destruction in the issues of the paper which appeared on 3, 10 June); *Suometar* 9, 23 June 1854; G. Högman's letter of 10 June 1854 to Elias Lönnrot and Frans Lönnrot's letter to Elias Lönnrot (Elias Lönnrotin kokoelma); SKS.

60. *HT* 10 June 1854.

61. *ÅU* 9 June 1854.

62. See tales of the Crimean war circulating among the farming community (Folk poetry collection: Crimean war/SKS).

63. *Ibid.*

64. *HT* 10 June 1854; *Morgonbladet* 15 June 1854 leading article; *HT* 17 June 1854.

65. August Schauman II 1922, p. 84; Topelius' letter of 29 December 1854 to August Schauman (August Schauman collection); HYK; also Krusius-Ahrenberg 1934, pp. 34–5.

66. Kaukiainen 1975, pp. 192–3.

67. On Russian news concerning the Kokkola battle, see *Journal de St Petersbourg* 15/27 June 1854 and *St Petersburger Zeitung* 17/29 June 1854. Nicholas I expressed his gratitude to the inhabitants of Kokkola who with 'our forces', had beaten the enemy (*Suometar* 7 July 1854). On decorations etc. given for the battle of Kokkola, see Schulman 1905, p. 85. On the farmer M. Kankkonen, see for example *Ilmarinen*

15 July 1854. On the destruction of Oulu and Raahe, see also the report of the Austrian embassy of 9 June 1854 to the foreign ministry.

68. Nicholas I's manifesto of 11/23 June 1854. In justification, it was stated for example that the enemy had 'been visiting unfortified coastal towns with fire and destruction'.

69. On the songs of the militia battalions, see for example *ÅU* 1 August 1854.

70. On conditions in Åland after the capture of Bomarsund, see Winter 1954, p. 18.

71. The proclamation of the military command of the western powers was read in the churches on Åland on 29 August 1854 (*Journal des Débats* 8 September 1854).

72. E.g. Gardberg 1924, p. 77.

73. Jäderholm 1977, pp. 27, 37–8.

74. *Finlands Allmänna Tidning*, passim; Tommila 1963, p. 106; *FAT* 24 August 1855; Governor-General Berg's account of the bombardment of Sveaborg.

75. E.g. Elmgren: *Päiväkirja* 24 September, 20, 31 December 1855.

76. E.g. the following: Elmgren: *Päiväkirja* 12, 14, 17 September 1855; Topelius' letter of 5 August 1855 to B.O. Schauman (B.O. Schauman collection); Fr. Polon's letter of 20 May 1855 to August Ahlqvist (August Ahlqvist collection); on the position of Yrjö Koskinen, see Suolahti 1933, p. 336–7; also Lindblad 1947, pp. 96–7.

77. Jansson 1961, p. 114.

78. Eriksson 1939, pp. 276–89; Jansson 1961, pp. 104–6.

79. On Oscar I's war plan for the conquest of Finland, see Jansson 1961, p. 109; Eriksson 1939, p. 288.

80. Eriksson 1939, p. 368; Anderson 1974, p. 352.

81. For example *Suometar* 14, 28 September, 5, 12, 26 October 1855; *ÅU* 9, 12 October 1855; *Viborg* 14 September 1855.

82. Särkilax II 1855, pp. 24–46; also Krusius-Ahrenberg 1934, p. 37.

83. August Sohlman 1855, pp. 1, 4, 12, 26.

84. Minute of the censorship committee of 23 November 1855 (*Sensuuriylihallituksen arkisto* Ca13/VA); Elmgren: *Päiväkirja* 12 September, 22 October, 11 November 1855.

85. Gabriel Rein's letters of 28 August, 16 October 1855 to Aleksander Armfelt (*Armfeltin kokoelma* II a 23b/VA).

86. On the 'Töölö squabble', see Klinge II 1967, pp. 37–9.

87. On the preliminary conditions for the peace conference, see the reports of the British ambassador in Paris of 18, 19 January 1856 to the Foreign Office (F.O: 27/1122). By then France had approved the British 'special condition' concerning Åland.

88. On the assessment of the situation in St Petersburg, see Meyensdorff 1923, pp. 214–16; Tarle II 1950, pp. 546–52.

89. On Oscar I's aims in January 1856, see Oscar I's memorandum of 18 January 1856 to the British government (F.O. 146/615).

90. On the British part in the Åland business, see Lord Cowley's report of 19 January 1856 to the Foreign Office (F.O. 27/1122). Also Palmstierna 1932, p. 36.

91. Rein II 1928, p. 135.

92. *Aftonbladet* 1 April 1856 leading article; 9 April 1856 leading article.

93. *Le Constitutionel*'s article (copy: Rein II 1928, p. 134).

94. *The Times* 28 March 1856 leading article.

95. *Le Siècle* 9 April 1856 leading article.

Chapter VII

1. Renouvin V 1954, pp. 297–8; Leslie 1964, pp. 310–11; Craig 1964, pp. 268–9.
2. *Suometar* 4, 18 January, 1, 8, 15, 29 February, 14 March 1856; *Viborg* 25, 29 January 1856; *OWS* 9, 16 February 1856; *HT* 2, 9, 16 January, 6, 13 February 1856; *FAT* 16, 17 January 1856. At the same time the censorship confiscated a large number of Swedish newspapers early in 1856 (documents received by the censorship committee in 1856 from the Post Office).
3. On the preparations for the peace in business circles, see Pipping 1972, pp. 34–5; *OWS* 2, 16 February 1856 (*J.W. Snellman G:sonin arkisto: saapuneet kirjeet* 1856/ OMA).
4. Governor-General Berg's speech of 29 April 1856. *FAT* 2 May 1856.
5. Transition to peacetime in Åland. The restoration of the 'former system' had begun in Åland — after the departure of the western forces — in October-November 1854, which resulted in reports and explanations to the office of the Governor-General (KKK/*salaiset aktit* 1810–58/n.351). Later there was an attempt, via the crown bailiff, to ascertain who would be considered 'collaborators'. Documents refer to law cases, but they were ordered to be stopped by the Turku Court of Appeals in June 1856. In this connection they referred to the order given by Alexander II on 27 May 1856 (*Ahvenanmaalla toimivan kruununvuodin arkisto: Da 40 kirjekonseptit* 1856/TMA).
6. Heikel 1940, p. 525; Osterbladh 1933, pp. 99–100.
7. On the Polish question in the peace conference at Paris, see Kukiel 1955, p. 302.
8. Tommila 1962, p. 271.
9. Alexander II's speech of 23 May 1856 to the leaders of the Polish nobility (*Recueil*, p. 117): 'Je vous porte dans mon coeur comme les Finlandais et commes mes autres sujets russes. Mais j'entends que l'ordre établi per mon père soit maintenu. Ainsi, messieurs, et avant tout, point de reveries, point de reveries.
10. Pipping 1972, p. 35; Nikula 1930, p. 2.
11. For example the imperial proclamation of 27 May 1856 on the development of Finnish shipping (*Samling af Placater* 1856).
12. Pihkala 1970, pp. 12–13.
13. Soininen 1974, p. 405; also Pipping I 1961, p. 531.
14. *Viborg* 15 February 1856 leading article; 28 March, 10 June leading article; *AU* 1 April 1856.
15. Paasivirta 1963, p. 16; Alma Söderhjelm 1974, p. 199.
16. *OWS* 1 March 1862.
17. Tommila 1963, pp. 254–7.
18. Rein II 1928, pp. 128–44.
19. M.G. Schybergson 1916, pp. 32–6.
20. Alexander II's manifesto of 15/27 May 1857 (*Suometar* 12 June 1857).
21. *Suometar* 12 June 1857; *ÅU* 27 February 1858.
22. *Litteraturblad* 1857 n.6 (June).
23. *HT* 17 June 1857.
24. Rein II 1928, p. 155; Mikko Juva IV 1966, p. 292.
25. *ÅU* 22 June 1858, 6 August, 14 December; *Wasabladet* 18, 24 December 1858. *Suometar* published a series of 22 articles on the war of 1808, between 12 February 1858 and 26 November.

26. *Litteraturblad* 1858 n.2 (February).
27. *Ibid.*, n.3 (March), n.7 (July).
28. *Suometar*, 16, 23 April 1858.
29. Rein II 1928, pp. 244–51.
30. *Ibid.*, p. 202.
31. Rauhala I 1915, pp. 349–50.
32. Proclamations for days of prayer of 24 November 1856, 23 November 1857 (*Samling af Placater XVI*), pp. 249, 622.
33. Mikko Juva 1950, pp. 155–9, 221–8.
34. Schauman II 1922, pp. 150, 178–9; Rein II 1928, pp. 167–74.
35. Berg's circular letter of 29 May 1859 to the censorship authorities (KKK/*salaiset aktit* 1848–65/n. 266).
36. Berg's instructions of 28 August 1860 on the handling of events concerning the unification of Italy (*Finska Förhållanden* IV, p. 9).
37. Paasivirta 1951, pp. 428–35.
38. Jussila 1969, pp. 217–18.
39. *Censur-Kalender* I (1861), pp. 15–38.
40. Leslie 1963, p. 102.
41. See the explanation given by Armfelt on 24 April 1861, and the Gracious Proclamation of 23 August 1861. On the situation in spring 1861, see Nordberg 1958, pp. 260–8; Schauman II 1922, pp. 263–73; Krusius-Ahrenberg 1934, pp. 245–52, 290–1.
42. Nordberg 1958, pp. 274–82. Also the report of the French consul in Helsinki to the foreign ministry of 1 June 1861 AAEF (CPC/Russia 1856–61).
43. *Hämäläinen*, 24 January 1862; *Suometar* 22 November 1861. Also *Tapio* 4 January 1862. 'The past year made it clear for the nation once and for all what it wanted and wished for.'
44. On the vehement debate in the press of September–October 1861, Elmgren (*Päiväkirja* 4 October 1861) described as 'the most belligerent time in the world of the newspapers which we have had for a long time'. On the controversy over Snellman, see Elmgren: *Päiväkirja* 19 November 1861; Krusius-Ahrenberg 1934, pp. 280–9; on the birth of a public opinion, see Puntila 1947, pp. 473–92, and on the relaxation of censorship, see Nordberg 1958, pp. 272–4.
45. *The Times* 30 November 1861.
46. The Paris newspaper *Patrie* had published an article on Finland in August 1861; this was reported by *Kölnische Zeitung* and after that by *Indépendence Belge* (*ÅU* 5 September 1861); also Elmgren 27 September 1861.
47. *Kölnische Zeitung* 18, 20 September, 8 October 1861.
48. *Aftonbladet* published 'Letters from Finland' from 1856, for which see *Finska förhållanden* I, pp. 7–68, 137–58, II, pp. 3–36, III, pp. 3–6, 10–47. *Nya Dagligt Allehanda*, on the other hand, kept an interval of several years and published such letters only from 1860. See *Finska förhållanden III*, pp. 48–56, IV pp. 3–15, 24–44, 56–73.
49. *Aftonbladet* 15 June 1861; *Nya Dagligt Allehanda* 30 April 1861.
50. On Snellman's article 'Nyåret 1861', publication of which was prevented by the censor (*Censur-Kalender I*, 1861).
51. Posten 1975, p. 66.
52. *Ibid.*, pp. 66–8.

Chapter VIII

1. *Suometar* 27 May, 3 June 1859; *OWS* 18 January 1862. — On Wecksell's poem 'Italienaren', see Alhoniemi 1969, p. 241. On the Finns in Garibaldi's army see H. Liikasen *kokoelma*/VA.

2. *Hämäläinen* 24 January 1862.

3. Reino Kero 1967 pp. 9–11; Also *Litteraturblad* 1861 n.4 (April).

4. Hautala 1956 pp. 277–8.

5. Lobanov-Rostovsky 1954, pp. 228–9; Leslie 1964, pp. 341–3.

6. R.H. Seton-Watson 1968, pp. 432–8.

7. Kaiser 1932, pp. 24–7; Birke 1960, pp. 201–2.

8. Elmgren: *Päiväkirja* 22 March, 27 September 1861. For mention of the Polish situation in the provincial press see *Hämäläinen* 24 January 1862.

9. Elmgren: *Päiväkirja* 27 September, 16 October, 1861.

10. For example *Helsingfors Tidningar* published on 29 January, 3, 12 February 1863 excerpts from the news concerning the Polish revolt in *Journal de St Petersbourg*. The same feature was repeated in other newspapers.

11. *HD* 16 February 1863 (source of the news items *Breslauer Zeitung* and *The Times*) and 28 February, 14 March; *ÅU*, 24 February, 3 March 1863; *HT* 5, 12 March 1863 (source of the news items *Indépendence Belge*); *HU* 5, 9 March 1863; *Hämäläinen* 20 March, 17, 24 April 1863; *OWS* 18 April 1863.

12. *HD* 11 March, 1 April 1863; *ÅU* 1 April 1863 (partly censored); *HT* 13 April 1863. Also Gardberg 1824, pp. 98–9.

13. Salmihen 1963, p. 16.

14. *HT* 21 April 1863; *Wecko-Krönika* (this paper used the expression 'weapons fever'); *Tapio* 9 May 1863. Also Leo Mechelin's letter of 25 April 1863 to Idestam (Mechelin 70).

15. *Wasabladet* 20 June 1863.

16. M.S. Andersson 1976, pp. 165–6; Hinsley 1967, pp. 96–101, 118–19.

17. Paasivirta 1964, pp. 327–30.

18. *HD* 26 January 1863 leading article; Paasivirta 1963, p. 18.

19. *HD* 5 June 1863 *Finska konsulater*.

20. *HD* 15 April 1863 leading article. Emil von Qvanten got letters from Helsinki which were sent under the pseudonyms 'Ljusblå' or 'Nestor', or which were completely anonymous. One such, sent on 17 May 1863, may describe the general views of the Liberal inner circle: 'It seems to me Sweden should look about herself. Now is the time to test the half-forgotten ideal; otherwise, after fifty years they will probably only find enemies on this same shore. Your diplomats probably know better than we do how hollow Russia is at present' (Qvanten collection/KB).

21. *ÅU* 18 April 1863 leading article.

22. *HD* 5 June 1863. On the censorship, see Gardberg 1924, p. 99.

23. *ÅU* 30 April 1863.

24. *ÅU* 9 May 1863, 6 June.

25. *HT* 21 April 1863; *Tapio* 9 May 1863.

26. E.g. *Helsingin Uutiset* 5 January 1863.

27. *Post och Inrikes Tidningar* 16 April 1863; *Litteraturblad* 1863 n.5(May) (published 9 July).

28. J.V. Snellman's letters of 8 May and 8 June 1863 to J.V. Snellman G:son (J.V. Snellman G:son collection/VA); Korhonen 1963, p. 19.

29. *HU* 10 July 1863 leading article; *Tähti* 24 July 1863.

30. *HD* 10 July 1863, 11 July.

31. *Ibid.*, 10 August 1863.

32. *Suometar* 8 September, 11 September 1863 ('Why could Finland not be made as free of wars and conflicts between foreign states as Switzerland and Belgium?').

33. *Päivätär* 5 September 1863.

34. *HT* 4 May 1863; *FAT* 1 June 1863; Hulkko 1963, p. 10.

35. *HD* 29 May, 10 June, 1, 15, 18 July 1863; *Helsingin Uutiset* 16 July 1863.

36. *HT* 9 June 1863.

37. *OWS* 2 May 1863.

38. *Wasabladet* 18 July 1863; *OWS* 18 July 1863; *HU* 30 July 1863.

39. *Nya Dagligt Allehanda* 13, 15 April 1863; also leading articles in the same newspaper on 17, 18, 22, 24 April 1863; *Post och Inrikes Tidningar* 16 April 1863.

40. E.g. the report of French ambassador to Stockholm of 4 May 1863 to foreign ministry (AAEF 332/Suède).

41. *Aftonbladet* 7 April 1863.

42. *Nya Dagligt Allehanda* 26 May 1863.

43. *Ibid.*, 18 May 1863; *Aftonbladet* 18 May 1863.

44. Statement of the Swedish committee for Poland, signed by Qvanten *et al.* (*Journal des Débats* 10 May 1863); also Carr 1937 p. 289.

45. *The Times* 24 April 1863; *The Morning Post* 24 April 1863; *The Standard* 24 April 1863; *The Morning Herald* 24 April 1863; *The Daily Telegraph* 24 April 1863; *La Patrie* 25 April 1863; *L'Opinion Nationale* 25 April 1863, *La Presse* 25 April 1863.

46. *Morning Post* 30 July 1863 leading article. *Nya Dagligt Allehanda* published this article 6 August 1863.

47. 'Revue de la semaine' column in *Aftonbladet*.

48. *Journal des Débats* 8 June 1863.

49. For example *Journal des Débats* 1 August 1863; *Le Pays* 1 August 1863.

50. *Journal des Débats* 7 June 1863.

51. *Ibid.*, 10 July 1863.

52. Report of British ambassador to Berlin of 24 March 1863 to Foreign Office and Bismarck's statement of 24 April 1863 to Prussian ambassador to Vienna (*Die Auswärtige Politik Preussens 1858–1871 III*, pp. 507–11).

53. British ambassador to Stockholm to Foreign Office 27 May 1863 (F.O. 73/332).

54. Report of French ambassador to Stockholm of 27 May 1863 to foreign ministry (AAEF 332/Suède).

55. For example the report of British consul in Helsinki of 2 June 1863 to embassy in St Petersburg (F.O. 181/420).

56. The report of the Swedish chief consul in Helsinki of 22 July 1863 to the foreign ministry/RA.

57. Revunenkov 1957, p. 297.

58. Prussian ambassador to St Petersburg to Bismarck 7 April 1863 (*Die auswärtige Politik Preussens 1858–1871 III*, p. 451).

59. Reports of Russian ambassador to Stockholm of 22 March/3 April, 12 April/24 April 1863 to foreign minister Gorchakov (Central archive Moscow — on film, Riksarkiv).

60. Also in addition to the foregoing the reports of the Russian ambassador to Stockholm of 29 April/11 May 1863, 7/19 May 1863 to Gorchakov.

61. On traces of censorship in the newspapers, see for example *ÅU* 30 April 1863; *HD* 15 May 1863; *HT* 27 May 1863. Also directive of the censorship authority of 7 May 1863 to the Governors/(*I Sensuuriylihallitus: kirjekonseptit* 1860–4); and on the censorship of Swedish newspapers (*HT* 1 June 1863). The confiscation of Swedish newspapers seems to have intensified at the end of April and was extensive in the summer months.

62. On the role of A. Armfelt and Stjernwall-Walleen in the matter of the address, see Rein II 1928, pp. 321–3.

63. Krusius-Ahrenberg 1934; 389–90.

64. *Ibid.*, 392–4.

65. *HD* 27 May 1863 leading article; *ÅU* 16 June 1863; *HT* 28 May 1863; *Suometar* 23 June 1863; *FAT* 26 May. Also Rein II 1928, p. 322. A. Armfelt's letter of 27 May 1863 to Snellman (J.V. Snellman collection 3/HYK); report of British consul in Helsinki 30 May 1863 (F.O. 181/420) which mentions that the Finnish Diet will meet in the autumn.

66. *HT* 11 May 1863.

67. On the programme of 'six points', included in the note of the western powers in June, see R.W. Seton-Watson 1968, p. 435. The report of the French ambassador to St Petersburg of 18 July 1863 to the foreign ministry (AAEF 231/Russie).

68. Krusius-Ahrenberg 1954, p. 175.

69. On the Parola review see for example *AU* 13 August 1863. Foreign observers noted that the imperial war and naval ministers were present but of the foreign military attachés, only the Prussian representative. See the report of the Swedish chief consul in Helsinki to the foreign ministry 3 August 1863. Report of British consul in Helsinki of 30 July 1863 to Foreign Office (F.O. 65/648).

70. Armfelt and Snellman had participated in drafting the opening speech of the Emperor to the Diet. (Rein II 1928, pp. 333–6.) A delegation of Finnish ship-builders, expressing a wish for Finnish consuls, called on Gorchakov in Helsinki. Report of the Swedish chief consul of 23 September 1863 to the foreign ministry.

71. On rumours about the holding of military exercises *HT* 7 September 1863. News of the tour of inspection in Finland by General Todleben, *Suometar* 4 September 1863; *ÅU* 10 September 1863; *Hämäläinen* 11 September 1863. Description of the parade *Helsingin Uutiset* 17 September 1863.

72. *Helsingin Uutiset* 21 September 1863.

73. See the speech by the farmer Juho Idänpään-Heikkilä in connection with the Parola review — *ÅU* 13 August 1863.

74. *HD* 18 September 1863 leading article. See letter of Ljusblå, 16 September 1863, to Qvanten (Qvanten collection): 'Now we are in the thick of our emperor fever . . . The proclamation of the Diet from the Senate steps was simple, but very ceremonial. The intolerable number of soldiers is expected to disappear after yesterday's parade.'

75. *The Times* 24 September 1863; *Daily Telegraph*, 21 September 1863; *The Globe* 21 September 1863; *The Standard* 21 September 1863; *Morning Herald* 21 September 1863, *Daily News* 21 September 1863.

76. On the British withdrawal from the Polish question, see Mosse 1956, pp. 50–1; Bell II 1966, pp. 349–50.

77. E.g. Alexander's speech was published in *Le Temps* 25 September 1863, *La Patrie* 24 September 1863, but not in *Le Constitutionnel*. When *Le Moniteur* did not publish

the speech, *Le Nord*, the usual advocate of a pro-Russian policy among the Paris newspapers, took the matter up (25 September 1863 summary). *Le Moniteur* only published the speech on 26 September. On the attention aroused by the incident, see for example *La Patrie* 27 September 1863, *Le Temps* 26 September 1863.

78. *Journal des Débats*, 24 September 1863.

79. E.g. *La Patrie* 24, 28 September 1863; *La Presse* 21 September 1863.

80. *Augsburger Allgemeine Zeitung* 6 July, 14, 17 July, 21 August, 28, 29 September 1863; *Kölnische Zeitung* 21, 24, 26 September 1863; *National-Zeitung* 26 September 1863; *Hamburger Börsen-Halle* 15, 19, 21, 23, 25 September 1863.

81. E.g. *Kölnische Zeitung* 3, 9, 14, 20, 22 October 1863; *National-Zeitung* 3 October 1863; *Augsburger Allgemeine Zeitung* 5, 22 October, 25 November 1863.

82. The general attitude of the Swedish newspapers is illustrated by *Post och Inrikes Tidning, et al.*

83. *Aftonbladet* 28, 29 September 1863.

84. *Nya Dagligt Allehanda* 23 September 1863 leading article.

85. *Helsingin Uutiset* 1 October 1863 leading article; *Suometar* 30 September 1863; *HU* 5 October 1863.

86. Katz 1966, p. 119; Krusius-Ahrenberg 1954, p. 194.

87. Katz 1966, p. 134.

88. Krusius-Ahrenberg 1954, pp. 199–208.

89. *Ibid.*, p. 209.

90. According to the assessment of the Swedish chief consul (report of 18 April 1864 to the foreign ministry) the content of the Emperor's speech was 'a sensation', and furthermore the Governor-General read it in Russian. As well as the Emperor's speech, Senator J.U. Gripenberg criticised the work of the Diet but was forced, because of the sharp reaction, to modify his words. *FAT* 3 April 1864, 26 April 1864.

91. *Suometar* 26 February 1864.

92. *Ibid.*, 2 July 1864; *HT* 11 May 1864.

93. On the economic performance of 1863, see Pipping 1928, p. 370 (table); Nikula 1948, p. 271.

94. Paasivirta 1969, p. 15.

95. J.L. Runeberg: *Samlade Skrifter I* (1873), p. 111: 'He is the strongest outpost of western culture against the east.'

Chapter IX

1. Hinsley 1967, pp. 244–9; Strang 1961, pp. 179–83.

2. Renouvin V 1954, pp. 259–63.

3. Soininen 1974, p. 406.

4. *Uusi Suometar* 4 January 1870.

5. Knoellinger 1959, p. 65.

6. Jutikkala 1968, pp. 210–12; Virrankoski 1975, pp. 107, 131.

7. Paasivirta: lecture on the history of the workers' movement given at a congress in Linz, autumn 1973 (unpublished).

8. Steinby 1963, pp. 43–52; Hyvämäki 1964, p. 31.

9. Reference to foreign cultural links are an indirect deduction from the material which has emerged in the course of the study.

10. On the increased mobility of the farmers, together with the development of agriculture, see Virrankoski 1975, p. 181.
11. Gitermann III 1949, p. 220.
12. Hanho II 1955, pp. 166–9, Ruutu 1963, pp. 176–7.
13. Misprint in text.
14. On the relations of church and state in the light of the church law of 1869, see Brotherus 1923, pp. 135–44, 170.
15. By 1867, southern Finland had cable links with Stockholm and St Petersburg. Hyvämäki 1964, p. 38.
16. *Soumetar* 2 July 1864.
17. *HT* 11 May 1864.
18. Snellman, *Kootut teokset II*, p. 310.
19. Maija-Leena Kero 1970, pp. 175–9.
20. *Ibid.*, pp. 184–7.
21. Rein 1918, p. 215.
22. *HD* 2 January 1868.
23. *Kirjallinen Kuukausilehti* 1869 n.1 (January).
24. *HD* 2 and 4 August 1870; *ÅU*, 5, 6, 8 August 1870. Also Gullberg 1952, pp. 252–60, 278–90.
25. *Uusi Suometar* 18, 21, 28 July, 4 August 1870.
26. *ÅU* 16 July 1870 leading article.
27. *Uusi Suometar* 8, 19 September 1870 leading articles.
28. Jalava 1948, p. 75.
29. *HD* 5, 7 September 1870 leading articles; *ÅU* 16 February 1871.
30. *Uusi Suometar* 17 July 1871.
31. *Kirjallinen Kuukausilehti* 1870 n.10(October).
32. *HD* 4 March 1871 leading article.
33. For example *Hufvudstadsbladet* 21, 22, 23, 25 March 1871; *HD* 25, 27, 28 March 1871; *Uusi Suometar* 22, 24, 27, 31 March, 3, 17, 26 April, 12, 19, 24 May 1871.
34. *ÅU* 21 August 1871.
35. *Uusi Suometar* 15 March, 6 December 1872.
36. *HD*, 20 June 1871.
37. Nieminen 1977, pp. 68–9.
38. Yrjö Koskinen: *Kansallisia ja yhteiskunnallisia kirjoituksia* III, pp. 238–49; *Morgonbladet* 16, 19, 20, 26, 27 August 1873. Waris 1956, p. 295; Palmgren 1948, pp. 116–17.
39. *OWS* 27 July 1878; *Tampereen Sanomat*, 23, 30 July, 10, 24 September 1878; *ÅU* 1, 2, 4 August 1878.
40. *Morgonbladet* 14, 16 August 1878.
41. *HD* 3 January 1879 leading article.
42. *Tampereen Sanomat* 18 June 1878; *Hämeen Sanomat* 30 April 1879.
43. Proclamation of a day of prayer 30 November 1871 (*Finlands författningssamling* 1871/n.35).
44. *Suomen virallinen tilasto I*, 4, p. 12.
45. Pihkala 1970, pp. 57–9.
46. For example, Pipping I 1961, pp. 470, 533; Nikula 1953, p. 72; Tigerstedt II 1952, pp. 425, 508, 514, 517.

47. *Uusi Suometar*, 3 January 1876.
48. Helander 1949, pp. 175–6.

Chapter X

1. On the limitations on the exchange of political views, e.g. the discussion in the Diet from 1867 on the question of getting commercial agents abroad and the 'muffling' of the general discussion of the question of parliamentary responsibility.
2. Paasivirta 1961, pp. 19–20.
3. Of Finnish volunteers in the Serbian army, e.g. Colonel Becker.
4. On the stockpiling of goods and raw materials in the autumn of 1876, see Nikula 1948, p. 365.
5. Virkkunen II 1938, pp. 561–2; Meurman 1909, p. 216.
6. Virkkunen II 1938, p. 565.
7. Snellman's speech of 26 May 1877 (*Landtdagen år 1877. Protokoll: Adel II*, p. 955; *Morgonbladet* 27 April 1877.
8. *HD* 2 January 1877 leading article.
9. *Uusi Suometar* 1 May 1877.
10. *Morgonbladet* 31 December 1877.
11. *HD* 13, 25 April 1877.
12. Meurman 1909, pp. 217–21; Virkkunen II 1938, pp. 561–6.
13. Kansanaho 1965, pp. 200–3.
14. Proposal of J.I. Berg of 4 May on the Estate of clergy (*Landtdagen år 1877–8. Protokoll: Prestestândet*, pp. 658–9). Also Virkkunen II 1938, pp. 567–71; Rein 1918, pp. 275–6. See note 7.
15. *ÅU* 8 May 1877 leading article.
16. *HD* 3 May 1877 leading article and 9 June.
17. Montgomery's speech of 26 May 1878 and M. von Born's speech of 26 May 1878 *Landtdagen år 1877–8. Protokoll: Adel II* pp. 947, 962. Also Rosen 1977, p. 52.
18. On Leo Mechelin about the departure of the Guard Battalion for the war, see Seitkari 1951, p. 319; Nordenstreng I 1936, p. 170.
19. Speeches of H. Molander and R. Furuhjelm, *Uusi Suometar* 5 September 1877.
20. On the celebrations for the departure of the Guard Battalion in Helsinki, see *Uusi Suometar* 5, 7 September 1877; *HD* 7 September; *ÅU* 5 September, *OWS* 15 September; *Tampereen Sanomat* 15 September.
21. On the Finnish officers in the Turkish war, see Screen 1976, p. 282. During that war the total of Finnish officers in the Russian army approached 300.
22. On the increase in the circulation of newspapers during the Turkish war, see Hyvämäki 1964, pp. 31, 33.
23. *Ibid.*, pp. 64, 65.
24. On folk ballads of the time of the Turkish war, Folk poetry archives/SKS and Ballad collection/HYK.
25. Seitkari 1951, p. 280.
26. On newspaper reports, see for example *Uusi Suometar* 29, 31 October 1877; *HD* 30 October 1877; *Hufvudstadsbladet* 30 October; *Tapio* 31 October; *Björneborgs Tidning* 31 October; *Hämäläinen* 1 November; *Tampereen Sanomat* Extra 3 November.
27. *HD* 26 September 1877.

28. Seitkari 1951, pp. 323, 335, 334; *OWS* 17 October 1877.

29. Leo Mechelin's journalism: *HD* 26 September 1877; *ÅU* 6 June 1863.

30. *Morgonbladet* 27 April 1877.

31. *OWS* 27 October 1877.

32. Letters from the censorship officials to the printing authority during 1877. (*III Painoylihallitus: kirje- ja anomuskirjat 1877*).

33. E.g. *Aftonbladet* 12 May 1877. In addition *Aftonbladet* 1, 3, 5 May 1877. On the debate in the Diet on the conscription law, see the report of the British consul in Helsinki of 31 March 1877 to the Foreign Office (F.O. 65/976).

34. On the 'bold Turks', see for example *OWS* 29 August 1877; *Vuosi* 1877; *Tampereen Sanomat* 28 April 1877; and the fennoman provincial papers generally.

35. *HD* 27 October 1877; also Mechelin's article in note 29.

36. Tigerstedt II 1952, p. 595.

37. On the growing difficulty of Finnish trade with east and west, see Halme 1955, p. 74, 76; for contemporary writing for example *Hufvudstadsbladet* 2 January 1878; *HD* 4 April 1878.

38. On the decline of total imports and consequently customs revenue, see *Suomen Virallinen Tilasto I*, 4, p. 8 and tables 9 and 10.

39. Pihkala 1970, p. 122; Laine III 1952, pp. 438, 451–2, 464; Tigerstedt II 1952, pp. 276, 436; Jutikkala I 1957, pp. 108, 114.

40. Pipping 1961, p. 536.

41. *Hufvudstadsbladet* 2 January 1878 article '1877–1878'.

42. *ÅU* 2 January 1878.

43. Speech of the Speaker of the Estate of farmers at the closing of the Diet (*Valtiopäivät v. 1877–1878/Pöytäkirjat: Talonpoikaissääty III*, p. 2163).

44. The Senate supported paid regular troops, Seitkari 1951, pp. 391–2.

45. *HD* 5 March 1878; 29 March leading article.

46. *Uusi Suometar* 5 March 1878 leading article; 6 March, 1 April leading articles.

47. *Uusi Suometar* 6 May 1878.

48. On the argument over the auxiliary cruisers, see Hyvämäki 1964, pp. 77–103.

49. On the view of the Senate, see Hyvämäki 1964, pp. 108–9.

50. In the press of the capital there was continuous reporting of the Congress of Berlin, with press comment and assessment from different directions (St Petersburg, London, Berlin, Vienna etc.). The news often covered as much as 3–4 columns in the papers. *Helsingfors Dagblad* published a series 'Bref från Berlin'.

51. *Uusi Suometar* 15 July 1878; *ÅU* 16 July; *OWS* 20 July.

52. *HD* 14 July 1878 leading article.

53. *ÅU* 2 January 1879.

54. *Uusi Suometar* 15, 17 January 1879; *OWS* 4 January 1879.

55. See note 53.

56. *Hufvudstadsbladet* 2 January 1879 leading article.

57. *HD* 2 January 1879 leading article.

58. See note 53.

59. Proclamation of a day of prayer 22 October 1877 (*Finlands författningssamling 1877/n.29*).

60. Proclamation of a day of prayer 14 October 1878 (*Finlands författningssamling 1878/n.21*).

61. Paasivirta 1961, p. 53.

62. Rein II 1928, p. 564.
63. *Ibid.*, p. 568.

Chapter XI

1. Renouvin VI 1955, pp. 10–26.
2. Barck 1953, pp. 18–42; von Federley 1958, pp. 63–8.
3. Salminen 1963, pp. 68–9.
4. Kauppinen 1952, pp. 109–12; Kohtamäki 1956, pp. 316–22.
5. Mikko Juva 1951, pp. 210–27; Rytkönen I 1940, pp. 122–35.
6. Henning Söderhjelm 1960, p. 70; Fellman 1974, pp. 163–6.
7. Engman 1978 pp. 164, 165, 172–4; Screen 1974, pp. 81–2.
8. Nokkala 1958, pp. 78–92, 98–117, 217–21, 247–69.
9. Russian mobilisation plan for 1888: report of French military attaché in St Petersburg to ministry of war (SHAF/FN 1471). On the joint exercises at Tsarskoe Selo, see Hyvämäki 1964, pp. 204, 206.
10. Paasivirta 1968, pp. 17, 18.
11. Korhonen 1967, pp. 63–70; von Rauch 1953, pp. 126–30.
12. Pohlebkin 1969, p. 136. According to Pohlebkin, Alexander III 'did not like' the Finnish constitution but 'only tolerated it'.
13. Katz 1966, pp. 165–77; Freeborn 1966, p. 123; Katkov 1971, p. 13.
14. Rothfels 1962, pp. 184–96. Also report of French military attaché in St Petersburg to ministry of war 26 October 1889 (SHAF/FN 1471).
15. Paasivirta 1969, p. 17; Pohlebkin 1969, pp. 114–17.
16. Hyvämäki 1964, pp. 162, 163, 170, 176–7, 199.
17. Höjer 1944, pp. 181–96.
18. Paasivirta 1968 p. 18.
19. Leo Mechelin, *Précis du droit public du Grand-Duché de la Finlande* (1886) and *Das Staatsrecht des Grossfürstentums Finnland* (1889).
20. On Ordin's work, see Osmonsalo 1947, p. VIII.
21. On the postal manifesto, see Osmonsalo 1949A, pp. 266–8.
22. Grüning 1929, pp. 48–9.
23. Sinkko 1976, pp. 208–9 (supplement).
24. Leo Mechelin's letters of 1 January 1892, 6 December 1894 to Harald Wieselgren (Harald Wieselgren collection/KB) and 21 December 1893 to S.A. Hedin (S.A. Hedin collection/KB).
25. Epstein 1973, pp. 147–8.
26. Marx's anti-Russian attitude was apparent from the Crimean war onwards.
27. On Criticism of the Dual alliance on ideological grounds in France, see Carroll 1964 pp. 137, 176, 194–5.
28. On the problems of British policy in Europe, see Taylor 1954, pp. 346–51; Hinsley 1963, pp. 255–7.
29. Lindberg 1958, p. 113. On the views of Oskar II, see the report of the German embassy in Stockholm of 17 January 1890 to the foreign ministry (AA/Russland 63).
30. For example *Le Matin* 26 July, 15 August 1890; also *Nya Pressen* 28 October 1890.
31. Paasivirta 1968, p. 25.

32. Finland had her own commissioner, Robert Runeberg, at the Paris world exhibition of 1878.

33. For example Mrs Alec Tweedie, *Through Finland in Carts* (1897).

34. On the book *Finland in the 19th century*, see Journal de Genève 23 March 1895; *Westminster Review* 1894/October; *Revue de Paris* 1895/n.18.

Chapter XII

1. On the internal development of Finland at the end of the 19th century, see Mikko Juva IV 1966, pp. 415–24.

2. Reports of the French military attaché in St Petersburg of 5 July 1890, 24 January 1891, 7 July 1893 to ministry of war (SHAF/FN 1472, 1565).

3. Edward C. Thaden, 'Russification in Finland: Official Russian views 1891–1914', *The fourth Conference on Baltic Studies, 12 June 1966* (mimeo).

4. Report of the French military attaché of 23 September 1893 to ministry of war (SHAF/FN 1473).

5. Hyyryläinen 1978.

6. On the Finnish press about the visit of the French squadron to Kronstadt, see *Päivälehti* 30 July, 5 August 1891; *Finland* 28 July 1891.

7. *Päivälehti* 21 August 1891; *Aamulehti* 8 January 1892; Hyyryläinen 1978.

8. On the extensiveness of the news, see *Hufvudstadsbladet* 11, 12, 13, 14 April 1897. On anti-Turkish attitudes, see for example J. Kangas, *Kolme uutta laulua sodasta Kreikan ja Turkin välillä* (1897) and Ballad collection/HYK.

9. Rommi 1964. pp. 81–4; Suni 1975, pp. 53–7, 64; Korhonen 1963 A, p. 23.

10. On Bobrikov's aims, see the report of the British ambassador to St Petersburg of 28 June 1899 to Foreign Office (F.O. 61/1518). Hardinge drew attention to the speculation that the Russian policy in Finland aimed to 'divide' the Finnish people politically and socially, as in the Baltic provinces and in Poland.

11. The Emperor's speech at the opening of the extraordinary Diet on 24 January 1899, 'Finland, inseparably joined to the empire, and under the protection and security of the whole Russian state, does not require armed forces separately from the Russian army' (*Valtiopäivät 1899, Keskustelupöytäkir jat Talonpoikaissääty*, pp. 14–15). On the Russian press, see the report of the German ambassador to St Petersburg, 28 November 1898, to foreign ministry (AA/Russland 63).

12. On the threat uttered by Bobrikov, see *Vossische Zeitung* 25 February 1899. Information received from *Dagens Nyheter*.

13. On Bobrikov's measures in 1899–1900, see Einar W. Juva V 1967, pp. 31–3.

14. Torvinen 1968, pp. 26–31; on the views of Johannes Gripenberg, see Rommi 1964, pp. 75–8.

15. Blomstedt 1969, pp. 149–55; Einar W. Juva I 1957, pp. 211–17.

16. Murtorinne 1964, pp. 27–9, 90–2.

17. Nordenstreng II 1937, p. 78; Copeland 1973, p. 30.

18. Paasivirta 1968, pp. 26–8; Nordenstreng II 1937, pp. 92–7; Werner Söderhjelm 1923, pp. 215–33. Also report of French consul in Helsinki of 29 October 1899 to foreign ministry.

19. Reuter I 1928, p. 39; Nordenstreng II 1937, p. 73.

20. Jellinek 1896, pp. 41–6; Jellinek 1905, pp. 478, 640–1, 740.

21. *Norddeutsche Allgemeine Zeitung* 26 February 1899; *Vossische Zeitung* 25 February.

22. *Vossische Zeitung* 28 February, 21 March 1899.
23. *Vorwärts* 26 February, 6 May 1899.
24. *The Times* 20 March 1899 leading article; 26 May leading article. Also Maude 1973, p. 329.
25. *Daily Chronicle* 23, 28 February 1899.
26. Reuter's letter, see *The Times* 20 March 1899.
27. *Le Temps* 25 March 1899; *Siècle* 22 March 1899.
28. *Journal des Débats* 5 April 1899.
29. Stjernholm 1973, pp. 41–50.
30. *Ibid.*, pp. 101–22.
31. On the hope of protests at the Hague peace conference, see *Aftonbladet* 21 April 1899.
32. Mechelin's letter of 24 December 1899 to Ivar Berendsen (Ivar Berendsen collection/VA).
33. Ernst Estlander, *Ofärdsårens politiska litteratur*, passim.
34. Report of British ambassador to St Petersburg of 22 March 1899 to Foreign Office (F.O. 65/1577) and British consul in Helsinki's report of 8 March to Foreign Office (F.O. 65/182); and Kerkkonen 1965, pp. 125–6; the report of French consul in Helsinki to foreign ministry, 1 April 1899 (AAEF — CPCC/Helsingfors II).
35. On the Russian publications, see Julkunen-Lehikoinen, *Finnish politics in the 19th and 20th century*, pp. 26–34.
36. Memorandum of the meetings of the leading constitutionalist groups 12 November 1902 (Mechelin collection 22/VA).
37. Soikkanen 1961, p. 182.
38. Murtorinne 1964, pp. 112–44.
39. Klinge III 1968, pp. 14–18; Kuusisto 1978, pp. 227–30.
40. Memorandum of the meeting of the Finnish emigrants in Stockholm 3–5 September 1903 (Mechelin collection 22/VA).
41. Lähteenmäki 1975, pp.64–76.
42. Copeland 1973, pp. 44–6.
43. Sunell 1959, pp. 97–112.
44. Parmanen III 1939, pp. 113–26.

Chapter XIII

1. Mechelin's letter of 2 February 1904 to Ivar Berendsen, and his memorandum to the Boden meeting, signed 20 February 1904. Also Parmanen III 1939, p. 617; Maissi Erkko's letters of 15 April and 17 October 1904 to Dagmar Neovius (Parmasen collection XXXIII).
2. *Fria Ord* 27 March, 8 November, 1 December 1903, 21 August 1904.
3. The stories, mostly about the naval battle of Tsushima, are not however deposited in the archives.
4. The later literary descriptions of the period and the interviews conducted are consistent in content.
5. On press reporting of Bobrikov's murder, see *Hufvudstadsbladet* 18, 19 June 1904; *Uusi Suometar* 17, 18 June.
6. On the emigrés' reaction to Bobrikov's murder, see for example Alexander Sikiö's letter of 19 June 1904 to Carl Mannerheim (Mannerheim family papers I–VA); P.

Aulin's letter of 12 August 1904 to Eero Erkko (*Parmasen* collection **XXXIII**).

7. *Fria Ord* 18 June 1906.

8. *Kölnische Zeitung* 20 June 1904.

9. *Vossische Zeitung* 17 June 1904.

10. *Vorwärts* 17, 18 June 1904.

11. *The Times* 17 June 1904 leading article; report of the British ambassador to St Petersburg of 19 June 1904 to the Foreign Office (F.O. 65/185).

12. *Journal des Débats* 19 June 1904 leading article: *Le Temps* 18 June 1904.

13. Copeland 1973, pp. 47–51, 74–5, 98–100.

14. *Ibid.*, pp. 165–72, 180–1, 197–8, 208.

15. Memorandum of the decisions made at the meeting of emigrés in Stockholm, 22–29 September 1904 (Mechelin collection 23/VA).

16. Memorandum of the congress held in Paris, 30 September–14 October 1904 (Mechelin collection 23/VA).

17. Zilliacus 1920, pp. 100–1.

18. Parmanen III 1939, pp. 663–76.

19. Futrell 1963, pp. 41–4; Copeland 1973, pp. 48–51, 71.

20. Parmanen III 1939, pp. 456–66.

21. Göran von Bonsdorff 1956, p. 48.

22. Gummerus 1933, pp. 164–7, 178–82; also Konni Zilliacus' letter of 21 June 1905 to Ivar Berendsen: 'The time for the finale draws nearer daily with giant strides.'

23. Screen 1976, p. 290. The number of Finnish officers in the Russian army fell from earlier levels.

24. Jutikkala I 1957, pp. 132, 145; *Suomen virallinen tilasto XVIII Teollisuustilasto* 1904 I, pp. 17–19; 1905 I, pp. 20–2; 1906, pp. 16–19.

25. Pihkala 1970 A, p. 127.

26. The general industrial situation improved and wages rose. Hjerppe *et al.* 1976, pp. 99, 107.

27. Roos 1907, pp. 51–9, 133–75.

28. Kalnins 1950, pp. 33–6; Hugh Seton-Watson 1962, pp. 236–8; von Rauch 1970, pp. 22–3.

29. Report of British embassy to St Petersburg of 9 November 1905 to the Foreign Office (F.O. 65/1703).

30. Soikkanen 1961, pp. 225–6; Rauhala II 1921, p. 528.

31. Parmanen IV 1941, pp. 406–8; Palmgren 1948, pp. 192–3.

32. Parmanen IV 1941 pp. 171–4, 462–3; on the position of Obolenski, see Jussila 1977, p. 78.

33. Rauhala II 1921, pp. 528–9; Seitkari 1958, pp. 14–15.

34. Kalnins 1950, pp. 37–41; Katkov 1971, p. 257.

35. Soikkanen 1975, pp. 89–92.

36. Svinhufvud's letter of 26 November 1905 to Ivar Berendsen.

37. Zilliacus' letter of 28 November 1905 to Ivar Berendsen.

38. *Kotimaa* 30 December 1905, 1 November 1906, in general Murtorinne 1964, pp. 296–300.

39. Klinge III 1968, pp. 299–300, 307–13; Kuusisto 1978, pp. 272–82, 297–308.

40. Eskola 1962, pp. 404–24; Borg 1965, pp. 536–70.

41. Soikkanen 1961, pp. 272–8, 338–9, and in general the publication *Alkutaipaleelta*.

42. Soikkanen 1961, pp. 241–4.

43. Seitkari 1958 pp. 156–7.
44. Soikkanen 1961, pp. 244–6; Salomaa 1966, pp. 116–18.
45. Blomstedt 1969, p. 220.
46. Soikkanen 1961, pp. 246–7; Salomaa 1966 pp. 119–21.
47. Edward Valpas speech: *Oulun puoluekokouksen pöytäkirja*, p. 209.
48. Ropponen 1968, pp. 150–1; Droz 1952, p. 491.
49. *Le Temps* 27, 29 October, 5, 7 November 1905.
50. *Ibid.*, 3 November 1905.
51. *L'Humanité* 28 October 1905 leading article.
52. *Ibid.*, 1 July 1905 leading article.
53. *Ibid.*, 3, 4, 5 November 1905.
54. *The Times* 6 November 1905 news, leading article.
55. *Morning Post* 2, 3 November 1905 leading articles.
56. *Daily Telegraph* 3 November 1905 leading article, news.
57. *Manchester Guardian* 3, 6 November 1905 leading articles.
58. *Kölnische Zeitung* 31 October, 2 November 1905; *Vossische Zeitung* 2 November 1905; *Hamburger Correspondent* 31 October, 2 November 1905; also report of the German embassy in Copenhagen on events in Finland 9 November 1905 (AA/*Russland* 63).
59. *Vossische Zeitung* 6 November 1905; *Hamburger Correspondent* 8 November 1905.
60. *Vorwärts* 3, 7 November 1905.
61. *Stockholms Dagblad* 2 November 1905.
62. *Dagens Nyheter* 4 November 1905; *Svenska Dagbladet* 3 November 1905.
63. *Social-Demokraten* 4, 6 November 1905.
64. *Stockholms Dagblad* 4 November 1905.
65. E.g. *The Times* 1, 2, 3 August 1906; *Vossische Zeitung* 3 August 1906; *Social-Demokraten* 1, 2, 3, 8, 11, August 1906.
66. *Vossische Zeitung* 3 April 1907; *Kölnische Zeitung* 29 March 1907; *Vorwärts* 21 April 1907; *L'Humanité* 29 April 1907; *Social-Democraten* 30 March 1907.
67. Soikkanen 1966, p. 90; Futrell 1963, p. 55; Wilson 1969, pp. 49–53.

Chapter XIV

1. Report of French military attaché in St Petersburg of 25 November 1906 to ministry of war (SHAF/7N 1477).
2. Reports of French military attaché of 6 March and 25 November 1906 to ministry of war (SHAF/7N 1477).
3. Report of French military attaché in St Petersburg of 8 December 1905 to ministry of war (SHAF/7N 1477); also Polvinen 1962, pp. 20–1.
4. Woodward 1965, p. 160.
5. R.W. Seton-Watson 1968, pp. 611–12; Renouvin VI 1955, pp. 221–4, 233; Milza 1968, pp. 191, 200–2.
6. Hugh Seton-Watson 1962, pp. 330–1.
7. Lindberg III, 4 1958, p. 227; Fink 1959, pp. 164–5.
8. Polvinen 1962, pp. 23, 27; Polvinen 1960, p. 39; also Report of French military attaché in St Petersburg of 5 August 1906 to ministry of war (SHAF/7N 1477).
9. Report of Norwegian minister to St Petersburg of 16 April 1909 to foreign ministry.

10. For example *Nya Pressen* 20 February 1909; *Hufvudstadsbladet* 1 January 1909; *Työmies* 8 January 1909.
11. Uola 1974, pp. 19–22.
12. Generally Jungar 1969, pp. 158–74.
13. *Helsingin Sanomat* 14, 18 October 1908; *Nya Pressen* 8 October 1908. 20 November.
14. *Uusi Suometar* 11, 25 October, 20 December 1908.
15. *Työmies* 22 October 1908.
16. *Helsingin Sanomat* 13, 14, 16, 21, 28 July 1911, and *Uusi Suometar* 16, 22, 29 July, 1, 8 August 1911.
17. *Nya Pressen* 11, 12, 13, 14, 15, 20, 25, 26, 27, 29 July, 1, 3 August 1911; *Hufvudstadsbladet* 11, 12, 13, 20, 23, 24, 27, 28, 29, 31 July, 3 August 1911; *ÅU* 11, 14, 18, 23, 25 July 1911.
18. The grounds for the opinion of the committee on procedure (*SDP:n puoluekokouksen pöytäkirja* 1911, p. 175).
19. Makkonen 1973, suppl. 5.
20. Rasila 1969, pp. 60–2; Copeland 1973, pp. 76–7; Salomaa 1966, pp. 145–7.
21. Maude 1973, p. 339; Harrison 1974, pp. 89, 91; also report of British ambassador to St Petersburg of 3 March 1908 to Foreign Office (F.O. 371/515.).
22. *The Times* 29 May, 1 June 1908; *Manchester Guardian* 26 May, 10 October 1910; also report of British embassy in St Petersburg of 19 May 1908 to Foreign Office (F.O. 371/515).
23. *Morning Post* 30 May 1908 leading article.
24. E.g. *Le Temps* 1 May 1908.
25. *Ibid.*, 19 February 1908.
26. *Journal des Débats* 4 June 1908; *Le Temps* 20 May 1908.
27. For example the four-part series of articles 'Lettre de Finlande' *Journal des Débats* 7, 14, 18, 25 July 1908; *L'Humanité* 13 July 1908.
28. *Vorwärts* 6 July 1910.
29. E.g. the reports of the Swedish military attaché in St Petersburg of 19 June, 7 August 1906 to the General Staff (*Generalstaben Utrikesavdelning/Ryssland* I).
30. For example *Svenska Dagbladet* 22 May, 11 June 1908.
31. Paasivirta 1968, p. 29; Nordenstreng II 1937, p. 435; Törngren 1930, p. 215–30.
32. Resolution of the socialist congress on the Finnish question (*Internationaler Sozialisten-Kongress zu Kopenhagen* 1910, pp. 18–19).
33. For example M. Borodkin, *Die finnländische Grenzmark im Bestande des russischen Reiches*, Berlin 1911; and in general the bibliography in Julkunen-Lehikoinen, pp. 26–34.
34. Paasivirta 1962 A, pp. 31–41.

Chapter XV

1. Seppälä 1969 p. 34; Polvinen 1962, p. 29. In the extensive Russian military exercises in the autumn of 1910, Sweden for the first time appeared as an 'enemy' beside Germany; report of Swedish military attaché in St Petersburg of 22 September 1910 to General Staff (*Generalstaben: Utrikesavdelning/Ryssland* IV).
2. The Memorandum of the French military attaché in St Petersburg to ministry of war for 1912 (SHAF/7N 1538) stresses the major political problems connected with the people of Finland from the Russian point of view.

3. Rasila 1976, pp. 51–2.
4. Jussila 1977, pp. 90–1.
5. *Uusi Suometar* 3 January 1912, 1 January 1913, 1 January 1914; *Helsingin Sanomat* 1 January 1911, 1 January 1913, 1 January 1914.
6. *Hufvudstadsbladet* 6 January 1912; *Dagens Tidning* 1 January 1914.
7. *Työmies* 31 January 1912, 3, 8 January 1913.
8. *Helsingin Sanomat* 3 January 1914.
9. *Uusi Suometar* 3 January 1914.
10. *Hufvudstadsbladet* 3 January 1913, 1 April 1914.
11. *Työmies* 9 January 1914.
12. *Helsingin Sanomat* 3 January 1912.
13. *Hufvudstadsbladet* 4 January 1912.
14. *Työmies* 11 January 1912.
15. *Uusi Suometar* 2, 19, 28 August; also Klinge 1972, pp. 97–8.
16. *Työmies* 1 August 1914; minutes of the trade union committee of 31 July 1914 and circular letter to the member unions dated 1 August.
17. *Kotimaa* 5, 25 August, 4 September 1914.
18. *Työmies* 3 August, 16 September 1914; *Työ* 4 September 1914; *Kansan Lehti* 5 September 1914; *Sosialisti* 7 September 1914; *Arbetet* 1, 4 September 1914.
19. Klinge 1972, p. 97; *Kansan Lehti* 5 September 1914; *Ilkka* 11 August 1914.
20. *Helsingin Sanomat* 2 August 1914.
21. *Kansan Tahto* 3 September 1914.
22. *Ibid.*, 8, 16 September 1914.

Bibliography

UNPUBLISHED SOURCES

FOREIGN

Public Record Office, London
Foreign Office archive (F.O.)
Reports of the ambassadors to St Petersburg.
Reports of the ministers to Stockholm.
Reports of the consuls in Helsinki.
Reports of the ambassadors to Paris.

Archives des Affaires Etrangères (AAEF), *Paris*
Reports of the ambassadors to St Petersburg.
Reports of the ministers to Stockholm.
Reports of the consuls in Helsinki.

Service Historique de l'Armée (SHAF), *Paris*
Reports of the military attachés in St Petersburg.
Expédition de Bomarsund, 1854.

Archives Nationales, Paris
Archives de la marine (AMF): reports on military operations in the Baltic, 1854.

Archiv des Auswärtigen Amtes (AA), *Bonn*
Reports of the German ambassadors to St Petersburg.
Reports of the German consuls in Helsinki.
Reports of the German minister to Copenhagen.

Riksarkivet (RA), *Stockholm*
Reports of the Swedish chief consul in Helsinki to the foreign minister (Muscovitica).
Reports of the Russian ministers to Stockholm to the foreign ministry (microfilm copies from the Central Archives, Moscow).

Kungliga Biblioteket (KB), *Stockholm*
S.A. Hedin correspondence.
Harald Wieselgren correspondence.
Emil v. Qvanten collection.

Krigsarkivet, Stockholm
Reports of the Swedish military attachés in St Peterburg.

Udenrigsdepartementets arkiv, Oslo
Reports of the Norwegian ministers to St Petersburg.

Hof-Haus- und Staatsarchiv (HHStA), *Vienna*
Reports of the ambassadors to St Petersburg.

FINNISH

Valtionarkisto (VA) *(National Archives, Helsinki)*
Rehbinder correspondence.
Archive of the office of censorship (SYH).
Riilahti collection.
C.G. Ottelin collection.
Stjernvall-Walleen collection.
Alexander Armfelt collection.
Mannerheim collection; family papers.
Luhtanen collection.
Ivar Berendsen correspondence (on microfilm).
Mechelin collection.
Mechelin correspondence.
Archive of the Governor-General (KKK).
Frosterus collection.

Suomalaisen Kirjallisuuden Seuran Arkisto (SKS) *(Archives of the Finnish Literary Society, Helsinki)*
August Ahlqvist collection.
Elias Lönnrot correspondence.
Antero Varelius correspondence.
Folk Poetry archives: ballads on the Russo-Turkish war; folk-tales on Napoleon's Russian expedition; folk-tales of the Crimean War.

Helsingin Yliopiston Kirjasto (HYK) *(Helsinki University Library)*
B.O. Schauman collection.
J.V. Snellman collection.
Ballad collection: ballads on the Russo-Turkish war 1877–8; ballads on the Greco-Turkish war, 1897

Työväenarkisto (TA) *(Labour archives, Helsinki)*
Archive of the Finnish Trade Union Organisation.

Turun Maakunta-arkisto (Turku Province Archives, Turku)
Archives of the Crown Bailiff (Åland).

Oulun Maakunta-arkisto (Oulu Province Archives, Oulu)
G. & C. Bergbom business archives.
J.V. Snellman G:son business archives.

OFFICIAL PAPERS, CORRESPONDENCE, ETC.

FOREIGN

Die Auswärtige Politik Preussens 1858–1871. III. Oldenbourg 1932.

Lettres et papiers de Nesselrode IX à XI. Paris.

Peter von Meyendorff: *Ein russischer Diplomat an den Höfen von Berlin and Wien. Politischer und privater Briefwechsel 1826–1863.* Berlin/Leipzig 1923.

Recueil des traités, conventions et actes diplomatiques concernant la Pologne 1762–1862. Paris 1862.

Internationales Sozialisten-Kongress zu Kopenhagen. Berlin 1910.

Russian War 1854. Official Correspondence. London 1943.

FINNISH

Borgå domkapitel: Circulär 1830–1870. Borga 1871.

Censur-Kalender. Samling af skeppsbrutet gods, tillhörigt den finska pressen I. Stockholm 1861.

Consistorii ecclesiastici i Åbo circulärbref: III 1808–12. Åbo 1812; IV 1813–18. Åbo 1819; XI 1846–50. Åbo 1851.

Domkapitlets i Kuopio Circulärbref: I *1851–56.* Kuopio 1857.

S.G. Elmgrenin muistiinpanot (Suomen historian lähteitä II). Helsinki 1939.

Finlands författningssamling 1869, 1877, 1878.

Finska förhållanden I–IV. Stockholm 1857–61.

Yrjö Koskinen: *Valtiollisia ja yhteiskunnallisia kirjoituksia* III. Helsinki 1916.

Henrik Gabriel Porthans bref till Mathias Calonius I–II (SSLS I). Helsingfors 1886.

J.L. Runeberg: *Samlade arbeten* I. Stockholm 1873.

Samling av Placater 1812, 1818, 1819, 1823, 1830, 1831, 1847, 1848, 1849, 1853, 1855, 1856, 1857, 1871, 1872

Snellman, J.V.: *Kootut teokset* II, XII. Porvoo 1931.

Landtdagen 1877–8, 1899.

Suomen Sosialidemokraattisen puolueen 5 edustajakokouksen pöytäkirja, Oulussa 20–27 1906. Helsinki 1906.

Suomen Sosialidemokraattisen puolueen 7 edustajakokouksen pöytäkirja, Helsingissä 4–10/9 1911. Helsinki 1911.

Suomen Virallinen tilasto: XVIII, *Teollisuustilasto* 1904–6.

NEWSPAPERS AND PERIODICALS

FOREIGN

Sweden

Aftonbladet 1856, 1861, 1863, 1877
Nya Dagligt Allehanda 1861, 1863
Post- och inrikes Tidningar 1863
Social-Democraten 1905, 1906, 1907
Stockholms Dagblad 1905
Svenska Dagbladet 1905, 1908

Britain

Daily Chronicle 1899
Daily News 1854, 1863
Daily Telegraph 1863, 1905
The Globe 1863
The Manchester Guardian 1905, 1908, 1910
The Morning Post 1854, 1863, 1905, 1908
The Morning Herald 1863
The Standard 1854, 1863
The Times 1808, 1854, 1856, 1861, 1863, 1899, 1904, 1905, 1906, 1908

Germany

Augsburger Allgemeine Zeitung 1854, 1863
Hamburger Correspondenz 1854, 1905
Hamburger Nachrichten 1854
Hamburger Börsen-Halle 1854, 1863
Kölnische Zeitung 1854, 1861, 1863, 1904, 1905, 1907
Lübecker Zeitung 1854
National Zeitung 1863
Norddeutsche Allgemeine Zeitung 1899
Vorwärts 1899, 1904, 1905, 1907, 1910
Vossische Zeitung 1899, 1904, 1905, 1906, 1907

France

Le Constitutionnel 1854
L'Humanité 1905, 1908
Journal des Débats 1854, 1863, 1899, 1904, 1908
Le Matin 1890
Le Moniteur 1808, 1854
Le Nord 1863
L'Opinion nationale 1863
La Patrie 1863
Le Pays 1863
La Presse 1854, 1863
Le Siècle 1856
Le Temps 1863, 1899, 1904

Russia

Journal du Nord 1808
Journal de St Petersbourg 1830, 1854
St Petersburger Zeitung 1854

FINNISH

Aamulehti 1892
Arbetet 1914
Björneborgs Tidning 1877
Borgå Tidning 1848
Dagens Tidning 1914
Finland 1891

Finlands Allmänna Tidning (FAT) 1820, 1821, 1823, 1830, 1831, 1833, 1848, 1853, 1854,
   1856, 1861, 1863, 1864
Fria Ord 1903, 1904
Helsingfors Dagblad (HD) 1863, 1868, 1870, 1871, 1877, 1878, 1879
Helsingfors Morgonblad 1833
Helsingfors Tidningar (HT) 1830, 1831, 1848, 1853, 1854, 1856, 1857, 1861, 1863, 1864
Helsingin Uutiset (HU) 1863
Helsingin Sanomat 1908, 1911, 1913, 1914
Hufvudstadsbladet 1871, 1877, 1878, 1909, 1911, 1912, 1913, 1914
Hämeen Sanomat 1879
Hämäläinen 1862, 1863, 1877
Ilkka 1914
Ilmarinen 1848
Kansan Tahto 1914
Kirjallinen Kuukausilehti 1869, 1870
Kotimaa 1905, 1914
Litteraturblad 1848, 1857, 1858, 1861, 1863
Morgonbladet 1848, 1854, 1877, 1878
Nya Pressen 1890, 1908, 1909, 1911
Oulun Wiikko-Sanomat (OWS) 1829, 1830, 1831, 1854, 1856, 1862, 1863, 1864
Päivälehti 1891, 1893
Päivätär 1863
Sosialisti 1914
Suometar 1848, 1849, 1854, 1855, 1856, 1857, 1858, 1859, 1861, 1863, 1864
Tampereen Sanomat 1877, 1878
Tapio 1877
Turun Wiikko-Sanomat (TWS) 1821, 1822, 1823, 1830, 1831
Työ 1914
Työmies 1908, 1909, 1912, 1913, 1914
Uusi Suometar 1870, 1871, 1872, 1876, 1877, 1878, 1879, 1908, 1911, 1912, 1913, 1914
Wasabladet 1858, 1863
Wiborg 1855, 1856
Åbo Allmänna Tidning (ÅAT) 1809, 1810, 1812, 1813, 1814, 1818
Åbo Tidning 1808
Åbo Tidningar 1848
Åbo Underrättelser (ÅU) 1830, 1841, 1846, 1848, 1849, 1854, 1855, 1856, 1857, 1858,
   1863, 1870, 1871, 1877, 1878, 1879, 1911
Östra Finland 1877

BOOKS, ARTICLES, DISSERTATIONS

FOREIGN

Key to abbreviations: HA = *Historiallinen Aikakauskirja*; HArk = *Historiallinen Arkisto*; HLS = *Historiska och Litteraturhistoriska Studier*; HTF = *Historiska Tidskrift för Finland*; SKHS = *Suomen Kirkkohistoriallisen Seuran Vuosikirja*; THA = *Turun Historiallinen Arkisto*.

Anderson, Edgar: 'The Crimean War in the Baltic Area', *Journal of Baltic Studies V* (1974).

Anderson, M.S.: 'The Ascendancy of Europe', *Aspects of European History 1815–1914*. London 1976.

De Bazoucourt: *L'Expédition de Crimée II*. Paris 1858.

Bartlett, C.J.: *Great Britain and Sea Power 1815–1853*. Oxford 1963.

Bell, Herbert C.F.: *Lord Palmerston (2 vols)*. London 1966.

Birke, Ernst: *Frankreich und Ostmitteleuropa im 19. Jahrhundert*. Köln 1960.

Björck, Staffan: *Heidenstam och sekelskiftets Sverige*. Stockholm 1946.

Bolsover, G.H.: 'Aspects of Russian Foreign Policy 1815–1914', *Essays presented to Sir Lewis Namier*. London 1948.

Borodkin, M.: *Kriget vid Finlands kuster 1854–1855*. Helsingfors 1905.

Brydolf, Ernst: *Sverige och Runeberg 1836–1848*. Helsingfors 1943.

Cadot, Michel: *La Russie dans la vie intellectuelle française (1839–1856)*. Paris 1967.

Carlsson-Höjer, Thorvald: *Den svenska utrikespolitikens historia III*: 1–2 1792–1844. Stockholm 1954.

Carr, E. H.: *Michael Bakunin*. London 1937.

Carroll, E.M.: *French public opinion and foreign affairs 1870–1914*. Hamden, Conn. 1964.

Copeland, William R.: *The Uneasy Alliance. Collaboration between the Finnish Opposition and the Russian Underground. 1899–1904*. Helsinki 1973.

Craig, Gordon: 'The system of alliances and the balance of powers', *The New Cambridge Modern History X*. Cambridge 1964.

Droz, Jacques: *Histoire diplomatique de 1648 à 1919*. Paris 1952.

——: *Europe between Revolutions 1815–1848*. Glasgow 1967.

Epstein, Fritz T.: 'Der Komplex "die russische Gefahr" und sein Einfluss auf die deutsch-russischen Beziehungen im 19. Jahrhundert', *Deutschland in der Weltpolitik des 19. und 20. Jahrhunderts*. Hamburg 1973.

Eriksson, Sven: *Svensk diplomati och tidningspress under Krimkriget*. Stockholm 1939.

Fink, Troels: *Spillet om dansk neutralitet 1905–09*. Aarhus 1959.

Freeborn, Richard: *A Short History of Modern Russia*. New York 1966.

Friese, Christian: *Russland und Preussen vom Krimkrieg bis zum polnischen Aufstand*. Berlin 1931.

Futrell, Michael: *Northern Underground: Episodes of Russian and Revolutionary Transport and Communications through Scandinavia and Finland 1863–1917*. London 1963.

Gerhard, Dietrich: *England und der Aufstieg Russlands*. München/Berlin 1933.

Gerschon, P.v.: *Versuch über die Geschichte des Grossfürstentums Finnland*. Odense 1821.

Gitermann, Valentin: *Geschichte Russlands III*. Hamburg 1949.

Gleason, J.H.: *The Genesis of Russophobia in Great Britain*. Cambridge, Mass. 1950.

Golovine, Ivan: *La Russie sous Nicholas Iᵉʳ*. Paris 1845.

Grüning, Irene: *Die russische öffentliche Meinung und ihre Stellung zu den Grossmächten 1878–1894*. Berlin 1929.

Grünwald, Constantine: *La vie de Nicholas Iᵉʳ*. Paris 1946.

Gullberg, Erik: *Tyskland i svensk opinion 1856–1871*. Lund 1952.

Göransson, Jean: *Aftonbladet som politisk tidning 1830–1835*. Uppsala 1937.

Harrison, W.: 'The British Press and the Russian Revolution of 1905–1907', *Oxford Slavonic Papers. New Series VII*. Oxford 1974.

Henry, Paul: *La France devant le Monde de 1789 à 1939*. Paris 1945.

Hinsley, F.N.: *Power and the Pursuit of Peace*. London 1967.

Holborn, Hajo: 'Russia and the European Political system', *Russian Foreign Policy* (Ivo Lederer, ed.) New Haven and London 1962.

Holmberg, Åke: *Skandinavismen i Sverige vid 1800-talets mitt*. Göteborg 1946.

Horn, David Bayne: *Great Britain and Europe in the Eighteenth Century*. Oxford 1967.

Höjer, Torvald: 'England, Russland och den central-asiatiska frågan 1869–1885', *Uppsala Universitets årsskrift*, 7(1944).

——: *Carl XIV Johan*. Stockholm 1960.

Jansson, Allan: *Den svenska utrikespolitikens historia III*: 3 1844–1872. Stockholm 1961.

Jellinek, Georg: *Über Staatsfragmente*. 1896.

——: *Allgemeine Staatslehre*. Berlin 1905.

Jerusalimski, A.S.: *Der deutsche Imperialismus*. Berlin 1968.

Jones, G.M.: *Travels in Norway, Sweden, Finland, Russia and Turkey*. London 1827.

Kaiser, Karl: 'Napoleon III und der polnische Aufstand von 1863.' *Beiträge zur Geschichte der öffentlichen Meinung in Frankreich*. Berlin 1932.

Kalnins, Bruno: *De baltiska staternas frihetskamp*. Stockholm 1950.

Katkov, George (ed.): *Russia enters the Twentieth Century 1894–1917*. London 1971.

Katz, Martin: *Michael N. Katkov: a Political Biography 1818–1887*. The Hague 1966.

Koht, Halvdan: *Revolutionsåret 1848*. Stockholm 1948.

Kukiel, M.: *Czartoryski and European Unity 1770–1861*. Princeton, New Jersey 1955.

Käiväräinen, I.I.: *Mezhdunarodnoe otnosheniya na severe Evropy v nachale XIX veka i prisoedinenie Finlyandii v Rossii v 1809 godu*. Petrozavodsk, 1965.

Lemberg, Eugen: *Nationalismus I*. Hamburg 1964.

Leslie, R.F.: *Polish Politics and the Revolution of November 1830*. London 1956.

——: *Reform and Insurrection in Russian Poland, 1856–1865*. London 1963.

——: *The Age of Transformation, 1789–1871*. London 1964.

Lindberg, Folke: *Den svenska utrikespolitikens historia III*. 4: 1872–1914. Stockholm 1958.

Lobanov-Rostovsky, Andrei A.: *Russia and Europe 1789–1825*. Durham, N.C. 1947.

——: *Russia and Europe 1825–1878*. Ann Arbor, Mich. 1954.

Malcolm-Smith, E.: *British Diplomacy in the Eighteenth Century*. London 1937.

Mardal, Magnus: *Norge, Sverige og den engelske trelasttoll 1817–1850*. Oslo 1957.

Marmier, X.: *Lettres sur la Russie, la Finlande et la Pologne I*. Paris 1843.

Martin, B. Kingsley: *The Triumph of Lord Palmerston: a Study of Public Opinion in England before the Crimean War*. London 1924.

Maude, George: 'The Finnish Question in British Political Life, 1899–1914.' THA XXVIII (1973).

Middleton, K.W.B.: *Britain and Russia*. London 1947.

Monas, Sidney: *The Third Section. Police and Society in Russia under Nicholas I*. Cambridge, Mass 1961.

Mosse, W.E.: 'England and the Polish Insurrection of 1863', *English Historical Review* LXXXI (1956).

——: *The European Powers and the German Question 1848–71*. London 1958.

Milza, Pierre: *Les rélations internationales de 1871 à 1914*. Paris 1968.

Nifontow, A.S.: *Russland im Jahre 1848*. Berlin 1954.

Odhner, C.T.: *Sveriges politiska historia under konung Gustaf III:s regering II*. Stockholm 1896.

Palmstierna, C.F.: *Sverige, Ryssland och England 1833–1855*. Stockholm 1932.

Petrie, Charles: *Diplomatic History 1713–1933*. London 1946.

Pohlebkin, V.V.: *Suomi vihollisena ja ystävänä 1714–1967*. Porvoo–Helsinki 1969.

Postén, Leokadia: *De polska emigranternas agentverksamhet i Sverige 1862–1863*. Lund 1975.

Rauch, Georg v.: *Russland: Staatliche Einheit und nationale Vielfalt.* München 1953.
——: *Geschichte der baltischen Staaten.* Stuttgart 1970.
Renouvin, Pierre: *Histoire des relations internationales IV–VI.* Paris 1954–5.
Revunenkov, V.G.: *Pol'skoe vosstanie 1863g. i evropeyskaya diplomatiya.* Leningrad, 1957.
Riassanovsky, Nicholas V.: *A History of Russia.* New York 1963.
Rothfels, Hans: *Bismarck, der Osten und das Reich.* Stuttgart 1962.
Ryan, A.N.: 'The Defence of British Trade in the Baltic 1808–1813', *English Historical Review* 1959.
Schiemann, Theodor: *Geschichte Russlands unter Kaiser Nikolaus I.* III–IV. Berlin 1919.
Schubert, Friedrich Wilhelm v.: *Reise durch Schweden, Norwegen, Lappland, Finnland und Ingermanland in den Jahren 1817, 1818 und 1820.* Leipzig 1823, 1824.
Screen, J.E.O.: 'Några synpunkter på officerutbildningen i Ryssland och Finland under autonomiens tid.' HTF 1974.
——: *The entry of Finnish officers into Russian military service 1809–1917.* London 1976.
Seton-Watson, Hugh: *The Decline of Imperial Russia, 1855–1914.* New York 1962.
——: *The Russian Empire 1801–1917.* Oxford 1967.
Seton-Watson, R.W.: *Britain in Europe, 1789–1914.* New York 1968.
Shukow, J.M. (ed.): *Weltgeschichte VI.* Berlin 1969.
Sohlman, August: *Det unga Finland.* Helsingfors 1880 (1st edn Stockholm 1855).
Stadelmann, Rudolf: *Soziale und politische Geschichte der Revolution von 1848.* München 1970.
Stjernholm: *Finland i svensk opinion och politik 1898–1899.* Historiska institutionen, Uppsala 1973.
Strang, Lord: *Britain in World Affairs.* New York 1961.
Sunell, Gunnar: *Ord och öden i ett tidninghus.* Stockholm 1959.
Suni, L.V.: 'Tsarismi ja yhteiskunnallis-poliittinen liike Suomessa 1880- ja 1890-luvuilla.' HA 69 (1975).
Särkilax, Peder: *Fennomani och skandinavism II.* Stockholm 1855.
Tarle, E.E.: *Krymskaya voyna* (vol.2). 2nd rev. edn, Leningrad, 1950.
Taylor, A. J. P.: *The Struggle for Mastery in Europe 1848–1918.* Oxford 1954.
Uvorov, S.S.: *Kejsaren Alexander och Bonaparte.* Åbo 1814.
Wilson, John Dover: *Milestones on the Dover Road.* London 1969.
Vogel, Barbara: *Deutsche Russlandspolitik. Das Scheitern der deutschen Weltpolitik unter Bülow 1900–1906.* Düsseldorf 1973.
Woodward, David: *The Russians at Sea.* London 1965.

FINNISH

Alanen, Aulis J.: 'Suomen historia 1809–1863', *Oma maa VIII.* Porvoo — Helsinki 1960.
——: *Suomen historia kustavilaisella ajalla.* Porvoo Helsinki 1964.
Alhoniemi, Pirkko: *Isänmaan korkeat veisut.* Helsinki 1969.
Anthoni, Eric: *Jacob Tengström och stiftsstyrelsen i Åbo stift 1808–1832 I.* Helsingfors 1923.
Apunen, Osmo: *Hallituksen sanansaattaja Virallinen lehti — Officiella Tidningen 1819–1969.* Helsinki 1970.
Barck, B.O.: *Arvid Mörne och sekelskiftets Finland.* Helsingfors 1953.
Blomstedt, Yrjö: *Johan Albrecht Ehrenström. Kustavilainen ja kaupunginrakentaja.* Helsinki 1963.
——: *K.J. Ståhlberg. Valtiomieselämäkerta.* Helsinki 1969.

Bonsdorff, Carl v.: *Opinioner och stämningar i Finland 1808–1814.* Helsingfors 1918.
——: *Åbo Akademi och dess män 1808–1828 I.* Helsingfors 1912.
Bonsdorff, Göran v.: *Svenska folkpartiet, tillblivelse och utveckling till 1917.* Helsingfors 1956.
Bonsdorff, L.G.v.: *Den ryska pacificeringen i Finland 1808–09.* Helsingfors 1929.
——: *Lars Gabriel von Haartman intill 1827.* Helsingfors 1946.
Borg, Olavi: *Suomen puolueet ja puolueohjelmat 1880–1964.* Helsinki 1965.
Brotherus, K.R.: *Valtio ja kirkko.* Porvoo 1923.
Castrén, Gunnar: 'Topelius fosterländska lyrik' in Z. *Topelius hundraårsminne.* Helsingfors 1918.
——: *Herman Kellgren. Ett Bidrag till 1840- och 50-talens kulturhistoria.* Helsingfors 1945.
Castrén, Liisa: *Adolf Ivar Arwidsson.* Helsinki 1944.
——: *Adolf Ivar Arwidsson isänmaallisena herättäjänä.* Helsinki 1951.
Danielson-Kalmari, J.R.: 'Walleenin memoriaali Suomen valtiosääntöön tehtävistä korjauksista.' HArk XXIV, 1, 3.
Engman, Max: 'Migration from Finland to Russia during the Nineteenth Century', *Scandinavian Journal of History* 1978.
Eskola, Seikko: *Sosiaalipolitiikka suomalaisen puolueen ohjelmassa vuonna 1906.* Jyväskylä 1962.
Federley, Berndt: *R.A. Wrede. Lantdagsmannen och rättskämpen 1877–1904.* Helsingfors 1958.
Fellman, Urban: 'Dreyfusaffären i finländsk pressopinion.' Unpubl. thesis, Un. of Helsinki, 1974.
Gallén, Jarl: 'La Finlande militaire au temps du Grande-Duché (1809–1917)', *Revue internationale d'histoire militaire* 23 (1961).
Gardberg, Carl-Rudolf: *Åbo Underrättelser 1824–1924.* Åbo 1924.
Gummerus, Herman: *Konni Zilliacus.* Jyväskylä — Helsingfors 1933.
Halila, Aimo: *Suomen kansakoululaitoksen historia I.* Turku 1949.
——: 'Porvoon valtiopäivät ja autonomian alkuvaihe' in *Suomen kansanedustuslaitoksen historia. I.* Helsinki 1962.
Halme, Veikko: *Vienti Suomen suhdannetekijänä vuosina 1870–1939.* Helsinki 1955.
Haltsonen, Sulo: 'Tadeusz Kosciuszko Suomessa vv. 1796–1797.' HA 1937.
Hanho, J.T.: *Suomen oppikoululaitoksen historia II.* Porvoo Helsinki 1955.
Hautala, Kustaa: *Suomen Tervakauppa 1856–1913. Sen viimeinen kukoistus ja häviö sekä niihin vaikuttaneet syyt.* Helsinki 1956.
——: *Oulun kaupungin historia 1809–1856.* Oulu 1975.
Havu, Ilmari: *Lauantaiseura ja sen miehet.* Helsinki 1945.
Heikel, Ivar A.: *Svensk vältalighet under 19:de seklet.* Helsingfors 1897.
——: *Helsingin yliopisto 1640–1940.* Helsinki 1940.
Helander A. Benj.: *Suomen metsätalouden historia.* Porvoo — Helsinki 1949.
Hirn, Yrjö: *Runebergskulten.* Helsingfors 1935.
Hjerppe, Reino ym.: *Suomen teollisuus ja teollinen käsityö 1900–1965.* Helsinki 1976.
Hornborg, Erik: *När riket sprängdes.* Helsingfors 1955.
——: *Suomen historia.* Porvoo — Helsinki 1965.
Hulkko, Jouko: *Siniristilippumme.* Helsinki 1963.
Hyvämäki, Lauri: *Suomalaiset ja suurpolitiikka. Venäjän diplomatia Suomen sanomalehdistön kuvastimessa 1878–1890.* Helsinki 1964.
Hyyryläinen, Veli-Pekka: 'Euroopan kansainvälis-poliittinen kehitys 1890-luvun

alkupuolella Helsingin horisontista.' Unpubl. thesis, Un. of Turku, 1978.

Jaakkola, Jalmari: *Suomen historian ääriviivat.* Porvoo — Helsinki 1945.

Jalava, Antti: *Tavallisen miehen tarina.* Porvoo — Helsinki 1948.

Joustela, Kauko J.: *Suomen Venäjän kauppa autonomian ajan alkupuoliskolla vv. 1809–65.* Helsinki 1963.

Julku, Kyösti: 'Englannin suunnitelmat ja toimenpiteet Ruotsi-Suomen auttamiseksi Suomen sodan aikana vv. 1808–1809.' THA XIII (1956).

Jungar, Sune: *Ryssland och den svensk-norska unionens upplösning.* Åbo 1969.

Junnila, Olavi: *Ruotsiin muuttanut Adolf Iwar Arwidsson ja Suomi (1823–1858).* Helsinki 1972.

Jussila, Osmo: *Suomen perustuslait venäläisten ja suomalaisten tulkintojen mukaan.* Helsinki 1969.

——: 'Vuoden 1905 suurlakko Suomessa.' HA 72 (1977).

Jutikkala, Eino: *Turun kaupungin historia, 1856–1917. I.* Turku 1957.

——(ed.): *Suomen talous- ja sosiaalihistorian kehityslinjoja.* Porvoo — Helsinki 1968.

Jutikkala, Eino and Pirinen, Kauko: *Suomen historia.* Helsinki 1973.

Juva, Einar W.: *P.E. Svinhufvud I:* Porvoo — Helsinki 1957.

——: *Suomen kansan historia V.* Helsinki 1967.

Juva, Mikko: *Suomen sivistyneistö uskonnollisen vapaamielisyyden murrosvaiheessa 1848–1869.* Helsinki 1950.

——: 'Valvojan ryhmän syntyhistoria.' THA XI (1951).

——: 'Suomen kielitaistelun ensimmäinen vaihe.' HArk. 58 (1962).

——: *Suomen kansan historia IV.* Helsinki 1966.

Jäderholm, Bo: *Greve Berg som Finlands generalkuvernör 1854–1861.* Jyväskylä 1970.

Kaukamaa, L.J.: *Porin puutavarakaupasta ja metsänkäytöstä kaupungin 'suuren laivanvarustustoimen' aikana 1809–56.* Helsinki 1941.

Kaukiainen, Yrjö: *Suomen talonpoikaispurjehdus 1800-luvun alkupuoliskolla (1810–1853).* Helsinki 1970.

——: *Koiviston merenkulun historia I.* Lahti 1975.

Kerkkonen, Martti: 'Suomen sortovuodet kansainvälisestä näkökulmasta. Näkökohtia ja poimintoja.' HA 1965.

Kero, Maija-Leena: 'Saksan kuva Suomen sanomalehdissä Preussin — Itävallan ja Saksan — Ranskan sotien välisenä aikana (v. 1866–1871).' THA XXIII (1970).

Kero, Reino: 'Yhdysvaltain kuva Suomen sanomalehdistössä 1800-luvun puolivälin jälkeen (noin vuosina 1850–1875).' THA XX (1967).

Klinge, Matti: 'Turun ylioppilaskunta 1800-luvun alussa. Yhteispyrkimyksiä ja aatevirtauksia.' HArk 61 (1967).

——: *Ylioppilaskunnan historia III, IV.* Porvoo — Helsinki 1967–8.

——: *Vihan veljistä valtiososialismiin. Yhteiskunnallisia ja kansallisia näkemyksiä 1910- ja 1920-luvuilta.* Porvoo — Helsinki 1972.

Kohtamäki, Ilmari: *Pietari Hannikaisen 'Kanava'.* Helsinki 1959.

Korhonen, Keijo: *Suomen asiain komitea, Suomen korkeimman hallinnon järjestelyt ja toteuttaminen vuosina 1811–1826.* Helsinki 1963.

——: *Linjoja puoleltatoista vuosisadalta.* Turku 1963.

——: *Autonomous Finland in the political thought of nineteenth century Russia.* Turku 1967.

Koskenvesa, Esko: 'Rukouspäiväjulistusten antaminen Suomessa kustavilaisen ajan lopulla ja autonomian ajan alussa.' HA 64 (1969).

Krusius-Ahrenberg, Lolo: *Der Durchbruch des Nationalismus und Liberalismus im politischen*

Leben Finnlands 1856–1863. Helsinki 1934.

——: 'Finland och den svensk—ryska allianspolitiken intill 1830/31 års polska revolution.' HLS 21–22 (1946).

——: ' "Dagbladseparatismen" år 1863 och den begynnande panslavismen.' HLS 30 (1954).

——: 'Synpunkter på April-manifestet.' HA 56 (1958).

Kuusisto, Seppo: *Hämäläis-osakunnan historia 1865–1918.* Helsinki 1978.

Lagerborg, Rolf: *Sanningen om Casimir von Kothen (1807–1880) enligt aktstycken och brev.* Helsingfors 1953.

Laine, Eevert: *Suomen vuorityö 1809–1887 III.* Helsinki 1952.

Lempiäinen, Pentti: *Turun hiippakunnan tarkistuspöytäkirjat isonvihan ajalta.* Helsinki 1973.

Lillja, Alexis A.: *Arsenjij Andrejevits Zakrevskij. Finlands generalguvernör 11/IX 1823–1/XII 1831.* Helsingfors 1948.

Lindblad, Märta: 'Politiska opinioner och stämningar under Krimkriget.' Unpubl. thesis, Åbo Akademi, 1947.

Lindström (Sarva) Gunnar: *Suomen kaupasta Aleksanteri I:sen aikana. I. Järjestäytymisvuodet 1808–1812.* Helsinki 1905.

Lähteenoja, Aino: *Rauman kaupunginhistoria IV. 1809–1917.* Rauma 1939.

Lähteenmäki, Olavi: 'Suomalainen siirtokunta Colonia Finlandesa.' Unpubl. thesis, Un. of Turku 1975.

Makkonen Tuula: 'Sosialistinen käännöskirjallisuus Suomessa vuosina 1898–1918.' Unpubl. thesis, Un. of Turku, 1973.

Mannerheim, C.E.: *Mannerheims egenhändiga anteckningar.* Helsingfors 1922.

Manninen, Pauli: *Selvitys Suomen elinkeinorakenteesta ja sen tutkimuksesta 1820–1970.* Helsinki 1976.

Meurman, Agathon: *Muistelmia.* Helsinki 1909.

Murtorinne, Eino: *Papisto ja esivalta routavuosina 1899–1906.* Helsinki 1964.

——: 'Sana aikanansa sanottu'. Papiston kannanottoja Itämaisen sodan aikana.' *Teologinen aikakauskirja* 1965.

Nervander, E.: *Blad ur Finlands kulturhistoria.* Helsingfors 1906.

Nieminen, Matti: *Suomen Kirjatyöntekijäin liiton historia I.* Jyväskylä 1977.

Nikula, Oscar: *Åbo sjöfarts historia Segelsjöfarten 1856–1926.* Åbo 1930.

——: *Malmska handelshuset i Jakobstad. Helsingfors* 1948.

——: *Rosenlew-koncernen. En hundra årig utveckling från handelshus till storindustri 1853–1953.* Helsingfors 1953.

——: *Turun kaupungin historia 1809–1856.* Turku 1972.

Nokkala, Aimo: *Tolstoilaisuus Suomessa. Aatehistoriallinen tutkimus.* Helsinki 1958.

Nordberg, Toivo: 'Huhtikuun manifestista tammikuun valiokuntaan.' HA 56 (1958).

Nordenstreng: L. Mechelin. *Hans statsmannagärning och politiska personlighet I–II.* Helsingfors 1936–7.

Nurmio, Yrjö: *Taistelu suomen kielen asemasta 1800-luvun puolivälissä.* Porvoo — Helsinki 1947.

Osmonsalo, Erkki K.: 'Hallituksen politiikka herännäisliikkeitä kohtaan Aleksanteri I:n ja Nikolai I:n aikana.' SKHS XII (1939).

——: *Fabian Langenskjöld I.* Helsinki 1939.

——: *Suomen valloitus 1808.* Porvoo — Helsinki 1947

——: *'Itsevaltiuden kausi.'* and 'Perustuslaillisen kehityksen kausi', *Suomen historian käsikirja II.* Porvoo — Helsinki 1949.

Paasivirta, Juhani: 'Kysymys Suomen autonomian oikeusperusteista erikoisesti silmällä pitäen J.V. Snellmanin ja Palménin kesken käytyä polemiikkia (1859–61). THA XI (1951).

——: *Becker Bey och hans idé om ett självständigt Finland 1880.* Ekenäs 1961.

——: *Suomen kuva Yhdysvalloissa. 1880-luvun lopulta 1960-luvulle.* Porvoo — Helsinki 1962.

——: *Suomen osallistuminen Tukholman olympialaisiin vuonna 1912. Diplomaattisia selvittelyjä.* Helsinki 1962.

——: *Plans for commercial agents and consuls of autonomous Finland.* Turku 1963.

——: 'Nuoren Leo Mechelinin näkemyksiä diplomatiasta ja ulkopolitiikan hoidosta.' THA XVII (1964).

——: *Suomen diplomaattiedustus ja ulkopolitiikan hoito. Itsenäistymisestä talvisotaan.* Porvoo — Helsinki 1968.

——: 'Suomen kuvan hahmottumisvaiheita toiseen maailmansotaan mennessä', *Suomen kuva maailmalla.* Helsinki 1969.

Palmgren, Raoul: *Suuri linja. Arwidssonista vallankumouksellisiin sosialisteihin.* Helsinki 1948.

Paloposki, Toivo: 'Vuoden 1734 valtiopäiväkutsun ja valtiopäivien vaikutus suomalaisten ulkopoliittiseen harrastukseen.' THA XIX (1967).

Pihkala, Erkki: 'Suomen ja Venäjän taloudelliset suhteet 1800-luvun lopulla ja 1900-luvun alussa.' HA 66 (1973).

——: 'Suomen Venäjän-kaupan puitteet autonomian ajan jälkipuoliskolla.' HA 65 (1970).

——: *Suomen Venäjän kauppa vuosina 1860–1917.* Helsinki 1970.

Pipping, Hugo E.: *Myntreformen år 1865.* Helsingfors 1928.

——: *Paperiruplasta kultamarkkaan. Suomen Pankki 1811–1877.* Helsinki 1961.

——: *'Efter Krimkriget — några följdverkningar i Finland.'* HTF 1972.

Pohjanpalo, Jorma: *Suomi ja merenkulku.* Helsinki 1965.

Pohjolan-Pirhonen, Helge: *Kansakunta etsii itseään 1772–1808.* Porvoo — Helsinki 1970.

——: *Kansakunta löytää itsensä 1808–1855.* Porvoo — Helsinki 1973.

Polvinen, Tuomo: *'Venäjän sotilaalliset tavoitteet Suomessa.'* In *Venäläinen sortokausi Suomessa.* Porvoo — Helsinki 1960.

——: *Die finnischen Eisenbahnen in den militärischen und politischen Plänen Russlands vor dem ersten Weltkrieg* (Studia historica 4). Helsinki 1962.

Puntila, L.A.: 'Yleisen mielipiteen muodostuminen Suomessa 1860-luvulla.' HA 52 (1947).

Rasila, Viljo: 'Lenin Suomessa.' HA (1969).

——: Jutikkala, Eino, Kulha, Keijo: *Suomen poliittinen historia II.* Vuodet 1905–1975. Porvoo — Helsinki — Juva 1976.

Rauhala, K.W.: *Keisarillinen Suomen senaatti 1809–1909 I–II.* Helsinki 1915–21.

Rein, Th.: *Muistelmia elämän varrelta.* Helsinki 1918.

——: *Juhana Vilhelm Snellman I–II.* Helsinki 1928.

Renvall, Pentti: 'Ruotsin vallan aika', *Suomen kansanedustuslaitoksen historia I.* Helsinki 1962.

Reuter, J.N.: *'Kagalen'. Ett bidrag till Finlands historia 1809–1905 I.* Helsingfors 1928.

Rommi, Pirkko: *Myöntyvyyssuuntauksen hahmottuminen Yrjö-Koskisen ja suomalaisen puolueen toimintalinjaksi.* Helsinki 1964.

Roos, Sigurd: *Suomen kansallislakko I, 1.* Helsinki 1907.

Ropponen, Risto: *Die Kraft Russlands.* Helsinki 1968.

——: *Die russische Gefahr. Das Verhalten der offentlichen Meinung Deutschlands und Österreich-Ungarns gegenüber der Aussenpolitik Russlands in der Zeit zwischen dem Frieden von Portsmouth und dem Ausbruch des ersten Weltkrieges.* Helsinki 1976.

Rosén, Gunnar: *Sata sodan ja rauhan vuotta.* Helsinki 1977.

Runeberg, C.M.: 'Krig eller fred. Studier i svensk presspolemik under 1800-talets världskrig.' HTF 1941.

Ruuth, Martti: 'Turun synodaalikokous 1842.' SKHS XXXI–XXXII. (1945).

——: *Helsingin suurkirkko satavuotias 1852–1952.* Helsinki 1952.

——: 'Carl Gustaf Ottelin piispuutensa alkuvaiheessa.' *Talenta quinque* (1953).

Ruutu, Martti: *Kahdeksan vuosikymmentä Arwidssonin tutkimusta. HAik 1955.*

——: *'Kansallinen herääminen ja kielellisen tasa-arvon saavuttaminen', Suomalaisen kansanvallan kehitys.* Porvoo 1956.

——: 'Koulumme muotoutumiskaudelta sata vuotta sitten.' *Kasvatusopillinen Aikakauskirja 1963.*

——: 'Suomalais-venäläisestä koexistenssistä historiallisten edellytystensä valossa.' *Suomalainen Suomi 1965.*

——: *Finland. De religiösa folkrörelserna och samhälletca. 1750–1850.* HA 63 (1968).

Rytkönen, Alli: *Päivälehden historia I.* Helsinki 1940.

Salminen, Johannes: *Levande och död tradition.* Borgå 1963.

Salomaa, Erkki: *Yrjö Sirola.* Helsinki 1966.

Schauman, Aug.: 'Från sex Årtionden i Finland', *Levnadsminnen I–II.* Helsingfors 1922.

Schulman, Hugo: *Händelserna i Finland under Krimkriget åren 1854 och 1855.* Helsingfors 1905.

Schybergson, M.G.: *Carl Gustaf Estlander.* Helsingfors 1916.

Schybergson, Per: *Hantverk och fabriker. I.* Helsingfors 1973.

Seitkari, O.: 'Suomen sotalaitos Venäjän sotilashallinnon osana 1800-luvulla', *Sotilasaikakauslehti 1939.*

——: *Vuoden 1878 asevelvollisuuslain syntyvaiheet. Suomen sotilasorganisaatio- ja asevelvollisuuskysymys 1860- ja 70-luvuilla.* Helsinki 1951.

——: 'Edustuslaitoksen uudistus 1906' in *Suomen kansanedustuslaitoksen historia V.* Helsinki 1958.

Seppälä, Helge: *Taistelu Leningradista ja Suomi.* Porvoo — Helsinki 1969.

Sinkko, Erkki: *Venäläis-suomalainen lehdistöpolemiikki 1890–1894.* Tampere 1976.

Soikkanen, Hannu: *Sosialismin tulo Suomeen. Ensimmäisiin yksikamarisen eduskunnan vaaleihin asti.* Porvoo — Helsinki 1961.

——: 'Vuoden 1905 tapahtumat ja niiden taustakehitys suomalaisen tutkimuksen näkökulmasta.' HA 1966.

——: *Kohti kansanvaltaa I 1899–1937.* Vaasa 1975.

Soininen, Arvo M.: *Vanha maataloutemme. Maatalous ja maatalousväestö Suomessa perinnäisen maatalouden loppukaudella 1720-luvulta 1870-luvulle.* Helsinki 1974.

Steinby, Torsten: *Suomen sanomalehdistö.* Porvoo — Helsinki 1963.

Suolahti, Gunnar: *Nuori Yrjö Koskinen.* Porvoo — Helsinki 1933.

Söderhjelm, Alma: *Raahen kaupunki 1649–1899.* Helsinki 1911.

——: *Sverige och den franska revolutionen* (2 vols) Helsingfors 1920, 1924.

——: *Jakobstads historia III.* Vasa 1974.

Söderhjelm, Henning: *Werner Söderhjelm.* Stockholm 1960.

Söderhjelm, Werner: *En samling resebrev.* Helsingfors 1923.

Takolander, Alfons: *Erik Gabriel Melartin I*. Ekenäs 1926.

Tarkiainen, Kari: *Vår gamle Arffiende Ryssen. Synen på Ryssland i Sverige 1595–1621 och andra studier kring den svenska Rysslandsbilden från tidigare stormaktstid*. Uppsala 1974.

Teljo, Jussi: *Suomen valtioelämän murros 1905–1908*. Porvoo — Helsinki 1949.

Teperi, Jouko: *Viipurilainen osakunta 1828–1868*. Helsinki 1959.

Tigerstedt, Örnulf: *Kauppahuone Hackman 1790–1879. II*. Helsinki 1952.

Tommila, Päiviö: 'Havaintoja uutisten leviämisnopeudesta ulkomailta Suomeen 1800-luvun alkupuolella.' HArk (1960).

——: *La Finlande dans la politique Européenne en 1809–1815*. Helsinki 1962.

——: *Suomen lehdistön levikki ennen vuotta 1860*. Porvoo — Helsinki 1963.

Torvinen, Taimi: 'Myöntyvyys- ja perustuslaillinen linja' in *Suomen ulkopolitiikan kehityslinjat 1809–1966*. Helsinki 1968.

Törngren, Adolf: *På utländsk botten*. Helsingfors 1930.

Uola, Mikko: *Suomi ja Etelä-Afrikka*. Tampere 1974.

Waris, Heikki: *Savo-karjalainen osakunta I. 1833–1852*. Porvoo — Helsinki 1939.

——: 'Hufvudstadssamhället' in *Helsingfors stads historia III, 2*. Helsingfors 1951.

——: 'Suomalaisen sosiaalipolitiikan kehitys' in *Suomalaisen kansanvallan kehitys*. Porvoo — Helsinki 1956.

Viljanen, Lauri: *Runeberg ja hänen runoutensa 1837–1877 II*. Porvoo — Helsinki 1948.

Winter, Helmer: *Anonyma anteckningar om kriget på Åland 1854*. Åbo 1954.

Virkkunen, Paavo: *Agathon Meurman II*. Helsingfors 1938.

Virrankoski, Pentti: *Suomen taloushistoria*. Keuruu 1975.

Vuorela, Tapani: *Keisarillisen Suomen kirkkopolitiikka 1809–1824*. Helsinki 1976.

Zilliacus, Konni: *Sortovuosilta. Poliittisia muistelmia*. Porvoo 1920.

Österbladh, Kaarlo: *Pappissääty Suomen valtiopäivillä 1809–1906, I 1809–1885*. Helsinki 1933.

INTERVIEWS

J.M. Granit, John Sundvall, Elsa Bruun, K. Rob. V. Wikman, Erik v. Frenckell, Lauri Pihkala, Gustaf Hackzell, Martta Salmela-Järvinen, Tyyni Tuulio, Carl Bergroth, Rainer Sopanen.

Index